It Sure Looks Different
from the Inside

It Sure Looks Different from the Inside

RON NESSEN

A Playboy Press Book

Trade distribution by Simon and Schuster
A Division of Gulf + Western Corporation
New York, New York 10020

Designed by Tere LoPrete

Library of Congress Cataloging in Publication Data

Nessen, Ron, 1934-
    It sure looks different from the inside.
    Includes index.
    1. United States—Politics and government—1974-
1977. 2. Ford, Gerald R., 1913- 3. Nessen, Ron,
1934- 4. Journalists—Washington, D.C.—Biography.
I. Title.
E865.N47   973.925   78-8185
ISBN 0-87223-500-9

Dedicated to Cindy and Edward, who suffered through it twice, once in the living and once in the writing.

Contents

	Acknowledgments	ix
	Cast of Characters	xi
	Introduction	xiii
1	The Nightmare Is Over	3
2	A Ron, but Not a Ziegler	9
3	First Impressions	15
4	Betty	19
5	Haunted by Nixon	29
6	Vodka with Strangers	40
7	Spies	54
8	A Ford but Not a Hoover	74
9	The Yellow Sickness	91
10	"Let's Look Ferocious"	117
11	Travels with Henry	132
12	Self-Inflicted Wounds	148
13	"Saturday Night" Live	163
14	Why Do These Things Keep Happening?	179
15	President Reagan?	192
16	Kansas City, Here We Come	225
17	What a Way to Start a Campaign	246
18	"Are There Any Soviet Troops in Poland?"	261
19	Troubles	279
20	The Ten-Day Orgasm	303
21	Defeat	313
22	Why; and What If . . . ?	326
23	Press Secretary to Superman	329

24 *Gossip and Trivia*   *341*
25 *Q and A*   *348*

    INDEX   *359*

Acknowledgments

I'm grateful to Bill Adler for encouraging me to write this book and for helping me through the discouraging moments I encountered as a first-time author.

Bob Gleason, the editorial director of Playboy Press, showed me how to make it a better book. I appreciate his patience and I admire his editorial skills.

A number of colleagues from the Ford White House shared with me their memories, including Senator Robert Dole, William Colby, Richard Cheney, Dean Burch, Michael Duval, James Cavanaugh, Foster Chanock, William Nicholson and Red Cavaney. They were most generous with their time.

Parts of the manuscript were read in the early stages by Lou Cannon of the *Washington Post*, Thomas DeFrank of *Newsweek* and James Shuman, former editor of the White House news summary, all friends. Their suggestions were helpful. But, of course, any shortcomings in the final manuscript are completely my responsibility.

Janice Barbieri, who served with dedication in the White House, made an important contribution to this book with her research and her other assistance in preparing the manuscript.

Finally, I wish to thank Gerald R. Ford for making this book possible by giving me the opportunity to see how the White House worked from the inside.

Cast of Characters

GERALD R. FORD, the accidental president. Behind the scenes, he was very different from his bland and clumsy image.

BETTY FORD, a frugal and jealous wife. In the White House she blossomed into an independent personality with controversial views on sex, abortion, etc.

RICHARD M. NIXON, former president. His resignation elevated Ford to the White House in 1974, but his ever-present specter contributed to Ford's loss of the White House in 1976.

SPIRO T. AGNEW, former vice president. I became the press secretary because I lived near his house.

NELSON A. ROCKEFELLER, vice president. Sniped at by conservative southern Republicans, he thought, "Who needs it?"

HENRY A. KISSINGER, secretary of state. Brilliant, visionary, egocentric, petty, hypersensitive to criticism. The truth was what he said it was.

DONALD H. RUMSFELD, White House staff coordinator, later defense secretary. He brought order out of anarchy in the Oval Office. But his manner and ambitions sparked rivalries.

ROBERT T. HARTMANN, chief speechwriter. Ford's top aide in Congress and the vice-presidency, he lost out in the White House power struggle. He took it badly.

JOHN O. MARSH, JR., counsellor to the president. A self-described "Virginia country lawyer," smart, steady and effective, but almost unknown to the public, he was the best of Ford's inner circle.

RICHARD B. CHENEY, Rumsfeld's deputy and later successor as staff coordinator. An easygoing manner and a very low public profile hid his steely control over the White House staff and the campaign organization.

BRENT SCOWCROFT, Kissinger's deputy and later successor as the president's national security assistant. He was the first to spot the East Europe blunder in the second debate.

DAVID HUME KENNERLY, photographer for the president. Irrepressible, irreverent, bearded, he was treated like a son by the Fords. He got into trouble taking nude photos of Elizabeth Ray.

WILLIAM M. LUKASH, M.D., White House doctor. Slim and graceful as a leopard from jogging and tennis, he put most of the White House staff on diets at one time or another. He had to break the news to the president that Mrs. Ford had breast cancer.

RONALD REAGAN, former movie actor, former governor of California. His stiff ultra-right primary challenge virtually destroyed the election hopes of moderate-right Jerry Ford. Reagan couldn't care less: better defeat than ideological impurity.

JIMMY CARTER, the new president. For once easygoing, nice guy Jerry Ford found someone to hate.

Introduction

My life inside the White House was the result of an accident of geography. It never would have happened if I hadn't lived a few blocks from Spiro Agnew.

Early one morning in August 1973 I received a phone call from an assignment editor at NBC in Washington, where I was a news correspondent. Some morning newspapers, he related, were carrying a story that federal prosecutors were investigating allegations that Vice President Agnew had taken payoffs from engineers and architects when he was governor of Maryland. The assignment editor directed me to meet an NBC camera crew in front of Agnew's home in Kenwood, a Maryland suburb of Washington, to catch his reaction to the stories.

I was called because I lived closer to Agnew's house than any other NBC correspondent.

For the next two months I crisscrossed Maryland and spent hours on the phone, tracking down the Agnew story through his friends, benefactors, enemies and prosecutors. Eventually I and eight other reporters were subpoenaed by Agnew to reveal the sources of our information about the investigation. Our lawyers advised us that if we refused, we probably would go to jail for contempt of court.

But we never went to jail, because the day before our hearing, Agnew dramatically appeared at the U.S. Court House in Baltimore, pleaded no contest to one charge of evading income taxes and announced he was resigning. He had struck a bargain with the Justice Department, removing himself from the line of succession to the impeachment-threatened Nixon in return for a promise that he would not be sent to prison.

With Agnew gone, my story was gone. But NBC figured since I'd covered the old vice president, I might as well cover the new vice president.

That's how I got to know, and like, Gerald R. Ford.

As a result of that friendship, Ford invited me to be his press secretary after he became president, giving me the chance to observe from close up as he moved into the ruins of Richard Nixon's White House and began repairing the damage. During that time I learned a lot about Ford.

The most revealing anecdote I know about Ford's character concerns an incident that occurred one Christmas when he was taking a vacation from the White House with his family at Vail, Colorado. One night while the family was eating dinner at their rented stone and glass chalet, one of their dogs had an accident on the floor. A red-jacketed White House steward rushed to clean up the mess. Ford got up from the table, took the rag away from the steward and wiped up the mess himself.

"No man should have to clean up after another man's dog," the president told the steward.

To use an inelegant, but accurate, metaphor, Ford's role in history was to clean up other people's messes. The messes he inherited included: the shattered faith of the people in their president as a result of Watergate; the lingering war in Indochina passed on from the four previous presidents; a sick economy ready to plunge precipitously because of mismanagement by earlier presidents and Congresses; and the accumulated sins of the government's intelligence and investigative branches, which were about to be judged unacceptable by the current morality of a free society.

While Ford worked to clean up those inherited "messes," as press secretary I had my own legacy from the past to deal with: the attitude of cynicism and self-righteousness held by the White House press corps.

When Ford offered me the post of White House press secretary, a few of my friends urged me not to take it. They warned that after the performance of Nixon's press secretary, Ron Ziegler, it would be the second hardest job in the government after the president's. They were right; I think it *was* the second hardest job. But I took it anyhow because, after more than two decades as a journalist watching from the outside as other people made history, I had the desire to be on the inside for once, taking part in events myself. At the time of my appointment as press secretary, a friend sent me a line written by Winston Churchill shortly after he gave up his career as a journalist to join the government. I had it framed and hung in my office because it summed up my feelings. Churchill wrote, "It is better to be making news than taking it, to be an actor rather than a critic."

And yet, I could not completely give up taking the news; I could not entirely stop being a critic. So, from inside the Ford White House, I watched the president and his government with the detachment of a lifelong outsider. I kept notes of my observations, tape-recorded at least once a week, often nightly, and transcribed later into almost 1000 typewritten pages.

The press secretary's post was a particularly good vantage point from which to view the workings of the Ford presidency. I was one of the president's nine senior advisers in his scheme of organization. More importantly, I was part of a small inner circle of Ford aides who spent far more time with the president, especially during private moments, than cabinet members and other senior officials dealing with policy matters. The members of this inner circle, who were almost like the monarch's personal chamberlains in a royal court, included the photographer, the staff coordinator, the doctor, the appointments secretary, the military aide and the press secretary.

During my years as a journalist, an outsider, I thought I knew what was going on inside the White House and the other institutions I reported on.

It sure looked different from the inside.

The presidency looked different; the press corps looked different; and I looked different to myself.

This book is all about what an outsider saw when they let him inside.

It Sure Looks Different
from the Inside

CHAPTER ONE

The Nightmare Is Over

A few hours after Spiro Agnew resigned in disgrace as vice president of the United States, House Republican Leader Gerald R. Ford received a clue that he might be President Nixon's choice to replace Agnew.

Ford and his wife, Betty, were relaxing in the airy family room of their suburban Alexandria, Virginia, home, overlooking a backyard swimming pool, when the phone rang. It was Melvin Laird, a friend and former colleague in the House, a former defense secretary and at that time a White House adviser to Nixon.

"Suppose the president asked you to be vice president, would you do it?" Laird asked Ford.

"I'm sure if I were asked I wouldn't turn it down," Ford replied.

Other possible nominees were mentioned, but the conversation kept coming back to Ford. Thinking about the phone call later, Ford concluded that Laird was calling on Nixon's behalf, to sound him out.*

When Ford hung up, he turned to Betty and asked, "What do you think?"

She replied, "If the opportunity comes, I don't see how you can say no."

Not that Betty Ford cared much for the life of a politician's wife. She did not like her husband's frequent absences for political trips. She did not like the travel, interviews and other demands made on her. She craved privacy. She was often in pain from

---

* Laird claims he urged Nixon to select Ford as his vice-presidential running mate in 1968, instead of Agnew.

arthritis and a pinched nerve in her neck, aggravated by the tensions of having to smile through a role she disliked. Mrs. Ford had her heart set on getting out of politics and getting out of Washington. Ford had promised her he would retire in 1976, after one more term in the House.

Now, instead of retiring, her husband was about to become vice president, with a good chance of becoming president soon.

On Friday night, October 12, 1973, in an elaborately staged, televised ceremony in the White House East Room, Nixon nominated Ford as Agnew's replacement. At a champagne reception after the announcement, Nixon put his arm around Betty Ford and said, "It's all yours."

She replied, "Mr. President, I don't know whether you're offering congratulations or condolences."

Nixon, struggling clumsily to make small talk, fell back on a graceless reference to money.

"Oh, well, the pay is better."

When he was named vice president, Ford had the image, as the *Wall Street Journal* put it, of "a pleasant but plodding wheelhorse who often speaks and apparently thinks in clichés." Nixon may have reasoned that the prospect of Ford in the White House would turn off congressional pressure for impeachment or resignation of the president over Watergate.

If so, his reasoning backfired.

By the time Ford was sworn in as vice president on December 6, 1973, many members of Congress had concluded that they preferred him to Nixon in the White House.

Ford's confirmation hearings in the Senate and House, widely reported on television and in the newspapers, gave Americans their first chance to size him up. They liked what they saw, especially when contrasted with Nixon. Ford came across as candid, likable, a commonsense guy. And, most of all, honest.

Ford was more thoroughly investigated than any other political figure in American history. More than 350 FBI agents from 33 field offices interviewed 1000 people all over the country. Every available record on his background was checked. The FBI report ran 1700 pages.

Nothing was found to disqualify him.

"The more they thought about Jerry Ford, the more they

thought of him," William Greider wrote in the *Washington Post* the day after Ford was sworn in as vice president. A Gallup poll a short time later found 46 percent preferred Ford for president, while only 32 percent preferred Nixon.

At the beginning of 1974, NBC broadcast its annual TV program in which news correspondents forecast what they expected to happen in the new year.

I expressed the view that Agnew's resignation had made a Nixon resignation more likely because (1) it reinforced the aura of corruption around Nixon and (2) it demonstrated that the Constitution and the political system could survive the resignation of a senior official.

"What about the new vice president, Jerry Ford?" the moderator asked.

"There's a Ford in your future," I predicted.

Covering Vice President Ford meant travel, travel and more travel. During his eight months as vice president, Ford visited forty states and flew 118,000 miles. No event was too small, from the dedication of a container wharf in New Orleans to a Saint Patrick's Day dinner of the Hibernian Society in Charleston, South Carolina, to a lunch with seventh graders in Honolulu. There was a joke during that period: If you were having a banquet and you couldn't get the local chief of police to speak, ask Vice President Ford.

In a single day Ford flew to White Sulphur Springs, West Virginia, to address a bankers' convention, flew back to Washington to speak to the Republican National Committee, drove to the suburbs to campaign for a Republican candidate for governor of Maryland, and finally drove back to Washington to attend an evening party for government officials. He was up early the next morning for a trip to Wichita Falls, Texas, and Tulsa, Oklahoma, where he held two news conferences, attended five receptions and made two speeches.

The trips provided a marvelous opportunity for a reporter to get to know Ford. He usually flew on a Convair, a small, propeller-driven plane on which he, his few aides and the handful of reporters assigned to cover him mingled easily.

Once, during a bumpy flight, magazine writer Patrick Anderson, who later wrote speeches for Jimmy Carter, was chatting with Ford when the plane hit an air pocket. Anderson's drink sloshed over Ford's head. The vice president laughed it off.

Another time, during the "streaking" craze, the traveling reporters presented Ford with a T-shirt emblazoned, "Keep on Streaking." About fifteen minutes after takeoff, Ford came running up the aisle wearing the T-shirt over his dress shirt and tie.

On one trip, newsmen informed the vice president that they had dubbed a rickety old navy plane assigned to fly him on a hop in Louisiana "Coonass Airlines." Ford's high, hard horse laugh rang through the aircraft.

While the traveling reporters liked Ford for his amiability and accessibility, they were critical of his zigzag position on Watergate. One day he would shout to the Republican audience, "I'm proud to be a member of the Nixon administration." The next day he would assert to another audience, "I'm my own man." He would praise the press as "a most significant contributor" to the exposure of the Watergate scandal, then turn around and read a speech written for him by the Nixon White House charging that the pressure for impeachment was an organized conspiracy by a small band of extremists.

A *New York Times* editorial chastised the vice president for his "rudderless tongue" on Watergate. Clearly, however, his inconsistency was the result of conflicting pressures he felt. By inclination and habit, Ford was loyal to the Republican party and a Republican president, but his integrity would not let him blindly defend the unfolding White House scandal. Moreover, his own political survival required him to keep clear of the sinking ship. Yet any overt criticism of Nixon might have been interpreted as personal ambition to move into the White House. Until almost the end, Ford insisted he had seen nothing to convince him that Nixon was guilty of an impeachable offense.

Then, on a trip to Mississippi and New Orleans the first weekend of August 1974, reporters traveling with the vice president noticed he suddenly stopped saying anything about Watergate in his speeches. He was asked about this at a news conference in the Hattiesburg, Mississippi, airport.

"In the limited time I have in these engagements, I think it's vitally important to speak about the affirmative things," Ford replied. "I don't want anyone to get the wrong impression. My views today are just as strong as they were two days ago. I believe the president is innocent of any impeachable offense and I haven't changed my mind."

However, two days earlier, White House Chief of Staff Alexander Haig had told the vice president that a June 23, 1972, tape was about to be released. It would be a bombshell. Haig asked Ford whether he was prepared to become president in the immediate future.

Returning from his Mississippi-Louisiana trip on Monday, August 5, 1974, shortly after the June 23 "smoking gun" tape was made public, the vice president issued a statement saying he would not make any more comments about Watergate "until the facts are more fully available."

Three nights later, Nixon went on television and announced his resignation. When the TV speech was over, Ford stepped onto the sidewalk in front of his home to address a forest of microphones. It was raining lightly. Outside the circle of camera lights, neighbors craned for a look at their friend who the next day would become president of the United States.

"I pledge to you tonight, as I will pledge tomorrow and in the future, my best efforts and cooperation, leadership and dedication that is good for America and good for the world," Ford told a badly shaken nation in a voice that sounded comfortingly calm and self-assured. He made his first personnel appointment right there in the wet street. He asked Henry Kissinger, whom he described as "a very great man," to stay on as secretary of state.

The next morning, Friday, August 9, 1974, after a tearful, rambling farewell to his staff and a last defiant wave, Nixon flew away from the White House by helicopter, bound for exile in San Clemente.

A short time later, standing on a raised platform in the East Room beneath a portrait of George Washington, Ford was sworn in as president by black-robed Chief Justice Warren Burger. A somber-looking Betty Ford held the Bible.

"I assume the presidency under extraordinary circumstances never before experienced by Americans," Ford began his inaugural speech. "I am acutely aware that you have not elected me as your president by your ballots and so I ask you to confirm me as your president with your prayers. . . .

"I believe that truth is the glue that holds government together, not only our government but civilization itself. That bond, though strained, is unbroken at home and abroad. In all my public and private acts as your president, I expect to follow my instincts of openness and candor with full confidence that honesty is the best policy in the end.

"My fellow Americans, our long national nightmare is over.

"Our Constitution works; our great republic is a government of laws and not of men. Here the people rule."

Less than an hour after taking his oath as president, Ford came to the White House press room to announce the appointment of Jerry terHorst, the Washington bureau chief of the *Detroit News*, as his press secretary. As a reporter for the *Grand Rapids Press*, terHorst had covered Ford's first campaign for Congress in 1948. They had been friends ever since.

I received a promotion from NBC. I was to follow Ford to the White House, to become a White House correspondent for the network.

CHAPTER TWO

A Ron, but Not a Ziegler

On Sunday morning, September 8, 1974, I covered, as a reporter, Ford's attendance at services at Saint John's Church across Lafayette Park from the White House. Church rarely produces a news story. Sending a correspondent and camera crew to church with the president is part of what the networks euphemistically call "protective coverage." That means they don't want to miss the pictures if someone takes a shot at the president.

After church I walked through the park, across Pennsylvania Avenue and up the driveway to the White House, expecting the normal announcement of a "lid," meaning no more news was expected for the rest of the day. But that Sunday the Press Office advised, "Stick around. There might be something."

Soon, reporters who never showed up on Sunday started streaming into the press room. They'd been called at home by the White House and told to come in. Something big was happening. Fidgeting on the green leather sofas in the press room and milling around the cubicles in their writing area, the reporters speculated on what the news might be. I guessed it was a big foreign-policy development, maybe the announcement of a major overseas trip.

Shortly before 11 A.M., I and the other newsmen were ushered into the Oval Office. Ford was seated behind his desk, facing a single TV camera transmitting pictures to all the networks. A canvas cloth was taped over the rug and floor to prevent damage from the television equipment. The office was exactly as Nixon had left it, except for a display of photographs of Ford's family on a table behind the desk.

A technician cued the president. In a tense voice, Ford announced he was granting a "full, free and absolute pardon" to Richard Nixon.

"My conscience tells me clearly and certainly that I cannot prolong the bad dreams that continue to reopen a chapter that is closed," Ford read solemnly from the papers on the desk. "My conscience tells me that only I, as president, have the constitutional power to firmly shut and seal this book. My conscience tells me it is my duty, not merely to proclaim domestic tranquillity, but to use every means that I have to insure it. . . .

"I do believe, with all my heart and mind and spirit, that I—not as president but as a humble servant of God—will receive justice without mercy if I fail to show mercy."

Ford picked up a pen from the green felt covering the desk and signed the pardon.

The public, stunned at first, quickly grew angry and suspicious. Ford insisted then and later that his only reasons for giving the pardon were to close the book on Watergate, avoid the lacerating national experience of a long Nixon trial and focus the nation's attention on the real problems of the present and the future. Nevertheless, speculation about a deal between Ford and Nixon sprang up almost immediately. The day of the pardon, during an NBC-TV news special, I said that many people suspected a deal but there was no proof.

Whatever my personal feelings about it, the president's announcement of the pardon changed my life, because it caused Jerry terHorst to resign as press secretary. In a letter to Ford, terHorst said he could not "in good conscience support" the pardon of Nixon "even before he has been charged with commission of any crime."

Some Ford staff members thought terHorst resigned because Philip Buchen, the president's legal counsel, had misled him a few days earlier by denying that a pardon was in the works. That caused the popular and conscientious terHorst innocently to mislead a reporter who'd gotten a tip that a pardon was imminent. Other Ford aides thought terHorst was simply overwhelmed by the amount of work and pressure in the Press Office and took the first convenient occasion to bail out. But whatever terHorst's reasons, his timing bothered Ford enormously. Ford never forgave terHorst for quitting at such a crucial moment, referring to his former friend in private conversations afterward as "that son of a bitch."

Nevertheless, terHorst's successor would have a tough act to follow. In fact, two tough acts to follow. The new man would have to live down Ziegler and live up to terHorst.

Four days after terHorst resigned I received a call from a man named David Smith who identified himself as a White House personnel recruiter. He asked if I was interested in the press secretary's job. I said I was, under certain conditions.

He asked me some routine questions about my background and my knowledge of the job. He also asked whether I felt someone from TV could be press secretary. (No TV correspondent had ever been the White House press secretary, although television was by far the most influential news medium.) I said yes.

Smith called back later in the afternoon.

"I just need to know one more thing. What's your full name?"

I figured he was running an FBI check on me.

Three days later, on a Sunday, I received a call from Robert Hartmann, counsellor to the president. Hartmann, a short, plump man with yellowing white hair and a bad smoker's hack, had been chief of staff to Vice President Ford and legislative assistant to Congressman Ford. He was a speechwriter and general adviser to the new president.

The phone conversation was long and elliptical. Hartmann said he had a list of possible press secretaries. I was on it. So were David Broder of the *Washington Post;* Robert McCloskey, a highly respected former State Department spokesman; and Bill Roberts, who had been on Ford's vice-presidential press staff and was then an assistant White House press secretary. Hartmann said Ford might be interested in a woman for the job. He didn't think Helen Thomas of the UPI or Marjorie Hunter of the *New York Times* was quite suited, but Bonnie Angelo of *Time* magazine might be all right.

Hartmann said Melvin Laird was pushing Jerry Freidheim, who had been press spokesman for the Pentagon when Laird was defense secretary. Laird was playing golf with Ford that afternoon and was probably pushing Freidheim, Hartmann grumped. Hartmann did not like Laird or Freidheim.

Hartmann never asked directly whether I wanted to be press secretary, but at one point he said, "I wouldn't want anybody to turn down the president to his face." When I didn't say I would turn him down, Hartmann took that to mean I wanted to be considered.

He was right. I was interested in the job because after twenty years as a journalist, as a professional observer at events, always standing on the sidelines watching others perform, I had the itch to be a participant. Besides, I was dissatisfied at NBC, despite the new White House assignment. I felt the one-minute or one-and-a-half-minute stories I was limited to on "The Nightly News" required so little effort that I was operating at only 10 percent of my capacity. I was frustrated by the need to cram the most complex subjects into 100 or 150 words. It drove me up the wall to have to argue with news producers for another five seconds, another ten words—and lose the argument.

Three days after our Sunday phone conversation, Hartmann called me back and asked directly if I was interested in being Ford's press secretary. I said I was. He told me to come to see the president the following day at either 3 P.M. or 6 P.M.

"I recommend three P.M.," he advised. "The president sometimes gets a little out of sorts late in the afternoon."

I took 3 P.M.

When you walk into the Oval Office you are struck by how quiet it is, and how bright with glareless light. It was still decorated with Nixon's furnishings: an almost garishly blue oval rug ringed with yellow stars; bright blue and yellow upholstery on the sofas and side chairs; ugly china birds by Edward Marshall Boehm on the shelves. The glass in the tall windows behind the desk is thick and green, bulletproof.

Ford looked at ease in the Oval Office. For most of the time I'd known him, I'd seen him only in a House member's role, part of a team, just one vote out of 435, and then in the vice president's role, traveling frenetically, delivering political speeches and performing trivial ceremonial duties. Now, for the first time in his life, Ford was in an executive's role with the sole responsibility for making important decisions. He appeared comfortable with it, tipped back slightly in the high-backed leather chair, turned away for the moment from the documents and decision papers cluttering his desk. In six weeks as president, Ford seemed to have grown more assured and forceful.

He quickly came to the point. He was surprised to hear that I was interested in the press secretary's job, since he thought it would require a big pay cut for a TV correspondent. I said I didn't even know what the job paid. He said he wasn't sure either, but he thought it was $42,500, the highest level then allowed for White House staffers.

He mentioned terHorst, with some anger. He complained that terHorst had never severed his loyalties to the press, had not given his loyalties totally to the president. Ford said he badly needed a replacement, someone who would not quit on him.

I told Ford I differed with terHorst on one point: I could see no reason why a press secretary needed to agree with every presidential decision. But I emphasized strongly that a press secretary needed to know everything that went on in the White House. The best press secretaries during my time in Washington were the ones who sat in on decisions, getting their information firsthand.

Ford assured me his new press secretary would be one of his top aides, with total access to the Oval Office, and would attend the meetings where the decisions were made.

I told the president I didn't believe I could be a huckster for his programs. The press secretary's job, I felt, was to announce the president's decisions, and why and how he had reached them. But I didn't think I could be a salesman.

"Well, if *I* can't sell the program, then the press secretary can't sell the program," Ford replied.

I explained that I was not a registered Republican. In fact, the last time I'd voted in a presidential election had been fourteen years earlier, in 1960, when I voted for John Kennedy. Every election since then I'd been traveling for NBC, following one candidate or another, and I had not bothered to get an absentee ballot.

"I would like you to take it," Ford finally said. "Would you like to think it over?"

"I really had the feeling this was in the wind for the last four or five days," I replied. "I've thought it over and I've talked it over with my wife, and there is really no need to think it over anymore.

"My answer is yes."

My appointment would be announced the next day, Ford decided.

On my way out of the White House after accepting the job, I bumped into several reporters who put two and two together and asked me if I was going to be the new press secretary.

"Not that I know of," I lied.

When I got home I had a call from John Hushen, the deputy press secretary. Hushen said I'd given a bad answer; I should not have misled the reporters. He advised me to phone all the reporters I'd lied to and tell them I was under consideration for press secretary but any announcement would have to come from the White House.

I reached the last reporter shortly before midnight.

It was a good lesson.

President Ford was scheduled to announce my appointment on Friday, September 20, 1974, immediately after a meeting with Soviet

Foreign Minister Andrei Gromyko. The meeting was supposed to last ninety minutes, but it ran nearly two and a half hours. During the wait, Assistant Press Secretary Bill Roberts took me on a tour of the White House offices, introducing me to members of the staff. I was surprised at how easily they seemed to accept me as one of them when only yesterday I'd been an outsider.

When I was finally ushered into the Oval Office just before the announcement, I jokingly asked the president, "Is it too late to back out?"

He didn't realize I was joking and responded seriously, "I hope you won't want to."

As we marched toward the press room for the announcement, I could see the brightness of the TV lights and the photographers jamming the doorway. I'd been on the other side of the lights so many times. For the first time I was getting my wish to be a participant instead of an observer.

Ford recalled to the White House press corps that he had gotten to know me when I covered his endless travels as vice president. "I admired his skill and objectivity as a reporter," the president said. "I enjoyed his company."

Mindful that some of the older newspaper reporters still considered television correspondents to be actors rather than real journalists, Ford felt compelled to point out that I had been a newspaper and wire-service writer before I went into TV.

I'd drafted some remarks for the ceremony.

"I hope the White House press corps is ready for another Ron," I began. "I am a Ron, but not a Ziegler, I can tell you that.

"I will never knowingly lie to the White House press corps. I will never knowingly mislead the White House press corps, and I think if I ever do you would be justified in questioning my continued usefulness in this job."

(I wondered later whether Jimmy Carter had stolen that line from me.)

I explained to the reporters my understanding with Ford: I didn't have to agree with the president's decision; I would not be a salesman for the president's programs; I would be kept informed of what went on in the White House; and I would transmit as much information as possible to the American people.

"I think it is probably too late to go back to a honeymoon," I concluded, referring to the relationship between the White House and the press. "But maybe we could have a trial reconciliation."

CHAPTER THREE

First Impressions

My first day on the job was a blur of phone calls, visitors, meetings and surprises as I learned about the problems and perquisites of being the president's press secretary.

I was surprised by the press secretary's heavy administrative duties. Forty-five people worked in the Press Office, one of the largest offices in the White House. It seemed most of them came to see me that first day to complain that they wanted less work, more money, a new title, a different job, more travel, less travel or a rival fired. One secretary came in to tell me she wasn't getting along with the other secretaries, they wouldn't talk to her, and she wanted a transfer to Mrs. Ford's staff. It wasn't exactly the kind of earth-shaking problem I thought I would be handling as a senior White House adviser.

I attended my first meeting with the president, a session with economic advisers to discuss Ford's speech to a White House economic conference the following weekend. I was dazzled. I kept thinking: "I'm sitting here six seats away from the president of the United States and I'm going to be doing this every day for the next few years." (In a short time the awe faded, but I never became blasé.)

Late in the afternoon I was faced with my first press problem. A reporter phoned requesting information on a story that Steve Ford, the president's son who had just graduated from high school, had failed to register for the draft within thirty days after his eighteenth birthday, as required by law. I asked John Marsh, a counsellor to the president, and Navy Commander Howard Kerr, a military aide, to come to my office to discuss the newsman's query.

Marsh, a former congressman from Virginia and former assistant defense secretary, was one of Ford's most steady and reliable advisers. He assured me that Steve had not intentionally tried to avoid the draft. He had just forgotten to register, Marsh said. Steve had registered for the draft seventy days beyond the deadline, and coincidentally, a few days after Ford announced an amnesty program for Vietnam draft evaders.

If I'd still been a newsman I might have questioned Marsh's explanation. But now I blithely passed it on to the reporter.

On my second day in the White House I spent more than an hour with Alexander Haig in his large corner office down the corridor from the Oval Office. He was a handsome former army general who had been Nixon's deputy assistant for national security affairs before being rushed in as chief of staff when H. R. Haldeman resigned. During Nixon's final days, Haig had been almost the acting president, keeping the routine White House machinery going while the president was preoccupied with Watergate, and holding everything together during the upheaval of the resignation.

Ford had kept Haig as chief of staff. But after six weeks of poisonous leaks to reporters and private complaints to the president from Hartmann and other Ford loyalists about retaining a top Nixon aide, the president concluded Haig had to go and appointed him military commander of NATO. He was leaving the White House in three days.

Haig looked cool and thoughtful, but weary, when I visited his office. He used the meeting to deliver his candid assessment of the Ford White House. He said he had come through Watergate with his integrity intact and he didn't want to stay around and have his reputation torn down by leaks from the Ford staff. Haig knew that some staffers objected to him. Hartmann and other aides who had come to the White House with Ford had been bad-mouthing Haig and other leftover Nixon staff members for alleged Watergate connections and for trying to isolate Ford from new ideas and old friends.

"They want a Nixon White House without Nixon," one Ford loyalist had grumbled to me in my NBC days.

I said something to Haig about the Ford people fighting with the Nixon people. Haig disagreed. The problem, he said, was Ford people fighting with other Ford people, meaning a traditional struggle for personal power in the White House hierarchy.

"I get the impression the president realizes that the people who were good enough for his staff in the House and the vice presidency might not be good enough for his staff in the White House," I told Haig. "I think he's going to bring in better people."

"I'm not so sure," Haig replied.

He said he liked and was impressed by Ford, but he had reservations about whether the White House was going to be able to operate effectively the way the president was organizing it. Ford had decreed that there would be no chief of staff after Haig left. Nine senior advisers would have equal access to the president. This was known as the "spokes of the wheel" theory of White House organization. The members of the senior staff were the spokes, all dealing directly with the president, the hub.

Every recent president—Nixon, Ford and Carter—promised to run his White House in this fashion in the interest of openness and accessibility, but it never worked well because a president doesn't have time to run the White House administrative machinery himself.

Leaning far back in his chair, Haig criticized the remarks I'd made at my announcement ceremony. He thought it was a mistake to proclaim that I would never lie or mislead. Let the reporters discover for themselves that you are honest, Haig advised. Then they will write stories about it. If you keep telling newsmen how truthful you are, you give them an incentive to try to catch you in a lie.

Haig also complained about my crack about being a Ron but not a Ziegler. "Ron had a tremendous belief in the truth," Haig insisted. "He never told a lie."

At one point Haig pointed to his head and said he was "a great computer," taking in and analyzing every bit of information about everything going on in the White House. He said the other two "computers" were the president and the press secretary.

Walking back to my office, I wondered about my capacity to be such a "computer." I was already having trouble keeping up with all the reading. Two thick briefing books had been dumped on my desk, one on foreign policy, one on domestic policy. I also was trying to get through a folder on an energy speech the president was making the following week and a tabbed notebook listing the administration's position on dozens of issues.

Haig offered some pertinent advice on handling the heavy work load. He told me one of the prime requirements for serving in the White House was sheer physical stamina.

The next day, Sunday, I arrived at my office at 9 A.M. No one else was there yet and I was so new I didn't know how to switch on the lights.

I received press queries about a Maxine Cheshire story in the *Washington Post* that morning saying the Ford White House had impounded 1100 boxes of gifts Nixon received from foreign countries and American admirers.

William Casselman, a lawyer from the White House Legal Counsel's office, gave me the information I needed to explain the situation factually to reporters.

"There's one problem," Casselman said. "Two pieces of jewelry are missing—a pin from Japan and a gold cigarette box from someplace else. They are simply missing."

Casselman said he hoped I wouldn't have to give that information to reporters.

"Well, the question may come up," I told him. "Maybe I can set up a briefing on the president's energy speech tomorrow and that might divert the reporters' attention," I suggested.

"Your attitude sure has changed in a hurry," Casselman commented.

"Well, it looks so different from the inside," I replied.

Asking pesky and embarrassing questions had been my job at NBC. Now such questions seemed to me to be aggravating diversions from the message I wanted to get out on Ford's substantive activities.

Earlier, at a staff meeting, I had asked my assistants for ideas to make press coverage of the White House more open "or at least to give the appearance of being more open." If I'd still been a reporter and heard the press secretary talk about giving the "appearance" of openness, I would have done a story accusing him of concocting phony media events to polish the president's image. I was surprised by how quickly I was shifting my loyalties and my attitudes.

After I'd attended my first few meetings with the president— listening to the blunt political talk, the construction of scenarios, the repeated question, "How will it play in the press?"—I began to understand why the Nixon transcripts sounded the way they did.

CHAPTER FOUR

Betty

I'd been the press secretary exactly one week when my first crisis arrived.

During Betty Ford's semiannual gynecological examination at Bethesda Naval Hospital, a lump about the size of a quarter was discovered in her right breast. The White House doctor, Navy Rear Admiral William Lukash, asked another doctor to reexamine Mrs. Ford at the White House early that evening. The second doctor confirmed the lump.

The doctors immediately informed the president and Mrs. Ford and recommended that Betty go into the hospital the next evening, Friday, for an operation on Saturday to remove the lump. If it was found to be cancerous, the doctors said they would remove Mrs. Ford's breast immediately.

I agreed not to announce the discovery of the lump and the impending operation until Friday evening, after Mrs. Ford already was in Bethesda Hospital. She wanted to go through her schedule on Friday as if nothing were wrong, and she wanted to get into the hospital without running through a gauntlet of cameras and microphones. I knew the reporters would be angry when they learned they had been kept in the dark. But, again, I felt my loyalties shifting fast.

Mrs. Ford stuck to her crowded schedule Friday: accompanying the president to the dedication of a Lyndon B. Johnson memorial park across the Potomac River in Virginia, dropping in at a Salvation Army luncheon and entertaining Mrs. Johnson at tea in the afternoon.

About 6 P.M. a military aide phoned to notify me that Mrs. Ford was in the hospital. I went to the Oval Office to clear my announcement with the president. He seemed worried and distracted. I suggested delaying the statement until he had left a reception he was about to attend for participants in a White House economic conference, so reporters could not bombard him with questions about Mrs. Ford.

"No, no. Get it out right away," he instructed.

Reporters were summoned from homes and offices. I read my statement and invited questions. I'd learned in just a week that White House press briefings lasted so long because every question was asked about a half-dozen times. My briefing on Mrs. Ford's operation was no exception. For example, this exchange:

Q.: Do you have a time for surgery, Ron?
NESSEN: Sometime tomorrow.
Q.: Morning or afternoon, do you know?
NESSEN: We don't know. . . .
Q.: When is it scheduled?
NESSEN: There is no scheduled time that I know of.
Q.: Can you say whether it is in the morning or the afternoon?
NESSEN: I don't know.

The operation began at eight o'clock the next morning. Within fifteen minutes the lump had been removed, examined and found to be cancerous.

The president was in his office, working with Bob Hartmann on the speech he was scheduled to deliver later that day to the closing session of the economic conference, when he was notified of the test results. Ford excused himself and stepped into a small bathroom off the Oval Office. When he returned in a few moments, Hartmann could see his eyes were red from tears.

"Go ahead and cry," Hartmann urged. "Do cry."

The two of them sat in the Oval Office and wept.

The president decided to visit the hospital before making his speech. It was raining hard, but someone had made the decision that the weather was marginally acceptable for a helicopter flight. John Marsh thought the president's chopper almost crashed into the Washington Monument while taking off from the White House in the driving storm.

The Fords' eldest son, Michael, then a seminary student at the Gordon-Conwell Theological Seminary in South Hamilton, Massachusetts, knelt in the aisle of the helicopter beside his father, clutching a Bible. The president bowed his head close to Mike's. Throughout the flight they prayed for Mrs. Ford and read passages from the Bible.

At the hospital Ford received a report from the doctors: They had removed the right breast, underlying muscles and lymph glands beneath the right arm. They would not know until the pathology report came back in a few days whether the cancer had spread beyond the lump and what further treatment might be needed.

The president visited his wife briefly in the recovery room, but she was too groggy to converse. Even at such a private moment of anguish, Secret Service agents and aides hovered near the president in the hushed hospital corridor.

It was raining harder than ever when the time came for Ford to leave the hospital for his speech to the economic conference. The Secret Service said a helicopter still could fly safely, but Marsh vetoed the chopper flight as too dangerous and ordered a motorcade.

I wondered how the president could remain outwardly calm under the tremendous strain of his wife's illness. And Betty's operation was not the only source of strain; the preparation of a major speech for the conclusion of the economic conference had caused problems too.

It had been a difficult speech to draft because the president had not yet made his decisions on new steps to combat what was then perceived to be the major economic problem—inflation. Hartmann finally stayed up all night before the president's appearance to write the speech. One paragraph was inserted in the holding room, just off the stage, only seconds before Ford walked out to deliver it.

The attendees at the economic conference—economists, members of Congress and representatives of business, labor and consumers—awaited the president's speech in a huge hotel ballroom in downtown Washington, along with live TV cameras.

On the way from the hospital, the president had written out on a sheet of paper, with much scratching out and rewriting and editing, an opening paragraph, which he now began to read:

"Just one personal note, if I might. I just returned from the hospital where I saw Betty as she came from the operating room. Dr. Lukash has assured me that she came through the operation all right. It has been a difficult thirty-six hours. Our faith will sustain us, and Betty would expect me to be here."

His voice cracked with emotion. His chin trembled. But he pulled himself together and went on with the speech, promising to re-organize the government's machinery for handling the economy, hold the federal budget below $300 billion and send his detailed proposals to Congress within ten days. The speech was pallid, but the press and participants were generally sympathetic because the president had come at all, under the circumstances. Hubert Humphrey said tears were streaming from Ford's eyes as he walked off the stage.

Except for the brief initial concealment of Mrs. Ford's plans to enter the hospital, we made the decision to be extraordinarily candid and complete in reporting on her operation and its aftermath. I announced that Mrs. Ford had cancer just moments after the president was notified, while she still had three hours to go on the operating table. We produced doctors for briefings, which were so detailed and technical in parts that they might have stumped a medical class.

As a result of the heavy news coverage of Mrs. Ford's operation, millions of women rushed to their doctors to be tested for breast cancer. Some found they had it, including Vice President Rockefeller's wife, Happy, who underwent a mastectomy just three weeks after Mrs. Ford's operation. Doctors credited Betty's widely publicized experience with alerting women to the risk of breast cancer and the importance of early detection.*

Mrs. Ford recovered quickly from her operation. However, some cancer cells were found in the lymph glands removed, so she was given an anticancer drug for two years to prevent a recurrence. Dr. Lukash issued periodic reports saying Mrs. Ford appeared to be cured of cancer, but her health remained frail and she tired easily. She had some good days and some not so good.

During Betty Ford's first twenty-five years in Washington, life had not always been easy. Divorced from a first husband when she married Ford in 1948, Betty gave up her own career as a department-store fashion coordinator and a Martha Graham–trained dancer, only to find herself stuck away in the suburbs, the anonymous wife of a congressman from Grand Rapids, Michigan. From the beginning she learned that politics and sports were rivals for her husband's attention. On their honeymoon in October 1948, Ford took her to a University of Michigan football game and a speech

---

* However, after she recovered, Mrs. Ford shied away from participating in cancer charities, perhaps because she didn't want to be reminded of her close call.

by Republican presidential candidate Thomas E. Dewey before hurrying back to Grand Rapids to resume his first campaign for Congress.

After Ford won that election, he and Betty moved to the Washington suburbs, where the children came one after the other, first Michael, then Jack, then Steve and finally Susan. Ford was away much of the time on political business—sometimes two nights out of three—leaving his wife to raise the children and run the household. That was a heavy burden, occasionally becoming almost more than Betty Ford could handle. The pressures aggravated the pinched nerve in her neck, forcing her to give up the skiing and golf she enjoyed and subjecting her to periods of intense pain.

At one point during Ford's congressional career, Mrs. Ford consulted a psychiatrist to help her cope with her problems. And over the years—including the White House years—she sought relief in alcohol, pain-killers and tranquilizers. The drugs, combined with the drinking, sometimes induced a state of drowsiness and slow, slurred speech. Mrs. Ford's family and friends were concerned about her dependence, but kept the problem a closely guarded secret from the public.

Finally, fifteen months after leaving the White House, Mrs. Ford checked into the alcohol and drug rehabilitation center of the Long Beach, California, naval hospital for treatment.

"Over a period of time I got to the point where I was over-medicating myself," Mrs. Ford said in a statement when she entered the hospital. "It's an insidious thing and I need to rid myself of its damaging effects." Ten days after she was admitted to the hospital, Mrs. Ford publicly acknowledged her alcoholism. "I am not only addicted to the medication I have been taking for my arthritis, but also to alcohol."

Mrs. Ford's son Steve elaborated on the problem when he told a television interviewer that she's "fighting a very, very rough battle against the effects of Valium and alcoholism . . . I know the problem exists. She does drink but to what extent I couldn't tell you. Anytime you mix alcohol and drugs you have a problem."

Ford was away on a speaking trip when his wife was admitted to the hospital. But he returned to California and enrolled in a series of seminars to better understand her problem and treatment.

Ford once confided to me during a moment of introspection that he regretted being away from home so much when his children were growing up. He rationalized that he had made up for his lack of companionship by achieving successes in public service of which his children could be proud. Despite Ford's frequent absences, the parents and children were close and affectionate, because of Betty's influence and because of the annual family vacations in Vail, Colorado, and Palm Springs, California, during which Ford put aside politics and devoted time to his wife and children.

However, one effect of Ford's travels away from home over the years was to make Betty jealous of other women who showed attention to her husband. I learned about that trait early in my term as press secretary when Vicki Carr, an attractive singer of Mexican ancestry, was invited to entertain at a White House state dinner. She flirted with the president and he responded. As Ford was escorting the singer out to the front portico at the end of the evening, Miss Carr asked, "What's your favorite Mexican dish?"

"You are," the president responded, in Mrs. Ford's hearing.

"That woman will never get into the White House again," the First Lady later snapped. "She was too familiar with my husband."

Another time, when Raquel Welch came to the White House as the representative of some charitable campaign, Mrs. Ford asked me how the men on the staff had liked her.

I replied, honestly, that I wasn't overly impressed by her looks.

"Oh, sure," Betty responded disbelievingly. "I'll bet my husband paid plenty of attention to her."

Mrs. Ford often nagged the president mildly about newspaper photos or television films that pictured him with attractive women. Once, when a front-page picture appeared showing the president enthusiastically kissing a drum majorette during a campaign trip to Texas, a few members of the staff drafted a mock briefing paper for Ford, suggesting how to explain the photo to Betty when he got home. In the section of the paper where suggested presidential remarks were normally outlined, we proposed that Ford say, "Yes, dear . . . yes, dear . . . yes, dear . . ."

Mrs. Ford's jealousy also was aroused when the president left for Martinique in December 1974 for conferences with French President Valery Giscard d'Estaing. Before one meeting, Kissinger introduced Ford to a stunning red-haired girl named Nicole attached to the French press office. Ford joked to Giscard that he would trade his press secretary for the attractive Nicole. News photographers snapped the scene and a picture of Ford, Nicole, Kissinger, Giscard and me appeared on the front page of the *New York Times*.

One of the first things Mrs. Ford wanted to know when the president got back from Martinique was who the hell was Nicole.

Ford occasionally gave his wife grounds for jealousy. At one White House dinner where the actress Elke Sommer was a guest, Mrs. Ford approached the president several times to dance. Each time he looked past her and made a beeline for Elke Sommer. Finally, the First Lady, in exasperation, commandeered a handsome military aide to dance with her.

Another attractive woman who caught Ford's eye at a White House dinner was Phyllis George, the CBS sportscaster and former Miss America. As the guests adjourned to the East Room for dancing after the dinner, George—the date of bachelor congressman David Bowen of Mississippi—zeroed in on the president and asked him for a filmed interview about football. A few minutes later the luscious sports reporter tracked me down on the dance floor to inform me that Ford had agreed to do the interview the next day. I figured she had mistaken the president's usual politeness in such situations for assent, so I did nothing to arrange the interview.

But the next morning Ford had not forgotten. He asked me what time Phyllis George was coming to interview him. "She's awfully attractive," the president added.

I got the picture. Trying to cover my inaction, I told Ford I didn't know how to get in touch with her.

"If her date is half the man I think he is," Ford advised, "you can reach her through his office."

The president was right. I located George through Congressman Bowen and told her to come to the White House right away for her interview.

While the CBS camera crew was setting up its equipment in the Oval Office, I guided the stunning George into a small presidential hideaway office next door and left her alone with Ford. When I knocked discreetly twenty minutes later to announce that the camera crew was ready for the filming, Ford led George into the Oval Office, grinning like a schoolboy.

I thought to myself, There's nothing wrong with a woman reporter using her sex appeal to get an interview with the president, and there's nothing wrong with a healthy man in his sixties enjoying a few minutes of private conversation with a woman as attractive as Phyllis George. And thank God Betty Ford didn't find out about it!

On one of the rare trips when Mrs. Ford accompanied the president, she caught him openly ogling a pretty girl at one event, having forgotten that his wife was along.

"Jerry!" the First Lady hissed through clenched teeth, just like any wife in those circumstances.

During a visit to Helsinki in the summer of 1975, Ford—like most of the men in the American delegation—was attracted to the lovely, friendly Finnish girls. One girl, whose job it was to shepherd news photographers, particularly caught the president's eye. He flirted with her and commented about her to aides several times.

Aboard *Air Force One* leaving Helsinki, I mentioned to the president and Mrs. Ford how much I and others on the staff had enjoyed the visit and how much some of us wished we could come back sometime.

"The next time we will come without the ladies," Ford joked.

"The hell you will!" Mrs. Ford retorted.

The years of struggling to manage a home and family on a congressman's salary made Mrs. Ford careful about money, a characteristic she brought to the White House. She phoned me in the Press Office one morning in December 1974 to ask whether the Senate vote that night on Nelson Rockefeller's nomination for vice president was likely to interfere with a White House Christmas reception for the press corps scheduled for 7 to 9 P.M. The Fords had engaged an orchestra from New York City to play at the reception, paying the band's fee and transportation out of their own pocket.

"I don't want them to go to waste," Mrs. Ford fretted. I assured her the Rockefeller vote would be over in time for her to get her money's worth from the orchestra.

In the same phone conversation, Betty told me that the family had decided to fly by commercial airliner, tourist class, to Vail for its annual Christmas skiing vacation. Mrs. Ford explained that she and the president were miffed by an Internal Revenue Service ruling—which grew out of the Nixon family's use of government aircraft for personal activities—requiring Ford to pay first-class air fares for his wife and children on *Air Force One* or else count their travel as the equivalent of income on his tax return. Mrs. Ford informed me that rather than fork out first-class fares, the president intended to buy the family tourist-class tickets to Vail on a commercial airliner, as he had done every year before moving to the White House. Eventually Ford was talked out of that idea on security grounds.

The characteristic which Betty Ford's husband, children and friends found most irritating was her habitual tardiness in arriving for appointments and functions. Some friends suspected her lateness was an assertion of independence during the years when she may have felt left out of Ford's political life. Ford occasionally displayed irritation when Betty was not ready on time, but mostly he accepted it with resignation.

After moving to the White House, where she had greater social responsibilities and a staff to help her stick to her schedule, the First Lady was less often late. Major Robert Barrett, the president's army aide and a particular favorite of Mrs. Ford's, was frequently assigned to make sure Betty was ready on schedule for major events.

But Betty is primarily a very strong woman, and this deep inner strength became increasingly apparent when she became First Lady. For Betty Ford's life in the White House was shadowed by a series of tragedies. And each time, she met the crisis with poise.

Once, while Mrs. Ford was seated at the head table at a banquet in New York City, a man receiving an award collapsed with a heart attack practically at her feet. While doctors vainly tried to save the man's life, the First Lady moved coolly to the podium microphone and asked the audience to join with her in a prayer for the victim.

Probably the most shocking personal tragedy to befall Betty Ford in the White House was the suicide of the husband of her assistant and friend, Nancy Howe. James Howe, a professor and retired army major, shot himself to death in the bathroom of his home on April 10, 1975, after learning that the *Washington Post* was working on a story charging that he and his wife had accepted free lodging at a resort in the Dominican Republic from Korean wheeler-dealer Tongsun Park.

Police alerted the White House about the suicide just as the president and First Lady were leaving for the Capitol, where Ford was to deliver an important foreign-policy speech. The news of Howe's death was withheld from Mrs. Ford until she returned to the White House after the speech for fear that she might be overwhelmed by grief in public if told before she took her place in the gallery.

Two years before, Nancy Howe had volunteered to help Betty handle the new demands on her when Ford became vice president. The two women formed a close relationship, almost like sisters. Nancy called Betty by the affectionate nickname "Petunia." When Ford became president, Nancy virtually moved into the White House to be with Betty.

But Mrs. Howe was badly shaken by her husband's suicide. The Secret Service took away her White House pass on grounds that in her distraught state she might cause harm. Betty Ford lost her confidante and companion. No one else filled the role. However, the fact that Ford, as president, spent more time at home with Betty than he had for years helped to ease the loss.

Indeed, after they moved to the White House, Betty Ford blossomed into an outgoing, witty and warm public personality with strong and independent views. Reporters loved her because she was always good for a colorful quote. The years as an anonymous housewife were over. She was no silent, smiling, plastic politician's wife.

In the White House, Betty Ford became a leading advocate of the Equal Rights Amendment and more liberal abortion laws. This was no act to create a chic media image; she was equally outspoken on these matters in private. Once, after the president had explained his own conservative views on limiting abortions in a TV interview with Walter Cronkite, Mrs. Ford sent him her reaction scrawled in the margin of the transcript of the program: "Baloney! This is not going to do you a damn bit of good."

Mrs. Ford gained a reputation for speaking openly about sex and other delicate subjects in press interviews and public appearances. That reputation stemmed in part from her interview with Morley Safer for "60 Minutes" on CBS-TV. The First Lady didn't duck when Safer asked her a silly, insulting question, "What if Susan Ford came to you and said, 'Mother, I'm having an affair'?"

"Well, I wouldn't be surprised," Mrs. Ford replied. "I think she's a perfectly normal human being like all young girls."

The answer was a sensation to reporters and the public, accustomed to First Ladies who came out foursquare for marriage and morality, when they said anything at all. It sent a shiver through Ford's political advisers, who worried about the reaction of conservative voters. But ultimately Mrs. Ford's candid views on this and other subjects, delivered at a time when American women generally were struggling to break out of their stereotyped roles, endeared her to far more people than were offended.

CHAPTER FIVE

Haunted by Nixon

I had hanging in my White House office a framed quotation from a column by Jerry Greene in the *New York Daily News:*

"Watergate is harder to wash away than the spray of a skunk."

The specter of Richard Nixon haunted the Ford White House from the first day to the last. The White House press corps, particularly, remained obsessed with Nixon. It was difficult for many journalists to come down from the high of Watergate. They were addicted. Lies! Tapes! Exposures! Drama! Officials caught, disgraced, jailed! A president driven from office! The valiant press vindicated! Its wicked accusers discredited! Who could be happy again covering mundane matters like budgets, energy and legislative proposals?

At my first White House briefing I got a taste of things to come. Much of the thirty-eight minutes was devoted to questions about Nixon, his phone calls to Ford, his former staff members still on the White House payroll, his health, the intelligence briefings being provided to him, and so on. The reporters paid less attention to two major news items involving Ford: his appointment of NATO Ambassador and former White House staff member Donald Rumsfeld as White House coordinator, replacing Alexander Haig, and some tough words the president had directed at the Arabs the day before in an energy speech.

Phone conversations between Ford and Nixon were always the subject of obsessive questioning. I was sensitive, probably oversensitive, about discussing these talks because I felt stories about them incorrectly implied a close relationship between Ford and Nixon, perhaps a sinister relationship.

In answering questions about one phone call shortly after becoming press secretary, I said only that Nixon had made a "passing reference" to public reaction to the pardon. Ford later gave *Time* the full quote: Nixon said he was sorry for all the trouble the pardon caused and he would send it back if that would help. Ford did not consider the offer a serious one and brushed it off.

When *Time* printed this full version of the conversation, one reporter lectured me for not giving the details earlier.

"Ron, you had said when you took over this job that you would never intentionally mislead the press. Are you saying to us now that you are defending the proposition that that particular part of the conversation was not relevant and was not germane and was not interesting and was not news, and therefore you didn't mislead us?"

I noticed that long and intense sessions of Nixon questions at my briefings frequently did not produce any news stories. Watergate junkies were just getting their periodic Nixon fix. A Gallup poll about that time showed that a huge majority of Americans listed inflation as the most important issue facing the country, while far fewer listed Watergate, the pardon or corruption in government as the most important issues. That did not reflect the relative interest in the White House press room.

I was frustrated by the barrage of Nixon questions during my first few weeks in the White House because I wanted to talk about Ford and his activities. I lost my temper after one briefing taken up almost entirely with Nixon. I told my staff I intended to call one briefing after another, on into the night, until the reporters started asking me about Ford. When I cooled down, I was talked out of it.

Questions about Nixon staff members still on the White House payroll dominated my early briefings. But I couldn't provide many answers. Haig declined to deal with the problem in his last days, Rumsfeld was too new, and Ford felt the carry-overs should be given time to find new jobs. Some Nixon people had gone to San Clemente with the former president—Ziegler, for instance—but were still on the White House payroll because Congress had not yet appropriated any money for Nixon's staff. Two categories of Nixon staff people remained in the Ford White House—those who were identified in some way with Watergate and those who had absolutely nothing to do with any aspect of Watergate. Ford wanted to keep most of the untainted Nixon staffers, for a while at least, until he and his people learned how to run the government.

Even Bob Hartmann agreed, in a graphic metaphor, that Haig had to stay at first because "he's the only one who knows how to fly the plane. We're not going to shoot him in the cockpit before we learn to fly the plane or design a new plane."

After a few weeks Rumsfeld directed members of Ford's senior staff to decide whether to fire or keep the Nixon people assigned to their offices.

I decided to keep Jerry Warren, a slim, mild pipe-smoker, who had been Ziegler's principal deputy. Warren had kept his self-respect and the respect of the press corps during the ordeal of conducting the White House briefings in the last months of Watergate after Ziegler declined to take the daily pounding anymore.

I decided to fire Father John McLaughlin, a Jesuit priest who lived at the Watergate apartments and spent most of his time giving speeches and interviews defending Nixon, and Kenneth Clawson, roly-poly former *Washington Post* reporter who masterminded maneuvers to get Nixon favorable press treatment.

McLaughlin refused to go, insisting he had a promise from Haig to find him a job. Rumsfeld phoned Haig, who reported he'd tried to get McLaughlin a job at the State Department, but they didn't want him.

I called McLaughlin and told him nothing more could be done. I asked him to submit his resignation in time for me to announce it the next morning. The conversation became heated.

"I'm not going to send anything to you until I've had a chance to talk to Rumsfeld or the president," McLaughlin insisted.

"Well, I'm going to announce your resignation tomorrow morning whether you send me a letter or not," I advised the last-ditch Nixon defender.

The next morning at ten o'clock he sent in his resignation.

In my frustration over the nagging questions about Nixon staff members, I made one bad mistake. Announcing the McLaughlin resignation and a list of other Nixon holdovers leaving the White House, I failed to make clear which ones were being squeezed out because of Watergate connections and which ones were leaving on their own for personal or career reasons. Rumsfeld chewed my ass for smearing innocent people with a Watergate taint. I deserved it.

Some of the press questioning about Nixon and the Nixon staff became vicious and uncharitable. Once, in an effort to defuse the vengeful mood, I tried reading a passage from the Bible at my briefing: "Let all bitterness and wrath and anger and clamor and slander be put away from you with all malice and be kind to one another, tenderhearted, forgiving one another as God and Christ forgave you" (Ephesians 4:31 and 4:32).

That didn't help much.

I removed Ziegler's massive briefing rostrum, which gave the impression of a barricade between the press and the White House, and replaced it with a simple music stand to signal a new regime of openness.

That didn't help much either.

Nixon's greatest disservice to the Ford White House was severing the fundamental bond of trust that had existed between a president and the public and press.

Theodore H. White wrote in *Breach of Faith:* "The myth he broke was critical—that . . . at one particular point—the Presidency —justice will be done beyond prejudice, beyond rancor, beyond the possibility of a fix. It was that faith that Richard Nixon broke. . . ."

Before Nixon, reporters held that faith, too; it was inconceivable that a president would commit a crime. Watergate showed that nothing and no one should be considered above suspicion, that the most unthinkable evil could fester, hidden, in the highest places.

The result was what Brandeis Professor Douglas J. Steward called in the *New Republic* "the flowering of contempt" among reporters toward the president and other public figures. Ford became the first victim of that new and deep journalistic cynicism toward government officials. And the press's contempt was increased by the embarrassment of those correspondents assigned to cover the White House on a regular basis. They were acutely embarrassed because they had failed to expose Watergate. It was uncovered by Bob Woodward, Carl Bernstein and other reporters who never went inside the White House gate.

The TV networks, radio stations, wire services and some newspapers expect their White House reporters to stay in the press room all day, every day, lest they miss some official announcement. This means they cannot be investigative reporters. But in their frustration over missing Watergate, some correspondents became make-believe investigative reporters in the Ford White House, pretending to be digging out corruption by asking sarcastic and accusatory questions at briefings and news conferences. Feeling that they had not been suspicious enough of Nixon (and Ziegler) early enough, they became doubly suspicious of Ford (and Nessen) from the beginning.

Like generals who always make the mistake of fighting the previous war, White House correspondents made the mistake, during the Ford years, of covering the previous president.

Far from banishing the specter of Nixon, the pardon focused new attention on the former president and his relationship with Ford. In fact, the very next month, October 1974, Bella Abzug and other members of Congress demanded that Ford answer a list of questions about the pardon. When written answers failed to allay the suspicions, Ford agreed to undergo questioning at a public hearing by the House Judiciary Subcommittee. Historians believed it was the first time a president in office had appeared before a congressional committee. (There were unconfirmed reports that Lincoln once went before a congressional committee to deliver a short, sharp defense of his wife, who was suspected of being a Confederate spy.)

Ford's two-hour hearing was held in a jammed conference room of the Rayburn Building on Capitol Hill and was broadcast live on radio and TV. The president sat alone at the witness table, facing two tiers of committee members.

Ford reiterated that he had granted the pardon "out of my concern to serve the best interests of my country." The only fresh revelation was the president's testimony that Haig had outlined to him a week before Nixon's resignation a number of options then under consideration in the White House. Some involved pardons, before or after resignation. Haig asked Ford for his recommendation. Ford replied that he wanted time to think and talk to his wife. He phoned Haig the next day and said he did not wish to make any recommendations or to have their conversation taken into consideration in Nixon's decision.

In their questions the committee members were probing but polite, except for Representative Elizabeth Holtzman, a humorless, dark-haired woman from Brooklyn with a grating voice. She reeled off eight accusatory questions about the pardon without pausing to let the president answer. He finally broke in. "There was no deal, period."

Press reaction to the president's testimony generally took the view that those who were suspicious of the pardon before did not have their suspicions either confirmed or refuted.

I jotted down a prediction in my private notebook the day of the hearing: "I honestly think that maybe the . . . appearance put the pardon behind now as an issue and it will begin to fade out."

I was a bad forecaster.

During Ford's presidency, he saw Nixon in person only once. It was a dramatic meeting in a California hospital, at which I was one of the few witnesses.

In late October 1974, Nixon was operated on in Long Beach, California, to remove blood clots caused by phlebitis in his leg. He went into shock and nearly died. Shortly afterward, Ford flew to California and other western states to campaign for Republican candidates in the 1974 congressional elections. The day before the trip I had this exchange at my briefing:

Q.: Is there any chance now that the president will call on Mr. Nixon?

NESSEN: There are no plans for the president to visit the former president.

Q.: In view of the pardon and in view of statements which come from that rostrum about mercy relating to other Nixon officials and in view of the fact that the man is acknowledged to be very sick, how can the fact that Mr. Ford is going to California and not seeing Mr. Nixon be acknowledged as anything but a snub?

White House reporters taking up for Nixon? Consistency is not required.

Ford phoned Pat Nixon from his hotel room in Los Angeles. I was in the next room and didn't mean to eavesdrop, but the president always speaks very loudly on the phone.

"Hello, Pat? This is Jerry Ford. How is the president?"

There was a long pause while Mrs. Nixon described her husband's condition.

"I don't want to push it," Ford said, "but would it help if I came down there?"

There was another pause. Ford told me later Mrs. Nixon had replied, "I can't think of anything that would do him more good."

"Well, I have a tight schedule," Ford concluded, "but I will get my schedulers to look at it and we will decide in the morning."

A military helicopter was put on standby at a base near Ford's hotel, ready to fly him to Nixon's bedside. The next morning, after Nixon's doctor told Dr. Lukash, the White House physician, that a visit from Ford would be a good boost for the former president's morale, the decision was made to go.

Ziegler phoned me in Los Angeles to arrange the press coverage of Ford's visit to the hospital. I had not talked to him since I'd proclaimed, "I'm a Ron, but not a Ziegler." Picking up the phone I didn't know what his attitude would be. He seemed friendly, if subdued, and cooperative.

I accompanied Ford on the chopper flight to the hospital and on the elevator ride to the seventh floor, where Nixon was being treated. No reporters were allowed inside the hospital, so I promised to make notes and give the press a description of what happened during the visit.

Nixon's room was at the far end of a row of intensive-care units. Ford hugged, in turn, Mrs. Nixon, Julie and Tricia, who greeted him in the seventh-floor corridor, and then put his arms around all three and hugged them together. Instead of going into Nixon's room immediately, Ford went with the three women into an unoccupied room.

Then Ziegler appeared, looking thin, haggard and tense. He explained that the door to Nixon's room had somehow become locked from the inside. There was no way to open it from the outside. Nixon was in the room all alone, hooked up to tubes and machines, too sick to get out of bed to unlock the door.

Ford couldn't get in. And if Nixon suffered a medical emergency, there would be no way for the doctors to get in either.

A workman was summoned to cut open the lock with a hacksaw.

Once Ford was in Nixon's room, Ziegler motioned me to follow him to the end of the corridor to look in from about ten feet away. Nixon was squirming in bed, trying to find a comfortable position. He looked drawn, his hair tousled and grayer than I remembered, his voice husky. Over the bed, electronic monitoring equipment blinked and flashed.

At one point, Ford asked him whether he'd had a good night.

"None of the nights are good," Nixon croaked.

Hordes of reporters waited outside the hospital to question Ford about the visit with Nixon. Before going out to face them, the president met with Ziegler and me in an empty hospital room to discuss what to say to the press. Ziegler urged Ford not to say that Nixon looked better than he'd expected. I wondered whether that was part of some strategy to support the contention that Nixon was too ill to testify in the Watergate trials.

At a news conference in the hospital driveway, Ford finessed the question by telling reporters, "Obviously, he's a very, very sick man, but I think he's coming along very, very well. . . . The [former] president was very alert. He was interested, but it was very obvious to me that he had been very, very ill. But he showed a great deal of strength."

In giving reporters my promised detailed description of the visit, at Ziegler's urging I did not disclose that the door to Nixon's room had to be cut open. To account for the time spent waiting for the lock to be sawed off, I reported that Ford was with Nixon for eight minutes. Actually they were together only about four minutes. It was a relatively minor matter, but for the first time I had broken my promise never knowingly to mislead the White House press corps. Ironically, my first lie was to cover up for Nixon.

Before Ford's western trip I had recommended that the president not visit Nixon. I argued that such a highly publicized event would raise new suspicions about the Ford-Nixon relationship. And, I contended, such a vivid reminder of the scandals in a Republican White House just three days before the congressional elections would hurt GOP candidates. Aboard *Air Force One* leaving California after the Nixon visit, I again raised with Ford my concern about possible political damage.

"If compassion and mercy are not compatible with politics, then something is the matter with politics," he replied.

Ford had not been a close friend of Nixon's before Watergate. Theirs had been mostly a political relationship. After becoming president, Ford maintained only occasional, correct telephone contact with his predecessor, aside from the hospital visit, because Nixon had violated Ford's simple, old-fashioned sense of ethics. Ford trusts people until they prove untrustworthy. Then he drops them. Ford never forgave Nixon for lying to him about Watergate.

To me, Ford's choice of words in referring to Nixon was a strong indication of his attitude toward the former president. Ford used first names and nicknames in talking about the other presidents he had known—"Harry Truman," "Ike," "Jack Kennedy," "Lyndon." But when he spoke of Nixon it was always just "Nixon," no first name, no title.

The Republicans were clobbered in the elections of November 5, 1974, losing forty-eight House seats, six Senate seats and six governorships.

"Maybe people were expressing their feelings about the Watergate era," I told my briefing the next day, in a massive understatement.

Yet there was almost a party atmosphere as the president watched the returns on TV with Mrs. Ford and a few friends and staff members. Because, after all, the outcome was no surprise.

Four TV sets were set up in the Oval Office, one tuned to each network for the election returns, and the other to an independent station that was showing a musical movie. At one point Mrs. Ford did a little dance in imitation of an actress in the musical.

"Here, here, now. None of that in the Oval Office," the president chided her good-naturedly, distracted for a moment from the dismal returns. "It's not allowed."

That night I was the master of ceremonies at a mock retirement ceremony for Dean Burch, the wry, wise, rumpled White House political adviser who was going back to private life.

"We are holding this ceremony because today's election was the crowning achievement of your political career," I kidded Burch, "although some would argue that nineteen sixty-four was the crowning achievement." Burch had been Barry Goldwater's campaign manager in the 1964 presidential debacle.

With the president and Mrs. Ford joining the spoofing tribute in a conference room across the hall from the Oval Office, I presented Burch with a white football helmet decorated with stick-on presidential seals "for playing politics."

There were some laughs and some drinks, the president's dog, Liberty, romped around, bearded White House photographer David Kennerly took pictures and showed off his airline stewardess date, and there was no visible gloom. The president, having seen enough of the bad election news, went to bed at 1:30 A.M.

The next morning I jokingly asked him, "If we had a party like that when we lost, what's going to happen when we win?"

"We." That's the term I found myself using to refer, collectively, to the Republican president, the Republican party and the recently apolitical me. Less than three months before, I had told the president and the world that I was no Republican. I had turned down invitations to speak at Republican gatherings because, I told my secretary, I wanted to keep my "political virginity."

But as Ford began his heavy campaigning for Republican candidates in the 1974 elections and clashed with the Democratic Congress, I found myself more and more acting as the president's advocate in political matters. I should have anticipated that part of the job, but I hadn't. It was the education of the "virgin."

In that autumn of 1974 a question mark hung over Ford's intentions in the 1976 presidential elections.

He had told his vice-presidential confirmation hearings that he would not be a presidential candidate in 1976, regardless of whether Nixon finished his term in the White House. But shortly after assuming the presidency, Ford directed Jerry terHorst to announce that he "probably" would run in 1976.

In mid-November 1974 Ford was interviewed by *U.S. News & World Report* on his first 100 days as president. He was asked about his plans for the 1976 campaign.

Q.: Previously, you have said you probably would run. . . .
FORD: I intend to run.

That was the big news, the president's first flat declaration that he would run for a full term in 1976.

But *U.S. News & World Report* could not print the interview until the following week. A few nights later Ford revealed his plans to a group of southern political leaders. But, for once, nothing leaked. He held a news conference. Nobody asked.

Here was a story the president wanted out, but it was remaining one of the few secrets the Ford White House ever kept!

Finally a reporter picked up the rumor and asked me at a briefing what the president's answer would have been if he'd been asked at his news conference about running in 1976.

Q.: He was not asked that. Can you tell us if he is going to upgrade that from "probably" to "will"?
NESSEN: Yes.
Q.: He will definitely run?
NESSEN: Yes. He intends to run in 1976.
Q.: What changed "probably" to "definitely"?
NESSEN: Well, I guess you have heard him . . . a couple of times say how much he enjoys being president.

There were several practical reasons for Ford making known then his intention to run for a full term. For one thing, it was supposed to keep other Republicans from going after the nomination. (That didn't work, obviously.) It also was a warning to the new, heavily Democratic Congress not to try to ignore or trample Ford as a lame duck, because they might have to deal with him until 1980. Similarly, it was a signal to foreign countries—friends and adversaries—that they could not simply mark time in their relations with the United States, waiting to see who would be president after 1976.

Not coincidentally, Ford's disclosure that he would run in 1976 was made just a few days before he began his first foreign trip as president, to Japan, Korea and the Soviet Union.

CHAPTER SIX

Vodka with Strangers

Ford's Far East trip was intended to assure Japan and Korea that the United States did not intend to abandon its friends in Asia after withdrawing its troops from Indochina, and to allow the new American president and Russia's leaders to size each other up.

Before the trip began, the Soviet Union threw a monkey wrench into press plans for Ford's stop in Vladivostok, in far eastern Russia. When the Press Office submitted the list of 155 correspondents, photographers and TV technicians who had signed up for the trip, the Soviet Union replied that only 40 would be allowed to accompany the president, and only American citizens.

In negotiations in Moscow and Washington, the Russians raised their ceiling to sixty. At that point I asked Secretary of State Henry Kissinger to intercede with Soviet Ambassador Anatoly Dobrynin.

"Do you want a fight or do you want an excuse?" Kissinger asked.

"Both," I replied.

I wanted him to fight to persuade the Russians to admit more newsmen. But if the Soviet Union maintained its hard-nosed position, I knew that Kissinger's involvement would convince the press corps that I had done all I could to help them.

Kissinger phoned me at home early the next morning to say he had persuaded the Russians to let ten more newsmen in, a total of seventy, only Americans. This meant that at least one representative of each American news organization that had signed up for the trip could go, with five from each network and four each from AP and UPI. It was the best we could do and nearly double the original Russian limit of forty. But of course the networks grumbled that we gave too many spaces to the writing press, and the wire services complained we gave too many spaces to the networks.

One of my assistants, Bill Roberts, reported in a memo, "The general feeling seemed to be—and was expressed by a number of reporters—that the White House was wrong in compromising, and should have stood firm on the principle that everyone accredited for the trip should have been permitted in, or the president should have canceled the trip."

Nobody ever accused the White House press corps of lacking a sense of self-importance.

Two days before departure, Kissinger gave reporters a briefing on the trip and answered questions. That was traditional before every presidential overseas visit. The purpose was to give accompanying correspondents background information and a preview of the issues to be discussed at each stop so the reporters would be better able to understand and analyze developments along the way. However, many White House correspondents, particularly those from the TV networks, radio stations and wire services, considered it a waste of time to spend forty-five minutes with Kissinger solely for the purpose of storing up information for later use. They wanted a headline for that day. So sixteen of the twenty-five questions at Kissinger's pretrip briefing dealt with war rumors then sweeping the Middle East. Only six questions were about the president's impending journey.

Just before leaving, the National Security Council's liaison man with the Press Office, Les Janka, warned me that I should not let Kissinger see me reading classified briefing books during the trip. "Henry doesn't think anybody should have the briefing books," Janka declared, "including the president."

Preparations for the trip were interrupted by one of those events that occasionally cause an explosion of emotion among the White House press corps. Reporters drop all pretext of being dispassionate chroniclers and become open, angry advocates in their questioning, if not in their stories.

The *Washington Post* ran a story quoting General George Brown, chairman of the Joint Chiefs of Staff, in an appearance at Duke University a month earlier, as saying a new Arab oil embargo might prompt Americans to "get tough-minded enough to set down the Jewish influence in this country and break that lobby." Brown was quoted as saying that Jews "own, you know, the banks in this country, the newspapers. You just look at where the Jewish money is in this country."

After Ford read the story in the *Post*, he instructed me to announce at my briefing that he considered the remarks ill-advised
and poorly handled, that they did not represent the views of his
administration. When I relayed the president's views to the reporters at my briefing, it did not satisfy demands for Brown's scalp.

Q.: Ron, I don't think the statement either made by the president
   or what you have said here today meets the problem. General
   Brown made statements that disturbed greatly every Jew in
   the United States and there are six million of them, and a lot
   of other people who are interested in this. For the president
   to say this is ill-advised is certainly a very pusillanimous view
   of it and unless he does something about it, the only implication we can draw, the only inference I should say, is that
   the president is not really concerned about this. He is letting
   the man stay in his job; he has not contacted him personally;
   he has not asked him to apologize. He has done nothing about
   it. What kind of situation is this?
NESSEN: Is that your question, what kind of situation is this?
Q.: Yes, in the White House by the president.
NESSEN: I have given you the president's reaction to this, which I
   emphasize he holds quite strongly. He disassociates himself
   from this view expressed by General Brown. It in no way
   represents the views of anybody else in the government. . . .
Q.: Let me ask you this, Ron. What would you advise American
   citizens, regardless of their religious backgrounds, who are
   angered and outraged by General Brown's statement? What
   would you advise them to do? How would you advise them
   to make their feelings known?
NESSEN: I would not presume to advise American citizens. . . .
Q.: . . . Are you going to discuss this, bring to the president the
   concern certainly that you hear in this room from Jew and
   Gentile alike, or not?
NESSEN: I will.
Q.: Thank you.

As a journalist and as press secretary, I held a purist view of
briefings and news conferences. I believed they should be used
exclusively for the purpose of obtaining information to write
news stories. Reporters should not use them to state their own
views, argue against a president's decision or let off steam.

The morning after that briefing Ford called Brown to the Oval Office at 7 o'clock and chewed him out in person. Brown apologized and said his quoted statements did not accurately reflect his personal feelings. Ford told Brown he never wanted to hear such remarks about Jews again.

I watched Brown leave the Oval Office with his head down, looking grim. He rubbed his palms together as if they were sweaty and he was trying to rub them dry.

In Tokyo, first stop on the president's Far East trip, Ford and his party were put up at the Akasaka Palace, a scaled-down replica of Versailles, decorated with marble, brocade and velvet furnishings of the Louis XVI period. The president slept in a pink canopied bed. The menu for all four formal meals in Tokyo was French. We might as well have been in Paris.

After relaxing the first afternoon and evening to recover from jet lag, Ford and his staff lined up on the palace's portico the next morning for the arrival of Emperor Hirohito for the official welcoming ceremony. The president and his entourage were dressed, as required, in swallow-tail morning coats, black and gray striped trousers, gray vests, wing collars and black and gray ascots. As we stood in protocol ranks waiting for the emperor of Japan, former god-king, to roll up to the red carpet in his limousine, Philip Habib, the down-to-earth assistant secretary of state for East Asian and Pacific affairs, whispered, "What's a boy from Brooklyn doing in a place like this?" I had a similar sense of awe. I wondered if the president was thinking, "What's a boy from Grand Rapids doing in a place like this?"

I became irritated later because some of the stories and photographs of the ceremony made a point of the fact that the president's formal pants seemed to be too short, ending at or above the ankles. Barry Schweid, the AP's State Department reporter, felt the matter was important enough to mention in the fourth paragraph of his story: "Wearing striped pants two inches too short, Ford began the day bowing to the Emperor. . . ."

The "pool" reporters—those chosen to cover the ceremony for the newsmen who couldn't attend—wrote: "Mr. Ford then reviewed the guard, with his long strides emphasizing that his trousers were considerably shorter than those of the others who were wearing formal dress." In addition, Richard Growald of the

UPI wrote a lengthy story suggesting that the president appeared confused at one point in the ceremony and almost walked past the Crown Prince without noticing him.

I was overly protective of the president's image and my temper flared at what I considered emphasis on inconsequential matters instead of on the diplomatic and symbolic importance of the trip, the first visit ever by an American president to Japan. I felt some reporters were concentrating on trivia because they had frittered away their opportunities to obtain substantive background information from Kissinger at the pretrip briefing and two briefings on *Air Force One*.

Ford explained later that when he first came to Washington in 1948, his hometown tailor had made him a set of morning clothes, assuring him that as a member of Congress he certainly would need them. Over the next twenty-five years Ford had occasion to wear the outfit only twice. When it came time to go to Japan the president decided to order a new coat and vest, but, for some reason, to make do with the old trousers.

The ceremonial high point of the Tokyo visit was the emperor's banquet for the president at the Imperial Palace. Dress this time was white tie and tails. Before dinner the American party was escorted to an enormous reception hall about the size of six tennis courts, a vast, tastefully austere open space. Kissinger cracked, "You would think that after spending this much for a palace they could afford to buy some furniture."

During dinner I watched the president talking to the emperor through a translator. I wondered what they found to talk about. Kissinger said it was difficult conversing with the emperor because, by tradition, he never expressed an opinion on anything, even the most minor matter.

After the banquet we trooped back to the reception hall. A palace official asked each person in Ford's party, "Would you like to speak to a member of the royal family?"

"Of course," I replied.

The official looked around to see who was available. "Would you like to speak to the empress?"

I made small talk with the doughty empress through an interpreter for a while, but out of the corner of my eye I kept glancing at Princess Michiko. I'd spoken to her briefly before dinner and was enchanted by her beauty, her intellect and her British-accented English, spoken in an ethereal way. As soon as someone else arrived to talk to the empress, I excused myself and sidled over to resume my conversation with Michiko. I laughed to myself at the absurdity of being attracted to a Japanese princess.

Ford's next stop was Seoul, Korea. He was welcomed by a huge and enthusiastic crowd. Korean officials estimated the number of people at more than two million. As Ford's motorcade drove into Seoul through cheering crowds ten deep, Sid Davis, then with Westinghouse Broadcasting, commented, "A repressive government can turn out the people, but it can't make them smile."

My wife is Korean, born in Pusan, now a naturalized American citizen. Her mother, who also lives in the United States, was on a visit to Korea at the time of the president's trip. I was concerned that the Korean authorities might exploit my mother-in-law's presence in Seoul during Ford's visit to emphasize that one of Ford's senior staff members had personal ties in Korea. I was especially alert to any Korean efforts along those lines because of an intelligence cable shown to me the previous month by Brent Scowcroft, Kissinger's deputy at the NSC. The cable indicated that the Korean CIA was gathering information about me and my wife, our associates and backgrounds, in hopes of finding something that might be used to influence me in favor of Korea's interests.

(Two months after Ford's trip to Korea, Kissinger gave me a list of three Koreans he said I and my wife should avoid because they were suspected of intelligence activities or other illegal behavior. The only name I recognized was Tongsun Park. The other names, Hancho Kim and Park Bo Hui, turned up later in the investigations of Korean efforts to buy influence in the U.S. government.)

My concern about Korea exploiting my mother-in-law's presence during Ford's visit was justified. Korean officials made sure she was in the official greeting area at the airport for Ford's arrival. The authorities also invited her to a reception for the president that night at the National Assembly Building. At the reception she introduced me to a man who she said had been very helpful in escorting her to all the events. I assumed he was an agent of the Korean CIA. I learned later that a member of the Korean National Assembly had offered to help my mother-in-law with her expenses in Seoul. My wife ordered her firmly to spend only her own money.

In Vladivostok, Ford and Soviet leader Leonid Brezhnev held their first discussions during a ninety-minute ride aboard an ornate green and gold railroad train from the airport to the meeting site, a health resort for government workers and trade union members. They sat across a table from each other, sipping refreshments, laughing at each other's anecdotes and getting acquainted.

Reporters and photographers were ushered into the railroad car at one point to record the meeting. Brezhnev, through a translator, told Ford the press wasn't always reliable in transmitting accurate information. He quoted what he said was an Arab proverb: "If you want to know what's really going on, you have to put on your fez and go down to the market." Brezhnev picked up a white linen napkin from the table and put it on his head as a make-believe fez to illustrate his story.

Ford replied, "Yes, in the United States, too, you have to get out and around the country if you really want to find out what's going on."

Early that evening I went to a dinner for the delegations at the conference hall. I found members of the American and Russian staffs milling around the tiled lobby and slumped in the heavy, over-stuffed sofas and chairs. Waiters in wrinkled white jackets circulated with trays of soft drinks, juice and hors d'oeuvres.

Ford, Brezhnev and a few senior aides were closeted in a meeting room at the rear of the lobby, overlooking a glass-enclosed garden. The delegations faced each other across a long, cloth-covered table set with dishes of refreshments and bottles of mineral water. The air was fogged with smoke from Brezhnev's chain-smoked cigarettes and Ford's pipe. The American president and the Soviet party chairman, both big, bearlike men with a broad sense of humor and a ready laugh, seemed to hit it off. They bantered easily, and several times when they were standing together Brezhnev hugged Ford.

The two leaders were discussing a new agreement to limit the U.S. and Russian arsenals of strategic nuclear weapons, the so-called SALT II agreement. It was an incredibly complex tangle of issues, vitally important to the survival of the two superpowers. Both sides were interested in slowing down the arms race in order to ease the enormous financial burdens. But Ford and Brezhnev each sought an agreement that would allow his country to keep its advantages in nuclear weapons while forcing the rival to make sacrifices.

The Russians had missiles capable of carrying much larger warheads than American rockets. This meant that even a near-miss by the bigger Soviet warheads might be able to destroy American missiles in their concrete-and-steel silos. On the other hand, the U.S.

rockets had more accurate guidance systems, enabling them to drop their smaller warheads closer to their targets in the Soviet Union.

The Russians had plans to build more missiles than the United States, while we had plans to rely on B-52 bombers and unmanned robot planes, called cruise missiles, for part of our strategic strike force.

The United States was ahead of Russia in developing multiple warheads (MIRVs) for its missiles, each warhead programmed to strike a different target. The United States was also ahead in missile-firing submarines, but the Russians were gaining fast.

While the two sides discussed these matters, a Russian general usually sat close to Brezhnev, serving as the Soviet leader's technical adviser on the complicated issues involved. Ford acted as his own technical adviser, drawing on his years as a member of the House Appropriations Subcommittee, which handled the Pentagon's budget.

Ford thought he'd found a compromise approach to a SALT II agreement which might meet the needs of both the United States and the Soviet Union. He suggested that ceilings be set on the number of nuclear weapons and the number of MIRVs each country could possess. The ceiling on weapons would be low enough to cause a cutback in the planned size of the Soviet arsenal, but the ceiling on multiple warheads would be high enough to let Russia catch up in this development. The United States and Russia would have to abide by identical ceilings. Photographs taken by spy satellites circling overhead would be used to verify compliance with the ceilings, eliminating the need for on-site inspectors.

Ford's idea seemed to interest Brezhnev. The conference was making progress.

Normally, every detail of a presidential trip is carried out with clockwork precision exactly as outlined in the official schedule. But in Vladivostok it didn't work that way. The first negotiating session between Ford and Brezhnev was supposed to last ninety minutes, ending at 7:30 P.M., in time for the dinner of the two delegations. Instead it ran on and on, until 12:30 in the morning, with only occasional short breaks. The dinner was canceled.

When the meeting finally broke up, Ford invited Kissinger, Rumsfeld, Kennerly, me and several other aides to his *dacha* for a snack. We tramped 400 yards along a dark road, our breath steaming in the subzero night air. Ford wore a parka made of gray wolf fur, given to him at the refueling stop in Anchorage, and a Russian-style mink hat given to him by Soviet Ambassador Dobrynin when he left Washington.

The servants, not expecting a crowd for supper so late, had to scramble to throw together a meal. They turned out a delicious thick Russian soup, black bread, butter, caviar, cheese, salami, Russian beer and vodka. And for dessert, ice cream.

After the early-morning supper, Kissinger and I rode the mile or so to the press hotel for a news briefing on the discussions. On the way, Kissinger told me Ford was a better negotiator than Nixon. He said Ford was more personable and was getting along well with Brezhnev. He said Ford seemed comfortable taking part in a genuine give-and-take, whereas Nixon followed a prepared scenario and would never really bargain. Kissinger said Nixon could not look Brezhnev or other foreign leaders directly in the eye when negotiating with them.

Kissinger walked a careful line at his briefing, giving just enough indication of progress so that any agreement the next day would not be dismissed as a last-minute, trumped-up public-relations gesture, but avoiding too much optimism so that failure to reach an agreement would not be perceived as a sudden collapse.

Kissinger was asked whether a stroll he and Ford took outside the conference hall during a break in the meeting was for relaxation or to confer privately away from possible Russian listening devices.

"It was to take relaxation in private," Kissinger quipped.

After Kissinger's briefing, I sat cross-legged on the edge of the stage and passed on to five or six reporters what he had told me in the car about the Nixon and Ford styles in diplomatic negotiations. (Later William Safire, the columnist and former Nixon speech-writer, accused Kissinger of programming me to disparage Nixon in an effort to build up Ford.)

The first thing Ford did when he awoke the next morning was to ask his military aide, Major Robert Barrett, the score of the Michigan–Ohio State football game which had been played while he slept. The president's school, Michigan, had lost 12–10. Ford asked for details. Barrett gave them. A president cannot live by diplomacy alone.

On the second day of the conference, Ford and Brezhnev

arranged to meet from 10 A.M. to 2 P.M., when the delegations would attend a lunch in place of the canceled dinner.

But the meeting ran late again, until nearly 4 P.M. Near the end, the president called me in to make arrangements for distributing a joint statement announcing that the negotiations had resulted in a breakthrough on arms limitations. Ford and Brezhnev had agreed to set a ceiling for each country of 2400 missiles and bombers capable of carrying nuclear warheads, with no more than 1320 of the missiles to be equipped with multiple warheads.

It was the first time the two countries had agreed to limit themselves to an equal number of offensive nuclear weapons and MIRVs.

Ford believed at the end of the previous night's meeting that Brezhnev was on the brink of making the deal, but he did not know for sure until the Soviet leader formally accepted the terms at the morning session.

Kissinger and I drove to the press hotel for a briefing on the agreement while Ford, Brezhnev and the other members of the delegations sat down for the delayed lunch of bear meat and venison. Kissinger told the reporters that technical negotiations would begin in Geneva in January 1975 to settle on procedures for verifying compliance, to decide whether U.S. cruise missiles and Soviet Backfire bombers qualified as strategic weapons to be counted under the ceiling, and to write the actual treaty.

"We believe that with goodwill on both sides, it should be possible to conclude a ten-year agreement by the time that the general secretary [Brezhnev] visits the United States at the summit, and at any rate we will make a major effort in that direction," Kissinger told the press. He added, "The negotiations could be difficult and will have many technical complexities, but we believe that the target is achievable."

After the briefing, Kissinger and I rushed back to the health resort for a champagne signing ceremony and a drive through Vladivostok, the concluding event of the visit. A reporter, Leroy Hansen of *U.S. News & World Report*, asked to hitch a ride to the signing ceremony in Kissinger's limousine because he could find no other transportation. Kissinger agreed.

In the car I bubbled over with enthusiasm about the agreement and what I perceived to be the reporters' reaction.

"I think they were dazzled," I told Kissinger. "I think they were amazed. I don't think they were expecting an agreement like this. The president will be returning home in triumph," I exulted.

"I think the president should be modest," Kissinger cautioned. "The agreement speaks for itself. The back of the arms race has been broken."

I thought of Hansen as a guest in the car, not as a reporter. But he typed up his recollections of what was said in the car and distributed them to the other reporters. I didn't know it then, but Hansen's report set off a new flap between me and the press.

Ford and Brezhnev rode side by side in the back seat of a Russian limousine during an hour's drive through the drab streets of Vladivostok. They peered out at 50,000 or 60,000 people standing silent in the waning afternoon light. Only an occasional bystander waved. Throughout the drive Brezhnev held Ford's hand as a gesture of friendship.

During the train ride back to the airport, Ford joined his staff in the wood-paneled dining car for some convivial relaxation. Cheese, salami, black bread, beer and vodka were on the tables. I began drinking vodka as soon as I sat down.

Ford and his entourage were in exuberant spirits, unwinding at last from the long hours and tensions of a hard trip and celebrating the success of Ford's first foreign-policy outing. The reporters, sitting at other tables in the dining car, asked Ford how he brought off the agreement.

"Just good negotiating," he gloated, "good give-and-take."

I kept downing vodka, and the more I drank the more enthusiastic I became about the president's triumph. At one point I told the reporters, "It was something Nixon couldn't do in five years. But Ford did it in three months."

By the time we got back to *Air Force One* and took off for home, I was all but proclaiming Ford the diplomatic genius of the age. I babbled to the reporters on the plane that the Vladivostok agreement was "one of the most significant agreements since World War II." "Richard Nixon could not achieve this in five years," I repeated. "President Ford achieved it in three months."

Having issued those judgments, I staggered up to the VIP lounge to sleep. The lounge was empty because Kissinger, Rumsfeld and many other members of the delegation had dropped off for another diplomatic mission, to China. I yanked off my clothes, stretched out on the couch in my underwear, pulled a blue air force blanket over me and slept off the exhaustion and vodka for the next nine and a half hours. I slept right through the refueling stop in Alaska.

We got home on a Sunday night, early enough to watch the

11 P.M. news. My quote about Ford doing what Nixon couldn't was a lead item. I began to get a queasy feeling that I had overstated the success of Vladivostok. In the sober light of Monday morning, I knew I was in a full-fledged mess. Mostly because of inexperience, I had exaggerated the triumph at Vladivostok and I had not given sufficient emphasis to the fact that lower-level negotiators still had to resolve many technical details before a treaty could be signed. The crack about Nixon was gratuitous. He had, after all, concluded the SALT I agreement with the Russians, taking the first steps toward limiting nuclear weapons.

The *Wall Street Journal* that Monday morning ran a boxed article saying one development during Ford's Far East trip was my emergence as an outspoken advocate for the president. Similar comments mounted in the next few days. The *New York Daily News* referred to my "gushing" praise for the president's negotiating ability. The *Boston Globe* wrote about White House "puffery." The *Globe* ran a savage cartoon showing Ford thinking, "I got from the Russians in three months what Nixon couldn't get in five years," and Brezhnev thinking, "We got from Jerry Ford in three months what we couldn't get from Nixon in five years."

I mentioned to Ford this growing reaction, but he brushed aside my concern. Kissinger, however, sent a cable from China suggesting that I back away from my extravagant claims for the Vladivostok agreement and my slap at Nixon. Someone at San Clemente phoned the White House and complained. But again Ford indicated he was content with what I'd said.

A few days later at my briefing I was asked whether the president had been critical of my remark.

"No," I answered honestly.

At that point, without checking with Ford, I decided to dissolve the controversy by making a graceful retreat from my crack about Nixon.

"I think it was probably a hasty and oversimplified remark," I told the reporters. "It is clear to me now, looking back, that what happened in Vladivostok was really kind of a culmination of steps that have been taken over the years."

When I told the president what I'd done, I thought he might be displeased at me for seeming to take some of the credit away from him.

"No, no, I think you handled it right," he told me.

Hartmann, who also was in the Oval Office, commented, "It was all right, what you said in Vladivostok, because it got us a lot of stories we wouldn't otherwise have gotten. And it is all right to apologize later, or reverse yourself later, after you've gotten all the benefit out of it."

One night shortly after the trip the president was half-watching a television interview in which Richard Perle, an aide to Senator Henry Jackson, was critical of the Vladivostok agreement. Ford thought he heard the aide say something about "drinking vodka with strangers." Ford concluded that the aide was implying that he'd been drunk during the negotiations. He angrily ordered the White House operator to get Jackson on the phone.

The president was unaware that Jackson was in the hospital recovering from a minor operation. In his condition, Jackson must have been bewildered to have the president come on his bedside phone and berate him for letting one of his aides impugn Ford's sobriety.

In the end, the agreement I had hailed so loudly in Vladivostok was aborted. The technical negotiations in Geneva foundered, unable to resolve the remaining issues. The agreement at Vladivostok could not be translated into a SALT II treaty during the Ford presidency.

In the meantime, however, I learned a few days after the trip that *Time* and other news organizations were preparing stories critical of my performance in the Far East.

I invited fifteen or so reporters to my office, served drinks and peanuts and tried to reverse my deteriorating relationship with the press corps.

"One of my predecessors felt that contrition was bullshit," I began. "But if that is the case, I'm going to give you some bullshit. I really feel confession is good for the soul and I want to confess that we messed up a little bit on this trip."

I explained that the Far East tour was the first foreign trip for me as press secretary and for most of the others in the Press Office. We'd found we had a lot to learn about handling press problems and distributing information under the pressures of foreign travel. I apologized for my ill temper, a petulant midnight briefing in Seoul and my frequent absences from the press room to attend official functions. I asked the reporters to be understanding while I tried to improve the White House press operation.

The meeting lasted nearly two hours. Many of the reporters voiced specific complaints about the Press Office performance during the trip and about my attitude.

"The president's pants being too short was a big story," UPI's Helen Thomas insisted, "and you can't expect us not to write about it."

By the end of the meeting, much of the heat had been let out of the press complaints and the critical stories were softened somewhat. But the trip ended whatever honeymoon I had with the press. After that I was never able to recover fully the lost opportunity to build a relationship of mutual respect and friendship with the White House press corps.

CHAPTER SEVEN

Spies

When Ford flew to Vail, Colorado, on Sunday, December 22, 1974, for his annual Christmas skiing vacation, *Air Force One* was loaded, as usual, with stacks of fat Sunday papers.

The president's attention was caught by a front-page *New York Times* article in which Seymour Hersh, a reporter specializing in investigative revelations, reported that the Central Intelligence Agency had engaged in a massive and illegal program of spying on Americans in the United States during the late 1950s and the 1960s. According to the article, the CIA tapped the phones of Americans, kept them under surveillance, read their mail and broke into their homes and offices. Also, the reporter alleged that the agency kept files on 10,000 Americans involved in the antiwar movement and other dissident activities.

The "pool" reporters flying to Vail aboard *Air Force One* asked me to find out if Ford had read the article, what his reaction was and what he was going to do about the charges. When I passed on this inquiry to Ford, the president decided to walk to the rear of the plane himself to discuss the matter with the press pool. I was glad he did. Reporters always asked the president easier questions than they asked me.

Ford told the newsmen that CIA Director William Colby had phoned him on the plane and assured him that nothing comparable to the domestic spying alleged in the *Times* was being done by the CIA at that time. "I told him that under no circumstances would I tolerate any such activities under this administration," Ford declared.

A reporter asked Ford whether he'd had any knowledge of domestic spying activities before he read the *Times* article.

"I had some partial information," the president replied. He did not elaborate and he was not questioned further. (Later I learned that during a meeting on another subject a few days earlier, Colby almost casually mentioned to Ford that the *Times* was coming out with the Hersh article. The president, concentrating on the primary subject of the meeting, had not picked up the significance of Colby's remark. This was a favorite trick of government officials—to mention troublesome problems to the president in an offhand way while he was focused on another matter. Then, if the problem blew up into a major crisis and the president demanded to know why he hadn't been forewarned, the official could claim, truthfully, that it had been mentioned.)

At my news briefing the day after Ford arrived in Vail, the press bore down hard on the CIA story. There was an air of anticipation. The story had the whiff of another Watergate, or perhaps even a continuation of Watergate, offering the exciting prospect of weeks and months of sensational news revelations. John Hushen, my deputy at the time, had advised me that reporters hoped to trap me into saying something similar to Ron Ziegler's early dismissal of Watergate as a "third-rate burglary." I was careful not to confirm or deny the allegations in the article.

Nixon's frequent protestations of innocence and of ignorance of the Watergate cover-up had so damaged the basic fabric of trust that White House reporters were suspicious of any presidential promise to investigate allegations of wrongdoing. Therefore when I announced during my briefing that Ford had sent instructions to Colby to prepare a report on the *Times* allegations and forward it to Vail within a few days, one reporter spoke up to express the skepticism of the press corps.

"We remember President Nixon saying, 'Nobody will tell me anything.' He ordered this investigation and that investigation and said never did the facts come to him."

Different president, different situation, but the disbelief lingered on.

After that briefing, reviewing the attitude of the reporters, I began to worry that Ford was not taking the problem seriously enough. Given the post-Watergate mood, I grew concerned that he would be hurt in public opinion if he did not act quickly to ascertain and punish past misdeeds in the CIA and to make sure misdeeds were not continuing in his administration.

I also worried that Ford might have known about CIA domestic spying in his roles as a member of the congressional committee over-seeing CIA activities, House Republican leader, vice president or president. But in private conversations he assured aides during the first days in Vail that he had not previously known of CIA activities within the United States.

When I expressed my concern about Ford's reaction to the CIA allegations to Rumsfeld, he asked me how big I thought the story was. I replied that I thought it would be one of the major issues of 1975. Rumsfeld then read me a memo he'd written by hand on a yellow legal pad saying the Ford White House should learn the lessons of Watergate and should avoid making the same mistakes in handling the CIA matter. Rumsfeld's memo said Ford's real problem was not public relations but the need to make policy decisions to prevent any repetition of CIA wrongdoing.

Kissinger also sent his advice to Vail in a "confidential/sensitive" memo saying, "We're concerned that we not act in such a way as to give credence to the allegations of the *New York Times* story and create an impression that a major problem actually exists and that the Ford Administration is confronted with a scandal of major proportions."

The report Ford requested from Colby arrived in Vail in a few days by courier from Washington. The CIA director confirmed some of Hersh's allegations, but denied that they added up to a "massive" domestic spy operation. Colby had seen some evidence of illegal activities. The evidence was contained in a set of highly classified documents known as "The Family Jewels." The "Jewels" were filed as responses to James Schlesinger when, during his brief tenure as CIA director in 1973, he asked officials of the agency to notify him of any past CIA activities which they felt were improper.

On January 3, 1975, the day after Ford returned to the White House from Vail, Colby revealed to the president the contents of "The Family Jewels" for the first time. The next day Ford appointed a special commission to investigate the allegations of domestic spying by the CIA, determine whether it was illegal and make recommendations on how to prevent future misdeeds by the agency. The president named Vice President Rockefeller as chairman of the commission* and selected the other seven commission members

---

* Ford's first choice for chairman was Erwin N. Griswold, former dean of the Harvard Law School and former Solicitor General. But he was dropped and Rockefeller was substituted at the last minute after Ford was informed that Gris-

from a list of more than two dozen prominent Americans. It was difficult to choose a panel that would have the appearance of integrity because so many of the candidates had been involved in one way or another with the CIA over the years. Some members picked for the commission had connections with intelligence activities in the past, and this drew some criticism in Congress and the press. There were suggestions that Ford set up the commission to whitewash the CIA.

Some thought they detected the shadow of another Watergate cover-up. The morning after Ford appointed the investigating commission, Daniel Schorr constructed a convoluted analogy for his CBS viewers as a way of expressing his suspicions about the true motives of the CIA investigation:

> The thing to do, said the president's advisers, is to convene a special presidential commission and then ask that congressional hearings be held in abeyance until the panel serves its purpose. The president was not Ford, the adviser not Kissinger, the subject not the CIA. It was John Ehrlichman on March 22, 1973, counseling President Nixon on how to stave off a Senate investigation of Watergate. That was back in the dark ages. It would be unfair to suggest that the Rockefeller blue-ribbon panel on the CIA is a stall. It would not be unfair to suggest that blue-ribbon panels have as one of their purposes the postponement of issues until the excitement has abated.

Schorr himself saw to it that the excitement did not abate. On Friday night, February 28, 1975, he appeared on Walter Cronkite's "CBS Evening News" with a sensational story: Schorr said that Ford had warned government officials that if investigations of intelligence operations went too far, they could uncover several assassinations of foreign officials in which the CIA was involved. Schorr said the president felt such a revelation would embarrass the U.S. government and damage relations with at least one foreign country.

"Details of the assassinations are being very closely held," Schorr reported. "They're believed to have numbered at least three, and to have occurred during the nineteen sixties or late fifties."

Ford was almost certainly the indirect source of Schorr's story.

---

wold had been investigated by the Watergate special prosecutor for possibly committing perjury in his congressional testimony on the ITT antitrust case.

A month and a half earlier, the president had attended a private, off-the-record lunch at the White House with the top brass of the *New York Times:* "Punch" Sulzberger, "Scotty" Reston, Abe Rosenthal, Tom Wicker, Clifton Daniel, John B. Oakes and Max Frankel. I also joined the lunch. Naturally the Timesmen were interested in pursuing their Seymour Hersh story on CIA domestic spying. Puffing on his pipe, Ford emphasized that the discussion had to be "completely off the record." He then disclosed how, shortly after he returned from Vail, Colby had revealed to him what he called CIA "horror stories," referring to the CIA director's briefing on "The Family Jewels."

"I was shocked," the president said in a tone that sounded genuinely appalled. "I couldn't believe it. If you knew what they were doing, it would curl your hair." He specifically mentioned CIA involvement in efforts to assassinate foreign leaders, but gave no details. He said he had issued firm orders to the agency not to commit any "horror stories" during his administration.

I've always believed that Ford's off-the-record remarks to the *Times,* and to a few other private visitors, reached Schorr, who followed up and broke the assassinations story.

"If he weren't president of the United States," I said to Brent Scowcroft of the National Security Council, "I guess he would have his security clearance taken away."

Deputy Staff Coordinator Richard Cheney, Scowcroft and I agreed that my initial response to press questions about Schorr's assassinations story would be to "stonewall." We actually used the word. We didn't know what involvement the CIA had in assassination plots against foreign leaders, and could not find out in a hurry. We simply didn't have the answers. So at my next briefing I refused to say anything about the assassinations story.

After the briefing, Schorr phoned and said he wanted to compliment me.

"What do you mean?" I asked.

"You didn't lie about the assassinations," he said. "I warned CBS that you were probably going to lie and flatly deny my story. But you didn't. You just said you weren't going to talk about it. I was pleasantly surprised. That's an amazing improvement over Ziegler."

After Schorr's story came the deluge, a year-long flood of allegations in the press, almost always attributed to unnamed "sources," that the CIA had been involved in seemingly far-out escapades, including assassination attempts against Cuba's Fidel Castro, Haiti's

François "Papa Doc" Duvalier, Rafael Trujillo of the Dominican Republic, Patrice Lumumba of the Congo, Cambodia's Prince Norodom Sihanouk and other foreign leaders, even Charles de Gaulle. Nothing seemed too farfetched to be reported. *Time* printed that the CIA once recruited Sam Giancana and John Roselli of the Mafia to use their expertise in the long-running effort to assassinate Castro. A woman named Judith Campbell Exner was reported to have been John Kennedy's bed partner in the White House at the same time she was dating Giancana and Roselli.

Some White House officials and journalists suspected that the unfolding CIA revelations eventually might confirm two chilling conspiracy theories which were whispered about in Washington: (1) that the CIA had engineered Watergate in a plot to dump Nixon; and (2) that Castro had ordered John Kennedy's assassination in retaliation for the CIA's murder plots against the Cuban leader.

Anticipating a question at my news briefing about a Castro-Kennedy connection, I raised the matter one day with Ford, expecting him to brush it off. I was surprised when the president, who had been a member of the Warren Commission which investigated Kennedy's death, began a serious review of the conclusions of the commission.

"We were very, very careful when we wrote our final report not to say flatly that Lee Harvey Oswald acted alone and was not part of a conspiracy," he recalled. "We argued against the staff, which wanted to say there was no evidence that Oswald was part of a conspiracy."

He got up from his desk, walked into his adjoining study and returned with a copy of the Warren Commission's final report. He flipped to a well-worn page and read out loud the conclusion: " 'The Commission has *found* [emphasis Ford's] no evidence that either Lee Harvey Oswald or Jack Ruby was part of any conspiracy, domestic or foreign, to assassinate President Kennedy.'

"You see," Ford said, "we were very careful to say we 'found' no evidence of a conspiracy." He said he doubted the CIA had told the Warren Commission everything it knew about Oswald, especially about his period in Russia, his relationship with Cuba and his visit to Mexico.

Ford said he had spent an hour and a half the day before pondering a possible connection between the Kennedy murder and CIA efforts to kill Castro, and was considering reopening the investigation of Kennedy's assassination.

I was shocked. Speculation that Kennedy was killed in revenge for attempts to assassinate Castro had circulated for years, but it had been dismissed as a farfetched theory of the conspiracy freaks. Now a president of the United States was thinking about ordering a new investigation of such a link. I felt like I was living in the pages of one of those Washington thriller novels.

In the hallway outside the Oval Office after the meeting, presidential counsellor John Marsh told me I ought to urge Ford to "get out ahead" on a possible connection between Castro and the Kennedy assassination. "There are enough people in this town who can put two and two together," Marsh said. "It's mind-boggling."

Later that day, at a lunch with editors and writers of the *Washington Post*, I learned that people already were putting two and two together. A reporter named Donnie Radcliffe, who usually covered social events but often extracted hard news stories from them, asked me if I had read a book called *The Tears of Autumn*. When I said I hadn't, she began to explain the plot. But I knew all about the book. It had been written by a former CIA agent named Charles McCarry. In novel form, he told about the Diem family of South Vietnam hiring a killer to murder Kennedy because they believed he plotted the assassination of President Ngo Dinh Diem.

Radcliffe asked me whether Castro might have engaged in such revenge against Kennedy. Pretending that someone at the other end of the lunch table was talking to me, I turned my back on Radcliffe and ignored her disquieting question.

As more and more stories about alleged CIA abuses were printed and broadcast, my daily news briefing was almost totally taken up with reporters' questions about the intelligence agency. I sometimes spent more than an hour a day with Ford discussing possible answers. Rumsfeld encouraged me to continue bringing the questions to Ford's attention as a way to prod the president into making policy decisions to deal with the allegations of CIA misdeeds. I was happy to play that role because I was anxious for Ford to take some action.

Since virtually all the abuses had stopped before Ford came to the White House, staff members warned the president that he could be hurt by the scandal only if he appeared to be covering it up. Ford agreed with that. But he also was concerned with other considerations. The president firmly believed in the necessity of a strong American intelligence organization for both gathering information and conducting covert operations. He viewed covert operations as a "third option," to be used to advance America's interests overseas when diplomacy failed but military action was too drastic. This reflected Ford's view of the world and of America's role in the world, which had been formed in the 1950s, in the chilliest and most dangerous days of the Cold War.

Ford and others in the White House were troubled by the idea that intelligence activities ordered by previous presidents and other former officials to meet the circumstances of the time were being judged in hindsight under different world conditions and in a different moral climate. He was determined to deal with the CIA scandal in a way that would not damage America's necessary intelligence capability. He believed he would be held accountable if he allowed the intelligence services to be crippled by excessive exposure and unwise restrictions.

Two congressional investigations of the CIA were undertaken, one in the Senate headed by Senator Frank Church and one in the House headed by Congressman Otis Pike. The White House believed the Church Committee had a first-rate staff but was never able to conduct a serious inquiry because Church and other members were more interested in sensational headlines. This was demonstrated at their first hearings when exotic CIA equipment, including a dart gun, was displayed for the cameras, but no effort was made to examine the fundamental shortcomings in the intelligence system. On the other hand, the White House admired Pike for understanding the right basic questions to pursue, but his staff frittered away the committee's respectability by an unending series of leaks to reporters.

Once these two committees began their investigations, Ford found himself spending long hours trying to settle disputes among Congress, Kissinger, the National Security Council, the CIA and other agencies over access to classified documents and procedures for handling them. There were no orderly and uniform rules for responding to congressional demands for documents. A committee would subpoena the same document from six different agencies. Each of the six agencies would censor out what it thought was too sensitive. The committee would put the six different versions together and get most of the original document.

There also were no guidelines for protecting the methods and sources the United States used to gather intelligence. And there was no strategy for focusing the attention of the congressional investigation on important issues rather than on the sensations.

To correct this, Ford created a top-level committee to deal with the problems, headed by Marsh with an aide named Michael Duval as the executive director. The committee and Duval met every morning at 9 A.M. in the White House Situation Room to review new allegations and resolve congressional requests for documents. Duval believed that Ford never did learn everything the CIA had done in years past. In fact, Duval thought the president might have been lied to.

While the Church Committee, the Pike Committee, the Rockefeller Commission and the Marsh-Duval Committee all pushed on with their work, a new CIA sensation burst into the headlines.

On March 19, 1975, Jack Anderson disclosed in a broadcast that the CIA had paid the Howard Hughes organization more than $250 million to build a unique deep-sea exploration ship named the *Glomar Explorer*. Anderson reported that in August 1974 the ship had recovered part of a Russian missile submarine which had sunk in 1968, 750 miles northwest of Hawaii.

(The decision to raise the submarine was one of the first important questions Ford faced in the White House. On August 10, 1974, his second day as president, he was told that the *Glomar Explorer* was on station, awaiting his orders. He was warned that a Soviet trawler was lurking nearby and might try to stop the recovery operation, possibly setting off a dangerous clash. Ford gave the order to go ahead. The trawler did not interfere, but as the sub was raised, the portion containing the nuclear missiles and the code books broke off and fell back to the bottom.)

It was decided that nobody in the government would answer any press questions about the *Glomar Explorer* after the Anderson broadcast. Even Ford told reporters bluntly, "No comment," when they asked him about the ship, a rare response from him. The total refusal to acknowledge the *Glomar Explorer* story was essential to avoid serious repercussions from the Soviet Union. If the United States government officially confirmed the *Glomar Explorer*'s accomplishment, the Soviet Union would feel it had been made a fool of in the eyes of the world and might be tempted to retaliate.

My first inquiry from the press, the day before Anderson's revelations, was not about the story itself. Rather, a reporter asked me if Colby was visiting news organizations all over town, asking them not to print or broadcast the story.

I checked and found that Colby had indeed contacted a number of news organizations and persuaded them not to run the *Glomar* story on grounds that it would provoke the Russians into interfering with an impending attempt to salvage the rest of the sub. Colby was on the phone with Anderson until five minutes before his broadcast, begging him not to break the *Glomar* story. Anderson ran the story anyhow, and the effort to retrieve the rest of the Russian sub was canceled as a result.

By early June 1975 the Rockefeller Commission had completed its report on domestic spying by the CIA. While Ford was on a European trip to Brussels, Madrid, Salzburg and Rome, Rockefeller led reporters to believe they would be handed copies of the 299-page report on Thursday, June 5, 1975, for publication and broadcast on Sunday, June 8. The problem was that Rockefeller had not cleared that timetable with Ford. The president wanted to read the report first and make the decision on when and whether the report would be released to the press and public.

Rockefeller had also let the anticipation build up among newsmen that the report would contain a section on CIA plots to assassinate foreign leaders, even though the commission had decided at least three weeks before that it could not finish its investigation of the assassination charges in time for the report. (This coincided with Ford's wishes. He did not believe that his White House should sit in judgment of covert activities conducted under previous presidents. Ford concluded that the best course was to turn over information about the assassination plots to the Church Committee.)

Ford returned from his European trip about 1 A.M. on the morning of Wednesday, June 4, 1975, and took off just seven and a half hours later for West Point to deliver the commencement speech at the military academy. Obviously neither he nor his staff was focusing on the Rockefeller Commission Report, which reporters expected to receive the next day. When the White House finally realized the problem, we forced the Rockefeller staff to issue a statement announcing that, contrary to expectations, the report would not contain any findings on assassination charges and a decision on whether to release it publicly would be made after the president read it over the weekend.

The press corps blew up. Reporters thought they caught the strong scent of another Watergate, another cover-up, lies, Ziegler. At my next press briefing I tried to explain for almost an hour why publication of the report was delayed and why there were no findings on assassination, while being careful not to publicly put the blame on Rockefeller for his overenthusiastic promises to the press. It was perhaps the nastiest briefing I ever faced. One reporter called me a liar.

The experience of being called a liar publicly, and of not being able to convince my briefing that I was telling the truth, really shook me. Although I sometimes used minor circumlocutions on sensitive issues and was occasionally overprotective in acknowledging Ford gaffes, I always tried to tell the truth, or at least never to tell a lie. That wasn't an attitude I adopted when I became press secretary. It was an attitude instilled in me from childhood by a strict and moral mother.

After the vicious briefing I phoned nearly a dozen reporters and explained to them privately what I felt I couldn't say openly: Vice President Rockefeller and some members of his staff were responsible for the foul-up. I indicated I expected the report to be made public after the president read it. I didn't see why Ford should be portrayed as considering suppression or censorship of the report while Rockefeller came off as being enthusiastic about publishing the whole thing immediately.

The flap with the press dissolved after Ford read the Rockefeller report and authorized its release to the reporters and public just three days later than Rockefeller had promised. The commission found that over a span of twenty-eight years the CIA had engaged in some activities that were "plainly unlawful and constituted improper invasions upon the rights of Americans," although the majority of the agency's actions was judged to be legal. Some of the illegal activities, the commission reported, "were initiated or ordered by the president, either directly or indirectly."

Among the illegal and improper CIA operations:

—For twenty years the agency inspected and opened mail between the United States and the Soviet Union, even though it knew this was against the law.

—The CIA administered LSD and other drugs to persons without their knowledge for more than ten years as part of a program to test the possible usefulness of such substances for intelligence activities.

—In the late 1960s and early 1970s, at the time of anti-Vietnam protests, the CIA set up Operation CHAOS in response to presidential requests to collect information on dissident individuals and groups. Ostensibly designed to determine whether any foreign influence was involved, the operation eventually compiled files on

7200 Americans and created a computerized index of 300,000 names of individuals and organizations.

—The CIA placed thirty-two wiretaps, planted thirty-two electronic bugs, broke into twelve establishments and inspected tax records of sixteen persons in the course of investigating suspected security risks.

The commission reported no evidence that illegal CIA activities continued in the Ford administration.

In the process of its investigation, the commission learned that the Soviet Union had installed electronic equipment at its embassy in Washington for eavesdropping on phone calls at the White House four blocks away, at the Capitol and indeed on any call transmitted by microwave. The Rockefeller Commission wanted to disclose this Russian spying as a means of justifying the need for a strong American intelligence organization.

However, Kissinger objected. He thought such a public accusation could anger the Russians into pulling back from detente, and could give conservatives in Congress ammunition to campaign against detente and even to demand retaliatory steps against the Russians. In addition, charges of Soviet electronic eavesdropping in Washington probably would lead to Russian denunciation of American snooping in Moscow.

Kissinger accepted a watered-down paragraph on foreign spying which carefully avoided any specific mention of the Soviet Union.

I once told Rumsfeld that by the time the intelligence investigations were over, most Americans would have become paranoid because of the revelations. Some members of the White House staff became a little paranoid because of unpublicized findings.

For instance, it was discovered that the Secret Service had concealed a TV camera in the vending-machine room of the Executive Office Building in hopes of catching a guard suspected of stealing sandwiches from the dispenser. Instead, the Secret Service captured eight minutes of videotape of a middle-level executive, frustrated by the machine's refusal to give him his food after he'd deposited the money, tearing off hunks of sandwich through the balky door and popping them into his mouth. Nabbed by the Secret Service, the executive explained that he was sick and tired of the machine taking his money day after day and not delivering his sandwich.

The worrisome aspect of the episode was that no one in authority in the White House knew the Secret Service had installed the camera. It raised questions in the minds of some staff members about what other spying devices might have been planted around the White House by various agencies.

When Rumsfeld moved into the chief of staff's office, previously occupied by Haldeman and Haig, he found recorders, other electronic devices and stacks of tapes in the cabinets. He had them removed without listening to them.

Ford, immediately after becoming president, ordered all listening and recording devices removed from the White House complex. What concerned the staff members was: If Ford didn't know what bugs had been installed, how could he be sure they'd all been removed?

I was horrified when Mike Duval, the executive director of the committee coordinating the administration's response to the various intelligence investigations, informed me that serious consideration was being given to criminal prosecution of three newsmen—freelancer Tad Szulc, Nicholas Horrock of the *New York Times* and Bob Woodward of the *Washington Post*—on charges of violating the Signals Intelligence Act. (The Signals Intelligence Act makes it a crime to publish classified information obtained through bugs, taps and other sophisticated electronic eavesdropping methods, or to reveal the procedures used to intercept the information.) I told Duval that criminal prosecutions would destroy Ford's image of openness toward the press and would bring back memories of Nixon's efforts to stop publication of the Pentagon Papers. I warned that the president would be accused of using the Signals Intelligence Act to conduct a new cover-up to hide misdeeds by the intelligence apparatus.

Duval said Kissinger, Schlesinger and Scowcroft were pushing for prosecutions. Attorney General Edward Levi was weighing the evidence. Among the news stories Levi reviewed for possible prosecution were: a Horrock article saying presidents Johnson and Nixon received reports on what prominent Americans were doing and saying on overseas trips, obtained from electronic listening devices; a Woodward article claiming the National Security Agency had monitored the phone calls of antiwar leaders and other dissidents; and a Szulc article in *Penthouse* on the NSA.

The most serious concern was a story being prepared by the *New York Times* saying that American submarines had crept close to the Russian coast off Vladivostok and tapped underwater cables for Soviet messages. An American sub was off the coast of Vladivostok at the time and officials feared the Russians might try to sink or capture it if the story was published.

Duval asked what I thought of the idea of Levi phoning Horrock and urging him not to write the submarine story. I replied that it was a terrible idea—Levi was not good at handling press questions. Duval agreed. He said Levi seemed shocked by some of the things he was learning from the intelligence investigations. "Levi sometimes looks like a rather stunned little boy whom you want to take in your arms and comfort," Duval said.

Mitchell Rogovin, a special counsel to the CIA director and former lawyer for Neil Sheehan of the *New York Times* in the Pentagon Papers case, did phone the *Times* several times urging that the submarine story not be printed and warning of possible prosecution for violating the Signals Intelligence Act. As a result the paper prepared a restrained version of the submarine story and delayed publication until after the American sub had left Soviet waters.

Ford was purposely kept out of deliberations on the explosive matter of prosecuting newsmen. If Levi decided to bring charges, we wanted to be able to say it was purely a legal decision by the attorney general with no political or public-relations considerations from the White House. We also wanted to be able to put the responsibility on Levi in case the Reaganite conservatives demanded to know why newsmen were not being charged with printing secrets.

Levi eventually concluded that too many secrets would have to be revealed in a criminal trial, so no charges were brought against the newsmen.

Press stories and congressional investigations of electronic spying led to disclosure of the only questionable intelligence practice found to have taken place during the Ford administration. This was "Operation Shamrock." Under the operation, the National Security Agency scanned virtually every phone call and Teletype message between the United States and foreign countries, with the cooperation of the international communications companies, looking for intelligence information. The program was begun by President Truman shortly after World War II and was ended by the Ford administration in May 1975, on grounds that it might be an improper invasion of the privacy of American citizens.

Some White House staff members thought Ford should seize the initiative on reforming the intelligence system. We argued that the time was right. The intelligence agencies had opposed reform efforts by previous presidents, but now they were under concentrated attack from Congress, the press and the public. Ford was the only force standing in the way of a rout. The intelligence agencies couldn't afford to oppose his reforms at that point.

Ford agreed to look at proposals for reorganizing the intelligence services, but he insisted that he was not committed to do anything before the 1976 election.

After conferring with intelligence experts back to the Kennedy administration, Duval compiled several thick loose-leaf notebooks for Ford, outlining the existing organization of the intelligence system, describing vicious internal jurisdiction battles, challenging Ford to decide what his principles and objectives were, and raising such fundamental questions as whether agencies should compete in the gathering and analysis of intelligence and whether military or economic intelligence was more important.

The president agreed in late 1975 to propose a sweeping reorganization and reform of the American intelligence services, partly because he saw the plan—the first major reorganization of the intelligence system since just after World War II—as a chance to put his imprint on an accomplishment of long-range significance.

The details were hammered out in a series of long and intense meetings in the Cabinet Room. Kissinger, Scowcroft and some other senior advisers opposed the reforms, but the president was determined to go ahead. He announced his reorganization on February 8, 1976, fourteen months after Seymour Hersch's *New York Times* article set off the spy scandal. The major features of the plan were:

—Legally binding restrictions on the intelligence agencies, forbidding them to experiment on humans with drugs without consent, plant secret agents in other government offices, spy on Americans within the United States, infiltrate dissident groups and in other ways violate the rights of U.S. citizens.

—A promise to meet with congressional leaders to draft legal safeguards against electronic surveillance and mail opening.

—Support for legislation prohibiting intelligence agencies from assassinating foreign leaders.

—Establishment of a new intelligence command structure with the National Security Council to set policy; a new Committee on Foreign Intelligence headed by the CIA director to manage all intelligence activities; and a new Oversight Board of three private citizens to monitor the entire intelligence operation.

—Proposed legislation making it illegal for a government employee to reveal certain highly classified intelligence secrets.

—An invitation to Congress to set up a joint Senate-House committee to oversee intelligence activities.

"As Americans, we must not and will not tolerate actions by our government which abridge the rights of our citizens," Ford declared in announcing his reforms. "At the same time, we must maintain a strong and effective intelligence capability in the United States. I will not be a party to the dismantling of the CIA and the other intelligence agencies."

Even before announcing these reforms, the president fired William Colby as director of the CIA, a step Ford felt was essential to restore public confidence in the agency. He chose as the new CIA chief George Bush, America's envoy in Peking, former congressman from Texas and former chairman of the Republican National Committee.

Ford drove to the CIA headquarters in Langley, Virginia, to preside at Bush's swearing-in. The ceremony was in a large modernistic auditorium which was open to visitors and the press. Afterward, when the president went into the main CIA office building to address several hundred employees, the reporters and cameramen were not allowed to follow him, to prevent photos from being taken of agents and to safeguard other secrets.

One of the secrets is a Lucite case in the lobby containing a memorial book listing the more than thirty CIA operatives killed in the line of duty. Some of the agents are listed by name. Others are commemorated only with a black star. These black stars designate persons whose families don't even know their deaths were connected with CIA activities.

By late 1975 the Senate's Church Committee was ready to issue its report on CIA assassination plots. There was some concern among White House aides that publication of the report might gravely damage the reputation of the United States, perhaps even provoking a United Nations investigation into the assassination plots. Some of the classified information in the Church report already had been disclosed during the yearlong deluge of leaks to the press. But that same information in an official document from a branch of the U.S. government might force a foreign government to take face-saving retaliatory action.

Consequently, Ford wrote Church asking him not to release the report, at least until administration officials were allowed to censor sensitive material. "Public release of these official materials and information will do grievous damage to our country," Ford wrote to Church. "It would most likely be exploited by foreign nations and groups hostile to the United States in a manner designed to do maximum damage to the reputation and foreign policy of the United States. I am convinced that publication at this time will endanger individuals named in the report or who can be identified when foreign agents carefully study it."

Nevertheless, the Senate voted to publish the report after considering it in a dramatic secret session.

"The committee believes the truth about the assassination allegations should be told because democracy depends upon a well-informed electorate," the report explained. "Despite the temporary injury to our national reputation, the committee believes that foreign peoples will, upon sober reflection, respect the United States more for keeping faith with its democratic ideal than they will condemn us for the misconduct revealed."

The committee concluded the following:

—The CIA had concocted numerous plots to kill Castro, all unsuccessful.

—The agency had plotted to kill Lumumba of the Congo, but when he was killed by Congolese rebels the CIA apparently had nothing to do with it.

—The United States had supplied weapons to dissidents in the Dominican Republic, but the evidence was conflicting on whether these weapons were used to assassinate Trujillo.

—The Kennedy administration had encouraged South Vietnamese plotters to overthrow Diem, but his murder was spontaneous, not prompted by U.S. officials.

—The CIA had supported a military coup designed to block Marxist Salvador Allende from becoming president in Chile, but the evidence indicated the United States was not responsible for the killing of General René Schneider during the coup.

—There was some evidence of CIA involvement in plots to kill President Sukarno of Indonesia and Duvalier of Haiti.

—Despite all this plotting, "No foreign leaders were killed as a result of assassination plots initiated by officials of the United States," and except for a "reasonable inference" that Eisenhower authorized a plan to assassinate Lumumba, there was no solid evidence that any American president approved any assassination plot against any foreign leader.

So there it was, out at last. The sky didn't fall. No country broke off diplomatic relations, although Russia publicly scolded the United States. America was not hauled before the United Nations. In fact, the Senate investigators' report seemed a disappointing anticlimax compared to the cornucopia of rumors, gossip, revelations, leaks, allegations and scoops that had filled the headlines and TV news for a year.

Three months after the Church Committee published its report on assassination plots, the Pike Committee in the House was ready to issue its findings on a broader range of intelligence abuses. Again Ford implored the investigators not to release their findings until he had a chance to excise material "detrimental to the national security." This time the appeal was heeded. The House voted 246 to 124 to keep the Pike Committee Report secret. Ford issued a statement praising the House for its "proper and responsible action" to deny classified information to "our enemies and potential enemies."

But Daniel Schorr of CBS voted 1 to 0 to release the Pike Committee's report.

Someone leaked a copy of the report to Schorr. After broadcasting a few excerpts on CBS, Schorr passed on the document to the *Village Voice* for publication in return for the promise of a cash payment to the Reporters Committee for Freedom of the Press.

(After the year of leaks, the Pike Committee Report also contained few new revelations. Pike examined some less sensational but more important issues, such as the accuracy of American intelligence, the distribution of intelligence findings through the government and the use of it in reaching foreign-policy decisions.)

Schorr's arrangement with the *Village Voice* was supposed to be a secret, but some members of the Reporters Committee blabbed to the *Washington Post.* "I deeply regret that the Reporters Committee has not been able to maintain the confidentiality of the arrangement," Schorr grumbled when the story of the deal was published. But, he added, "I am fully aware of the irony of my complaining about leaks."

Indeed.

The correspondent was first suspended, then released by CBS. The House conducted an investigation to determine who leaked the report to Schorr, but never found out. Schorr, who is abrasive and aggressive with a large ego, was not well liked by some of his colleagues at CBS and in the press corps. Nevertheless, a pantheon of media stars trooped before the House investigators to defend Schorr's First Amendment right to reveal the Pike Committee Report and his journalist's right to refuse to name his source.

I think Schorr was wrong. As a journalist for more than twenty years, I am a stout defender of the First Amendment and of the necessity to protect confidential sources. But there is something that bothers me about one newsman, with mixed motives, superimposing his judgment over the judgment of 246 elected representatives of the people. After all, Watergate grew from this same attitude among men in places of power and influence that their own judgment of what was right and in the national interest took precedence over laws, ethics and decisions of Congress.

A final irony of the press corps' long spy chase was that it ignored one of the CIA's biggest authentic foul-ups.

In May 1976 the CIA made a public confession that for ten years, and perhaps longer, the American intelligence services had badly underestimated the proportion of the Soviet gross national product spent on defense. Russia was actually spending twice as big a percentage of its GNP on military programs as the United States thought it was, the CIA conceded, and this estimate might go even higher after the matter was studied further.

White House aides held a flurry of meetings to prepare for the expected deluge of press inquiries. Duval prepared a long memo containing dozens of tough questions and suggested answers: What effect would the error have on future American military spending? What did the revised estimates reveal of Soviet economic inefficiency and of the allocation of funds for consumer needs versus defense needs? Who was to blame for the massive intelligence error? Were they going to be fired?

I never got a single press question about the matter.

Maybe this genuine intelligence gaffe was considered suspect because it was revealed through a public CIA announcement instead of a leak.

CHAPTER EIGHT

A Ford but Not a Hoover

Some of Ford's chief advisers were in a gloomy mood as 1975 began. They were concerned and frustrated because Ford seemed to be drifting, unable to rally the public with inspiring leadership, haunted by the specter of Nixon, unwilling to bring in an all-new Ford team, hobbled by a lackluster speechwriting office.

For a time, after Haig departed, the White House was close to anarchy. Literally, no one was in charge of the staff. Advisers wandered in and out of the Oval Office, often taking up the president's time with minor matters. (I once listened to a second-level staff aide discuss in the Oval Office his airline connections to get to a speech.) Ford's schedule was overcrowded with time-wasting appointments that should have been skipped. There was no one to make sure the necessary background and option papers were prepared before decision-making meetings. As time went on, Don Rumsfeld gradually took over the chief-of-staff duties, although without the title. So much for the spokes-of-the-wheel theory.

The most serious cause for gloom was the economy. It was suddenly and precipitously plunging into a recession. At the White House Economic Conference in late September 1974, economists from all points on the ideological spectrum assured Ford that inflation, then over 12 percent, was the big problem. A few cautioned that there could be a downturn in the economy. But none saw a sharp drop.

As a result Ford announced an economic program to a joint session of Congress in early October 1974 designed to combat inflation: a tight lid of $300 billion on the federal budget; a $5-billion surtax on corporations and higher-level personal income to soak up excess purchasing power; and the WIN program, "Whip Inflation Now."

Ford was earnest about the WIN program, based on the homespun notion that the average citizen, in little ways, could help whip inflation. When the president unveiled his economic program to Congress, he wore a red and white WIN badge pinned to his lapel. There were only two handmade WIN badges in existence and until more could be mass produced they were passed back and forth among officials to wear at briefings, speeches and TV shows.

The day after Ford's speech to Congress, WIN "enlistment forms" were printed in newspapers all over the country, recruiting volunteers for the great citizens' crusade against inflation. A week later, in a speech to the Future Farmers of America in Kansas City, Ford reported on some of the inflation-fighting ideas he'd received from WIN enlistees:

"From Hillsboro, Oregon, the Stevens family writes they are fixing up their bikes to do family errands. . . . Bob Cantrell, a fourteen-year-old in Pasadena, California, gave up his stereo to save energy. . . . Rick Jacobsen of the fifth grade at Sault St. Marie, Michigan, writes the White House that 'we planted our own garden so we could save on vegetables.' "

In the Future Farmers speech, Ford advised WIN volunteers to "take all you want but eat all you take" at meals and he urged every family to make a one-hour "trash inventory" to find waste.

It was easy to laugh at the WIN program. And, boy, was it laughed at, by political opponents, comedians and cartoonists. I never found out who was responsible for dreaming up the WIN program. Nobody claimed credit.

Ford wanted his Future Farmers speech carried live on television because he felt he was talking directly to the American people, giving them their marching orders for the war on inflation. But the networks refused to carry it, ostensibly on grounds that it contained no news. I suspected the real reason was that the networks felt Nixon had misused TV coverage to promote his political goals and they weren't going to let Ford get away with the same thing.

On the morning of the speech, when I told the president the networks would not carry his speech voluntarily, he directed, "Well, do what you have to do."

That meant "requesting" time from the networks, virtually commandeering the airwaves. Traditionally such requests were never rejected. So the networks carried the speech on TV, but under protest. Walter Cronkite canceled an interview scheduled with Ford the following weekend to demonstrate his displeasure. Arthur Taylor, then president of CBS, wrote the president that "these kinds of tactics" threatened the free, vigorous and independent press in America.

Despite the flap, I still felt there were occasions when a president had the right to speak directly to the American people on an important issue.

Within weeks after Ford announced his program to fight inflation, he and his advisers were scrambling to find solutions to a deepening recession. The outlook had shifted in an incredibly short period of time. Unemployment was rising. Auto sales were dropping. The automobile and other industries were laying off workers. The gross national product, a measurement of the total output of goods and services, was down. The sharp and unexpected drop in the economy created a sticky problem of what to say to the press that wouldn't unduly alarm the public or increase the political damage to Ford.

At a White House news briefing in mid-November 1974, Phil Shabecoff of the *New York Times* asked whether "the president is now prepared to concede that the national economy is in a recession."

I heard another reporter mutter, "Oh, yeah, never are they going to do that."

But I surprised the press corps by acknowledging, "When the statistics come in from November and are analyzed, it will probably appear that this month we are moving into a recession." That cautious admission had been carefully drafted by the president and his economic advisers.

Someone asked me at the briefing, "Is it simply coincidence that the White House is declaring a recession one week after the election of nineteen seventy-four?" For once, the reporters' cynicism was not misplaced.

While we were conceding publicly that the country was moving into a recession, privately there was apprehension in the White House that the economy might be plunging out of control. Alan Greenspan, chairman of the Council of Economic Advisers, told some presidential aides at an informal meeting, "We think that this is going to be a rather deep but short recession, but we could fall off the cliff."

On Saturday afternoon, December 21, 1974, Ford convened a

meeting of all his senior aides in the Cabinet Room to find a solution to the recession. The economic advisers had met that morning and all the previous day to chart the seriousness of the problem and draft recommendations. Vice President Rockefeller, sworn in the night before, was attending his first official meeting.

The mood was somber, almost frightened.

The president asked Roy Ash, the budget director, to give the good news.

"That will take about four seconds," Ash replied bleakly.

There was plenty of bad news. The economic advisers, who previously had forecast peak unemployment of 7 or 7 ½ percent, now said it might to go to 8 percent. They also hedged their previous assertion that the economy would hit bottom in the spring and start improving in the second half of 1975. Now they weren't sure when the recovery would begin.

Greenspan, speaking in a soft voice, said economists had not seen such a recession before. Until a few weeks before, it had followed the pattern of a normal economic downturn. Then something new happened. Businessmen and consumers suddenly seemed to lose all confidence in the future. Greenspan said the economy was getting worse and, frankly, he didn't know where the bottom was.

There was absolute silence in the Cabinet Room. The president and his aides looked grim.

After listening to the bad news and his advisers' ideas for coping with it, Ford sat forward in his high-backed leather chair at the side of the long cabinet table and announced his decisions for trying to reverse the recession. The major initiative, he proclaimed, should be an immediate tax cut to increase the purchasing power of individuals and to reward businesses for undertaking job-creating expansions. This represented a complete reversal of the $5-billion tax increase Ford had proposed less than three months earlier to fight inflation.*

The president decided at the meeting to announce his new economic strategy in his State of the Union speech to the new Congress the following month. The president wanted to impress Congress and the American people with the seriousness of the situation, which he likened to the grim days of World War II. He suggested that the speechwriters for his State of the Union address read FDR's State of the Union speeches of 1942, 1943 and 1944 to catch the

---

* A reporter asked me at a briefing whether Ford's new antirecession program was a 180-degree shift from his anti-inflation program. No, I wisecracked, it was only a 179-degree shift.

tone he wanted. He directed that the speech be written in language that would jolt the American people back into a sense of confidence that something was being done to halt the recession.

Nevertheless, the meeting broke up in a mood of apprehension, as if these powerful men, who commanded such enormous influence over the nation's course, realized that they were not entirely in control of the sick economy.

During that period of White House doldrums in late 1974, Rumsfeld, his deputy Richard Cheney, Greenspan, John Marsh and I frequently gathered in Rumsfeld's office at the end of the day to drink beer and worry over the recession and other White House problems.

At one session Rumsfeld said he'd been urging Ford to get away to Camp David to think about and discuss his long-range goals and aspirations for America, for inclusion in the State of the Union speech. Ford thought that such a meeting should consider a shopping list of practical legislative proposals and budget items, while Rumsfeld wanted the president to think about broader matters like the changing relationship between the people and their institutions, new ways of viewing the economy, and so forth.

Don looked discouraged. He wasn't getting anywhere with this idea and he wasn't getting anywhere with suggestions that Ford put his own stamp on the government with a major cabinet shake-up.

Rumsfeld said Ford was tottering on the brink. I thought he meant tottering on the brink of going ahead with the Camp David meeting. But Rumsfeld meant he considered Ford to be on the brink of a long, unbreakable slide in public esteem which would rob him of any chance to win the election in 1976. According to Rumsfeld, Ford had a maximum of three months to determine his future. "At the end of three months, the Ford administration will either have the smell of life or the smell of death," he declared. "If it's the smell of death, this White House is going to be torn to pieces by the press, by the Democrats, even by other Republicans who will challenge the president for the nomination in nineteen seventy-six."

Ford looked forward to a respite from his troubles when he and Mrs. Ford and their children flew to Vail for their annual Christmas and New Year's vacation of skiing and partying. But the problems followed the president to the snowy Colorado mountains. Because time was growing short before the State of the Union speech, Ford summoned his chief advisers to Vail to discuss the issues—final decisions on his antirecession economic program and a related energy program to meet rising foreign oil prices.

The meeting was held in the wood-and-stone family room of the president's rented chalet, in front of a blazing fire. Everyone was dressed in the casual Vail style—sweaters, slacks, boots, après-ski clothes—everyone, that is, except Arthur Burns, the courtly chairman of the Federal Reserve Board. Conservative in outlook and formal in dress, he wore a suit and tie. (After the meeting had been under way for about fifteen minutes, Burns stood up and, without saying a word, took off his jacket and loosened his tie. For him, that was casual.)

A tax cut, which had been approved so readily at the earlier White House meeting, now was reconsidered. Some advisers argued that the federal budget deficit was going to be so large, due to falling tax revenues and increased unemployment payments caused by the recession, that a reduction in taxes was not justified. Their view was that a tax cut could raise the federal deficit to an enormous $60–$80 billion, frightening businessmen and consumers so much that the goal of restoring confidence in the economy would be aborted.

The meeting had been going on for four hours when the question of the tax cut was brought up. I could see the president was itchy to go skiing. Whether for that or some other reason, after only a perfunctory discussion of the tax cut the president decided to put off a final decision until he returned to Washington.

The economy and energy were not the only problems that plagued the president in Vail. The *New York Times* ran a front-page story saying that Richard Bass, the Texas businessman and friend from whom the president was renting the house in Vail, stood to make $100 million from his coal holdings if Ford vetoed a bill Congress had sent him regulating strip mining. The story suggested a conflict of interest.

President and Mrs. Ford were outraged by the implication. Ford said he didn't even know Bass owned coal land until he read it in the *Times* and, besides, he wasn't going to base his decisions about the legislation on the business interests of a man from whom he rented a house. (Ford vetoed the strip-mining bill during his stay in Vail on grounds that it would restrict mining at a time when the

United States needed to expand production of coal as a substitute for oil.)

Over a drink at a New Year's Eve party at his Vail house, Ford grumbled to me about other news stories criticizing his vacation as an unwarranted waste of time, money and resources. He was particularly irked by a CBS report that pointed out that Ford's energy advisers consumed 14,000 gallons of jet fuel getting to Vail for a meeting to discuss how to conserve fuel.

Back in Washington after New Year's, 1975, Ford decided he would unveil his economic and energy programs in two speeches, the formal State of the Union message to Congress in mid-January and a more informal fireside chat aimed directly at the American people a few nights earlier.

It was recognized in the White House that the speeches were perhaps the last opportunity to blow away the rising public doubts about Ford. If the speeches demonstrated leadership and competence to find solutions to the complex problems nagging the country, the Ford presidency would at last be launched on an upward path of popularity and acceptance. If the speeches misfired, I worried in a note to myself, maybe "the Ford Presidency is never going to get off the ground and he is going to be a President for 2 ½ years and that is all."

The fireside chat was to be delivered in the seldom-used library on the lower level of the White House. For the first time since becoming president, Ford would use a TelePrompTer.

Starting about a week before the speech, he practiced using the prompter and cameras. Until the speech was ready, parts of old statements and even stories clipped from the newspaper were put on the prompter for rehearsals. One day someone put on the device a story from the *New York Times* about a poet who had won an award for his work. After stumbling through the unfamiliar material, Ford complained in exasperation, "I don't use that kind of language."

When a draft finally arrived from Bob Hartmann's speechwriting office three days before the fireside chat, it was awful—ten minutes too long, full of clichés, flowery, with the major points blurred. Before transferring the speech to the TelePrompTer, I fixed it up a little, although I had no authority to rewrite speeches. While Ford rehearsed my edited version, Hartmann kept leafing through his text, trying to find out what happened to his draft. "Those are not my words," he muttered. "I wonder whose words those are."

After the rehearsal I retreated to Rumsfeld's office to discuss the sad state of the speech.

"Do you think it can be salvaged?" he asked.

"Yes," I replied, "with very, very heavy editing. The basis of a good speech is there, but it needs to be put together better."

"Well, if you think you can do it, why don't you write the speech," Rumsfeld urged.

I wrote a draft overnight. It was the first direct challenge to Hartmann's status as Ford's speechwriter. (I found out later that Rumsfeld had ordered still another draft from Alan Greenspan and Robert Goldwin, the White House liaison with the academic community.)

The fireside chat was scheduled for Monday night, January 13, 1975. The Saturday before, I asked Rumsfeld which speech I should put on the TelePrompTer for the day's rehearsal, Hartmann's latest version or mine.

"You have to put the Hartmann version on the machine," he advised. Hartmann was still, officially, the president's chief speechwriter. "But put your speech on another sheet and have it ready," Rumsfeld suggested. "Of course, if you make a mistake and put the wrong speech on the TelePrompTer, I guess nobody could do anything."

Hartmann became aware of the alternate versions of the speech. Watching him at the Saturday rehearsal, I sensed that Hartmann—who had a large ego and a combative attitude toward rivals—was building up to an explosion over the challenge to his speechwriting authority.

That night he invited me to share his car for the ride home. He bitched the whole way about White House staff members trying to horn in on his speechwriting duties. I was uncomfortable, knowing I was one of those who was horning in. He complained that speechwriting was the only area where staff members from other White House offices felt free to meddle.

The next day, Sunday, Hartmann made a tactical error. He failed to come to the rehearsal to fight for his version of the fireside chat. He sent an assistant, Robert Orben, a tall, crew-cut author of joke books, who was no match for Rumsfeld.

After Ford read through the Hartmann speech in the library and watched a videotape playback, Rumsfeld suggested that the president go through the text again to mark the TelePrompTer copy for emphasis and pauses. But that was just a ruse to open up the speech for major changes. First, individual words were changed, then phrases, then sentences, then whole paragraphs. The process took more than two hours, conducted in full view of the network television crew.

While waiting for the changes to be typed, Ford, Rumsfeld, Cheney, Greenspan and I went up to the president's residence on the second floor of the White House to watch the Super Bowl game between the Pittsburgh Steelers and the Minnesota Vikings on TV. At half time, the staff members left the president and trooped to Rumsfeld's office, where we were joined by William Seidman, director of the White House Economic Policy Board, and Frank Zarb, the energy administrator, for a final rewrite of the speech. Rumsfeld, who was suffering from an eye ailment, was gray with fatigue and pain. Every once in a while he clutched his eye in agony.

After three hours of writing and editing, our version of the speech was done, incorporating parts of my draft, the Greenspan-Goldwin text and Rumsfeld's ideas. Rumsfeld's strategy was to send it to the president with a note saying it was the draft unanimously recommended by the staff members involved and urging Ford to direct Hartmann to incorporate our changes into the final text. Hartmann would never accept the suggestions directly from us, but he could hardly refuse to make changes if Ford ordered them.

The president did finally settle on a speech that was an amalgam of Hartmann's draft and our rival version. And after all the jockeying, it turned out to be a pretty good speech. Ford taped his final rehearsal Monday afternoon, a smooth performance. But he decided to do the broadcast live at 9 that night. "If I drop dead before tonight, you can still use the tape," he joked morbidly.

A fireside chat required a fire, of course. Special logs, made of compressed sawdust, were used because they burned quietly, without crackling, and therefore would not interfere with the sound of the president's voice on TV.

Rather than delivering the entire speech in the standard presidential posture, staring across his desk, Ford had practiced changing his position during the address, from sitting at a small antique desk to leaning against the desk to standing beside the desk. The TelePrompTer printed the words on a mirror directly over the camera lens, so the president was reading his text but appeared to be looking the television audience square in the eye.

The library is a small room, lined floor to ceiling on three sides with shelves of books. Even with some of the furniture removed, it was crowded with television equipment and technicians. Rumsfeld and I hunched in chairs against one wall, watching intently, as Ford read from the TelePrompTer a speech that could have an important affect on public perception of his presidency.

Ford delivered the speech virtually flawlessly, with only one minor stumble over a word. He outlined his economic and energy program in a relaxed way but with a tone of authority.

"Without wasting words, I want to talk to you tonight about putting our domestic house in order," the president began. "We must turn America in a new direction. . . . We must wage a simultaneous three-front campaign against recession, inflation and energy dependence."

He listed his proposals:

—Raise taxes on imported and domestic fuel to encourage conservation of petroleum and natural gas.

—Return revenues from these taxes in the form of special payments to individuals, businesses, state and local governments.

—Speed the development of nuclear, geothermal and solar power and increase incentives to produce more coal and oil within the United States.

—Cut taxes $16 billion in the form of rebates to individuals and in incentives to companies which expand their plants and hire more workers. (The doubts about the tax cut, raised at Vail, had been resolved.)

—Veto new federal spending programs, other than energy projects, and limit increases in government and military pensions and social-security benefits to 5 percent, to combat the still-persistent inflation.

"We know what must be done," Ford concluded. "The time to act is now. We have our nation to preserve and our future to protect."

I grabbed Rumsfeld's arm excitedly as the camera's red light blinked off.

"We did it! We did it!"

I felt Ford's fireside chat had accomplished what needed to be done, giving his tottering administration the boost it needed. It was a well-conceived program and a well-delivered speech. Ford conveyed a sense of assuredness, competence and leadership.

Eric Sevareid, on CBS, concurred: "Mr. Ford now has his second wind and his second chance. He is seizing a chance for the vigor and decisiveness he has not shown before. . . . He is in motion at last."

The upbeat mood in the White House over the fireside chat vanished by noon the next day, when Ford's aides realized that the president was scheduled to deliver his State of the Union speech to a joint session of Congress in exactly twenty-four hours, spelling out the details of his proposals, and no acceptable address had been written. Again, Hartmann's speechwriting operation had produced a draft that was long on hackneyed rhetoric and short on vision or clear statements of policy.

On occasion Hartmann showed a knack for creating memorable phrases ("Our long national nightmare is over"), but he was weak in complex areas of substance. One reason was that he boycotted the daily senior staff meetings, where such matters were discussed, as long as Rumsfeld presided.

Early in the afternoon the day after the fireside chat, Rumsfeld summoned me to his office. His usual cool manner had disappeared. He was clearly concerned about whether the president's State of the Union speech could be written in time.

For the next eight hours Rumsfeld, Cheney, Greenspan, Seidman, Zarb and I sat around the conference table in Rumsfeld's office feverishly writing, rewriting, scissoring, pasting, editing and boiling down a State of the Union speech to rival Hartmann's effort. We munched cookies, peanuts, and steak sandwiches, washed down with beer, as we worked, racing to complete our draft by 9 P.M., when Ford had said he would return to the Oval Office from dinner to make his final decisions on the speech text.

Ford came back to his office dressed casually in a blazer and gray pullover shirt. The Rumsfeld group and Hartmann pulled chairs up to the president's desk. Ford placed the competing speech texts in front of him, ours on his right, Hartmann's on his left, and began flipping through the pages, deciding which version he liked best. I could feel Hartmann radiating hostility toward Rumsfeld's rebels. The mood was tense.

Ford accepted the first four or five pages of the Hartmann draft and turned down ours. I ventured the suggestion that the president cut out the next portion of the Hartmann speech.

Denied.

Hartmann seemed to grow cocky. I thought, Uh-oh. We're going to be massacred.

But then Ford accepted our section on tax cuts and passed over Hartmann's. Next he took our section on budget cuts, and our section on energy. I was encouraged; the revolt against Hartmann's draft wasn't a total failure after all. When Ford reached the end of the two speeches, he chose Hartmann's longer, more cliché-ridden peroration over our shorter version. But we had won most of the major skirmishes.

Ford went back to the beginning of the patched-together speech to review it one last time. The meeting degenerated into haggling over individual words. It dragged on until 3:30 in the morning.

When Ford delivered the speech to Congress that afternoon, the most memorable feature was its blunt candor.

"I must say to you that the state of the Union is not good . . . I have got bad news and I don't expect much, if any, applause."

He didn't get much.

Obviously the long, bitter struggles required to produce a fireside chat and a State of the Union address were not the way to write presidential speeches. It was a wasteful and divisive process. It exposed a serious weakness in the Ford White House organization.

More distressingly, it exposed Ford's unwillingness to get tough with his staff, to demand a better speechwriting operation and less infighting.

A few weeks after the State of the Union speech, President Ford was confronted with new evidence that the economy was dropping fast. He had to decide whether additional rescue measures were needed. Unemployment shot up one full percentage point in January 1975, adding one million people to the jobless rolls in just thirty-one days and exceeding the worst prediction the economists had given the president. Ford convened an emergency meeting in the Oval Office to decide what, if anything, to do about the worsening situation.

Ford was told at the meeting that federal money was available for new highway, sewer and water projects, which would hire unemployed workers, or he could funnel more federal money to the states and cities to allow them to hire additional workers.

James Lynn, the new budget director, argued that Ford should not approve such steps until computer print-outs determined whether the money would actually create any jobs quickly or would merely be a symbolic gesture of the president's concern. Hartmann argued that if Ford announced additional steps to bolster the economy at that point, it might be viewed as a sign of panic and it certainly would be seen as an admission that his economic recovery program, announced to Congress only a few weeks before, was inadequate.

Hartmann's view prevailed and Ford decided to do nothing further at the moment to spur the recovery.

Still, I was worried because Ford's advisers did not seem to be able to give the president an accurate prediction of how bad the economy was going to get before turning around. At the end of the meeting I asked Greenspan whether he could forecast how high the unemployment rate was going to climb and, if not, how Ford could be sure he had done enough to prevent the economy from nose-diving into a calamity.

Greenspan talked and talked, but didn't answer the questions. So I asked him the same question again in different words. He talked and talked but didn't answer. When I asked him a third time and he still didn't answer, I dropped the matter.

Ford sat behind his desk, watching and listening to the exchange, without saying a word.

In the first months of 1975, Ford and the heavily Democratic Congress tilted over the president's economic and energy proposals. Members of Congress, fearful of antagonizing their constituents, shied away from raising petroleum prices, the foundation of Ford's fuel-conservation program. In the absence of legislation, the president used what authority he had to increase the price of imported oil until Congress stymied that approach.

Naturally, the most popular part of Ford's economic program— the tax cut—was approved quickly by Congress, in just eleven weeks. But the members increased the cut considerably, to $24.8 billion. With Congress racing to get out of town for its 1975 Easter recess, and Ford anxious to leave for his annual spring golfing holiday in Palm Springs, the president seriously considered vetoing the increased tax cut on grounds that it would raise the federal budget deficit to an irresponsibly high level and send interest rates soaring.

Some White House advisers, led by Hartmann, argued that a veto of a tax cut would be political suicide. A smaller group, led by Treasury Secretary William Simon, contended that Ford should veto the tax cut as dangerously excessive. The decision was complicated by concern over how it would look to veto a tax cut heavily weighted in favor of lower-income persons just before jetting off to play golf with millionaires in Palm Springs. Besides, the economy did need the stimulation of a tax cut.

There were strong arguments on both sides for signing or vetoing the tax cut. At the end of one meeting to discuss the pros and cons, Ford instructed his chief economic advisers to send him their individual recommendations.

Arthur Burns, the conservative Federal Reserve Board chairman, a fierce opponent of large government deficits, asked Ford in his rumbling voice, "How do you propose that we get a recommendation directly to you without anyone else seeing it?" Perhaps Burns was thinking of the trouble he had seeing and sending memos to Nixon through Haldeman. I wondered whether Burns was having the same trouble with Rumsfeld.

Ford directed Burns and the other economic advisers to seal their tax-cut recommendations in envelopes and give them directly to his secretary without going through Rumsfeld. Burns seemed to be reassured.

By late afternoon of Good Friday, 1975, Ford had made up his mind to sign the tax-cut bill, despite misgivings about its size. Staff members strongly recommended that the president delay his departure for the Palm Springs vacation, scheduled for the next morning, Saturday, so he could explain his decision on nationwide television from the Oval Office in prime time on Easter Eve.

Tired and irritable after a period of long days and intense pressure, Ford didn't want to delay his vacation. Instead he proposed taping his explanation speech and leaving it behind for broadcast Saturday night. He was told that would be a public-relations disaster.

"Then we'll do the speech tonight," Ford snapped. "We'll do it at seven-thirty tonight."

It was then 5:30. I doubted that a speech could be written and the technical arrangements made in two hours. After more arguing, Ford gave in and agreed to make the speech Saturday night, delaying his golfing trip. Forty-five minutes after going off the air, the president took off from Andrews Air Force Base for Palm Springs.

Statistics on the economy continued to grow worse even after the president signed the tax cut. Unemployment increased month after month, reaching 8.9 percent of the work force in May 1975, the peak.

Ford instructed me on several occasions during the recession not to feed reporters unduly optimistic assessments of the economy, as previous administrations had done in similar circumstances. If anything, the president directed, I should err on the side of pessimism. Ford's reasoning was that when the economy eventually did begin to improve, the statistics would have more credibility with the press if the White House had been honest about the bad news.

The bad news kept coming. In October 1975 Ford concluded that a further tax cut of $28 billion was needed to stimulate economic recovery. In order to avoid the inflationary effects of the increased federal deficit resulting from such a large tax cut, the president proposed that Congress reduce government spending by a matching $28 billion. The unique coupling of a tax cut and budget cut brought charges from the Democratic Congress that Ford was grandstanding, that he only wanted to get credit with the voters for trying to hold down government spending, when he had no real anticipation that Congress would go along with the cut.

At my daily briefings I used increasingly tough language to criticize Congress for not approving the president's proposed spending cuts. Max Friedersdorf, Ford's congressional liaison officer, told me my performance amounted to kicking House and Senate Democrats in the ass. I had just about abandoned my initial vow not to be a partisan salesman for Ford's programs.

As the Christmas, 1975, recess approached, Congress was on the verge of approving Ford's $28-billion tax cut without his proposed reduction in spending. The president searched for some way to impress the members of Congress with his determination to force them to pass the budget cut. Drawing on his years of experience on Capitol Hill—and on his sly sense of humor—Ford instructed Friedersdorf to ask the parliamentarian of the House about the procedure for calling Congress back from its Christmas recess to a special session on the budget.

"Tell the parliamentarian the president wants him to keep your inquiry to himself," Ford grinned to Friedersdorf. "That will get the message around Congress faster than Western Union."

But the threat of losing its Christmas vacation did not frighten Congress. It approved the tax cut and ignored the spending cut. Ford vetoed the tax-cut bill. Congress then repassed it with a vaguely worded addition promising to try to hold down spending. Figuring that was the best he could get, the president gave up the fight and signed the tax cut in that form.

Ford hailed it as a "hundred-percent" victory. It was not a victory at all, except perhaps for some public-relations benefit with voters who appreciated the president's efforts to limit government spending.

By the end of 1975 the economy was on the upswing. Unemployment dropped; employment increased to record levels; the gross national product shot up; the housing, automobile and other industries began to recover. The inflation rate, over 12 percent when Ford became president, was down by half.

But the recovery was slow, and in the months just before the 1976 presidential election unemployment took an unexpected uptick. Ford's economists reported that the recovery had hit a "pause." It hurt Ford in the 1976 election.

In general, however, Ford should get good marks for his handling of the economic and energy problems. His energy proposal was one of the outstanding—and underrated—accomplishments of his presidency. He was not successful in selling Congress or the American people on the need to accept the discomfort and higher costs required to reduce dependence on expensive foreign oil; most of his energy plan died. But at least he began the public discussion of the hard choices which eventually will have to be faced.

The sharp rise in the cost of imported oil, and the economic policies of earlier presidents, were responsible for the recession during Ford's term, the deepest since the Great Depression of the 1930s. He stuck to his conservative philosophy in combating the recession. He opposed heavy-handed government interference in the economy, resisted excessively expensive emergency federal jobs programs, fought to keep the budget deficit down and continued to regard inflation as a major threat.

As a result of his conservative approach, the nation pulled out of the recession only gradually, but without igniting a new spurt of inflation that would have led to greater economic problems in the future.

When I came to the White House I had moderately liberal views on the government's role in stimulating the economy and helping the less fortunate members of society. Listening to Ford and his economic advisers discuss their conservative philosophy during long Cabinet Room meetings on the recession, at first I thought to myself, What am I doing here? I had that reaction, for instance, during one meeting when Arthur Burns grumbled that extending unemployment benefits beyond a certain minimum period would only encourage the jobless to be choosy in accepting new jobs, instead of grabbing the first ones that came along.

But the more I listened to the conservative arguments at the economic meetings, the more I found my own views becoming more conservative. Once a supporter of heavy government spending to cure every ill of society, I soon became a convert to Ford's view that the cost of these proliferating programs—in taxes and inflation—had become too high for the public to bear.

CHAPTER NINE

The Yellow Sickness

=====================

From my first day in the White House I had a fantasy that at some point I would stand up in front of a news briefing and announce the end of the Vietnam War. My fantasy began to come true early in January 1975 when the North Vietnamese launched what was to be their final offensive. That offensive scored its first big success on January 7, 1975, with the capture of Phuoc Long Province and its capital city, Phuoc Binh, only thirty-five miles from Saigon.

That morning, after the senior staff meeting, I told Brent Scowcroft I wanted to talk to him about what I should say to reporters, since so many previous spokesmen had gotten into trouble over Vietnam. Rumsfeld, who was standing nearby, said sarcastically, "Yeah, that's the important thing around here, to protect the press secretary."

I admit it, my initial concern was selfish. I worried about my credibility. But given the number of times government information officers had been caught misleading reporters about the war, my reaction was understandable. I felt even more justified when Les Janka, who was then the NSC's liaison to the Press Office, handed me his formula for handling newsmen's questions about the offensive and any possible U.S. involvement. Janka gave me two artfully worded, bland answers and the advice to duck all other inquiries.

"Look, Les," I said, more strongly than I intended, "too many press secretaries have gone down the tubes on the Vietnam issue by being misled and misleading reporters. If the day ever comes when I'm misled or lied to, then either I leave or the guy who lied to me leaves."

At a tense meeting in my office I took him through a long list of anticipated press questions, dragging the answers from him. "Are you sure that's absolutely right?" I demanded after each answer he gave me.

Following my news briefing that day, Janka complained, "You really blew one."

He didn't like my answers in this exchange:

Q.: Is there any possibility that the president would send troops back into Vietnam?
NESSEN: He is forbidden by law to do that. . . .
Q.: Does the president interpret the law as forbidding any air action by the United States over South Vietnam?
NESSEN: In what sense?
Q.: Bombing?
NESSEN: Oh, yes.

Janka felt I had closed the door too firmly on possible future American intervention in Vietnam. He said the NSC wanted to scare the North Vietnamese a little, or at least leave them guessing about American intentions. I replied that I didn't think Hanoi devised its strategy according to my answers.

"Oh, yes. The North Vietnamese know what you say at your briefings," Janka asserted. He said North Vietnamese Foreign Minister Le Duc Tho had once quoted a Ziegler press statement to Kissinger. Nevertheless, I promised myself I would resist NSC efforts to use my press briefings to frighten North Vietnam, because such threats also could needlessly alarm the American people.

Janka persisted in trying to convince me that my answers could influence Hanoi. He showed me a classified intelligence report quoting sources who had been in touch with the North Vietnamese and Viet Cong missions in Paris. The sources claimed Moscow was urging the Vietnamese Communists to be cautious in their attacks because the Russians were not sure whether the United States would resume its bombing raids. If the Russians became convinced that there was no chance of new American intervention, they would encourage Hanoi to go all out for a quick victory, the intelligence report said.

Whatever message the North Vietnamese received from my briefings, their offensive continued to roll. Throughout February and March 1975, South Vietnam's troops fell back on all fronts, abandoning cities and bases, sometimes without a fight. In Cambodia, the Khmer Rouge Communists also were on the attack, encircling and closing in on Phnom Penh, the capital.

As the situation worsened, Ford requested from Congress $300 million in emergency aid for South Vietnam and $222 million for Cambodia. Congress balked. Most members—most Americans—wanted the war to go away.

At the end of March 1975, Ford sent Army Chief of Staff General Frederick C. Weyand to Saigon "to express the support of the United States for the government and people of South Vietnam, to assess the military situation and to inform the president about what assistance South Vietnam needs from the United States at this critical time."

I knew that if the assistance to South Vietnam included a resumption of American bombing or other U.S. military intervention, my conscience would not allow me to defend that action and I would have to resign. I had seen too much of the war firsthand to continue as Ford's spokesman if his Indochina policy clashed with my beliefs. On other issues I could announce and explain his decisions without necessarily agreeing with him, but I was too emotionally involved in the war.

For the past decade, my thirties, one-quarter of my existence, virtually every major event in my life involved Vietnam. I made my reputation as a journalist covering the war. I was there for the arrival of the American combat troops, for the Tet offensive, for the so-called peace accords. I met my wife there. I grew into a man there. I almost died there.

As NBC's White House correspondent in 1964 and 1965, I reported on Lyndon Johnson's first retaliatory air strikes against North Vietnam, the beginning of full-scale bombing raids on the North, the dispatch of the first two American marine battalions to Danang. Johnson sometimes amused guests by doing a malicious imitation of me standing in front of a TV camera solemnly describing the latest Vietnam crisis.

The last story I covered at the Johnson White House was the president's July 1965 news conference at which he announced that he was ordering 50,000 American ground combat troops to the war. And then NBC sent me to Vietnam for what was supposed to be a two-and-a-half-month stint as a substitute for various vacationing correspondents. I stayed eleven months, until I was wounded, and went back for four other reporting stints, finally being expelled after the 1973 American troop withdrawal for asking a question of

President Nguyen Van Thieu which was considered impertinent.

Even now, rarely a day goes by that I don't recall some vivid image from Vietnam:

—Sitting on the bodies of two dead marines on a helicopter flight out of Hue during Tet because there was no other place to sit . . .

—Asking someone about two piles of charcoal beside a road and being told they were two children burned to death in the fighting . . .

—Watching a Vietnamese soldier clown with the body of a dead Viet Cong and having the brains plop out at my feet . . .

—Bleeding in the grass beside a stream in the Central Highlands, a grenade fragment in my lung, telling a soldier I didn't want to die . . .

—Climbing a mountain with the elite 101st Airborne at three o'clock in the morning and wondering what my mother would think. She had been overprotective, not even letting me join the Boy Scouts . . .

—Being swarmed over at a Saigon orphanage by dozens of children starved for the touch of a caring adult and unable to stop my tears for those poor doomed babies . . .

—Discovering I was not a coward in the face of danger—but also discovering one day when I could not force myself to board a convoy into a battle area that sometimes fear wins . . .

—Thinking I had descended into hell during my last trip to Saigon, on the terrace of the Continental Palace Hotel, once a sedate oasis for French colonials and American newsmen, now populated by heroine-addicted whores; midget whores; deaf-mute whores; twelve-year-old whores; transvestites; drowsy drugheads; crippled beggars; thieves snatching briefcases and racing away on waiting motorcycles; left-behind Americans and Frenchmen with strange eyes. . . .

And, as I've already mentioned, Vietnam had an even more personal impact on my life. A month after arriving in Saigon I met a Korean girl named Cindy, a singer, in the Caravelle Hotel bar, where she was having a drink with a mutual friend, an NBC cameraman. We were attracted to each other, but I was leaving the next morning to cover the fighting farther north and she was leaving soon to continue her singing tour in Bangkok and Europe. Fortunately we talked by phone just before I boarded my plane for the battle area. She decided to cancel her tour and wait for me to return.

We lived together happily for the next ten months in a suite on the top floor of the Caravelle Hotel, a cool and homey refuge from what was going on outside, complete with a fluffy white dog purchased at the sidewalk animal market on Christmas morning.

Then, in July of 1966, I was wounded. I'll never forget the sight of Cindy's stricken face outside the rear windows of the army ambulance carrying me to a medical evacuation flight to the United States. It took her two months before she could cut through the immigration red tape and come to New York City, where we were married.

Now, in March 1975, as the end of the war drew near, I was swept by conflicting emotions. Like many Americans, my attitude toward the war had progressed through stages of support, then doubt, to the point where I felt strongly that America's involvement had been wrong and destructive beyond belief. And yet, there is something seductive about Vietnam and its people which made it painful for me to see them going under. What was going to happen to the people? That was the thought that would not go away.

I was haunted by a news film I saw on TV in those last weeks of the war showing an Indochinese mother holding out her paralyzed baby to the cameraman, begging him to do something for the child, whose arms and legs flopped uncontrollably. I could not get the picture out of my mind. That baby symbolized all the helpless Vietnamese who were about to be swallowed up by defeat.

On my first trip to Saigon, a decade before, the late Bernard Fall, the French writer and expert on Indochina, told me I'd come down with the *mal jaune*, the "yellow sickness," an incurable affection for Asia and Asians.

My case became virulent in the last days of the war.

By the end of March 1975 the deteriorating situation in South Vietnam was brought home graphically to Americans by television films showing panicky soldiers and civilians clawing their way onto evacuation planes out of Danang as the Communists closed in.

Ford was scheduled to leave in a few days for his annual Easter golfing vacation in Palm Springs. Several people on the staff, including me, urged him not to go while Vietnam was collapsing. How would it look if he was on the golf course when Danang fell? I had a mental picture of Ford on the eighteenth green, dressed in golf clothes with a putter in his hand, surrounded by reporters and cameramen clamoring to know what he thought of the terrible massacre in Danang.

But Ford was worn out and testy from a hectic period of domestic and foreign crises. He insisted on going to Palm Springs. One friend and admirer in the press said, sadly, he'd never seen Ford act more like an imperial president.

Aboard *Air Force One* flying to Palm Springs, the president came back to the staff compartment to chat with Rumsfeld, Alan Greenspan and me. While we were talking, a flight attendant handed me a brown envelope from the radio operator. Inside was a Teletype message, "Danang has fallen," and some sketchy details. I passed it around to Ford and the others. They read it in silence. Ford shook his head slowly. No one said anything for a long time.

Night after night while we were in Palm Springs, the news from Vietnam grew worse. The army was disintegrating, soldiers dropping their weapons and fleeing by the thousands and tens of thousands, sometimes beating women and children out of the way to scramble aboard evacuation planes and evacuation ships.

Pictures of these horrors were shown nightly on TV—along with pictures of President Ford playing golf. I was under tremendous pressure at my news briefings to explain the president's seeming insensitivity. I dreaded stepping up to the podium, knowing what the subject of the questions would be:

Q.: I mean, is he not a bit worried about what the look of his playing golf, in view of this crisis, would have on his administration?

NESSEN: . . . I don't know that his personal activities would have any effect on the military situation in Vietnam. . . . Would it prevent anything from happening in Vietnam if he did not play golf?

Q.: That still begs the question. The question is, is the president concerned about how the public views him in a place like Palm Springs when Danang and other places are being pictured in complete chaos?

NESSEN: He is spending time every day on the problem and other problems.

Q.: How much time is accorded to Vietnam?

NESSEN: He spent from about 7:00 A.M. until he left for the golf course on business. As soon as he returns he has a full afternoon of business, all afternoon.

The president himself was bombarded with similar questions by reporters at the Bakersfield airport when he left Palm Springs for a day to inspect the Elk Hills oil reserve. Ford, normally a most accessible public figure, ran from the newsmen. The picture of him sprinting ahead of a pack of pursuing reporters was on TV and front pages all over the country. At my next briefing I braced for the inevitable derisive questions about Ford's odd behavior:

Q.: Ron, can you tell us, then, exactly why the president ran at Bakersfield airport?

NESSEN: I am sorry. I did not see what has been described as running.

Q.: He ran almost as fast as the South Vietnamese Army. [laughter]

In addition to trying to explain the unexplainable and being torn by emotion as I watched the destruction of a people and a country with which my life had been intertwined for so long, I had to deal with the fact that my wife had left me that week. I didn't know when or whether she would return.

The demands of my White House job had frayed our relationship. Harried, rarely home, I no longer had the time or inclination to share my problems with her or listen to hers. She left when I vented on her the anger and helplessness that had built up in me as a result of the Vietnam tragedy. I had always thought of my relationship with Cindy as a metaphor for America's relationship with Indochina: I felt fascination beyond explaining; I displayed a paternalistic attitude which created in her a sense of being condescended to. She had a maddening custom of speaking and acting by indirection. We made repeated efforts to understand more about each other, but ultimately came to the realization that because of our different cultures we never would understand each other fully. All those characteristics of my life with Cindy mirrored America's attitude toward Indochina. How fitting, I thought, that just when America was ending its relationship with Vietnam, I seemed to be ending my relationship with Cindy.*

By the time Thomas DeFrank of *Newsweek* came to talk to me in my office in Palm Springs to gather material for an article on the end of the war, I was an emotional wreck. He asked me about my personal memories of Vietnam. I started talking about my Vietnamese friends caught in the collapse, especially the brave camera-

---

* Cindy later returned. Our relationship survived the White House, barely.

men with whom I had worked closely, shared foxholes and
C-rations, shared fear and narrow escapes. I was worried about
what would happen to them.

"There is nothing you can do, is there?" DeFrank asked sym-
pathetically.

I got out the word "No" before I broke into tears. I put my head
down on the desk and wept. The tears released some of the pressures.

But there was no relief from the pressure on the South Vietnamese, or on Ford to mount a last-ditch effort to save them. General
Weyand flew from Vietnam to Palm Springs during Ford's vacation to report his findings to the president. Kissinger came from
Washington to attend the meeting.

Weyand's report was pessimistic about the outlook for South
Vietnam's survival. He recommended that Ford request from Congress another $722 million in aid as quickly as possible. Weyand
also recommended that Ford use American air power to help Saigon
avoid defeat. The general added, "I realize the political and legal
questions involved in this."

We kept that recommendation a secret and never carried it out.

After the meeting, Kissinger drove to the press center to give a
briefing. "Why don't these people die fast?" he moaned in the car.
"The worst thing that could happen would be for them to lin-
ger on."

Although clearly distraught, Kissinger was eloquent in arguing at
his briefing for serious consideration of more American aid to Vietnam:

> Regardless of the probable outcome of the war, I think it is a
> serious question . . . and I really believe that at this moment,
> having paid so much in our national unity on this issue, we
> should conduct this debate, not with an attitude of who is
> going to pin the blame on whom, but with an attitude that we
> are facing a great tragedy in which there is involved something
> of American credibility, something of American honor, some-
> thing of how we are perceived by other people in the world,
> on which serious people may have different questions but in
> which, for God's sake, we ought to stop talking as if one side
> had the monopoly of wisdom, morality and insight.

David Kennerly, Ford's semihippie photographer, who had won
a Pulitzer Prize for his sensitive coverage of the war as a camera-

man for UPI, had accompanied Weyand to Vietnam and gave the press in Palm Springs his own assessment of the situation: "It is really shitty and you can quote me."

That night, after a second meeting with Kissinger and Weyand, the president flew to the San Francisco International Airport in a rainstorm to welcome a chartered jet bringing 325 South Vietnamese children to safety. Some of the children were ill, many were exhausted and terrified. Ford joined other volunteers carrying the children off the fetid aircraft to ambulances and buses. Some reporters considered the president's participation to be a staged White House media event to associate the president with the humanitarian babylift. But Ford would have been content with no press coverage. He went because he was genuinely moved by the plight of the children caught in South Vietnam's fall. Feeling helpless, like everyone else, the president wanted to do something for the innocents.*

Even in the midst of the collapse of Vietnam, we were still plagued by more mundane problems—like the Frank Sinatra affair.

The night before returning to Washington from Palm Springs, Ford invited the reporters covering him and their wives to a reception around the pool of the house he was renting. When I arrived at the house, I found Hartmann just inside the front door, in a state of agitation. He pulled me into a guest bedroom and explained the problem. It seemed Kissinger had invited the president and Mrs. Ford to his house that night to have dinner with Frank Sinatra.

"We just can't let the president go out there for dinner," Hartmann exclaimed. "Sinatra is Agnew's friend and he was Kennedy's friend."

"Why don't you call Kissinger?" I asked.

"He'll never listen to me," Hartmann replied. "Why don't you call him?"

I agreed that it would damage Ford's image further to have dinner with Sinatra at the end of a week in which the president had been criticized daily for lazing in the millionaires' playground while Vietnam burned.

I phoned Kissinger and told him it would put the president and Mrs. Ford in an embarrassing situation to have dinner with Sinatra, who had been so publicly identified as Agnew's friend and who had a questionable reputation.

---

* Joseph Laitin, the Pentagon spokesman, told me later of reports that some genuine orphans were forced to give up their seats on the evacuation planes and their identifying armbands to the children of Vietnamese government officials and military officers.

"How am I going to get out of it?" Kissinger asked. "It's all arranged."

"Look," I told him, "it's better to hurt Sinatra's feelings than to embarrass the president."

Kissinger agreed to disinvite Sinatra. I suggested he tell Sinatra he had to discuss business with the president at dinner.

As soon as I hung up, Hartmann kissed me on the forehead. But he predicted the matter was not over. "I'll bet Kissinger calls the president within five minutes."

In ten minutes, with guests for the press reception milling around, the phone in the living room rang. I answered. It was Kissinger for Ford.

I hovered close by and when the president hung up I asked, "Well, are you going?"

"I'm going," he replied. "I made the decision and I'm going."

"You are the president," I said, "and you can do whatever you want."

"I know you don't approve, but Sinatra has done nothing illegal or immoral," Ford said. "It probably won't play very well in the press, but I feel I have a right to have dinner with whomever I want to."

Win some, lose some, I thought.

At that point, Kissinger gave an illuminating insight into his character and methods. Having demonstrated his power by winning Ford over to his view in a clash with rivals on the staff, with his clout reaffirmed and his ego boosted, Kissinger then did what was best for the president and told Sinatra not to come to dinner.

Ford had postponed any decisions on Vietnam until he returned to Washington. He arranged to announce his recommendations in a foreign-policy speech to Congress four days after getting back to the capital. Four days was not a long time to prepare such a major pronouncement and Rumsfeld complained that he was unable to persuade the president to spend much time on the Vietnam speech in Palm Springs because of the enticements of golf and parties.

"Maybe I'm just going to stop trying to get him to be the kind of president I think he should be," grumbled Rumsfeld, "and let him be the kind of president he wants to be."

But once back at the White House, Ford knuckled down to write the speech. He sought opinions from a wider range of advisers than just Kissinger and the usual foreign-policy, military and intelligence aides. I was probably the strongest advocate of sending no more aid and certainly no direct American military intervention, in order to bring the war to a close and stop the killing. I felt conquest by the Communist forces was inevitable and saw no sense in prolonging the agony.

I had voiced that opinion in Palm Springs, and on the flight home to Washington Kissinger told me I took that view because, as he said, "you are a newsman."

I looked puzzled.

"What I mean is, you are saying that because it is the popular thing in the public and Congress," Kissinger elaborated. "But they are wrong, and within two years they will be proven wrong."

Back in the White House, as Ford's speech was prepared, I was concerned that Kissinger, with so much of his personal diplomacy invested in trying to save South Vietnam, would convince Ford to try one more increase in aid or even a new military involvement as a last desperate effort to avoid defeat for the old policy. But, in my view, if Ford requested more aid for Vietnam, Congress would almost certainly turn him down, thus getting credit for ending the war over the president's seeming determination to continue it.

I felt so strongly about the need for Ford to announce steps to end the fighting that I wrote and submitted a draft for the president's speech:

> I have decided it is time to put the divisions and the horrors of this war behind us and to lead this nation and the world in a new direction. God willing, it will bring peace at last and stop the agony in the tortured lands of Indochina. . . .
>
> None of my advisers was able to assure me that . . . additional money would enable South Vietnam to stabilize the military situation and continue the fight.
>
> When the outcome is so doubtful, I cannot in good conscience ask the American people to bear a further burden after they have given so much. We have done our best for many, many years. To continue along this same course would merely prolong the agony of the Vietnamese people who already have suffered far too much. Given the realities of the situation, it would be wrong for America to contribute further to the killing.

We must now devote all our efforts to the healing, both in Vietnam and here at home. . . .

I believe that these decisions I have made represent the will of the majority of the American people and their representatives in the Congress, and, after all, we are a democracy, where government must reflect the will of the majority.

I realize now that my proposal was naïve and probably not the best way to achieve the peace I desired for the Vietnamese people or the safe rescue of the Americans left in Vietnam. Rumsfeld told me it read like I had "vomited out" all the emotion I felt about the war.

Ford, of course, did not accept my view. In fact, in his speech to Congress he scathingly rejected the idea that the United States should "shut our eyes and wash our hands of the whole affair," leaving South Vietnam to save itself "if it can" and abandoning thousands of Vietnamese who had worked with America to save themselves "if they can." He blamed the deteriorating situation on North Vietnam for violating the peace accords, on Congress for reducing and threatening to end American aid, and on the Saigon government for hastily ordering and poorly executing the strategic retreat which had led to panic and rout. "The options before us are few and the time is very short," Ford intoned grimly.

He made the following recommendations:

—Another $722 million in military aid to South Vietnam, as General Weyand had proposed.

—Modification of the restrictions on U.S. military involvement in order to evacuate the remaining Americans and those Vietnamese "whose lives may be endangered should the worst come to pass."

—"A maximum humanitarian effort" to help the refugees.

Anticipating resistance from a Congress and public weary of the war, Ford justified his request for more aid on grounds that it could help South Vietnam "stabilize" the military situation and perhaps persuade the communists to negotiate a settlement. The president also said other friendly nations "must not think for a minute that the United States is pulling out on them or intends to abandon them to aggression." He told Congress he wanted them to approve his plan in nine days.

Congress was not receptive to the speech. One member booed

loudly. Another hissed. And about half the members had stayed away to demonstrate their opposition to Ford's request.

In background briefings on the speech, Kissinger and other officials confided to reporters that the $722-million request was partly a symbolic gesture of support to prevent morale from collapsing in Saigon.

Vietnam was not the only Indochina ally on the verge of collapse. The night after his speech to Congress, Ford ordered the evacuation of the Americans left in Phnom Penh. U.S. Ambassador John Gunther Dean had notified him that time had run out for Cambodia.

The president followed the evacuation from his residence, fed information by phone from Scowcroft. It took only two hours for helicopters from American carriers offshore to remove 82 Americans, 159 Cambodians and several dozen others of various nationalities. About 350 additional Cambodians had been expected to leave on the American helicopters, including all the government leaders. But most of the Cambodian government unexpectedly decided to stay and carry on the fight, even though the Khmer Rouge Communists were on the outskirts of Phnom Penh and the evacuation meant the United States considered the war lost.

"The Cambodians won't go," Scowcroft informed me.

"In other words," I said, "the Cambodians are telling us, 'Okay, you chickenshits, go ahead and bug out, but we're going to stay and fight.' "

Scowcroft shuddered at my crude but accurate paraphrase of the situation. Normally frail, and exhausted from eighteen- and twenty-hour days, he looked at that moment like he might crumble. Scowcroft was deeply anguished because the long American effort in Indochina was ending in failure.

But the American involvement in Cambodia wasn't quite over. The morning after the evacuation, Scowcroft came running into my office.

"We are going to ask for aid to Cambodia after all because the government has stayed," he exclaimed. "Go right in and see the president."

I found Ford in his private study with Kissinger. They already had a press statement prepared, calling on Congress to approve more aid to Cambodia quickly. I suspected the request was made mostly so that the president could not be criticized later for prematurely abandoning an ally that was still fighting for its existence. Hundreds of tons of supplies were dropped by parachute to the hold-outs over the next few days before they finally surrendered to the Khmer Rouge.

With American aid to Cambodia ended, the White House press corps quickly found a new target for criticism. At a news briefing, I had this exchange with James Deakin of the *St. Louis Post-Dispatch*, who felt Ford had violated congressional restrictions on the use of U.S. military forces in Indochina by allowing Cambodians and other foreigners to escape from Phnom Penh on the American evacuation helicopters:

Q.: . . . What was the authority?
NESSEN: He sent the military forces there to save the lives of Americans.
Q.: Then is it your position that having done that, the military people on the scene then exceeded their authority by taking out about two hundred foreign nationals?
NESSEN: I don't think so.
Q.: Somebody did it, somebody authorized it, somebody permitted it. Who?
NESSEN: The president.
Q.: He doesn't believe he was in violation, although small, of these various congressional enactments?
NESSEN: No, because he was doing it under what he believes to be his inherent power to save the lives of Americans.
Q: What is the inherent power . . . to save the lives of nationals of other countries?

Finally, another reporter cut in and injected a note of charity:

Q.: Is the president at all ashamed of taking the opportunity to show a little mercy to a few non-Americans?
NESSEN: No.

I found the exchange disgusting, since networks, wire services and newspapers had been phoning daily, pleading with me to use my influence to make sure their Cambodian and Vietnamese employees were evacuated, regardless of any congressional restrictions.

With Cambodia gone, we knew it was only a matter of time before the scenario was repeated in Vietnam. As the moment approached to evacuate Americans and Vietnamese from Saigon, many members of Congress were troubled by the possibility that American military forces protecting the evacuation might become involved in a new and prolonged conflict with Communist troops. The Senate Foreign Relations Committee requested a meeting with the president to express its concern.

Kissinger began the session in the Cabinet Room by revealing that the United States considered more than a million Vietnamese, who had ties with America, to be in danger at the hands of the Communists after the war. Of these, 174,000 were in "overwhelming jeopardy" and should be evacuated if possible, he declared.

Senator Frank Church protested, "The evacuation of 174,000 South Vietnamese could involve a very large number of Americans in a very long war."

Ford assured Church and the other senators, "We do not envision a protracted U.S. military operation." But the president warned, "If you are going to say you are not going to get the South Vietnamese out, you are going to have a hard time getting the six thousand Americans out."

Kissinger, looking weary and depressed, added that a Saigon official had informed him, "If you pull out the Americans and leave us in the lurch, you may have to fight your way out through a South Vietnamese division."

The safety of the remaining Americans was a major concern of the committee. Senator Clifford Case, the respected senior Republican, said the consensus of the members was that the number of Americans left in Saigon should be reduced to the point that they could be evacuated on one flight when the end came.

"We don't want the Americans held hostage," Senator Charles Percy elaborated.

Ford responded that the number of Americans in Saigon was being reduced, steadily but quietly, to about 1500. To remove most of the Americans all at once would seem to the South Vietnamese to be "pulling the plug," the president cautioned, possibly setting off panic and attacks on the remaining Americans. "The quickest way to put them in jeopardy is not to vote the assistance money," Ford warned. "I can't guarantee that if we say 'no more money' Thieu . . . won't do something totally irrational."

The senators grasped the dilemma: Much as they opposed more aid to South Vietnam, it might be necessary to assure the safety of the remaining Americans. "I don't want to vote any more money for a government headed by Thieu," Senator Jacob Javits declared. "But I'll pay any ransom to get our people out."

Senator Joseph Biden was more blunt in expressing his view of the problem: "I'm not willing to pay any money to get Vietnamese out unless we can't get any Americans without buying 174,000 Vietnamese. In that case, I'm willing to buy the 174,000 Vietnamese."

Even with more aid money, and some good luck, Kissinger conceded that the outlook was not encouraging for the endangered Vietnamese. "I personally don't believe we'll get out anything like the 174,000," he acknowledged glumly. "We have an obligation to get out as many as we can, if we can get any out."

At the end of the meeting, Ford warned the senators that if reporters learned that the entire session had been devoted to discussing evacuation, it might encourage North Vietnamese attacks and destroy South Vietnamese morale. "Say we talked about how we might stabilize the situation," the president instructed.

After the meeting, Kissinger stuck his head into my office and, in disgust at the senators' cut-and-run mood, exclaimed, "Have you ever heard such bullshit in your life?"

In the last days of Saigon, the ghost of Nixon rose once again. Senator Henry Jackson charged that in 1972 and 1973, Nixon had given Thieu secret assurances of American military support in case North Vietnam violated the peace accords.

After lengthy consultations involving Ford, Kissinger, Scowcroft, Rumsfeld and me, I was authorized to acknowledge that Nixon and Thieu had exchanged private letters, but to say, "The public statements made at the time reflected the substance of those private communications."

Similarly, in a letter rejecting a request from the Senate Foreign Relations Committee to see the Nixon letters, Ford wrote, "I have reviewed the record of the private diplomatic communications. . . . Since the same policy and intentions contained in these exchanges were declared publicly, there was no secret from the Congress or the American people."

In fact, Nixon's private assurances to Thieu seemed to go beyond public statements of support at the time.

Seven private Nixon letters to Thieu were found in the NSC files. In an effort to cajole the reluctant Thieu into signing the Paris peace accords, which would allow the withdrawal of all American troops, Nixon promised continued American assistance. For instance, in an October 16, 1972, letter hand-delivered by Kissinger, Nixon told Thieu, "I can assure you that we will view any breach of faith on their [North Vietnam's] part with the utmost gravity; and it would have the most serious consequences." A month later Nixon was more explicit: "You have my absolute assurance that if Hanoi fails to abide by the terms of this agreement, it is my intention to take swift and severe retaliatory action." And on January 5, 1973, Nixon wrote, "You have my assurance of continued assistance in the post-settlement period and that we will respond with full force should the settlement be violated by North Vietnam."

But in 1975, with the war nearly lost and congressional limitations blocking American military involvement, the question of carrying out these secret Nixon promises to Thieu was moot. Why then did the Ford White House fudge on the truth and play word games to avoid revealing the now-irrelevant contents of Nixon's letters?

Mostly, to protect the principle of confidentiality, the necessary ability of a president to communicate privately with foreign leaders. But also because the letters could be used as ammunition in any postwar recriminations over who was responsible for losing the war. Thieu and American hawks might claim that Ford failed to carry out Nixon's commitments. Doves in Congress might claim they blocked further aid because Ford never informed them of the secret promises.

Ford wrote his own secret letters to Thieu in the final weeks of the war, but their assurances were sharply limited by a clear recognition of congressional restrictions and public opposition. The president told Thieu on February 24, 1975, "We strongly support your efforts to resume negotiations and will make every effort to provide the assistance that is so necessary to your struggle until peace comes." And on March 22, Ford wrote in another letter, "I, for my part, am determined to stand firmly behind the Republic of Vietnam at this crucial hour. With a view to honoring the responsibilities of the United States in this situation, I . . . am consulting on an urgent basis with my advisers on actions which the situation may require and the law permit." The president gave Thieu similar assurances in a letter on March 25, 1975.

Twenty-nine days later, Ford boarded *Air Force One* for a flight to New Orleans to make a long-scheduled speech at Tulane University. The president himself had outlined what he wanted to say about Vietnam at Tulane and instructed Hartmann and a sensitive speechwriter named Milton Friedman to draft it. Kissinger was not consulted.

The final lines were typed on the plane flying to New Orleans, including a key sentence declaring that the Vietnam War "is finished as far as America is concerned."

I was excited when I read through the speech text, given to me several hours in advance of delivery for distribution to the reporters. The speech was so different from Ford's Vietnam address to Congress just two weeks before in which he requested more American aid to stave off a Communist victory. Now, in the Tulane speech, Ford had decided to acknowledge that Vietnam was lost and America could do no more to save it.

Riding down an elevator with Ford on his way to deliver the speech, I worried whether he would deliver his dramatic message well. He had been through a tiring day and had just come from a reception, where he had sipped a cocktail. I suggested discreetly that he read the speech slowly and with care.

"Mr. President," Kennerly cut in, "what he's trying to tell you is, 'Don't screw it up.' "

Ford exploded into one of his great high-pitched horse laughs. He did not screw up the speech.

"America can regain the sense of pride that existed before Vietnam," Ford declared to the thousands of students jamming the university field house. "But it cannot be achieved by refighting a war that is finished as far as America is concerned."

The students cheered and applauded loud and long.

The president did not say a single word about further assistance to South Vietnam, nor did he repeat earlier charges about North Vietnam's violations of the peace accords. He spoke only about the future, after the now-inevitable defeat of Saigon.

"As I see it, the time has come to look forward to an agenda for the future," Ford intoned to the receptive audience. "I ask that we stop refighting the battles and the recriminations of the past . . . I ask that we accept the responsibility of leadership as a good neighbor to all peoples and an enemy of none."

The speech was a milestone in contemporary American history. Ford did something no American president had been able to do for thirty years: He spoke of the Indochina war in the past tense.

When the speech was over, the Tulane field house exploded with the deafening sound of approval. I and others on Ford's staff shared the students' enthusiasm.

On the flight back to Washington on *Air Force One* late that night, one senior Ford aide raised his drink in a toast: "Fuck the war."

Five days later, Scowcroft slipped into an energy-economic meeting in the Cabinet Room and passed Ford a note saying the North Vietnamese were rocketing the airport in Saigon. Two American marines had been killed. The end was at hand. Ford whispered instructions to Scowcroft to assemble the National Security Council at 7 P.M.

At the NSC meeting, Ford decided against an immediate, final helicopter evacuation. American C-130 transport planes had been shuttling out Americans and "high risk" Vietnamese for days and the president ordered the airlift continued for at least one more day, if possible.

While he waited to find out if the C-130s could still land at Saigon's Tan Son Nhut airfield, Ford retired to his residence for a corned beef and cabbage dinner with Mrs. Ford. The other staff members involved drifted restlessly from office to office, awaiting the report from Saigon. Communications circuits were hooked up directly from Kissinger's NSC office to the U.S. Embassy in Saigon and to a navy task force off the coast. If necessary, the White House could even listen in on conversations with individual pilots in the planes.

The C-130 transport planes reached Saigon and reported that no rocket fire or artillery shells were hitting the airport. The pilots were cleared to land to continue their airlift. But when they circled lower, they found the runways blocked by abandoned South Vietnamese planes and by thousands of people desperate to escape.

Kissinger got on the phone with Ambassador Graham Martin in Saigon. Martin, a sixty-one-year-old career diplomat, had for days resisted evacuating the remaining Americans, but now, with no hope of further airlifts, tired, emotional, despairing, he recommended that the long-planned final helicopter evacuation be launched.

Kissinger phoned Ford at his residence, explained the situation and relayed Martin's recommendation. Pondering only a moment, at 10:51 P.M., April 28, 1975, Ford gave the order for "Operation Frequent Wind" to begin, the withdrawal of the last Americans and endangered Vietnamese from Saigon.

Halfway around the world, the president's order was flashed by radio to an armada of American navy ships steaming in the South China Sea off the Vietnamese coast. Thirty-four evacuation helicopters lifted off from their carrier ships and whirled toward Saigon. The first choppers carried heavily armed marines to guard the evacuation pads at the U.S. Embassy and the airport. Jet fighter-bombers screamed through the morning sky, providing aerial protection for the pickup.

Back in the White House, as the long night unfolded, Marsh and members of Ford's congressional liaison office phoned key members of Congress to notify them of the president's use of military forces, as required by the War Powers Act. Marsh reported later, "The general response was one of relief that the evacuation was under way."

Ford, grim-faced, visited the Situation Room, a hushed spyproof crisis center in the White House basement, for a briefing. On the way back to his residence, the president paused outside Rumsfeld's office. Ford, Rumsfeld, Cheney and I stood there silently, staring at the carpet, alone with our thoughts, unable to say anything appropriate. A spring rain pinged against the windows.

Finally the president started away.

"Sleep well," I called after him, "if you can."

There was some gallows humor exchanged as the staff waited nervously to find out whether the last Americans would have to fight their way out of Saigon. Kissinger came to Rumsfeld's office and said, "I'm the only secretary of state who has ever lost two countries in three weeks. I lost one country in my capacity as secretary of state and I lost another country in my capacity as national security adviser."

"If we give you another title," I asked, "will you lose another country?"

Kennerly, snapping candid photos of the vigil, cracked one of his endless good news–bad news jokes. "The good news is the war is over. The bad news is we lost."

With almost no Communist opposition, the evacuation went on all that night and throughout the next day until early evening, much longer than anticipated. The reason was that thousands of South Vietnamese clamored to be evacuated in scenes of chaos and panic. The decision on when to cut off the evacuation was left to Ambassador Martin and he kept extending it.

Finally, as a second dawn approached in Saigon and the helicopter pilots reported they were growing dangerously fatigued, Ford indicated it was time to end it. Only nineteen more helicopter loads of evacuees would be picked up. But Martin would not conclude the evacuation and leave unless he received a direct order from Ford. The order was sent.

The ambassador flashed a Teletype message: "I'm going out on the last chopper, which is expected to take off at 4:30. This is our last communication. I'm destroying the communications equipment."

By the time Martin's helicopter lifted off from the roof of the American Embassy and flew away into the dawn, about 1000 Americans and 6000 Vietnamese had been carried to safety. The long war ended a few hours after the final helicopter departed when the South Vietnamese government surrendered to the advancing Communists.

At the White House, it was time to pronounce the official benediction over America's now-finished involvement in the Indochina War. A few minutes after Ambassador Martin left Saigon, Kissinger and I walked into a news conference to announce the end. (When Kissinger heard the news conference was going to be carried live on television, he rushed to the White House barbershop for a quick haircut.)

The news conference was held in the theater of the Executive Office Building, an ancient and ornate structure of Victorian design next door to the White House. The turnout of reporters was surprisingly small considering the historic moment, but late-afternoon deadlines were at hand for morning newspapers and evening TV shows, so many reporters had decided to watch the conference on television in their offices. The reporters who remained, scattered among the tiered seats of the auditorium, were weary from the long wait for the evacuation to be completed.

Standing on the stage, surveying the small audience, I thought to myself: The war seems to be ending with neither a bang nor a whimper, but with a yawn.

Waiting to begin my statement until the TV cameramen and still photographers on a platform at the back of the theater had adjusted their lenses, I was acutely aware that my fantasy was about to become a reality. After being so intimately involved in so many phases of the war, I was about to announce its end. My emotions at that moment were a mixture of fatigue, sadness and nervousness.

"I would like to read a statement by the president," I began in a shaky voice. The only sounds in the room were the whir and click of cameras.

"The evacuation has now been completed.

"The president commends the personnel of the armed forces who accomplished it, as well as Ambassador Graham Martin and the staff of his mission who served so well under difficult conditions.

"This action closes a chapter in the American experience. The president asks all Americans to close ranks to avoid recriminations about the past, to look ahead to the many goals we share, and to work together on the great tasks that remain to be accomplished."

Kissinger then stepped to the podium to answer the reporters' questions. A chief architect and implementer of America's war policy for seven years, he stood now in the ashes of that policy. The loss was too fresh and too painful for him to draw any eloquent lessons.

"What lessons we should draw from it, I think, we should reserve for another occasion," he said softly in his accented English. "But I don't think that we can solve the problem of having entered the conflict too lightly by leaving it too lightly, either. . . .

"One lesson we must learn from this experience is that we must be very careful in the commitments we make, but that we should scrupulously honor those commitments that we make."

As Kissinger and I stepped off the stage into a small anteroom at the end of the news conference, Scowcroft was waiting there with some stunning news. The evacuation had not been completed, as we had announced. There were still 129 marine security guards inside the American Embassy compound in Saigon waiting for helicopters to return and take them out.

"How could this happen? It's unbelievable!" Kissinger exploded when Scowcroft informed him. "This is the most botched-up, incompetent operation I have ever seen!"

While we waited for helicopters to rescue the marines, more black humor was exchanged. Someone suggested the left-behind marines had gone to Tu Do Street to locate old girl friends, or had stopped off for a drink and a screw.

Finally, two and a half hours after I had announced the evacuation was over, the marines climbed aboard helicopters and were flown toward the carriers at sea. This time, it was really over.

At the White House, we haggled over how to explain to the press the delayed evacuation of the marines and the premature pronouncement that the rescue mission was completed. Kissinger wanted to blame the Pentagon's military communications center, although the false announcement resulted from his own incorrect assumption that Martin's departure meant the end of the evacuation.

To ease the tension, Kissinger tried a bleak joke: "I guess you could say the evacuation is at hand," a reference to his premature declaration in 1972 that peace was at hand.

"Maybe we could say the evacuation was so popular we decided to do an encore," I suggested. More seriously, I proposed that we simply ignore the delayed completion of the evacuation.

"No," Rumsfeld declared. "This war has been marked by so many lies and evasions that it is not right to have the war end with one last lie. We ought to be perfectly honest and say that at the time we said the evacuation was over it really wasn't over."

Which is what we did. And I have to admire Rumsfeld for insisting on truthfulness at the end.

The day concluded with a final incongruity. While Kissinger was in his office, changing into his tuxedo for a state dinner for visiting King Hussein of Jordan, Kennerly flung open the door and snapped a memorable photograph of the secretary of state half-naked.

The next morning at my news briefing, the reporters had many follow-up questions on the evacuation of Saigon, including a round of niggling inquiries about why Ford allowed Vietnamese to be rescued on American helicopters. I was in no mood to explain patiently the legal justification and I snapped back at the questioners:

Q.: Ron, can you tell us what authority the president used to use American military forces to evacuate the South Vietnamese?
NESSEN: The president decided that to leave those people there would endanger their lives. . . . The president is proud that he took them out.
Q.: . . . I don't think your answer really addressed itself to the question.
NESSEN: The answer is the answer the president wants given and it is the answer he feels extremely strongly about. He took the people out because they would have been killed otherwise and he is proud he did it.
Q.: The point is—
NESSEN: The point is that is the way he feels and that is why he did it, and the answer is not going to go any further, no matter how much you push on it. . . .

Q.: Then I guess we have to ask, does he feel he broke the law?

NESSEN: He did it because the people would have been killed otherwise. . . .

Q.: So you are unable to cite a legal rationale for it?

NESSEN: I am citing a moral rationale for it.

The next day this line of questioning persisted:

Q.: I wondered if you pursued that matter with the president after your remarks yesterday.

NESSEN: . . . I had done some research on my own . . . after that briefing and found that any number of news executives and newsmen had been in touch with me or other White House or State Department officials in the past couple of weeks about evacuating their Vietnamese employees. . . . None of the news executives ever asked me whether the president had legal authority to take their employees out. . . . I suppose that mirrors the fact that they had the same concern about the lives and safety of their employees—some of whom are our friends —that the president exhibited when he decided that as many Vietnamese as possible should be taken out.

That stopped the questioning about why Ford evacuated endangered Vietnamese.

But the questions reflected an uncharitable attitude toward the refugees by many Americans who worried that they would cost too much to take care of, compete for jobs, crowd schools, threaten neighborhoods and introduce an alien culture into the United States. Two days after the evacuation, the House of Representatives, catching what it thought was the mood of the country, voted down a bill to spend $327 million to help the refugees.

"God damn it, I just don't understand it," the president exclaimed when I brought a wire-service report on the House vote to him in the Oval Office. Clearly incensed, the president directed me to have a tough statement prepared denouncing the uncharitable House action.

About fifteen minutes later, while I was in my office working on the statement, Terry O'Donnell, the president's appointments secretary, arrived with further instructions from Ford. The more the president thought about the rejection of the refugee funds, the angrier he got, O'Donnell informed me. Therefore the president wanted the statement criticizing the House action to be extra strong.

When the draft of the statement was ready for Ford's approval, I found him in the White House barbershop getting a haircut. While Ford, in the barber chair, read through the statement, Kennerly looked over his shoulder and asked, "What's this, some criticism of those pricks on the Hill?"

Kennerly, who was sympathetic toward the refugees, asked Ford to let him read the statement for the reporters and cameras. He promised to add some critical language of his own. Instead, Ford directed me to read the statement to the press on his behalf. I was glad to get the task because I, too, was outraged by the House action. I left the barbershop, returned to my office and summoned the press to the briefing room to receive the statement. I read it forcefully:

> The president is saddened and disappointed by the action of the House of Representatives today. . . .
>
> This action does not reflect the values we cherish as a nation of immigrants. It is not worthy of a people which has lived by the philosophy symbolized by the Statue of Liberty. It reflects fear and misunderstanding rather than charity and compassion. . . .
>
> The president urges the members of the House of Representatives and of the Senate to approve quickly new legislation providing humanitarian assistance to the South Vietnamese refugees. To do otherwise would be a repudiation of the finest principles and traditions of America.

Those principles and traditions were not always displayed when the refugees arrived in the United States for resettlement. Outside the refugee camp at Fort Chafee, Arkansas, demonstrators carried signs reading "Go Home" and "Gooksville." One demonstrator told a reporter, "They say it's a lot colder here than it is in Vietnam. With a little luck, maybe they'll take pneumonia and die." And the mayor of a town near the refugee camp at Eglin Air Force Base, Florida, told ABC cameras, "We're concerned with not only what's happening in general but what's going to happen to our clean beaches."

Some newspapers across the country fanned the antirefugee sentiment by running a vicious cartoon by Pat Oliphant showing a stream of Vietnamese refugees filing past the Statue of Liberty with a parody of the inscription, "Send me your tired and huddled masses, your generals, your wealthy and privileged classes, your crooks and pimps and bar girls, yearning to breathe free. . . ."

Ford later campaigned resolutely for help for the refugees. He visited the refugee camp at Fort Chafee to dramatize the need. Largely because of the president's efforts, congressional and public opinion was turned around and the refugees were assisted in finding a place in American society.

It was probably Ford's finest effort at moral leadership.

Ford inherited the Vietnam War after Americans had long since grown sick of it. Kennedy, Johnson and Nixon had not been able to end, win or abandon the war. But when the North Vietnamese swept into Saigon, Ford gracefully concluded America's role once and for all. Given the deep and bitter divisions in America over the previous decade caused by the war, Ford should have received more credit than he did for presiding over the end of the conflict in a way that avoided a new era of recriminations in the United States about who lost Indochina. The president's call for national unity and his refusal to point the finger of blame set the tone for a reconciliation in American society.

I had hanging in my White House office, and I now have hanging in my home, a haunting photograph taken by Kennerly on his last trip to Indochina with General Weyand. It shows a little Cambodian girl, perhaps five years old, with matted hair and soulful eyes, a dogtag around her neck, tears rolling down her dirty cheeks and a look of unfathomable sorrow on her face.

I plan to keep it where it will remind me always of what we did in Indochina, and what we couldn't do.

CHAPTER TEN

"Let's Look Ferocious"

At 7:40 on the morning of May 12, 1975—thirteen days after the surrender of Saigon—President Ford was informed by Brent Scowcroft that a Cambodian patrol boat had fired on, boarded and seized an American merchant ship, the *Mayaguez*, in the Gulf of Siam.

Thus began a tense military confrontation which, in some ways, was more challenging for Ford than the evacuation of Phnom Penh and Saigon. In those crises, his role was to end a long-standing American involvement as best he could with few realistic options. But the capture of the *Mayaguez* was his problem from the beginning, to resolve successfully or disastrously. Throughout the crisis, Ford was acutely aware that supporters and critics at home and friends and enemies abroad were watching his performance closely to measure his determination and wisdom in dealing with this first international provocation of his presidency.

Scowcroft could tell Ford little about what was happening to the *Mayaguez*. A Mayday broadcast from the ship had been picked up in Djakarta, Indonesia, about four and a half hours earlier: "Have been fired upon and boarded by Cambodian armed forces at 9 degrees 48 minutes North and 102 degrees 53 minutes East." The message was reported to the U.S. Embassy in Djakarta, which flashed the word to the State Department.

The *Mayaguez* was an aging container ship with a crew of thirty-nine Americans on a run from Hong Kong to Sattahip, Thailand. The location it reported as its point of capture was sixty miles off the Cambodian coast, but only eight miles off a rocky island named Poulo Wai, which was claimed by both Cambodia and Vietnam.

There wasn't much Ford could do immediately. There were no

American navy ships anywhere near the area. For the time being, he ordered navy and air force planes based in Thailand and the Philippines to find the *Mayaguez* and keep it under observation.

Later that morning I went into the Oval Office for my daily meeting to discuss with Ford anticipated press questions. Before I could start through my checklist, however, he announced, "Well, I have some bad news to give you."

He informed me of the seizure of the *Mayaguez* and filled me in on the sketchy information available at that time.

"What would you do?" he asked, catching me by surprise. "Would you go in there and bomb the Cambodian boat and take a chance of the Americans being killed? Would you send helicopters in there? Would you mine every harbor in Cambodia?" His tone was pensive, as if he were saying, "So, you think it's fun being president, huh?"

Obviously I had no answers to the questions he posed.

The president summoned his chief diplomatic, military and intelligence advisers to a National Security Council meeting in the Cabinet Room at noon to review the latest information on the *Mayaguez* capture and to discuss what the American response should be. We decided not to announce the seizure of the ship to the American people until after the NSC meeting.

At the meeting, Kissinger argued that the United States must respond firmly to the capture of its ship and citizens in international waters. South Korea, the Philippines, Thailand, NATO, indeed the entire world, would be watching to see if the withdrawal from Vietnam and Cambodia signaled that America had lost its resolve to stand up against aggression. Kissinger said the capture of the *Mayaguez* gave Ford the chance to assert strongly that there was a point beyond which the United States would not be pushed.

Ford directed Kissinger to try for a diplomatic solution, asking the People's Republic of China to transmit a U.S. message to Cambodia demanding immediate release of the ship and crew. But diplomacy was not expected to work with the unpredictable new Communist rulers in Phnom Penh, so the president decided to begin preparations for a military rescue by ordering 1100 marines flown to Thailand. He also directed the aircraft carrier *Coral Sea* and the destroyers *Holt* and *Wilson* to hurry to the scene. But, as Scowcroft put it, they were "heartbreakingly" far away, at least two days' hard steaming.

After the forty-five-minute NSC meeting, I was authorized to issue a statement announcing the capture of the *Mayaguez* and threatening reprisals if the ship was not released. However, because the Press Office had advised the White House reporters that no news was expected before 3 P.M., most of the newsmen were out to lunch and were not expected back for nearly two hours. As a result we had to phone all the restaurants within several blocks of the White House and pass messages to the reporters eating there to reassemble in the briefing room. Within about forty-five minutes we had most of them back.

The reporters knew it had to be big news for the White House to summon them back from lunch. When a secretary walked into the briefing room to distribute my press release, they mobbed her and snatched the copies out of her hands. The reporters quickly scanned the release, which consisted of a Xerox map of the Gulf of Siam with an "X" marking the point where the *Mayaguez* was captured, and a statement which said: "We have been informed that a Cambodian naval vessel has seized an American merchant ship on the high seas and forced it to the port of Kompong Som. The president has met with the NSC. He considers the seizure an act of piracy. He has informed the State Department to demand the immediate release of the ship. Failure to do so would have the most serious consequences."

The reporters didn't waste much time asking frivolous questions on that occasion—they were too anxious to race to the phone to file the news of the international confrontation.

That afternoon Ford stuck to his schedule despite the crisis, meeting a delegation from *Time* to receive a special Bicentennial commemorative issue and presenting awards to five International Women of the Year, among other routine appointments. Kissinger flew off to keep a scheduled speaking engagement in St. Louis.

After filing their initial bulletins, several reporters came to my office to ask for additional details. Among other things, they wanted to know why there wasn't an air of crisis around the White House, as there had been during periods of international tension in the Kennedy, Johnson and Nixon administrations.

The answer was that Ford preferred to make his big decisions in an atmosphere of calm deliberation. Throughout the *Mayaguez* episode, Ford appeared cool, precise, and very low-key. Just as he rarely showed anger, whatever rage he had bottled up inside, he remained impassive during crises no matter how intense the pressures. By his own demeanor he tried to avoid generating a crisis mood. It was his style.

That evening, the Defense Mapping Agency's Hydrographic

Center issued a "Special Warning" to mariners: "Shipping is advised until further notice to remain more than 35 nautical miles off the coast of Cambodia and more than 20 nautical miles off the coast of Vietnam including off-lying islands. Recent incidents have been reported of firing on, stopping and detention of ships within waters claimed by Cambodia, particularly in the vicinity of Poulo Wai Island."

The statement was issued a little late to warn the *Mayaguez* away from that area.

News accounts told of a Panamanian freighter and a South Korean vessel being harassed by Cambodian patrol boats a few days before the *Mayaguez* was seized. Actually there were a number of similar incidents, beginning much earlier, which were never revealed. In addition, the United States had picked up intelligence that Cambodia intended to extend its territorial claims around the offshore islands, including Poulo Wai, and to enforce its claim by seizing ships that strayed too close.

If the United States knew this, why wasn't the warning to merchant shipping issued much sooner? It could have been simply a bureaucratic screw-up, one agency not knowing what another agency knew.

I never saw a shred of evidence that the *Mayaguez* was deliberately allowed to sail into a Cambodian trap in order to provoke an international incident.

Following Ford's order at the noon NSC meeting to try to win release of the *Mayaguez* through diplomatic means, Huang Chen, the head of the Chinese liaison office in Washington, was summoned to the State Department and asked to transmit to Cambodia Ford's demand that the ship and its crew be freed. George Bush, the American representative in Peking, delivered the same request there. The Chinese returned the messages without indicating whether they had been passed on to Cambodia. Bush also tried to enlist the help of exiled Cambodian Prince Sihanouk, then living in Peking. No luck. United Nations Secretary General Kurt Waldheim was asked to use his good offices. But one U.N. official said he didn't even know whom to deal with in Cambodia.

Shortly after 7 P.M., Ford left the Oval Office and went to his residence to have dinner with Mrs. Ford. There wasn't much more he could do until the marines and the navy ships were in position to launch a rescue operation.

At 9:16 P.M., Scowcroft phoned Ford with good news. When

the sun had come up over the Gulf of Siam a short time before, a navy reconnaissance plane had spotted the *Mayaguez* anchored not far from where it was seized, guarded by two Cambodian patrol boats. It had not been taken to the mainland port of Kompong Som after all. As long as the ship was still at sea, there was a chance that American military forces could reach it and free the crew before they were taken ashore, where rescue would be more difficult.

At 2:21 A.M., Scowcroft awakened Ford with bad news: The *Mayaguez* was being escorted toward the mainland.

I arrived at the White House shortly before 6 A.M. on the second morning of the *Mayaguez* crisis because the TV networks needed fresh information for their early morning news shows. I found Scowcroft asleep on the couch in Kissinger's office. His assistant, Marine Lieutenant Colonel Robert C. "Bud" McFarland, was asleep on a chair in his cubbyhole office. Spread out on his desk was a map on which he had plotted the movements of the *Mayaguez* during the night by monitoring radio reports from the reconnaissance pilots circling overhead. The *Mayaguez* was again at anchor, at an island called Koh Tang, about thirty-four miles off the coast. There was still a chance to save the crew before they were taken to the mainland.

At 10:22 that morning, Ford convened another National Security Council meeting. The U.S. Navy ships were still too far away for a rescue attempt. The only forces immediately available were jet fighters based in Thailand. Ford ordered them to stop any Cambodian boats trying to sail from Koh Tang Island to the mainland or from the mainland to the island.

As he made this and other decisions throughout the *Mayaguez* episode, Ford was mindful of the case of the *Pueblo*, the U.S. Navy intelligence ship captured by North Korea in 1968; it took nearly a year of negotiation and humiliation before the crew was released. Ford was determined to try to prevent the *Mayaguez* crewmen from being taken ashore because he feared it would require months or years to win their freedom.

On the second day of the crisis, Ford again stuck to his regular schedule of appointments, including a meeting to hear Governor Hugh Carey and Mayor Abraham Beame plead for federal financial assistance to save New York City from bankruptcy.

During the day, Joseph Laitin, the Pentagon spokesman, phoned to advise me that B-52s on Guam had been put on alert for possible raids on the airport at Phnom Penh and the airfield and naval base at Kompong Som as part of a military rescue operation. He said newsmen had been excluded from the air base on Guam so they couldn't see the planes being loaded with 1000-pound bombs. Laitin said a top-level debate was going on over whether to use big bombers, with Kissinger and Rockefeller the strongest proponents of B-52 raids. Laitin said Schlesinger was arguing against them because he felt B-52s were so widely identified with the unpopular American bombings in Vietnam that their use in the *Mayaguez* episode would turn world opinion against the United States.

The president called another National Security Council meeting at 10:30 that night. It was now clear that military force almost certainly would have to be used to free the *Mayaguez* crewmen. Ford made tentative decisions on the degree of force and the tactics to be followed from a list of options presented at the meeting. He ordered that the military units involved be put on alert, ready to move on one hour's notice.

Shortly before the meeting, the jet fighters circling over Koh Tang Island spotted Cambodian boats heading for the mainland. When the boats failed to heed warning shots, the planes attacked, sinking three boats and damaging four. The pilot of one plane, swooping down on another boat, radioed, "I believe I see Caucasian faces." This message was picked up at the White House and rushed in to the president while he was presiding over the NSC meeting.

Ford faced a tough decision. If he ordered the boat sunk and the "Caucasian faces" turned out to be the *Mayaguez* crewmen, the Americans would be killed by their own planes. But if he called off the attack, it might mean that some or all of the crew would be imprisoned on the mainland, out of reach of the rescue force.

Ford sent orders to the planes to stop attacking the boat. The jets tried to force the craft to turn back by exploding bombs and firing rockets and cannon in its path and even dousing the boat with tear gas. It kept steaming right into the harbor at Kompong Som. Ford's order not to sink the boat was fortunate because, though the president didn't know it then, all thirty-nine members of the *Mayaguez* crew were on that boat.

The third and climactic day of the *Mayaguez* incident was Wednesday, May 14, 1975. By midafternoon the time had arrived for Ford to make his final decisions on recovering the *Mayaguez*. He convened still another National Security Council meeting in the Cabinet Room shortly before 4 P.M. to review his options: The carrier *Coral Sea* and the destroyers *Holt* and *Wilson* were finally closing in on the *Mayaguez*. The 1100 marines were in place in Thailand. Diplomatic efforts had accomplished nothing. Intercepted Cambodian radio messages suggested that at least some of the *Mayaguez* crew members might have been moved to the mainland, although the broadcasts were not conclusive. The president concluded that he had no choice except to launch a military operation to rescue the crew and ship.

Less than an hour after the NSC meeting started, Ford's orders were relayed to the Pentagon:

—Marines were to be lowered to the *Holt* from helicopters and then board the *Mayaguez*.

—Other marines were to land on Koh Tang Island from helicopters to recover crew members.

—Jet planes from the *Coral Sea* were to bomb installations on the Cambodian mainland to prevent the dispatch of reinforcements to Koh Tang.

—The B-52 raids were canceled.

The troops, helicopters and planes began moving at dawn, Cambodian time, twenty-nine minutes after Ford issued his orders. It would take them several hours to reach the assault area.

Following the NSC meeting, the president invited the most important members of Congress to the White House for a meeting early that evening to inform them of the rescue operation.

When Ford strode into the Cabinet Room at 6:40 P.M.—brushing right past James Cannon of the Domestic Council, who was trying to stop him to sign a letter to Mayor Beame denying financial aid to New York City—the senators and House members, Democrats and Republicans alike, stood and applauded. For thirty-five minutes the president explained the history of the episode from the time the *Mayaguez* was captured. Then, pointing to maps of the Gulf of Siam and an aerial photo of Koh Tang Island propped against metal easels, Ford outlined the details of the military action he had ordered to recover the ship and crew.

The senators and congressmen murmured and nodded their assent as the president explained how the marines would assault the *Mayaguez* and Koh Tang Island. But Ford struck a raw nerve when he described the planned air strikes against Cambodian military facilities at Kompong Som and Ream on the mainland. Three of the most powerful members of the Senate—Democratic Leader Mike Mansfield, Assistant Democratic Leader Robert Byrd and Chairman John McClellan of the Appropriations Committee—spoke up strongly in opposition to the air strikes. Ford tried to quiet their criticism by explaining that the bombing raids on Kompong Som and Ream were designed to prevent 2400 Cambodian troops, eight large landing barges and seventeen planes at the facilities from attacking U.S. Marines. But, with memories still fresh of the escalating air strikes ordered by presidents Johnson and Nixon during the Indochina war, which never seemed to accomplish their announced purpose, the senators were not satisfied with Ford's explanation.

"I thought we were going to use minimum force," grumbled crusty old John McClellan. "Do we have to do it all at once? Can't we wait to see if the Cambodians attack before we attack the mainland?"

"It's too great a risk," Ford responded.

"I want to express my deep concern, apprehension and uneasiness at this near-invasion of the Indochina mainland," declared Mansfield, a lean, scholarly, enormously respected man. "We have plenty of firepower there in the two destroyers. Frankly, I have grave doubts about this move."

Byrd, known for his harsh partisanship, criticized Ford for not conferring with the Democrats in Congress earlier about the air strikes.

"I had a choice between doing too little and too much," Ford replied. "If I did too little and endangered the marines, I would have been subjected to very legitimate criticism."

"Allow me to press this respectfully," Byrd persisted. "Why weren't the leaders brought in when there was time for them to raise a word of caution?"

"We have a government of separation of powers," the president responded firmly. "In this case, as commander in chief, I had the responsibility and obligation to act. I would never forgive myself if the first wave of marines was attacked by twenty-four hundred Cambodians."

The argument ground on. But it was meaningless, since the president already had ordered the air strikes. When the senators and House members had expressed their views, Ford ended the meeting by asking the congressional leaders to join in a prayer for "the very best."

At 7:07 P.M., while the meeting with congressional leaders was going on, and only two minutes before the first American helicopter approached Koh Tang Island and was shot out of the sky, the domestic Phnom Penh radio service began a nineteen-minute propaganda tirade in the Cambodian language, concluding with an announcement that the *Mayaguez* would be released.

The broadcast was picked up and translated by the CIA. A summary was sent to the White House and other key officers on the CIA's Foreign Broadcast Intelligence Service Teletype at 8:06 P.M., just forty minutes after the Cambodian radio statement concluded, an impressive demonstration of the intelligence agency's abilities.

The broadcast made no mention of releasing the crew, only the ship, and it was too late to postpone the military operation in order to seek elaboration of the broadcast. Marines were under fire on Koh Tang Island and others were clambering aboard the *Mayaguez* when the CIA translation arrived at the White House. The first air strike was just fifteen minutes away from its target on the mainland.

As soon as the president was informed of the Phnom Penh statement, he directed that a message be sent to the Cambodians saying their broadcast had been heard and promising to call off the military operations as soon as the crew members were freed. The problem was there was no way to send a message to Cambodia quickly. The United States had no direct communications with Phnom Penh. But Kissinger, following the crisis from his spacious, art-decorated NSC office in the White House, had an idea: Maybe the international press wire services could be used to transmit Ford's reply to Cambodia. He phoned me in my office.

"Come down here right away!" Kissinger ordered in an agitated voice.

But despite his urgent tone, I didn't go right away because I was wrestling with several other problems. I didn't realize I was delaying Kissinger's desperate scheme to contact the Cambodians. When I didn't respond immediately to Kissinger's summons, he sent his deputy, Brent Scowcroft, to get me. Scowcroft burst into my office dressed in a tuxedo for a state dinner being held for the Dutch prime minister that night, grabbed me by the arm and literally pulled me to Kissinger's office.

"We have got to use you to get a message through to Cambodia!" Henry informed me excitedly. "They've got to read it on the AP!"

Kissinger had concluded that the fastest way, perhaps the only way, to reply to the radio broadcast was to release the American response to the press and hope that Cambodian officials in Phnom Penh or elsewhere in the world would see it on the news wires.*

I pointed out to Kissinger that the message to the Cambodians offered to call off the American military operation, but we had not yet publicly announced the beginning of the operation.

"Yes, do that first," he agreed, "and then do the message to the Cambodians. But hurry!"

I ran to the press room and climbed up on the small briefing platform. It was after 9 P.M., but the place was still jammed with reporters. There are no bigger stories than international military confrontations. I began to read the president's statement to the Cambodians at a very fast pace.

"Would you read it slowly, please?" the reporters shouted.

Oh, Lord! The press wanted me to read the statement at slow dictation speed so they could copy down each word accurately, while I was anxious to race through in order to get Ford's message moving toward Phnom Penh on the news wires as quickly as possible, perhaps ending the battle, then going on and saving lives.

"Listen to what I have to say!" I shouted at the reporters. "There is some urgency about it."

The newsmen realized that I had something important to announce and that speed was essential. The room grew quiet. The reporters let me read Ford's message to the Cambodians quickly:

"We have heard a radio broadcast that you are prepared to release the S.S. *Mayaguez*. We welcome this development, if true. . . . As soon as you issue a statement that you are prepared to release the crew members you hold, unconditionally and immediately, we will promptly cease military operations."

The reporters scribbled furiously to keep up with my words. I had to repeat one sentence for a newsman who didn't get it. When I finished the statement, I told the press corps why I had insisted on reading the message so fast. "We believe the news channels may be the fastest way for this message to get through," I explained. "Go file!"

The newsmen rushed to their phones and cameras to report that the military operation to rescue the *Mayaguez* was under way and to transmit the president's response to the Cambodian broadcast. I hurried back to Kissinger's office in time to watch on his TV set

---

* A plan to broadcast the U.S. reply over a radio frequency the Cambodians were known to be monitoring was considered also, but for some reason it was never put into effect.

as the networks interrupted their programs to broadcast the news I had just announced.

While all this was going on, while the president and his senior advisers were sweating out the tensions and uncertainty of the military strike, a glittering black-tie banquet was being held for visiting Dutch Prime Minister den Uyl and dozens of guests beneath the enormous chandeliers in the State Dining Room. Under the circumstances, of course, the dinner was a shambles. Ford was a half-hour late arriving and excused himself several times during the meal to take phone reports on the rescue mission. Defense Secretary Schlesinger left in the middle of the dinner. So did Rumsfeld. Kissinger and Scowcroft made only brief appearances at the end of the dinner. Den Uyl said, diplomatically, that he understood.

After the banquet, Ford, Kissinger, Rumsfeld and Scowcroft, still in their tuxedoes, returned to the Oval Office to await the outcome of the rescue. The president sat behind his desk, where he could take phone reports from Schlesinger, who was monitoring the operation at the Pentagon. The others settled back in chairs around the desk. At first the only news was bad: The marines were under heavy fire from Cambodian troops on Koh Tang Island and the *Mayaguez* crewmen had not been found aboard their ship. Then came an encouraging report that a fishing boat was approaching the destroyer *Wilson* and that people could be seen on the deck waving white shirts. It might be some of the *Mayaguez* crew members.

Finally, a little before midnight, the white phone on Ford's desk buzzed softly. It was Schlesinger again with stunning news: The entire crew was safe aboard the *Wilson*. The Cambodians had set them free more than two hours earlier, put them aboard a rickety fishing boat and pointed them toward the *Mayaguez*, anchored off Koh Tang.

"They're all out!" Ford whooped to the startled aides around his desk. "They're safe! Thank God!"

Kennerly, lurking off to the left side of the Oval Office, camera cocked, captured the instant of elation in a memorable photo showing the president coming half out of his chair with excitement and the others displaying their reactions in expressions and gestures of relief.

After a few moments of exchanging handshakes and congratulations with his advisers in the Oval Office, Ford decided he wanted the successful conclusion of the *Mayaguez* crisis to be announced from the White House. Cheney phoned me in my office and passed on Ford's directions to make arrangements to issue the statement.

"Call Laitin," Cheney instructed. "Don't let him put out the news from the Pentagon."

But it was too late. A secretary tossed a wire-service bulletin on my desk reporting, from the Defense Department, that the rescue had succeeded. The Pentagon spokesman, who from the very beginning of the operation had been leaking information about the *Mayaguez* to reporters before the White House could announce it, had scooped the president with the news that the crew was safe.

I rushed to the Oval Office to tell the president that Laitin had stolen our opportunity to announce the happy ending of Ford's first military test. "That goddamn Laitin has already leaked the news!" I informed the president. Curses were directed at the Pentagon spokesman by other aides in the Oval Office too.*

But I had an idea how Ford still could get press attention at his moment of success. "Look, we have one thing that Laitin doesn't have," I suggested. "We have the president. Why doesn't the president go out and announce the recovery of the *Mayaguez* and the crew on live television, in the middle of the Johnny Carson show?"

"That's a good idea," Ford agreed. The others thought so, too. Ford went to his residence to change out of his tuxedo into a brown suit. While he was changing, his statement was written in the NSC office. By the time he got back, it was done and the networks had been alerted to stand by for a Ford statement. But before the president went to the press room to read the statement for the cameras, a cautious Rumsfeld insisted that he phone Schlesinger from the Oval Office to make certain the entire *Mayaguez* crew had been recovered. (Remembering the marines left behind in Saigon?)

"I'm sure you can understand, Jim, under the circumstances I need to be absolutely assured that all the crew members are out," the president explained over the phone to the defense secretary. Schlesinger replied that it had been confirmed by three different sources.

There was one more important matter to consider before the rescue operation could be declared over.

"Is there any reason for the Pentagon not to disengage?" Scowcroft asked.

---

* When Ford fired Schlesinger later, I kidded him that he was really doing it to get rid of Laitin. The eternal bureaucratic survivor, Laitin turned up as Treasury Secretary Blumenthal's spokesman in the Carter administration.

"No, but tell them to bomb the mainland," Kissinger responded. "Let's look ferocious! Otherwise they will attack us as the ship leaves."

With a third and final air strike ordered against petroleum-storage facilities on the mainland, and the marines fighting on Koh Tang directed to withdraw, Ford walked from his office to the press room to read his low-key victory statement on television. I noticed he had forgotten to change out of his shiny black patent leather formal pumps. He seemed tired and nervous, muffing some words.

> At my direction, the United States forces tonight boarded the American merchant ship S.S. *Mayaguez* and landed at the Island of Koh Tang for the purpose of rescuing the crew and the ship, which had been illegally seized by Cambodian forces. They also conducted supporting strikes against nearby military installations.
>
> I have now received information that the vessel has been recovered intact and the entire crew has been rescued. The forces that have successfully accomplished this mission are still under hostile fire but are preparing to disengage.
>
> I wish to express my deep appreciation and that of the entire nation to the units and the men who participated in these operations for their valor and for their sacrifice.

After the TV appearance, the president and half a dozen aides trooped back to the Oval Office. I expected Ford to sit around with his staff for a while, reliving the crisis and winding down, but after accepting congratulations briefly, the president said, "I'm going home and going to bed."

"Sleep well," I told him.

"I will tonight," he said, walking out.

Ford took a sleeping pill that night, something he almost never did. He was keyed up from the drama of the past three days. But he had never let it show.

Public reaction to the president's decisive action was overwhelmingly favorable. By the end of the week the White House had received more than 14,000 letters, telegrams and phone calls expressing support for Ford, and barely a thousand opposed.

But a number of doubts and suspicious questions were raised al-

most immediately in press comments: Had Ford overreacted? Did
he make judgments in the episode on the basis of an excessive concern about boosting his own reputation for decisive leadership?
Was a desire to assert American resoluteness after the fall of
Indochina a major factor in deciding on a strong military response?
Why didn't Ford wait longer to see if Cambodia would comply
with diplomatic appeals? Why didn't he cancel the operation and
the air strikes immediately when he learned of the Cambodian
radio message? Did he know the crew had been taken to the mainland, and, if so, why did he order the marines to land on Koh Tang?

The suspicions were fanned by the fact that the Pentagon refused for days to announce an accurate and final casualty count,
as if it were trying to avoid dampening the good news of the
crew's safe return with the bad news of deaths and injuries among
the rescue forces. Despite prodding from Ford, the Defense Department stalled.

Finally, a full five days after the rescue, Laitin announced the
casualties: fifteen dead, mostly on the first helicopter shot down;
three missing; fifty wounded. Another eighteen men being trans-
ported from one base to another in Thailand for possible use in the
rescue were killed when their helicopter crashed.

The delay in releasing the casualty figures undermined the president's credibility with an already doubting press corps. The relatively high casualties—thirty-six dead or missing in order to rescue
thirty-nine—set off a round of stories suggesting Ford should have
found a less costly way of recovering the *Mayaguez.*

Ford also was criticized for not canceling the military operation
after the Cambodian radio broadcast offering to release the ship,
or after the *Mayaguez* crewmen had been set free on the mainland
to sail to their ship on the fishing boat. But a study of the sequence
of events shows that the crew was released only after the rescue
mission had begun. The crew left shore, bound for the *Mayaguez*
thirty-four miles away, at 7:29 in the morning, Cambodian time,
almost the exact moment marines were boarding the *Mayaguez.*
Other marines already were in a bloody fight on Koh Tang Island.

When the *Mayaguez* crew visited Ford later in the Oval Office,
they attributed their release to the marine assault on Koh Tang and
the previous day's jet strikes against Cambodian patrol boats. The
crew believed the Cambodians were afraid of being pulverized by
American military might if they didn't release the crew. The last
words to the crew from one of their English-speaking captors were,

"You will contact the American government when you get on your ship. Tell them to stop the jets."

In any case, Ford never had second thoughts about his decisions. He dismissed the criticism as carping hindsight by Monday-morning quarterbacks who didn't have to make life-and-death decisions under pressures of time, with incomplete information.

CHAPTER ELEVEN

Travels with Henry

As the White House official responsible for disseminating factual information to the press and public, I frequently had run-ins with Kissinger because he believed that the truth should be shaded or withheld if that would advance his foreign-policy objectives.

My first serious clash with Kissinger occurred in the spring of 1975 after I was misled about Vietnam peace efforts by a lower level staff member of Kissinger's National Security Council.

As North Vietnamese troops closed in on Saigon, this staff member assured me that "diplomatic initiatives" were under way, that a negotiated settlement was being sought. I passed this on to the press. But there were no diplomatic initiatives. I had to call a special briefing to retract my statement and apologize to the reporters. The episode was the inevitable result of a system, then in operation, under which Kissinger grudgingly gave the press office a minimum of information with which to answer press questions about important foreign-policy matters. For instance, one day I asked his liaison to the press office for information about a situation in anticipation of questions.

"Oh, that is something we don't talk about," she replied in the same tone she might use to brush off a pesky reporter.

Rumsfeld reported to Ford that I had been misled about Vietnam peace efforts. I was surprised he would bring up with the president the activities of a relatively minor Kissinger aide. I had the uneasy feeling that Rumsfeld was using the incident to drag me into a behind-the-scenes struggle to curb the power of Kissinger and NSC.

Rumsfeld had suggested several times that the president should seek advice on foreign-policy matters from a wider group than just Kissinger and the NSC. I agreed. For instance, the initial decision not to invite Soviet dissident Alexander Solzhenitsyn to the White House almost certainly would have been handled differently if Ford had received a broader range of advice, from aides dealing with Congress, politics, the press, etc.

I was aware that Ford had invited more than the usual circle of foreign-policy advisers to offer suggestions for a Vietnam speech he was preparing in the final weeks of the war. I was also told, secondhand, that Ford had been overheard saying, "In a short period of time I'm going to have to take over foreign policy myself."

For these reasons, when Bob Schieffer of CBS asked me after the "peace-initiative" flap whether his perception was correct, that Ford was pulling away from Kissinger a little, I nodded my head yes.

At the same time, other White House aides were confiding to reporters their concern that Kissinger had too much influence and their determination to encourage Ford to assert himself as the manager of foreign policy, in both image and reality.

The result was a flood of news stories saying the secretary of state was about to be fired from his second job as head of the NSC.

Kissinger angrily blamed me for some of the stories. I became a little uneasy. Kissinger had great clout with the president and was the survivor of innumerable backstage fights. I was concerned that he might demand that Ford reprimand or even fire me for leaking stories about his power waning.

I scrambled to get back in Kissinger's good graces. I began telling reporters that there was nothing to reports that Kissinger was losing influence. I also arranged a press photo of Ford and Kissinger alone in the Oval Office working on the Vietnam speech. While the photographers snapped away, Kissinger had a smug look on his face that seemed to say, "See? I'm still here."

And I did something I'm not proud of: I fired a member of my staff, telling Kissinger I suspected him of being the source of some anti-Kissinger leaks. Actually, I had decided previously to let the staff member go for inefficiency and an inability to get along with other members of the Press Office. I believed he *was* leaking some of the stories about Kissinger leaving, but I am angry at myself for letting Kissinger think I had offered a sacrificial lamb to appease him.

Kissinger immediately became more friendly and helpful. He invited me to attend his morning staff meetings with his chief aides from the State Department and the NSC so I could soak up more information about foreign policy. I wondered if it was a standard

Kissinger tactic—to bluster threateningly and then make his opponents grateful for small favors.

The episode was not over. A new round of press stories detailed an alleged plot by Rumsfeld, Marsh, Hartmann and Nessen to get Kissinger. The *Washington Star*, for instance, ran a long front-page story saying Rumsfeld was the leader of a coup against Kissinger, with me as front man, but the revolt had failed.

The day it appeared, I approached Kissinger before a cabinet meeting and told him jokingly, "The next time we try a coup against you, we're going to use T-28 fighter planes."

Kissinger assured me he didn't believe the stories, he felt our relationship was good. In fact, he wanted to take me more into his confidence, he said.

Another tactic? Magnanimity in victory?

As the flurry finally died down, with Kissinger unscathed, someone kidded me that I should win a National Rifle Association marksmanship award for taking a shot at Kissinger, hitting one of my own staff members by mistake and wounding myself in the foot at the same time.

Nearly two months later, Rumsfeld undertook a more subtle and more successful campaign to give Ford fuller control over foreign policy, and Kissinger less. Rumsfeld insisted that Ford convene two long staff meetings in order to give Kissinger instructions for several speeches he was scheduled to make at international conferences. Previously, Kissinger would have decided himself what to say in the speeches.

Rumsfeld continued his new campaign as Ford prepared to attend a NATO meeting in Brussels in May 1975. Don proposed that Ford should conduct the press briefings himself during the trip. Kissinger normally would have done the briefings. Rumsfeld also suggested that Kissinger be excluded from press photos of Ford and the leaders of the other NATO nations.

I told none of this to reporters. This time, I decided, I was going to stay out of the Rumsfeld-Kissinger jockeying. I remembered an old Vietnamese saying, "When the elephants fight, the grass gets trampled."

But I made a mistake. Actually, I made a joke that was taken seriously. On the flight to Brussels, Rumsfeld chatted with the pool reporters on *Air Force One*. Since Kissinger had flown ahead on another plane, I joked to the reporters that, for this flight only, Rumsfeld would play the role of the "senior American official," the title Kissinger affected when talking on background to newsmen.

Several news stories treated my joke as a serious indication that Rumsfeld was trying to cut in on Henry's turf. That fed a new wave of stories saying Kissinger was losing influence, Rumsfeld was gaining influence and Ford was more than ever exerting personal control over foreign policy.

As a result of these stories, Henry asked to see me privately the first day in Brussels. We met in my office, which was a curtained-off corner of the press room. The sounds of mimeograph machines, Teletypes and phones penetrated the alcove.

Kissinger said he was sick and tired of all the stories about him losing power. He said he wasn't going to take it anymore. If his rivals on the staff thought he was going to allow himself to be nibbled to death, they were crazy. When he got mad, Kissinger warned, he would show how he could strike back.

I assured him I was not responsible for the new round of anti-Kissinger stories.

"I think you are not involved, or, if you are involved, you are only involved at the periphery," he concluded.

"I made a conscious decision not to get involved when I saw this bubbling up a week or so ago," I explained.

"Well, I would have thought that if you saw it bubbling up, you would have warned me," he complained.

I learned later that Kissinger also had demanded meetings with Rumsfeld and Hartmann and had made similar threats.

The next morning I told Ford about my conversation with Kissinger. I wanted the president to know I was not leaking anti-Kissinger stories and I did not like being bullied by the secretary of state. Ford asked me whether I thought someone in the White House was leaking critical stories about Kissinger, or whether the news stories were the result of journalistic imagination. I replied that I thought someone on the staff was passing anti-Kissinger stories to reporters.

"You know how much I hate fighting on the staff," Ford declared. "It's the one thing that makes me mad."

But he didn't seem mad. I sensed that he was not unhappy at all about the stories describing Ford's control of foreign policy as getting stronger and Kissinger's role as getting weaker.

It became a ritual on virtually every foreign trip for Henry to blow up at least once about anti-Kissinger leaks, his tone bitter and arrogant, his voice high-pitched and quavery.

During one such Kissinger tirade aboard *Air Force One,* some-one asked, "Who leaked?"

Henry replied, "We have ways of finding out."

I felt a chill. I remembered the phones of Kissinger's staff mem-bers had been tapped during the Nixon years to catch leakers.

On another trip, to an economic summit meeting in France in November 1975, Kissinger said he wanted to talk to me alone in the president's *Air Force One* bedroom about fifteen minutes before landing in Paris.

"Ron, there is no question now that you are leaking stories about me," he said, perched on the edge of Ford's pale blue sofa-bed. "At least ten reporters have told me about your backgrounder briefings about me, and if it keeps up I'm going to go public."

"I don't know what you're talking about," I replied. And I really didn't. I told him truthfully that I admired him as a brilliant secretary of state who brought a long-range historic and philo-sophic perspective to the day-to-day conduct of foreign policy. It made no sense, I said, for a press secretary to try to bump off a secretary of state.

But Henry was not convinced. He accused me of telling re-porters that he was spending less time with the president and of hinting that Elliot Richardson was standing by to become the next secretary of state. Despite his strong protest, Kissinger seemed deflated. Ford had recently stripped him of his NSC job. He said he really didn't care whether he continued in the cabinet, he could easily leave the State Department.

"All the joy has gone out of it for me," he sighed as *Air Force One* settled onto the runway in Paris.

But the joy of power was not so gone that Henry gave up fight-ing for his place in the limelight. His ego would not tolerate anyone challenging his role. For instance, when Kissinger was late arriving for one session of the economic summit in France, Ford asked White House Economic Adviser William Seidman to sit at the con-ference table with him while news photos were taken. When Kissinger came bustling up to the door during the photo session, I suggested he wait until the picture-taking was over since the president had already invited Seidman to substitute. Kissinger brushed past me, rushed into the conference room, stopped directly behind Seidman and cracked sarcastically, "Well, *Mr. Richardson,* I see you are in my seat."

On the flight home from another European trip, *Air Force One* made a refueling stop in England. Richardson, who was ambassador, came to the airfield to visit with Ford and his party during the brief layover. In the airport lounge, where refreshments had been laid out, Kissinger noted a Bible displayed conspicuously on a table. He pointed it out to Ford, nodded at Richardson and joked tartly, "I wonder if we are going to administer an oath to someone here today."

Ford's trip to China in November and December 1975 provided new insights into Kissinger's character. On the long flight to Peking, Henry conducted a running argument with Richard Solomon, an NSC China expert, about a revolutionary ballet that the Chinese planned to perform for the president.

The ballet selected by the Chinese was entitled *Song of the Yimeng Mountains*. In song and dance, it told the story of Communist revolutionaries coming to the Yimeng mountains and executing an oppressive landlord, his friends of the mandarin class and Nationalist Chinese troops.

Kissinger believed the Chinese had chosen that ballet as a deliberate insult to the United States for its past and continuing support of the Nationalists. "The Chinese will see they have made fools of us if we attend that ballet," he fumed to Solomon, "and they will think we don't even know we have been made fools of."

Solomon promised to talk to the Chinese about changing the ballet. But Kissinger was resigned. "It's too late now."

As it turned out, the Chinese did stage *Song of the Yimeng Mountains* for the president. Several members of Ford's party, including me, were so tired we dozed off during the performance and awoke only when the make-believe gunfire on stage mowed down the evil landlord. So perhaps it was a good choice after all.

Kissinger was a demanding boss. On the flight to Peking he demonstrated that. After bickering for hours with Solomon about the wording of Ford's toast at the formal banquet in China, Kissinger concluded the discussion by declaring, "No use arguing. It's just a question of how much anguish you want to go through before I get my way."

Kissinger also got his way in handling the news during the China visit. He decreed that there should be a nearly total blackout on information during the four days of diplomatic discussions. Ford and the normally secretive Chinese agreed that the talks were more likely to succeed if conducted without publicity about daily ups and downs.

That was a foreign-policy decision, not a press office decision. But as the press secretary, I had to face the wrath of the frustrated reporters. Their news organizations had spent thousands of dollars to send them to Peking, but we gave them nothing of substance to report beyond banquet menus, sightseeing trips, and meaningless adjectives about "constructive . . . wide-ranging . . . significant" meetings.

The more enterprising American journalists were able to obtain some insight on Ford's talks from diplomats and reporters of other nations. The rest of the U.S. newsmen were forced to search for diplomatic meaning in the size and enthusiasm of street corner crowds for Ford's motorcades, or the quality of food at state banquets.

The strangest episode of the China trip was kept entirely secret from the reporters. About 5:30 in the morning of the next to the last day in Peking, I and others in the American delegation were awakened in our utilitarian guest compound by the sound of gunfire. Approximately twenty shots were heard, some about half a mile away from Ford's quarters and the others farther away, as if there were an exchange of fire. The Secret Service asked the Chinese what all the shooting was about. The Chinese denied there had been any shooting, even though a number of members of Ford's party heard it clearly. The press corps, staying at a hotel several miles away, was never told of the mysterious gun shots.

Even without Kissinger's determination to clamp the lid of secrecy on Ford's Peking discussions, the Chinese made life difficult for the American press corps—and for me. The Peking authorities informed the White House advance party before the trip that American officials were forbidden to give out substantive information to the press, verbally or in writing, during Ford's visit, without first obtaining permission from an executive of the information department of the foreign ministry.

I learned what this meant late on Ford's first night in Peking after the welcoming banquet in the cavernous Great Hall of the People. The information department refused to approve the press coverage arrangements for the following day and would not authorize my office to distribute the schedule to reporters until I went through an elaborate midnight ritual.

The ritual involved sitting around the press office on the tenth floor of the shabby Minzu Hotel until I received a phone call from Ma Yu-Chen, the young, smooth, English-speaking official in charge of dealing with foreign reporters at the information department.

Mr. Ma invited me to meet with him. I walked two flights down the stairwell to his plain office. He introduced me to his boss, the head of the information department, who spoke no English, and to several other Chinese men and women whose roles I never learned.

I was urged to take tea or a soft drink. The American protocol officers had advised us that it was an insult to refuse such refreshments. So I sipped, made small talk, laughed at comments that weren't funny or that I didn't understand, and killed the small hours of the morning. Eventually, when he was good and ready, or when some secret signal arrived through the Chinese bureaucracy, Mr. Ma suggested that perhaps it was time to review the press arrangements for the following day. He was excessively polite, but I tried to outdo him in excessive politeness. Without making any changes, Mr. Ma finally approved the coverage plans and granted permission to reproduce the schedule for distribution to the American press.

By then it was long past midnight.

It happened that way every night of the China trip.

Inscrutable. Even more inscrutable than Kissinger.

Finally, on the eve of Ford's departure from Peking, Kissinger came to the press center and spent nearly forty-five minutes trying to soothe the angry reporters by giving them a substantive report on Ford's meetings.*

Kissinger announced that as the only concrete accomplishment of the visit, China had promised to return the remains of two American airmen shot down during the Vietnam War and provide information on the deaths of five other Americans missing in action.

On the matter of U.S. detente with China's rival Russia, Kissinger indicated that Ford and the Chinese leaders had agreed to disagree. And on the thorny matter of finding a formula for establishing diplomatic relations with Peking without abandoning Taiwan, Kissinger told his briefing that China had suggested the United States follow the "Japanese model." (Japan had transferred its diplomatic recognition from Taiwan to Peking, but maintained a healthy trade and cultural relationship with the Nationalist Chinese.)

---

* Garry Trudeau, the *Doonesbury* cartoonist, who was along on the trip, drew a wonderfully appropriate cartoon showing Kissinger telling the briefing, "Good evening. The talks were significant. Have a nice flight back."

"We are satisfied with the visit," Kissinger summed up.

After returning to the United States from the China trip, I tried to take a short vacation in Florida with my family. But after a few days I was called back to the White House by Cheney to deal with a spate of critical articles about press problems in Peking.

Typical of the complaints was a column by Jim Squires in the Chicago *Tribune:* "During four days in China, [Nessen] appeared in the press room only twice—once to announce that he had nothing to say, and another time to say that he had nothing to announce."

It was maddening to be denounced for withholding information during the China trip when it was not my decision. Even if I had wanted to tell the reporters everything going on in the negotiations, I did not have the information because I had not been invited to attend the meetings.

While blaming me for the lack of news in China, Squires indicated he understood the real story of the problem. "There may be a good explanation for Nessen's Pacific vacation as a source of information," he wrote. "And that is that despite all the appearances of having access, he really didn't have any. Every indication was that Secretary of State Henry Kissinger had control of all the information during Ford's foreign tour."

The Kissinger character trait that troubled me most was his lack of commitment to the truth as a matter of morality. Kissinger bent the truth to serve what he believed were worthwhile foreign-policy maneuvers.

I saw that graphically illustrated during Ford's trip to Yugoslavia in the summer of 1975, when a translator made a significant mistake. At the conclusion of Ford's talks with President Tito in Belgrade, the two leaders appeared before reporters in the starkly modern Federal Executive Council Building and made brief statements on their conference. The woman translating Tito's remarks into English quoted him as saying, "Both sides have obviously expressed concern about the situation in the Middle East. I think our views are quite identical. . . ."

That was news. Only the night before, in his toast at the official banquet, Tito had denounced America's Middle East policy of supporting Israel and had demanded that Israel immediately withdraw to its 1967 borders.

As the American delegation trooped down the wide marble staircase after the Ford and Tito press statements, the American ambassador to Yugoslavia, Larry Silberman, rushed up and advised me of the translation error. What Tito actually had said was, "I think our views are quite identical *on the dangers* of the situation in the Middle East." Silberman asked me to make sure the reporters understood the mistake.

I informed Kissinger as we reached the bottom of the staircase.

"No, no. Don't bother correcting it," he directed. "Leave it vague like that. Leave them guessing for twelve hours and then you can correct it. Obviously, we have not changed our position. So, by leaving it incorrect that way, it gives the impression that Tito has changed *his* position on the Middle East."

Unforgivably, I went along with Kissinger's deception. I did not tell the reporters of the translator's error until the next day, back in Washington.

Earlier on the same European trip, before reaching Yugoslavia, Kissinger got caught tinkering with the truth and felt compelled to back down. It was in Helsinki, Finland, where Ford held a meeting with the leaders of Britain, France and West Germany to discuss the troubled international economic situation. After the meeting, Kissinger told newsmen, "No conclusions were reached. No decisions were taken."

But, a reporter pointed out to the secretary, a German press officer had just announced that decisions were made to hold a conference later that year on currency problems and to prepare for another conference on soaring interest rates.

"There was no agreement reached to hold a monetary conference while I or the president was in the room," Kissinger insisted.

"You seem to be leaving open an option," the reporter pressed.

"I believe this must be based on a misunderstanding of either the German press officer or the translation from the German," Kissinger replied. "No decision was reached to hold a particular conference . . . and I did not even hear a proposal that one should be held on currency."

That night while I was attending a large and loud press party at a Helsinki hotel ballroom, a waiter notified me that I had a phone call in the kitchen, in the banquet manager's office. It was Kissinger. He was concerned that his denial of any agreement on an international economic conference might be misunderstood. The Big Four leaders had agreed to explore the possibility of such a conference through private economists, Kissinger explained. Apparently worried that there were too many witnesses to the agreement for him to stick by his denial, Kissinger wanted me to straighten it out with the reporters.

Less than four months after Kissinger denied that Big Four leaders had agreed on an international economic conference, the conference took place in a château outside Paris.

One of my biggest clashes with Kissinger over the need for truthfulness with the press occurred aboard *Air Force One* on Ford's flight out of China after the Peking visit.

While I took a nap on the plane, Kissinger spent nearly two hours discussing the China visit with the pool reporters, James Naughton of the *New York Times*, John Roderick of the AP and Helen Thomas of the UPI. They typed up an eight-page report on Kissinger's remarks to hand out to the other reporters flying on the press plane. When Kissinger saw the report, he decided he had been too candid. He wanted some of his quotes attributed only to "a senior American official," and some of his remarks he didn't want quoted at all.

I was awakened and asked to solve the problem. Tired and grumpy, I complained to the pool reporters that they were cheating their colleagues out of valuable information by letting Kissinger censor his remarks. "You would never let *me* get away with this," I fumed. Indeed, it was an unwritten rule that the pool report was inviolate, not to be changed by White House officials.

Nevertheless, at the urging of Kissinger and Cheney, I went through the original report line by line with a felt-tip pen, excising entire paragraphs, removing quotation marks and eliminating attribution to Kissinger by name.

Naughton was especially anxious to have the revised version retyped before it was duplicated, so the other reporters would not see how much editing Kissinger had been allowed to do. But all the typists on *Air Force One* were busy, so I had to piece together the laundered pool report with scissors and tape before running it through the Xerox machine.

I thought I was on the right side of the argument, fighting for the dissemination of more information on the China trip and protesting the concealment of the source of the information. But several critical news reports appeared berating me and defending Kissinger. For example, John Osborne wrote in the *New Republic*,

"It most certainly was not the function, the place, the duty of the President's press secretary to object to deletions and to denounce reporters for agreeing to deletions that were in part intended to protect the President. According to reporters who were on the plane at the time, as I was not, it amounted to a display of venom that was shocking. . . ."

I like to think that most of my arguments with Kissinger were the result of my struggle to provide more news on foreign-policy developments for the press and public. But, I admit, some of our conflicts—including the one over the China pool report—resulted in part from a clash of personalities. Perhaps Kissinger and I were too much alike. We both had large egos. We both liked to put down critics with sarcastic wisecracks. And we both had a low tolerance for criticism.

Kissinger set off a flap in the press in January 1975 when he seemed to suggest in an interview with *Business Week* magazine that the United States might use military force in the Middle East to secure its oil supply. The interview reignited a rumor which had persisted in Washington for some time that the United States was planning to invade one or more Arab nations.

Several weeks before Kissinger talked to *Business Week*, Phil Shabecoff of the *New York Times* asked me to confirm that a meeting of the president's energy advisers at Camp David had discussed a "low-cost option," meaning an American invasion of the Middle East to seize the oil wells. I checked with Frank Zarb, head of the Federal Energy Administration. He said Michael Duval, a Domestic Council aide, had scratched on a note pad, "Let's go for the low-cost option," and passed it around the Camp David meeting as a joke. Everyone laughed, according to Zarb.

At my daily news briefings during that period I was asked repeatedly about the rumors of American plans to invade the Middle East. I gave an answer I had worked out with Ford—that the president knew of no plans for an invasion of an Arab oil nation. Actually, I was afraid that answer was too weak; it left the implication that, while the president did not know about any invasion plans, perhaps the Pentagon or the CIA did know.

Kissinger, however, thought it was too *strong*. He sent word to me through an aide that he was unhappy with my answer because he felt it would be interpreted as a firm denial of any American plans for military intervention in the Middle East. He wanted to leave some element of doubt about American plans in order to scare the Arabs.

Henry took care of that himself in the *Business Week* interview. He told the magazine: "I am not saying that there's no circumstance where we would not use force [against the Middle East oil nations] where there's some actual strangulation of the industrialized world."

Since Vietnam, any hint that the United States was considering military action anywhere produced a barrage of critical questions from the press. Knowing my briefing that day would be wild, I went over the anticipated questions about the Kissinger interview at length with the president. The most difficult question would be whether Ford agreed with Kissinger on using force in the Middle East. We searched for wording that would not put the president in the position of disowning Kissinger's statement, but would not embrace it too tightly, either.

The first thought was for me to repeat my previous statements that Ford knew of no contingency plans for a Middle East invasion. But that was rejected because it seemed to repudiate Kissinger. Rumsfeld suggested I say the president did not disagree with Kissinger. That was rejected because it seemed to align Ford too closely with Henry's saber rattling. Finally, the president agreed that I should say he considered Kissinger's statement to be a very highly qualified answer to a hypothetical question about some future contingency involving strangulation of the West, and he had nothing to add.

When I offered that fuzzy answer at my briefing later that morning, it confused the reporters. Different reporters interpreted it in different ways, as this excerpt shows:

Q.: Are you leaving us with the impression or would you want to leave us with the impression that the president did not necessarily agree with Secretary Kissinger?

NESSEN: He does not have anything to add on the subject.

Q.: It seems to me he is subscribing to Dr. Kissinger's statement by your reply.

NESSEN: Your colleague gets just the opposite impression.

Q.: Do you intend to leave it confused that way?

NESSEN: I intend to say that the president has nothing further to add on the subject. . . .

Q.: Would the president defy the United Nations Charter by invading another country?

NESSEN: . . . the president has nothing to add on the subject.

Later, when I read the transcript, I realized "stonewall" was the right word to describe my performance. But it had been necessary in order to avoid putting Ford in the position of either rejecting or accepting Henry's veiled invasion threat.

That afternoon, following a bill-signing ceremony in the East Room, Helen Thomas of the UPI cornered Kissinger.

"Were you slapped down by the president today?" she demanded.

"What do you mean, was I slapped down?" Kissinger responded.

I watched the exchange, worried that Henry would destroy my effort to keep Ford out of the controversy.

"Well, didn't he chew you out for saying that about war in the Middle East?" Thomas persisted.

"Oh, look," Kissinger declared, "I reflect the views of the president. I don't make major statements on foreign policy that do not reflect the views of the president."

Someone watching the scene in the East Room told me I made a face. No wonder. Kissinger had just swept away my carefully crafted statement designed to keep the president at arm's length from Henry's controversial views on a possible American invasion of the Middle East.

I walked over to Rumsfeld's office and told him what Kissinger had said.

"Oh, shit," Rumsfeld snapped in a rare outburst of profanity.

The final twist to Kissinger's Middle East invasion hint occurred when John Chancellor interviewed Ford live on NBC television in the living quarters of the White House on January 23, 1975. I almost fell off the camera case I was perched on when Chancellor asked the question:

"The *New Republic* this week has a story saying there are three American divisions being sent to the Middle East, or being prepared for the Middle East. We called the Pentagon and we got a confirmation on that, that one is air mobile, one is airborne and one is armor. It is a little unclear as to whether this is a contingency plan because we don't know where we would put the divisions in the Middle East. Could you shed any light on that?"

I could always tell when the president drew a blank on a subject raised in a press question. He would give a bland, cautious answer, but he would not flatly deny even the most farfetched allegation, just in case something was going on he hadn't heard about. When Chancellor asked his question, I could tell Ford knew of no American divisions going to the Middle East, but he answered equivocally:

FORD: I don't think I ought to talk about any particular military contingency plans, John. I think what I said concerning strangulation and Dr. Kissinger's statement is about as far as I ought to go.

CHANCELLOR: Then we have reached a point where another question would be unproductive on that?

FORD: I think you are right.

I was angry at Chancellor for putting Ford on the spot about the nonexistent Middle East invasion force. As soon as the program went off the air, I pulled Chancellor aside in the central hallway of the White House residence floor.

"You really are beating a dead horse on this Middle East war story," I told him. "Let me use a very blunt phrase: The press is jerking itself off with this story."

"No, no. This is serious," Chancellor replied. "We confirmed it with the Pentagon. Besides, if there is nothing to it, why does the president keep talking about it?"

"Why does the press keep asking about it?" I retorted. "Where did you get this story confirmed?"

"A young man in my office called the Pentagon and talked to a major, and the major confirmed it," Chancellor explained.

I found out the next day that the young man was a copy boy named Bob Dore who phoned the information desk at the Pentagon and talked to a major on duty. The major reiterated the army's previously announced plans to expand from thirteen divisions to sixteen. Dore somehow misunderstood this to mean that the three new divisions were being trained as a Middle East invasion force.

I became even angrier when I learned that this was the "confirmation" passed to Chancellor. I felt Chancellor had been irresponsible to ask the president a question on live national television about such an explosive subject based only on a copy boy's garbled conversation with a Pentagon information officer.

I knew we were going to have to knock down the invasion rumor once and for all. After the TV program, Ford told me flatly that no American expeditionary force was being organized. Secretary of Defense James Schlesinger called the speculation "bunkum." So, at my briefing the morning after the Chancellor interview, I issued an unequivocal denial without waiting for the question to come up:

"The United States is not creating any Middle East expeditionary force, it is not putting together three divisions to send to the Middle East, and the United States has no plans to develop any army divisions to send to the Middle East. . . . We are not trying to slip through any semantic loopholes on this. This is a clear, firm, hard answer."

That answer had the desired effect. On his news program that night Chancellor apologized for asking the question based on faulty information. And after that the Middle East invasion rumor gradually faded and died.

Looking back, I'm sure the Pentagon had contingency plans for military intervention in the Middle East if a new Arab oil embargo seriously threatened the economic collapse of the West.

I'm also sure that the rumors were kept alive by (1) Kissinger and others for the purpose of frightening the Arabs into a more cooperative attitude; and (2) reporters who were as anxious to spot another Vietnam as they were to spot another Watergate.

During one spate of Middle East invasion rumors, *New York* magazine ran on its cover a cartoon, in comic-book style, depicting Ford and Kissinger as battle-ready GIs storming ashore with guns blazing on some oil-rich beach. The dialogue balloon above the Ford-soldier read, "Are we gonna let these wogs kick sand in our faces?" and the headline screamed, "Would We Really Kill for Oil?"

I typed a note to Kissinger and attached it to the magazine cover: "The next time you want to send a message to the oil countries, mail them this picture and say, 'I'll see you soon.'" I showed it to Kissinger, whom I found getting a haircut in the White House barbershop.

He didn't think it was funny.

CHAPTER TWELVE

Self-Inflicted Wounds

My run-ins with Kissinger were not isolated episodes. I am appalled by the amount of time Ford's men devoted to fighting with, plotting against and leaking bad stories about each other. Friends from other administrations assure me that such jockeying goes on in every White House. I can't believe other administrations squandered as much effort on it as we did. During one particularly bad spate of staff feuding, I joked that when the Ford White House pulled its wagons into a circle, all the guns were pointed in.

Some news stories about staff infighting resulted from what Hartmann correctly identified as a tendency by reporters to reduce all situations to a conflict between two individuals. But there was plenty of real infighting, much of it stemming from personal ambition for power and position. Instead of helping and protecting a colleague who might be in trouble temporarily because of a mistake or because of criticism from outside, some members of Ford's staff took the opportunity to kick the colleague while he was down.

The staff fighting made Ford look like a president who could not select and inspire a united team.

The failure of Ford's staff to pull together smoothly and loyally was partly due to the fact that he came to the White House without a large group of tested aides dedicated to him. Most presidents reach the White House after years of campaigning, during which staff members demonstrate their abilities and find their proper places in the organization. Good aides are kept; the ones who don't measure up are dropped. Staff members develop loyalty and a personal relationship with the candidate and each other. Then, for the winning candidate, there is the two-and-a-half-month transition period to construct a White House organization, putting the members of his team into the jobs for which they have proven themselves best suited.

Ford did not have that luxury. He came to the White House literally overnight. At the last minute, a few friends secretly began planning a Ford presidency, but that was only days before Nixon resigned.

The Ford staff was made up of four separate groups which never completely melded into a unified team:

—Carry-overs from the Nixon administration (Henry Kissinger; Treasury Secretary William Simon; William Baroody, Jr., special assistant for public liaison; Max Friedersdorf, head of the Congressional Liaison Office; Jerry Jones, chief of scheduling; etc.)

—Old and trusted friends from Grand Rapids, the "Michigan Mafia" (Legal Counsel Philip Buchen; Economic Policy Coordinator William Seidman)

—Members of Ford's congressional and vice-presidential staffs (counsellors Robert Hartmann and John Marsh; Bill Roberts, assistant press secretary; Gwen Anderson, director of research)

—New people who had never worked for Ford before (Don Rumsfeld and his deputy, Richard Cheney; Ron Nessen; James Cannon, director of the Domestic Council; etc.)

Hartmann was a frequent target—and source—of staff sniping, dating from the anti-Haig campaign during Ford's first days in the White House. I felt sympathy for Hartmann, a baffled and frustrated man who had been the top assistant to Congressman Ford and Vice President Ford, but now was eclipsed by squads of competitors for power and position with President Ford.

In the spring of 1976, when Ford was in deep trouble in the primary elections, Hartmann told me he wished Ford were still vice president. "It was so much easier," he reminisced wistfully. "We had all the pleasure and all the pomp and circumstance, without any of the worries."

And without any rivals for Ford's attention, he might have added.

In the White House, however, Hartmann considered Rumsfeld a major rival. Rumsfeld's first move in this rivalry was to force Hartmann to "staff out" presidential speech drafts—i.e., to circulate the texts to the substantive offices such as the Domestic Council, National Security Council, Economic Policy Board, etc., for review and revision. Until then, Hartmann had operated casually, as in the old congressional and vice-presidential days, showing his drafts only to Ford.

Rumsfeld won an even more important early victory when he forced Hartmann to move out of an office close to the Oval Office. Following the dictum that proximity to the president is a sure measure of power, Hartmann at the outset of the Ford administration staked out for himself Rose Mary Wood's old office. It was small and had no view, but it was separated from the Oval Office by only a tiny presidential hideaway and it connected to the Oval Office by a private passageway. It allowed Hartmann to exercise what he called "peeking privileges," which meant he could peek into the Oval Office from the passageway and if Ford wasn't occupied he could slip in without going through the appointments secretary.

When Rumsfeld arrived, he took the large, sunny, southwest corner office formerly occupied by chiefs of staff Haig and H. R. Haldeman. Thus established, he almost immediately launched a scheme to exile Hartmann to the less prestigious second floor and take over for his own staff the entire south corridor between his office and the Oval Office, including Hartmann's coveted quarters.

Hartmann, of course, refused, and won the first skirmish with Rumsfeld. Within a few weeks, however, Rumsfeld triumphed. He convinced Ford himself to take over Hartmann's office as a private study. Hartmann could hardly refuse to move for the president.

Hartmann was shuttled to a large first-floor suite overlooking West Executive Avenue, formerly occupied by the congressional liaison officer. To reporters, I passed off the shift as a routine house-keeping matter designed to give Ford, Rumsfeld and Hartmann more room. But nobody in the White House or the press corps missed the significance of Hartmann's move, even if it was only a couple of dozen feet.

Shortly after that, Evans and Novak wrote a column highly critical of Rumsfeld, quoting "one old colleague" of Ford's as complaining that Don had not fulfilled the expectation that he would bring "imagination, ingenuity and managerial talent" to the White House. Many suspected that the complaint came from Hartmann, trying to get revenge.*

Despite Rumsfeld's occasional threat to take over jurisdiction

---

* Rumsfeld's deputy, Richard Cheney, also a frequent target of critical and sometimes inaccurate leaks to Evans and Novak, bitterly referred to the columnist team as "Errors and No-facts."

for speechwriting in the White House, Hartmann clung to his title as counsellor to the president and chief speechwriter throughout the Ford presidency, because of Ford's loyalty to longtime employees. However, the writing operation was so unreliable that other staff members were quietly recruited to produce presidential speeches and statements. Hartmann also eventually lost his duties as political liaison with the Republican National Committee and with Republican members of Congress, and he played no role in the 1976 election campaign other than writing some speeches.

Another White House staff feud broke out in January 1975 when another Evans and Novak column reported that Treasury Secretary William Simon disagreed with Ford's antirecession program, was horrified by the size of the anticipated budget deficit and might argue against the program when called to testify by Congress.

My immediate problem was that Simon was scheduled to be the chief speaker at a series of briefings to explain the program to the press. I was concerned that most of the questions would focus on Simon's support or nonsupport, rather than on the details of the program. Rumsfeld encouraged me to substitute William Seidman, director of Ford's Economic Policy Board, at the briefings.

I also sent Rumsfeld a memo complaining that Simon's Treasury Department was dragging its feet in preparing charts and fact sheets for press kits on the antirecession program. Rumsfeld rushed the memo to Ford. I suspected he was using the relatively minor logistics problem to snipe at Simon.

After the Evans and Novak column appeared, Rumsfeld made comments in private which I interpreted as a signal that Simon might be on his way out. I felt Rumsfeld was working against him. Some Ford aides believed Rumsfeld wanted Simon's job. Those aides were convinced that before Rumsfeld came to the White House he exacted a promise from Ford to appoint him secretary of state, defense or treasury, whichever opened up first.

A day or so after the Evans and Novak column on Simon appeared, I wandered into the press room, where I ran into Helen Thomas of the UPI. She had a way of blurting out questions about ticklish situations bluntly and with no preliminaries.

"Is Bill Simon leaving?" Helen demanded.

"Well," I began—and then paused to choose my words carefully I'd heard nothing specific about Simon being fired or resigning, but I thought I'd picked up vibes that he was in trouble. Ford seemed irritated with him and Rumsfeld clearly was.

My pause went on longer and longer as I tried to figure out the best way to answer Helen's question.

Finally she declared, "Oh, that's a very significant pause."

From my long pause, she wrote a 400-word story for the UPI wire which began, "Treasury Secretary William Simon is expected to leave the Cabinet soon, it was learned Wednesday. White House officials indicated that Simon lost out as one of President Ford's top economic advisers. . . ."

I'd known I could get in trouble by saying the wrong thing. That episode taught me I also could get in trouble by not saying anything!

As soon as Helen's story hit the wire, Simon phoned me and demanded a strong statement of support from the president. I told him I would make Ford aware of his request. When I hung up, I went to Rumsfeld's office and told him of Simon's call. Together, Rumsfeld and I marched to the Oval Office to inform the president.

Taking my usual chair on the left side of Ford's desk, I asked him how he wanted me to handle Helen Thomas's report that Simon was leaving and Simon's demand for a presidential endorsement.

Ford's immediate reaction was that I should tell the reporters he had never talked to Simon about leaving and had no plans to.

"Wait a minute," Rumsfeld cut in from the other side of the desk. "We don't want to go that far, do we?"

After a discussion in which Rumsfeld seemed to try to steer the president away from a firm commitment to Simon and Ford appeared uncertain about how strong he wanted his support to be, I was finally authorized to tell the press only that the president had not talked to Simon about resigning.

When I gave that answer at my next briefing, every newsman in town recognized a halfhearted endorsement when he heard one. After the briefing, several reporters came to my office to sort out what was going on. Frankly, I told them off the record, I didn't know for sure who was doing what to whom. But I probably led the reporters to believe Simon was leaving by thinking out loud about possible scenarios.

Maybe, I suggested, Simon was planning to leave anyhow, or anticipated being fired, and was himself the source of the stories that he opposed Ford's antirecession program, in an effort to shine up his conservative credentials before returning to Wall Street.

Or, I speculated, maybe Rumsfeld or others in the White House were out to get Simon and were using his opposition to Ford's economic program as a club to drive him out of the cabinet.

Several reporters interpreted my speculation as a deliberate tip-off that Simon was on his way out.

That evening Rumsfeld summoned me to his office. He appeared to be in an ugly mood. He had received a call from the respected columnist Charles Bartlett, who was agitated over the Simon affair. Another reporter had passed on to Bartlett my speculation about Simon leaving. Bartlett told Rumsfeld he had never seen such an "assassination" of a public figure. If Simon was "gunned down," he said, Ford's economic and energy programs would be in great trouble. Bartlett threatened to write a column charging that Rumsfeld, Hartmann and Nessen were trying to squeeze Simon out, Rumsfeld because he wanted to be treasury secretary.

Rumsfeld glared at me across the polished conference table in his office and accused me of spreading anti-Simon stories. I denied that my uninformed thinking-out-loud justified the press speculation that Simon was on his way out. Whatever the source, the Simon rumors had gotten out of hand.

"What do we have to do to straighten it out?" Rumsfeld asked.

"First of all, we have to determine what the president really wants to do," I replied. "If he wants Simon to stay, we have to issue a very strong statement containing all the right code words so the reporters will know he really means it."

"Does the president really want him to stay?" asked Cheney, who had wandered into Rumsfeld's office during the conversation.

Rumsfeld said he was seeing Ford shortly and would get an answer from the president.

The next morning, during a further discussion of the Simon matter in the Oval Office, Ford directed me to issue a strong statement affirming his intention to keep Simon:

"The president has assured Secretary Simon that he wants him to continue as secretary of the treasury. The president has not asked and has no intention of asking him to leave."

I phoned Bartlett and read him the statement. The columnist was still livid over what he thought was a Rumsfeld-Hartmann-Nessen effort to dump Simon.

"I have never seen a guy who was machine-gunned like this," Bartlett declared. "Hand grenades were thrown at him. It was a total assassination."

I still don't know what really happened.

Had Simon contrived to win a public vote of confidence from

Ford? Had Rumsfeld tried to oust Simon so he could become treasury secretary? Had someone in the White House tried to scare Simon back into line after his Evans and Novak threat to oppose the president's economic program? Or had I, by misreading what I interpreted as halfhearted presidential support and Rumsfeld opposition, inadvertently led reporters to think Simon was on his way out?

Cheney surmised that the Republican congressional leaders, Senator Hugh Scott and Congressman John Rhodes, might have been responsible for the Simon-is-leaving stories. Scott and Rhodes were in the Oval Office when Ford phoned Simon and told him forcefully that he must support the antirecession program. Cheney suggested that Scott and Rhodes, having overheard that conversation, might have spread the word among reporters that Simon was in trouble with the president.

The day I issued the president's statement of support for Simon, Rumsfeld assured me, "In a month I'll tell you what really happened."

He never did. Relations between Rumsfeld and Simon remained cool.

There was one footnote to the Simon affair. Several weeks after it was resolved, Eileen Shanahan, then an economics writer for the *New York Times* and later the press spokesman for President Carter's HEW Department, informed me that Simon had told her off the record that he would resign and join George Wallace and Ronald Reagan to fight government spending if Ford's budget deficit went over $40 billion.

The feuding among Ford's staffers continued throughout his presidency. Cheney once blamed Lyn Nofziger, Reagan's hardball political aide, for spreading some of the stories about fighting among Ford staff members. But we didn't need any outside help. Almost every week someone was squabbling with someone else in the Ford White House.

Rumsfeld tried, but failed, to persuade Ford not to select several close Rockefeller associates for the top jobs on the Domestic Council. Rockefeller later accused Rumsfeld of trying to drive a wedge between him and the president, and he accused me of doing Rumsfeld's "dirty work."

Rumsfeld grumbled that he could stamp out the staff fighting and make the White House run smoothly if Ford gave him more power as chief of staff. As it was, Rumsfeld had enough authority that some White House aides half-kiddingly referred to him as "a smiling Haldeman."

Rumsfeld once canceled my daily meeting with the president for two weeks while Ford recovered from a bad cold. When the meeting did not appear on Ford's schedule for the third week, after Ford was well again, I informed Rumsfeld I would not hold any more press briefings until my daily sessions with the president were restored. I threatened to tell the reporters why. I got my meeting back.

Even Ford's son Jack got into the squabbling, once complaining during an angry two-hour meeting in my office that inept members of the staff were responsible for bad speeches, bad scheduling, bad events and bad press coverage of the president.

"I wonder how people around here can go home at night and sleep when they realize they are letting my father down," Jack declared.

"I don't have any trouble when I go home and get in bed," I replied with some heat, "because I work down here sixteen or eighteen hours a day for your father and I'm pretty well tired out."

When Ford finally decided to reshuffle his staff and cabinet, it was a blockbuster.

The president was confined to his residence for several days in October 1975, suffering from a cold and sinus infection. The enforced inactivity and isolation gave him the rare leisure to consider the people who worked for him and to mull over advice he'd received about staff problems.

Immediately after Nixon's resignation, Ford had followed a recommendation from his transition team that he demonstrate continuity of policy and personnel in the sensitive areas of foreign relations, intelligence and defense. Now, after more than a year in the White House, Ford concluded it was time to place his own imprint clearly on the Pentagon, CIA and National Security Council.

Alone in the family room of his living quarters, Ford made his decisions:

—James Schlesinger would be fired as secretary of defense, replaced by Rumsfeld. Dick Cheney would be promoted to Rumsfeld's White House staff-coordinator job.

—William E. Colby would be fired as director of the CIA, replaced by George Bush, America's representative in Peking.

—Kissinger would be stripped of his White House post as national security adviser, but would remain as secretary of state. His deputy, Air Force General Brent Scowcroft, would be promoted to the top NSC job.

—Elliot Richardson would be brought back from his post as ambassador to England to become commerce secretary, replacing Rogers C. B. Morton, stepping down because of poor health and because he wanted to devote time to Ford's election campaign.

—Rockefeller would announce that he would not run for vice president in 1976.

Ford told only a few people about his plan, including Kissinger, Rumsfeld and Cheney, but not Schlesinger. He wanted to spring it on the nation as a surprise the following week. But by Saturday, November 1, 1975, five days before Ford intended to make his announcement, *Newsweek* had stumbled onto the Kissinger and Schlesinger parts of the shake-up.

Within hours, other reporters picked up rumors of these changes and phoned me at home that Saturday night requesting confirmation. But I knew almost nothing about the shake-up at that point because Ford had kept it a secret, even from most of the people involved. I phoned Rumsfeld late that night to ask his advice on how to handle the press questions. Rumsfeld told me to be careful of my credibility, to inform newsmen that I didn't know what was going to happen with personnel changes, but not to deny the rumors.

While I was talking to Rumsfeld on a White House phone on my bedside table, my private, unlisted phone rang. Thinking it was a relative or personal friend who knew my unlisted number, I lifted the receiver off the hook and placed it on the floor beside the bed while I finished my conversation with Rumsfeld. When I finally picked up the private call, I found it was Thomas DeFrank, White House correspondent for *Newsweek*, phoning to check on the Kissinger and Schlesinger rumors. He claimed he hadn't overheard anything useful from my end of the Rumsfeld call.

Colby was summoned to the Oval Office at 8 o'clock the next morning, Sunday, November 2, 1975, to receive his news. He was offered an ambassadorship, but declined. He accepted his dismissal like a gentleman. Colby had not been implicated by the congressional investigations of CIA wrongdoing, but Ford felt a new face in the top post at the CIA, his own choice, would help restore public confidence in the agency.

Schlesinger was next, at 8:30 A.M. He did not take his dismissal graciously. The meeting was difficult.

Schlesinger was fired because he rubbed Ford the wrong way. The dislike dated from Ford's days in Congress. The president was uncomfortable working with Schlesinger, resented Schlesinger's habit of lecturing him like a professor and worried that Schlesinger's disdainful attitude toward Congress could endanger the Pentagon's legislative program.

Much later, at a Christmas party less than a month before leaving the White House, Ford confided to some friends that he found Schlesinger "peculiar . . . strange . . . hard to get along with."

Within an hour after notifying Colby and Schlesinger of their dismissals, Ford flew to Jacksonville, Florida, to confer with visiting Egyptian President Anwar Sadat, still keeping the personnel shake-up a secret from the public.

While Ford and Sadat lunched on red snapper and avocado on the roof of a stucco boathouse at an estate overlooking the St. Johns River, Cheney and Marsh closed themselves into a tiny makeshift office on the estate and began running through a checklist written on a yellow legal pad, notifying people and making arrangements to announce Ford's mass reshuffling.

After the Sadat lunch, Ford motored to a borrowed private home alongside a golf course, where the notification and planning process continued. By then I'd been informed of the changes.

It was a chaotic afternoon of constant meetings and phone calls, punctuated by a swim in the backyard pool, during which Ford raised a welt on his temple when he dove into the shallow bottom. A TV set was kept tuned to an exciting football game between the Washington Redskins and the Dallas Cowboys.

More and more reporters were picking up parts of the story and demanding confirmation, especially after *Newsweek* issued a press release announcing its scoop. When Ford walked to a nearby house in the late afternoon for a second conference with Sadat, he was bombarded with press questions. Mostly he ignored them, once smiling, "I love you all."

My own answer to questions about the personnel shake-up, worked out in advance, was, "I don't have anything on it." And when Kissinger arrived for the meeting, his answer to the reporters was, "Hi, how are you?"

At the end of the meeting, as the participants departed, the questions and nonanswers were repeated. Openness and candor were sacrificed temporarily because Ford wanted to stick to his plan to announce all the changes at a news conference.

Flying back to Washington that night, Cheney, Marsh and I discussed the likely reaction to Ford's announcement, now moved up to the following evening because of the leaks.

I thought Kissinger might be perceived as the winner in a power struggle with Schlesinger, especially since Scowcroft would appear to be Henry's handpicked successor in the White House national security adviser's job. Marsh agreed, saying he had "broken his pick" arguing against announcing the Scowcroft appointment right away but had been overruled by Ford.

I suggested that the Schlesinger and Colby dismissals might seem to be a victory for Kissinger and other soft-liners against hard-liners in the administration's relations with the Soviet Union. I also worried that the president would be suspected of dumping Rocke-feller to appease conservative Republicans in the contest with Reagan.

All these concerns came true in the weeks ahead.

On the flight home, Marsh commented that Ford would appear to be springing a highly dramatic move in a precipitous manner, without consulting anyone and without even notifying his own staff until the last minute. Marsh said it might remind people of the pardon.

In fact, Ford did make the personnel decision and the pardon decision in a similar, secretive manner. He seemed to be following a pattern of acting alone and instinctively on important matters about which he had strong personal feelings.

As Ford ducked out of the helicopter that Sunday night on the south lawn of the White House at the end of the Florida trip, he exclaimed in a tone of anticipation, "It's going to be a big day tomorrow!"

The day began with a morning meeting between the president and the vice president. I was called in at the end and handed a letter from Rockefeller to Ford saying, "After much thought, I have decided . . . that I do not wish my name to enter your consideration for the upcoming Republican Vice Presidential nominee." I also was handed a short statement saying Rockefeller "acted on his own initiative."

Ford told Rockefeller at the end of their meeting, "Nelson, you're a hell of a team player."

Many reporters thought Rockefeller had been pushed, rather than that he jumped. Actually, it was some of both. Rockefeller had been irritated for some time by statements from Howard "Bo" Callaway, then the chairman of the Ford election campaign, and others suggesting that the vice president was a political liability in Ford's fight with Ronald Reagan for the GOP nomination, especially in the conservative South. Ford did not disavow the statements or reprimand Callaway.

Rockefeller finally decided: Who needs it? At his stage in life, after a long and distinguished career of public service, with wealth and honors, he refused to let himself be nibbled to death by people he considered moral and political midgets.

With Rockefeller's decision revealed, Ford announced the rest of his personnel shake-up that evening at a news conference in the East Room of the White House, broadcast to the country by television. Facing dozens of reporters fanned out before him in delicate gold chairs, the president explained the personnel changes, repeating again and again that his primary purpose was to place his "own team" in the key foreign-policy and national-security posts of his administration.

Press suspicions about hidden motives for some of the changes had sprung up with the first leaks to *Newsweek* and had flourished for three days, unrestrained by an official explanation. Consequently, at the news conference, Ford was put on the defensive, forced to deny rumors and speculation. Many of the questions focused on Kissinger and Rockefeller.

Q.: The vice president, by his action today, sacrificed himself on your political behalf, and have you in any way urged him to do so?

FORD: The decision by Vice President Rockefeller was a decision on his own. . . .

Q.: Mr. President, could you tell us why Mr. Schlesinger and Mr. Colby did not fit on your new team?

FORD: I think any president has to have the opportunity to put together his own team. They were kept on when I assumed office because I wanted continuity, but any president to do the job that is needed and necessary has to have his own team. . . .

Q.: There are reports . . . that Secretary Schlesinger was in conflict with your attitude on detente and with Secretary Kissinger's. Can you address yourself to that?

FORD: There are no basic differences. I wanted the team I have selected . . . and I have it. . . .

Q.: Did you ask for suggestions or did you do this largely on your own?

FORD: I did it totally on my own. It was my decision. I fitted the pieces together and they fitted excellently.

Q.: Mr. President, with all due respect, you have been talking about your desire to make your own team, but in fact, you have replaced half the team and you have not replaced the other half. Mr. Kissinger and Mr. Scowcroft are really part of someone else's team who you have elected to keep. It seems to me that you have not answered the question. . . .

FORD: I have affirmatively answered the question by saying I wanted my own team. . . .

One reason Ford had trouble convincing suspicious reporters was that his manner at the news conference was uncharacteristically gruff. He snapped out terse answers, sometimes only a few words or a sentence. His answers were so short that there was time for nearly twice as many questions as normal at the news conference. He gave the same explanation again and again—that he wanted his own team and that Rockefeller's letter needed no elaboration.

The shake-up was supposed to demonstrate that Ford had a firm hand on the helm of government. He should have won plaudits for his sweeping plan to place his own selections in major administration jobs. But because of premature leaks and unchecked speculation, it ended up looking like another sloppy example of White House ineptness, another case of high-level staff jockeying.

The press labeled it "The Sunday-Night Massacre."

Over the next few weeks there were endless articles, TV stories, columns and editorials suggesting there must have been more to the shake-up than met the eye. Rumsfeld was often named as the one who secretly put Ford up to it, on the theory that Don got his rival, Kissinger, out of the White House; got his rival, Bush, out of contention for the 1976 Republican vice-presidential nomination; and got himself a cabinet post.

Ford and Rumsfeld repeatedly denied this speculation.

A week after the big announcement, facing more suspicious questions about the reshuffle on NBC's "Meet the Press," the president told the panel that the simple truth doesn't always seem to be the truth because it's so simple.

"I told the simple truth," he declared.

The departure of Rumsfeld brought a pleasant improvement in the relationship among White House staff members. Three weeks after the shake-up I wrote a note to myself: "There has been a real change at the White House since Rumsfeld left, a change of mood, almost like a fresh breeze blowing through."

Cheney, as the new White House staff coordinator, was far more easygoing, at least at first. He did not create a mood of rivalry. Other members of the staff relaxed and let their guard down. Hartmann even started coming to senior staff meetings, which he had boycotted when his rival, Rumsfeld, was in charge. More staff members found they could spend more time with Ford.

Rumsfeld's departure solved a Press Office personnel problem for me. He took with him, as chief Pentagon spokesman, my deputy William Greener, a beefy, florid-faced career government and military press officer who was a favorite drinking companion of many reporters. Greener had served as Rumsfeld's press spokesman at several other government agencies. When I appointed him my deputy, some reporters wrote that he would look out for Rumsfeld's interests in the Press Office, and within a few months after Greener came to my staff, stories began to appear suggesting he would soon take my job. For instance, Richard Reeves, in *New York* magazine, quoted Rumsfeld as saying I was on my way out, quoted Greener as saying he would be my replacement and further quoted Rumsfeld as saying Greener wasn't good enough, that he wanted David Broder for press secretary.

"Absolute bullshit," Rumsfeld exclaimed when I confronted him with the article.

Other members of my staff informed me that Greener was telling White House reporters privately that he would soon take over as press secretary. When I questioned him about this, he denied it—sort of.

"If people ask me, I always tell them I'm available," Greener explained.

Some loyalty.

I wasn't sorry to see Greener go to the Pentagon.

Ford must share some of the responsibility for the staff fighting that went on throughout his presidency. He was too much Mr. Nice Guy.

Once in a while, though, Ford did indicate to his staff that he was unhappy about the squabbling and the news leaks about the squabbling. After less than two months as president, already aware that feuding and leaking by the staff were undermining his administration, Ford appeared at a meeting of his senior aides in the Roosevelt Room and declared, "I'm damn sick and tired of a ship that has such leaky seams. We are being drowned by premature and obvious leaks." During one upsurge of stories that Kissinger was losing his power, Ford pounded his desk and told a group of aides, "Goddamn it, I don't want any more of this." He threatened "dire consequences" for anyone who leaked stories against Kissinger.

But such blowups were rare. It wasn't Ford's manner to get tough, to stop the feuding and to fire those staff members who deserved to be fired.

The president acknowledged his weakness. Thomas DeFrank of *Newsweek* once asked Ford in an interview what he considered his greatest flaw.

"I'm probably too easygoing on people that work for me . . . I tend to overlook," Ford replied. "I don't get angry and stomp my feet and swear at people. Some people take that to mean that I'm too easygoing."

A man who worked for Nixon and wished he could have worked for Ford once commented to me: "With Nixon, you had to try to save him from his worst instincts. With Ford, you have to try to save him from his best instincts."

How can you get mad at a president who's too nice for his own good?

CHAPTER THIRTEEN

"Saturday Night" Live

Gerald Ford's biggest continuing problem in the White House —and mine, as the overseer of his press relations—was the portrayal of him in the media as a bumbler. This false image was perpetuated by news reports, photographs and TV film clips that magnified every presidential stumble. Alleged physical clumsiness was subtly translated into suggestions of mental ineptitude. Such ridicule in the press and on television undermined public respect for Ford as a leader and damaged his chances in the 1976 election. After all, no one wants a clown for president.

Ford was depicted, literally, as Bozo the Clown in a retouched photo on the cover of *New York* magazine. Chevy Chase, an unknown television comedian, became a household word by doing pratfalls in supposed imitation of Ford. The normally responsible *Washington Post* described Ford as "Our Top Fall-Down Comic" in a headline over a column by Nicholas von Hoffman referring to the president as "The Great Flub-Dub." Ford's alleged clumsiness was a regular topic of Johnny Carson's monologue. Even good reporters asked Ford whether he was smart enough to be president. And so on and on.

It was a sorry and mindless performance by the press. The idea that Ford was a not-very-bright klutz was just plain wrong, a false image spread by herd journalism at its worst.

In his sixties, Ford was a youthful, graceful, athletic man, still competently skiing, golfing, swimming and playing tennis. He had finished in the top third of a brilliant Yale Law School class which produced two Supreme Court justices, a secretary of state, a secretary of the army, a governor of Pennsylvania, a mayor of Philadelphia, a senator, etc.

Ford possessed a vast amount of practical knowledge and an intellect that could quickly absorb details of complex issues. At a thousand congressional meetings, Ford's specialty was picking his way through the budgets of the Pentagon, State Department and CIA. He considered this expertise to be the best training for the presidency. As a member of the House, Ford was invited to share his knowledge in seminars at the Aspen Institute, the University of Chicago, Kissinger's classes at Harvard, and elsewhere. After leaving the White House, Ford received invitations from 800 colleges to lecture or teach.

And yet, Ford could never shake the doubts about his intelligence, planted by Lyndon Johnson's malicious remarks that he played football too often without his helmet and that he was too dumb to walk and chew gum at the same time.*

Probably no other president was asked by reporters so often and so publicly to defend his mental competence for the office, beginning at the very outset of his administration. In Ford's first TV interview as president, Harry Reasoner of ABC told him a major public criticism was that "you have not got the magnitude of the grasp of the presidency. . . . Can you grow in this job, sir?"

Ford patiently recited his educational background and his twenty-five years of experience in Congress.

Reasoner followed by asking Ford about his ability to handle foreign policy, ending with the condescending question, "You are aware there is a world out there?" (ABC protected Reasoner's reputation by editing that question out of the broadcast.)

In Ford's next TV interview, live on NBC, Tom Brokaw hemmed and hawed, stammered and stuttered, but finally came out with it: "I have a question that isn't easy to phrase, so I will just bore straight ahead with it. As you know, I'm certain, because I have been told that you have commented on this before, but it has been speculated on in print not only in Washington but elsewhere and it crops up in conversation from time to time in this town—the question of whether or not you are intellectually up to the job of being president of the United States."

My inclination would have been to snap, "I'm smart enough to

---

* Political reporter Richard Reeves, in his book *A Ford, Not a Lincoln*, claims that Johnson's actual remark was, "Jerry Ford is so dumb he can't fart and chew gum at the same time."

be president. Are you smart enough to be a reporter?" But Ford, ever earnest, again reiterated his academic record and his knowledge accumulated in a quarter-century of public service.

By asking the president repeatedly to defend his intelligence, reporters in effect forced Ford to declare again and again, "Your president is no dummy."

Members of the White House staff were not without blame in perpetuating the myth that Ford was a dullard. Describing to journalists their role in briefing Ford for major decisions or overseas trips, staff members often made it sound like they were giving Ford a cram course, as if they were tutoring a backward schoolboy. Particularly bothersome to me were the stories suggesting that Ford was learning foreign policy at the feet of Henry Kissinger.

Whenever the president made an especially impressive appearance, the effect was frequently diluted by Ford staff members who rushed to tell reporters what a great job they had done coaching and rehearsing Ford, as if he were a brainless puppet they had to manipulate.

Poor planning by Spanish officials during an overseas tour by Ford in May 1975 was indirectly responsible for the episode which assured that the president would never be able to shed his reputation for clumsiness. For Ford's overnight stay in Madrid, the Spanish provided a narrow, short bed unsuitable for the president's tall, husky build. After repeated demands by the White House advance team for a bigger bed, the Spanish grudgingly agreed only to place a second bed next to the first. But the second bed was several inches higher than the first!

Ford tossed and turned and hardly slept at all that night because of the two-tier beds and a hard, round, European-style pillow. Consequently, when he arrived in Salzburg, Austria, the following day on the next leg of his trip, he was very tired. With fatigue compounding the usual stiffness in his knees from old football injuries, and the ramp slick from rain, Ford tripped and fell on the stairs descending from *Air Force One*, in full view of the reporters and cameras of the world.

Later that day there was another incident which furthered the impression among the press that Ford was ungainly. Ford's foot slid twice on a long, rain-slick staircase at the Residenz Palace in Salzburg when he arrived for conferences with Egyptian President Sadat.

That night, while I was attending a banquet given for Ford by

Austrian Chancellor Kreisky, I was summoned out of the dining hall to take a phone call from the White House press center across town in a Salzburg hotel. One of my assistants informed me that reporters were bombarding the Press Office staff with questions about the president's missteps. My assistant described some of the newsmen as nearly hysterical in their demands for more information and in their suggestions that something was wrong with the president.

As soon as the banquet was over, I drove to the press center and called the reporters together for a briefing which I hoped would calm the excitement over Ford's stumbles. The briefing was a classic example of the White House press corps losing all perspective on a minor matter:

Q.: This is serious. We are really concerned.

NESSEN: About what?

Q.: Apparently with the fall this morning there were several missteps this evening.

Q.: Colonel Blake [Lieutenant Colonel Robert Blake, Ford's air force aide] is aware of the misstep going up the steps and the misstep coming down the steps. Is it possible we could have Colonel Blake in to brief us?

NESSEN: I know you are kidding. . . .

Q.: Has Dr. Lukash examined him?

Q.: We would like to know if the president is really tired. Is there something he is misgauging? Is his balance off because he is exhausted?

NESSEN: No. The president is tired. I am tired. I assume you are tired.

Q.: You said he never got tired.

NESSEN: I don't remember saying that. . . .

Q.: Does the White House feel this incident is being overplayed?

NESSEN: I don't think the White House ever comments on news coverage.

Of course the president's slips in Salzburg were overplayed, and were exaggerated in some accounts. A UPI reporter originally wrote that Ford "toppled over and, for a moment, lay spread-eagled at the bottom of the airplane ramp," although photos showed Ford landed on both hands and one knee and straightened up almost immediately. An AP story, suggesting that Ford was barely saved from tumbling down twenty steps at the Residenz Palace, also was exaggerated. On CBS the slips were escalated into "a minor controversy over the president's physical condition."

There was a final story in the *Washington Post*, nearly a week later, an 800-word article on Ford's knee problem, illustrated with an anatomical diagram of a knee. The Great Salzburg Stumbling Episode then faded from the news.

But the image of Ford as a klutz would never fade away after that. After Salzburg, the press seemed to keep a special watch to catch and transmit every presidential stumble, real and imagined, physical and verbal. Any incident that supported the image was reported and filmed: Ford wrapped in the leashes of his frisky dogs; Ford bumping his head on the door of a helicopter; Ford locked out of his own news conference by a broken door handle; Ford falling down on skis.

They were the kind of everyday minor mishaps that befall everyone, but when they happened to Ford, cameras were always trained on him. Unbelievably, ABC once phoned me and asked whether the White House had any film footage of Ford bumbles to fill out a TV documentary on presidential bloopers.

The notion that Ford was a clumsy clod became so ingrained that some reporters considered it news when Ford did not stumble, as when Bob Schieffer of CBS reported that a campaign trip was "remarkably free of gaffes." Some were also disappointed. Tom Sharrock, for example, of the Lawton, Oklahoma, *Morning Press*, wrote, "I kept wishing the president would bump his head or skin his shins or suffer some small mishap for me to peg a paragraph on."

My first open confrontation with the press over its continuing portrayal of Ford as a bumbler occurred at Vail, Colorado, during Ford's skiing vacation there at Christmas 1975. Ford was rated as an advanced intermediate skier, a real accomplishment for a man in his sixties with bad knees. But like all skiers, at whatever level of ability, Ford occasionally took a spill. During that vacation, photos and films of him falling on the slopes were splashed on front pages showing Ford skiing down a mountain backward while an on- and evening news shows. The *Denver Post* ran a political cartoon looker commented, "I guess he learned to ski from the same people running his campaign."

One night at a party during that Vail stay, I asked Dick Cheney whether he had any ideas on how to combat the unending flow of photos, news stories, cartoons and jokes portraying Ford as a clumsy dimwit. Cheney replied that in private meetings and interviews with reporters he let them know he was angry about the inaccurate image of the president being portrayed in the press. He suggested that I also express anger in background sessions with newsmen.

The next morning I wandered into the press room and found half a dozen reporters sipping coffee and reading the Sunday newspapers. Many of the papers carried photos of Ford taking a tumble while skiing, and naturally the conversation turned to Ford's supposed clumsiness. Thinking I was chatting informally (but without explicitly putting my remarks off the record), I decided to try Cheney's suggestion. I told the reporters that stories portraying Ford as a bumbler were "the most unconscionable misrepresentation of the president. . . . The president is healthy, graceful, and he is by far the most athletic president in memory," I added.

It was a Sunday, there was no other news for the White House press corps, and thus my little informal complaint became a lead story. (The episode demonstrated the wisdom of the admonition one of my assistants had hanging on his office wall, "Don't screw up on a slow news day.") My comments set off a flood of articles, editorials and columns in publications ranging from *Forbes* to the Cherokee, Iowa, *Daily Times*. Art Buchwald wrote a funny column suggesting I explain that the president fell deliberately at Vail "so all the photographers would get the only picture they had made the trip for."

Perhaps the nicest comment was written by society columnist Betty Beale in the *Washington Star*. She said she had danced with all the recent presidents and found Ford the most graceful. She said Chancellor, Brokaw and Cronkite couldn't know how graceful Ford was because they had never danced with him. The president phoned and thanked her.

Initially, the reaction of the White House senior staff to my public complaint was almost 100 percent negative. They felt it merely called attention to the klutz image. However, within a few days that judgment softened when a number of editorials and columns appeared supporting me and chastising newsmen for overdoing the clumsy bit.

Still, by creating a new public controversy over Ford's physical and mental abilities, I felt I had mishandled a matter which, as

Cheney suggested, should have been discussed with reporters quietly and privately. So, on the flight home from Vail I told Ford that perhaps he needed a new press secretary who matched his own cool temperament and relaxed relationship with the press. I told him I was willing to resign if I was an embarrassment to him.

"I think you're doing a great job and I'm happy with what you are doing," he replied, patting me on the leg. "You just go and do what you think is best and ignore all this criticism."

Ford usually kept his resentment over being depicted as a clumsy clod hidden. But it bubbled to the surface during and after that 1975 winter vacation in Vail. Over a New Year's Eve drink in the dining room of his rented Vail chalet, Ford complained bitterly to me that many reporters half his age who were making fun of his ski spills got most of their exercise on barstools and couldn't make it down the beginner's slope.

In an interview with Lou Cannon and David Broder of the *Washington Post* on the flight back to Washington from Colorado on *Air Force One*, Ford declared, "I think it is an inaccurate depiction. . . . Most of the critics . . . have never played in a ball game, never skied. I don't know whether it is a self-defense mechanism in themselves or what, but I'm kind of amused at that. It doesn't bother me at all."

The next day, in a year-end interview with a score of reporters in the Oval Office, Ford dropped the pretense that the stories didn't bother him.

"Some of the things you read or hear or see, you know, it kind of hurts your pride a little bit because you know it isn't true," Ford told the reporters. "You have to be a little thick-skinned, and I think that comes from some experience."

Most reporters attributed my outburst at Vail to the news photos of Ford falling on the ski run. That was not correct. I boiled over because of a Tom Braden column. He began by quoting a Johnny Carson joke, that Timex wanted Ford for a commercial showing the president strapping on a watch and walking down the steps.

"It's a clear signal," Braden wrote, "when . . . comedians begin to treat a serious politician as a joke, he is through."

What disturbed me about the Braden column was that he correctly pointed out the political danger to Ford of the bumbler image, because it suggested mental and executive incompetence as well as physical clumsiness.

For example, in a year-end assessment of Ford broadcast by

CBS from Vail, correspondent Bob Pierpoint offered the view that skiing falls and other mishaps damaged the president's standing "because I think they have been almost symbolic of the Ford administration. It has stumbled. . . . That kind of thing has indicated that Mr. Ford is not always adept at handling himself both physically and politically."

On the same program, Bob Schieffer put his finger squarely on the real issue involved in Ford's public image: "I think that one of the main problems Mr. Ford had, from a political standpoint, was he had to demonstrate to the country that he was of presidential timber."

As the 1976 election year approached, the Ford campaign pollster, Robert Teeter, found in his surveys that Ford's public image had created doubts about his "Presidential timber." Teeter wrote in a memo a year before the election, "The President . . . gets mediocre or relatively poor ratings [for] being competent, strong, intelligent and a strong leader. . . . He needs to appear more Presidential. . . . Appearing more Presidential should help to improve his perception as being knowledgeable and competent."

In an effort to minimize news photos and TV film of Ford in unpresidential poses, we cut back Ford's attendance at public events involving football and other sports, curtailed pictures of him in such cutesy activities as playing with his dogs, and even skipped press coverage of the presentation of the annual White House Thanksgiving turkey. I also raised the ire of the press by banning photographers and cameramen from the south lawn, where they often caught the 6′2″ president bumping his head on the 5′9″ doorway of his helicopter.

But these tactics did not help Ford much to appear more presidential in the newspapers and on TV. The press, and especially television, invoked a maddening Catch-22: Many of Ford's most presidential actions and statements were not reported; or when they were, they were often described as calculated to "act" presidential.

The difficulty of meeting press demands that Ford prove himself presidential when his truly presidential activities were all but ignored was illustrated by television's near-blackout of Ford's participation in the Bicentennial celebration—apparently because the networks feared it would give him an unfair advantage over other candidates.

A special set of six speeches was prepared with extraordinary care for events during the Fourth of July, 1976, period, each one dealing with the accomplishments of the past and the challenges of the future in a particular area of American endeavor. They were among the best and most thoughtful speeches Ford ever made, but with the exception of the speeches at Valley Forge and Independence Hall on the Fourth of July, these "presidential" addresses received virtually no coverage.*

Other times, "presidential" activities or statements were ignored or played down in favor of trivia. For example, Ford once delivered a major explanation of his farm policy at Iowa State University. In beginning the speech, the president made a minor slip of the tongue, referring to "Ohio State," but quickly corrected it. ABC and CBS ran film of the meaningless slip and almost nothing of the "presidential" statement on agriculture.

Surely no other president, while performing his official duties, was so often described in the press as "acting presidential" instead of simply *being* president. That peculiar grammatical put-down ran through the press herd like a case of chicken pox in a kindergarten class.

Martin Agronsky talked about Ford putting aside politics "to assume a presidential posture" when the Lebanese civil war forced the evacuation of Americans from Beirut. After Ford canceled a campaign trip to Iowa to oversee the Beirut evacuation, Ann Compton explained to her ABC viewers that he was "acting presidential." And Peter Lisagor told his PBS audience that Ford was "going to play president" in the Beirut crisis.

Later, Helen Thomas of UPI wrote that Ford was going to emphasize his "presidential role" in the weeks before the Republican convention. Casting doubt on the motives for Ford's attendance at an international economic summit meeting in the summer of 1976, Barry Dunsmore said on ABC, "I don't think it will escape anyone's attention that the president's advisers have told him to look more presidential."

And so on and on.

---

* The press missed a number of stories on July 4. Shortly before Ford arrived on the flight deck of the carrier *Enterprise* to review the tall ships in New York Harbor, a sailor was struck in the back by a nearly-spent .38-caliber bullet. Its origin was never discovered. An intelligence report warned that a small boat in the harbor was carrying a bazooka to fire at one of the tall ships. That turned out to be a false alarm.

Dick Growald, UPI: "President Ford dons the role of statesman" to meet French President Giscard d'Estaing.

Phil Jones, CBS: Ford is "still trying to appear presidential."

Bob Schieffer, CBS: "President Ford's Labor Day strategy was to select the pose of a president at work."

And, most ridiculous of all, Marilyn Berger, NBC: Ford is going to stay at the Crown Center Hotel in Kansas City for the Republican Convention because "they say it's presidential."

The incessant and inexplicable use of such pejorative formulations drove me up the wall. Once, in exasperation, I wrote a needling article for the Op-Ed page of the *New York Times* referring to the White House press corps acting journalistic, news cameramen acting photographic, Congress acting legislative, the Supreme Court acting judicial, George Meany acting laborious, etc. I concluded: "The staff grammarian here at the White House, acting scholarly, says 'acting presidential' is not correct. It should be 'acting presidentially.' "

I let off some steam writing the spoof. But I never mailed it in.

I did, however, get involved in a far more elaborate spoof in an effort to counter Ford's distorted media image.

One Saturday night in 1976 I was home in bed, flipping around the TV dial, looking for something interesting to watch. I stopped dead at Channel 4. I couldn't believe what I was seeing and hearing. A tall, young comedian named Chevy Chase was falling down, bumping into things, uttering malapropisms and misunderstanding everything said to him. He was pretending to be President Ford. Actor-author Buck Henry was playing me, briefing the "president" for a news conference and trying to prevent him from hurting himself.

Live from New York, it was "Saturday Night," the hottest thing on TV, with an audience of twelve million, practically a religion among college students, a weekly satirical program on which a group of young entertainers performed a series of sketches that were usually funny, always irreverent and occasionally tasteless.

The Monday after I discovered "Saturday Night," I ordered a videotape of the entire program. After that I watched with fascination every Saturday, wincing at Chase's portrayal of the president. I worried that the act could further damage Ford's public image, but stirring in the back of my mind was the notion that perhaps the popularity of "Saturday Night" might make it the vehicle to counteract the bumbler image.

When Ford campaigned in New Hampshire in February 1976, I ran into a "Saturday Night" writer, Al Franken, who was gathering material for the show. He told me the producer hoped to recruit "non-show business" hosts for the program and asked me if I was interested. I talked by phone with the producer, Lorne Michaels, several times over the next few weeks and finally agreed to appear as the guest host on a program in April 1976.

I believed it was an opportunity to demonstrate that the Ford White House did not take itself too seriously, that we could laugh at our own foibles. I believed the sting could be taken out of the ridicule of Ford's alleged bumbling by co-opting it. How could jokes about the president be considered harmful if one of his senior staff members was willing to take part in the fun? I did not discuss my plan with the president before agreeing to take part in "Saturday Night," but several weeks before my appearance on the program, Ford himself gave a memorable demonstration that he could laugh at himself. And he did it with Chevy Chase sitting two feet away!

In March 1976 Chase was invited to perform at the annual black-tie banquet of the Radio-Television Correspondents Association in Washington. The president and Mrs. Ford also attended. While the band played "Hail to the Chief," Chase began his act by stumbling and falling across the entire width of the huge hotel ballroom to the microphone. On the platform, Chase went into his Ford bit, bumping his head on the rostrum and making such cracks as, "I have asked the Secret Service to remove the salad fork embedded in my left hand."

Ford, sitting next to the comic and puffing his pipe, laughed.

Then it was the president's turn. He had secretly developed and rehearsed a routine poking fun at himself. As he stood up, Ford pretended to get tangled in the tablecloth, yanking off a coffee cup and some silverware. The president next placed a sheaf of blank pages on the podium, supposedly his script, and proceeded to spill the papers all over the floor.

"Mr. Chevy Chase," said Ford, squelching the comic, "you are a very, very funny suburb."

Ford performed his bits like a pro. The audience roared. The president had topped his imitator.

Encouraged by Ford's enthusiastic spoofing of his klutz image,

I resolved my lingering doubts and confirmed that I would appear as guest host on "Saturday Night."

A few days before the show, I asked Ford to film three short lines to be inserted in the program. He agreed. Standing in the Cabinet Room, looking into a camera, Ford intoned, "Live from New York, it's 'Saturday Night,'" "Ladies and gentlemen, the press secretary to the president of the United States," and "I'm Gerald Ford and you're not."

When I arrived at the NBC studios in Rockefeller Plaza in New York City three days before the program to begin rehearsals, there was a wariness on both sides. In person, the mostly young cast and production team turned out to be even more eccentric in their language, dress and conduct than I had expected. As a spokesman for a Republican president, dressed in suit and tie, I must have appeared to them to be a direct descendant of Herbert Hoover.

After going through a few scenes in practice, however, I realized that the people I was working with were extremely talented and professional. And they realized that I was willing and competent to take part in the fun, having appeared on live TV probably more than they had during twelve years as an NBC news correspondent. In fact, I discovered that I had worked on news broadcasts over the years with several members of the technical crew. Soon we all relaxed about the unprecedented casting.

My major contribution to the program involved a sketch in which Chase portrayed the president and I played myself in a make-believe Oval Office meeting:

CHASE: Brief me on my schedule for tomorrow, Ron.

NESSEN: All right, sir. You'll be awakened at 5:30 A.M. in the usual manner.

CHASE: Ron, Betty and I are getting sick and tired of the twenty-one-gun salute. . . . Couldn't someone just speak in my ear or set the alarm clock?

NESSEN: We tried the alarm clock at the beginning, if you'll remember, sir. When it rang, you answered the telephone and broke your ankle.

CHASE: Well, it sounded just like the telephone.

NESSEN: We should have briefed you on that, sir. The telephone is a series of short staccato rings. An alarm clock is one long continuous ring.

CHASE: Well, Ron, when you play without a helmet all these years, everything sounds like an alarm clock. . . .

NESSEN: Shall I continue to brief you?

CHASE: Yes, go on.

NESSEN: Six-seventeen, shave and brush your teeth; 6:28, yawn and stretch; 6:30, get out of bed; 7:05, break the water glass by the sink and Mrs. Ford's shampoo bottle by mistake; 7:12, tumble down the stairs. . . .

Throughout, Chase was doing various clumsy bits—sticking a letter opener in his neck, stapling his ear, etc.

When I returned to the White House on Monday morning after the program, Ford told me he had watched at Camp David, laughed at some parts of it, didn't like others and couldn't understand why some subjects were topics of humor (presumably a mock commercial for a carbonated vaginal douche and a sketch about the Supreme Court inspecting a couple's bedroom habits).

The AP interviewed Mrs. Ford in Corpus Christi, Texas, and reported in the lead paragraph that the First Lady found some of the skits "distasteful." Buried in the sixth paragraph was a more favorable reaction from Mrs. Ford: "I thought the White House material was very funny and so did the president. We both laughed at it and had a good time."

Jack Ford, the president's twenty-five-year-old son, who often complained about the quality and loyalty of the White House staff, was deeply displeased by my appearance on "Saturday Night." He was traveling through the country, campaigning for the president, and grew angry when he started receiving more questions about the show than about Ford's policies. He dashed off an angry note in red ink on White House stationery and had it hand-delivered to me in Austin, Texas, where I was appearing at a seminar at the University of Texas.

"I thought as Press Sec. you're supposed to make *professional* decisions that get the Pres. *good press!*" Jack steamed. "If you get a min. I'd be happy to explain to you that your job is to further the Pres. interests, not yours or your family's!"

Jack's private plane happened to touch down that afternoon at Austin to refuel and I went out to the airport to try to mollify him. I explained that I had no intention of advancing my own interests at his father's expense, that I went on "Saturday Night" primarily to demonstrate that the Ford White House could laugh at itself and, thereby, defuse jokes about the president's clumsiness. Jack did not seem convinced.

Some press reaction to my appearance was downright silly.

At my first press briefing following the program, Sarah McClendon demanded: "Is this the type of thing that the president believes that the Federal Communications Commission should allow general audiences in the United States to see? Does he approve of the Federal Communications Commission permitting mixed audiences to see this?"

The *Chicago Sun-Times* thought the matter was of such magnitude that it ran a banner headline across the top of the front page reading: "Report Ford Turned Off by His Role in TV Skit."

My predecessor, Jerry terHorst, humphed that the show was "a privy party . . . a travesty of good taste . . . grossly offensive . . . kinky sex . . . bawdy crudity . . . a gross error of judgment."

Even Rona Barrett reported to her ABC "Good Morning America" viewers, "Usually reliable sources in Washington report that Ron Nessen's days at the White House are numbered, thanks in great measure to President Ford's negative reaction to NBC's 'Saturday Night.'"

Only John J. O'Connor in the *New York Times* perceived the real purpose of my participation: to defang the ridicule of Ford's supposed clumsiness.

"Obviously, the Ford people would be anxious to lick this image-making threat," O'Connor wrote. "So, in a familiar but still treacherous ploy, they decided to join their taunters. . . . Perhaps President Ford has defused the 'clumsiness issue' by goodnaturedly joining his detractors."

One of the show's writers, Michael O'Donoghue, put it more succinctly in a PLAYBOY interview: "Nessen did it to co-opt us and we did it to co-opt him."

At the time I appeared on "Saturday Night" I believed Chevy Chase's slapstick impression of Ford was well-intended fun, in the tradition of satirizing the peculiarities of national leaders, with no intention of deliberately harming the president. Now, I'm not so sure.

Chase had appeared at public events in support of Morris Udall's presidential campaign, and in a number of interviews revealed an antagonism toward President Ford. The comedian told a reporter for the *Washington Star:* "I wouldn't vote for him in a million years. I think he's a terrible president." And in an interview with the *Washington Post*, Chase said of Ford, "He's never supported any legislation to help people in his life. He is a totally compassionless man."

The author reporting under fire from Vietnam for NBC. Nessen—whose long personal involvement with Vietnam included five tours as a war correspondent and marriage to a woman he met there—suffered emotional turmoil when it fell to him as White House press secretary to announce the final collapse of Saigon.

Walter Cronkite explains to the press secretary why he was so insistent on interviewing Ford during a 1976 campaign swing in New York. "Beat Barbara Walters" was the name of the game. White House aides Don Penny (with cigarette) and John Carlson look on.

Relaxed and casually dressed, Ford and Nessen converse during a stroll beneath the trees at Camp David. Shortly after this photo was snapped, an aide to Mrs. Ford pushed Nessen, fully clothed, into the Camp David swimming pool.

Backstage, waiting to deliver his speech during a campaign trip, the president receives last-minute information by phone. Nessen checks wire-service copy for late news. A military aide was always near Ford, carrying secret codes needed to launch nuclear retaliation.

Ford pets golden retriever Liberty during Oval Office meeting with senior staff. Left to right: chief speechwriter Robert Hartmann; Nessen; staff coordinator Donald Rumsfeld; counsellor John Marsh; assistant for legislative affairs Max Friedersdorf.

Robert Redford, in Washington to research his role of reporter Bob Woodward in All the President's Men, *was invited to the Oval Office for a visit with Ford, daughter Susan, and Nessen. The president and the actor talked about their common passion: skiing.*

Betty Ford, Happy Rockefeller, Nessen and his wife Cindy hold up the reception line at a White House banquet to share a laugh. Betty loved to dance after state dinners, but sometimes had trouble getting her husband away from other attractive dancing partners.

The Rockefellers and the Nessens. The smiles masked an uneasy relationship. Nessen blamed the vice president for putting the White House on the spot over release of the Rockefeller report on CIA domestic spying. Rockefeller accused the press secretary of acting as Rumsfeld's front man in dumping him off the GOP ticket in 1976.

Christmas at Vail, Colorado—a Ford family tradition. Ford, often absent from home on political trips, set aside the annual Christmas ski holiday to spend time with his wife and children. Daughter Susan and son Michael watch Nessen participate in a spirited game of table-top soccer.

GOP vice-presidential candidate Bob Dole and his wife, Elizabeth, with the press secretary. Nessen and other White House aides urged Dole not to debate Democratic vice-presidential candidate Walter Mondale. Dole's reference to "Democrat wars" in the televised debate turned off some voters. But Nessen contends Dole helped the ticket, especially in the West.

Ford reads statement to reporters in White House press room while press secretary sits on edge of platform looking worried. Nessen believes his short temper and thin skin, plus suspicious post-Watergate mood, contributed to his troubles with the press corps. Nevertheless, he cites as one of Ford's accomplishments greatly improved relations between the White House and the press.

In the bedroom of hotel suite during presidential trip, Ford confers with staff coordinator Richard Cheney and Nessen. Press secretary says small inner circle of personal aides was like a king's royal court, occasionally seeing the emperor with literally no clothes.

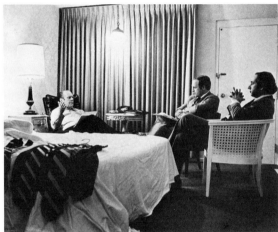

Henry Kissinger and Donald Rumsfeld discuss foreign-policy problem aboard Air Force One during overseas trip while Nessen looks on. Kissinger's hypersensitivity to real or imagined criticism often boiled over on such foreign journeys.

Betty Ford and press secretary grin during light moment aboard Air Force One *while president discusses more serious business with economic advisor Alan Greenspan. Nessen, initially concerned over Betty Ford's public views on sex, abortion, and other subjects, concluded that her warm, witty, outspoken manner won her more friends than it lost.*

Kissinger and Nessen clashed frequently. Press secretary accused secretary of state of shading the truth and withholding information from the public on occasion. The night of the Mayaguez *rescue, Kissinger snarled, "Let's look ferocious."*

Bad news from the primaries, reflected in the expressions of Ford, Cheney, and Nessen. Press secretary receives report by telephone that the president has lost the primaries in Indiana, Georgia, and Alabama to Ronald Reagan.

Waving to tourists and staff members, Ford crosses White House south lawn from Oval Office to helicopter. He's trailed by look-alike Secret Service agent Richard Keiser, and press secretary.

In a PLAYBOY interview later with the cast of "Saturday Night," Chase had this to say: "It's not that Ford isn't a nice fella. It's just that he never gave a shit about people. . . . Anybody who was so guilty about being president that he kept trying to kill himself [by being clumsy] was inherently funny. . . . It was a revelation to look at the man's eyes. . . . It was like looking into the eyes of fifty milligrams of Valium."

During the revealing PLAYBOY interview, Chase claimed that his mocking imitations of Ford were a factor in the president's election defeat.

"The election was so close that had he taken New York, he would have tied the electoral vote," the comedian told PLAYBOY. (Actually, Ford would have won the election with New York.) "It's the most heinously egotistical thing to say I had anything to do with it, but I think I must have had some influence."

So, it wasn't all innocent fun and games after all.

Looking back, it's obvious that my attempt to smother the ridicule of Ford by joining the laughter on "Saturday Night" was a failure. Ford's reputation as a bumbler persisted and was a factor in the election outcome, as Chevy Chase claimed.

The political reporter Richard Reeves was as responsible as any journalist for spreading the misconception that Ford was a clumsy boob. He wrote the article which *New York* magazine illustrated with the cover picture of Ford as Bozo the Clown.

But after the 1976 election, Reeves wrote another article for *New York* entitled, "Mea Culpa: The Candidates Were Not the Only Clowns," in which he had this to say:

> There was something very wrong with this campaign and in the final analysis, it was not them [the candidates] and it was not the American people; it was us, the Press. . . . I don't think there is anything wrong with making fun of politicians and presidents—actually, I make a living doing it. They *are* laughable a good deal of the time. But there is more to them than that, and if we don't start showing what it is, we are going to be the ones laughed at—or stoned—by someone more credible than Spiro Agnew.

Thanks, Dick. But it was a little late.

A few weeks after Jimmy Carter's inauguration, virtually every newspaper in the country ran a photo of the new president losing his footing on the ice outside the Oval Office.

I didn't laugh.

I thought: This is where I came in.

CHAPTER FOURTEEN

Why Do These Things Keep Happening?

Ford visited Sacramento, California, in early September 1975, the last stop on a West Coast trip, to deliver a speech to a joint session of the California legislature, confer with Governor Jerry Brown and do some politicking.

The morning of September 5 was so lovely—warm, clear and sunny—that the president decided to walk the short distance from his hotel to the state Capitol across the street. He strolled slowly along a walkway through the park surrounding the Capitol, shaking hands with a crowd four or five deep on his left. I was strolling behind and to Ford's right, about ten or fifteen feet away from him, with Bob Hartmann and James Shuman, editor of the president's daily news summary.

Suddenly, there was a commotion. I saw someone charge into the crowd, driving a spectator back. For an instant I caught a glimpse of an upraised gun. The circle of people around the president—Secret Service agents, policemen, aides, newsmen—abruptly surged forward and into the Capitol.

"What happened?" Hartmann asked.

"Somebody pulled a gun on the president," I replied, grasping his shoulder to hurry him into the building in case there was still a danger of shots being fired.

Inside the Capitol, Ford went directly into his meeting with Brown as if nothing had happened. In fact, nobody bothered to tell the governor about the assassination attempt on his lawn. After forty minutes of discussion about economic and energy problems, Rumsfeld interrupted the meeting to deliver a report to Ford on the episode. That was the first Brown knew of it.

Immediately after the incident, Rumsfeld, the Secret Service and local and state police gathered in a commandeered office to piece together an account of what had happened. Just outside the door, a mob of reporters, photographers and cameramen clamored for information.

The basic details of the assassination attempt were assembled amazingly quickly, in no more than fifteen or twenty minutes:

As Ford shook hands with the crowd, a red-haired woman named Lynette Alice Fromme, nicknamed "Squeaky," a follower of Charles Manson, pulled a loaded .45-caliber pistol from beneath her skirt, raised it between two spectators in front of her and pointed it directly at the president from two feet away. Secret Service Agent Larry Buendorf grabbed the gun and twisted it out of the woman's hand. With the help of another agent and a local policeman, Buendorf subdued the woman, handcuffed her and sent her off to jail. The president was not hurt. Fromme had not had the time, or strength, to pump a bullet into the firing chamber of the .45.

As soon as the report was compiled, Buendorf—a young, handsome, popular agent—phoned it to Secret Service headquarters in Washington, as regulations required. Clutching a bloody handkerchief to a cut on his hand sustained when he grabbed the gun, Buendorf held on while a secretary located Richard Keiser, head of the White House Secret Service detail. Keiser had been suffering for several days from a case of nonstop hiccups.

"Wait until he hears this," somebody cracked. "That will cure his hiccups."

As Buendorf dictated his report, I copied it down for the press with a shaky hand. Once, he was interrupted by a local policeman flashing a photo. "Is this the girl?" the cop asked.

It was. The identifying information said she was twenty-six years old. Buendorf had estimated her age as forty or forty-five.

With Buendorf's report in hand, I stepped into the jam of TV lights, cameras, microphones and reporters and read it in a quavery voice. Just thirty-two minutes had elapsed since Lynette Fromme pulled her gun. Later, newsmen complimented the White House on delivering such a full and accurate account so quickly. It was one of my better moments as press secretary.

After the meeting with Governor Brown, Ford went ahead with his scheduled speech to the California legislature, on the subject of crime. In the holding room before the speech, Hartmann kidded Ford about having the foresight to choose crime as the topic of his address on the day of an assassination attempt.

After the speech, the Secret Service drove the president's car into the basement of the state Capitol to transport Ford back to his hotel. They didn't want him exposed on the streets again. Rumsfeld and I climbed into the back of the limousine with him.

Rumsfeld felt it was important for the president to demonstrate to the press and public that he was unhurt and unruffled, so we radioed ahead for the reporters and cameramen to assemble in the hotel lobby.

At a mini–news conference in the lobby, the president made several points we had hastily worked out in the limousine: He praised the Secret Service; said the actions of one individual would not sour him on California; and promised not to let the episode deter him from traveling and mingling with the American people.

The reporters wanted to know his personal recollections of coming face-to-face with death.

"I saw a hand coming up behind several others in the front row and, obviously, there was a gun in that hand," Ford related. "I then saw almost instantaneously very quick and very effective action by the Secret Service in taking care of the matter."

"Your own thoughts, sir?" a reporter prompted.

"Well, I was very thankful," Ford replied. "I was very thankful to the Secret Service for doing a superb job. But once I saw that they had done it, I thought I'd better get on with the rest of the day's schedule."

As usual, Ford kept his deepest emotions to himself. It was no calculated facade; it was a genuine reflection of his imperturbable response to crises.

Rumsfeld, Kennerly and I accompanied the president to his hotel suite after his meeting with the reporters. Rumsfeld suggested that the incident might boost Ford's popularity in the public-opinion polls, as the *Mayaguez* rescue had.

"It should create a wave of sympathy," I suggested.

Ford agreed.

I was aghast that we were discussing possible political benefits such a short time after the president had nearly been murdered.

On the plane returning to Washington that night, the president recounted his memories of the incident again and again in conversations with the staff and the Secret Service, apparently as a way of discharging pent-up emotions. He referred to Fromme as "the oddest person I've ever seen," believing, like Buendorf, that she looked much older than twenty-six. The president demonstrated how Secret Service agents had violently shoved him into a bent-over position and rushed him away when the gun was spotted. He said his good physical condition probably helped him absorb the rough treatment without harm.

Frank Ursomarso, the advance man for the Sacramento trip, was ribbed about being a jinx because he also had been the advance man for Salzburg, where Ford had tripped on the plane steps. Ursomarso produced a diagram he had used for logistics planning in Sacramento showing the path of the president's walk from the hotel to the state Capitol. Ford autographed copies for all the staff members on the trip. (Hartmann grumbled that so many copies were made that it would cheapen the value.)

The president was anxious to see news film of the episode. *Air Force One* has a television set that can pick up channels from cities beneath its flight path, but the plane traveled so fast it was in and out of a station's range in moments, so it was not possible to see the news programs from the air. However, the White House Communications Agency transmitted to the plane the sound track of the NBC "Nightly News" coverage of the assassination attempt. Ford listened intently to the plane's stereo system.

Mrs. Ford, who was back at the White House, was notified almost immediately of the assassination attempt and of the president's escape by Richard Keiser of the Secret Service. Kennerly and Dr. Lukash phoned her shortly afterward to assure her that Ford was fine, but the president did not call her until he was aboard *Air Force One* flying home, many hours after the incident.

Rumsfeld asked Lukash to keep an eye on Ford in case he had any delayed reaction to the scare. Apparently there was none, except for an almost obsessive desire to talk about the incident. The next morning, back in Washington, Ford held a meeting on energy legislation with Democratic congressional leaders. Before getting down to business, the president gave a detailed account of the episode, dwelling on the sight of the gun. That night, at a promotion party for two military aides, as the president moved around the room shaking hands, he recounted the assassination attempt again and again.

Nevertheless, the incident did not really seem to rattle the president. Playing golf at the Burning Tree Club the day after the episode, he shot an eighty-five, a good score for him.

Hartmann told me that he himself had a violent reaction to the episode, getting sick to his stomach immediately after the assassination attempt and twice more during the day.

I had a delayed emotional reaction in the middle of the night after we'd returned to Washington. In a shallow sleep, I reached over to touch my two-year-old son, who was sleeping between me and my wife. His arm felt cold and limp. I thought I'd suffocated him by accidentally flinging a pillow over his face. Still half-asleep, I felt his chest to see if it was rising and falling. I put my ear to his mouth to listen for breath. I tickled him to see if he'd move.

He was, of course, alive and unharmed. I lay awake in the dark a long time, my heart racing. Witnessing Ford's brush with death had affected me more deeply than I realized.

Less than three weeks after the Sacramento incident, Ford returned to California for a series of speeches and appearances, ending in San Francisco on September 22, 1975.

I had planned to take some time off during the president's California trip, rejoining him at the San Francisco airport at the last minute for the flight home. But after the episode in Sacramento, I had a premonition that I should stick close to Ford.

Others had premonitions, too. An NBC cameraman I knew stopped me on the street near the St. Francis Hotel, where Ford's San Francisco activities were centered, and asked me how much longer the president was going to be in the city.

"Another three hours or so," I replied, consulting my schedule.

"Get him out of town as fast as you can," the cameraman advised. "These are not good people." He nodded at the motley groups demonstrating for a variety of causes in front of the St. Francis and across the street in Union Square.

While the president was completing his final San Francisco event—a thirty-minute taped interview with a local TV station in a suite at the St. Francis—Kennerly went down to size up the crowd waiting for the president outside the hotel's Post Street entrance. The photographer didn't like what he saw or felt. He suggested to the Secret Service agents that they not let Ford shake hands in the crowd. The Secret Service shared Kennerly's apprehension. Instructions were radioed to the agents with Ford that he was to get directly into his limousine outside the hotel.

During the TV interview—conducted in a stuffy room too small for all the lights, cameras and participants—Ford was asked about his views on gun control in light of the Sacramento episode. Ford reiterated his opposition to registration of guns or gun owners, but said he supported mandatory jail sentences for anyone convicted of using a gun in the commission of a crime.

"I prefer to go after the person who uses the gun for illegal or criminal purposes," Ford explained. "That, to me, is a far better approach than the one where you require registration of the individual or the gun."

After the interview, Ford descended by elevator to a small, side-street lobby of the St. Francis, waved to some workmen crowding a corridor leading to the main lobby and passed through the glass doors onto Post Street. Outside, the president started toward the front of his limousine as if he were going to cross the street and shake hands with the crowd on the other side. But he followed the Secret Service's advice and walked to the rear of the car. The door was not open. While an agent reached to open it, Ford waved to the crowd. I was behind him and to his left.

There was a sharp, loud pop.

I tried to persuade myself it was a firecracker. But I knew it was a gun.

For an instant there was absolute silence. Nothing moved. News photos froze that moment, showing Ford starting to crouch, his eyes glassy with shock and fear.

Then, pandemonium. People screamed. Rumsfeld and Secret Service agents Jack Merchant and Ron Pontius shoved Ford down behind the car. Police and agents rushed the person in the crowd with the gun. Cameramen scurried. I involuntarily reached for the arm of Dr. Lukash, walking next to me, then realized the danger and crouched.

"Get him in the car!" an agent yelled.

Ford was bundled into his limousine. I knew I was going to be left behind if I didn't find a seat in the motorcade fast. I ran to the first car behind the Secret Service vehicle and jumped in.

The motorcade took off immediately at high speed. As we raced away from the scene, I caught a glimpse of a gray-haired woman being carried out of the crowd in a horizontal position by policemen. She was Sara Jane Moore, a middle-aged woman whose .44-

caliber pistol and 113 bullets had been confiscated by police the day before as a threat to Ford. She had obtained another gun—a .38-caliber revolver—in time to fire at the president.

(I can set this all down in an orderly way now, but at the time it was a blur of images and instinctive reactions—everything happening so fast. Just a few seconds elapsed between the time Ford stepped through the hotel's glass doors and the time the motorcade roared away. The one shot Moore fired, before spectators grabbed her, struck the wall of the hotel to Ford's right, ricocheted, struck the curb to Ford's left and, now spent, bounced up and hit a taxi driver in the groin. *Time* magazine ran a chart showing the path of the bullet, indicating it passed directly in front of Lukash and me as it ricocheted off the wall. I was more frightened when I saw that than I was at the time.)

Racing away from the hotel, I found myself in the telephone-equipped car reserved for the wire-service reporters. Helen Thomas of the UPI was in the front seat next to the driver. Thomas, doyenne of the White House press corps, epitome of the hard-boiled newswoman on talk shows and in lectures, was very upset. She pleaded with the driver to help her get a phone call through to the UPI office. "Please, give me a line, give me a line," she asked over and over again.

She finally reached her office on the car phone, and was hardly able to dictate her story. "There was a shot . . . the president . . . someone fired . . . the president . . . there was the noise of gunfire. . . ."

"What kind of gun was it?" she blurted to the rest of us in the car. "Was it a shotgun?"

Perhaps the driver nodded, whereupon Thomas dictated that one observer thought the shot sounded like a shotgun blast. Finally I told Thomas in three or four sentences what I had seen outside the hotel and, beginning to calm down, she dictated that information to her office. At that point she switched on the car radio and dictated as her story what she heard other reporters broadcasting.

One radio reporter announced that the shot might have been fired from a shotgun. He was, of course, repeating Thomas's guess about the shotgun from the UPI wire while she was listening to him for more information to dictate to the UPI wire, an almost laughable example of media feedback.

After two assassination attempts in California in two and a half weeks, something in me snapped in the car.

"God damn California!" I shrieked, pounding the door and the front seat with my fist. "These motherfuckers in California! Why the fuck did we ever come back here? I hope we never come back to this fucking state!"

The last I had seen of Ford, he was being pushed into the back of his limousine by Rumsfeld and the two Secret Service agents. Until the motorcade hit the freeway I wasn't sure we were going to the airport and not to a hospital.

Robert Mead, Ford's television adviser, who was in the car with me, had a walkie-talkie tuned to the circuit used by the White House staff, known as the "Sierra frequency." But not a word came from the radio, and it was against the rules to ask for information over the radio in a time of emergency. Not until we reached the airport did I learn for sure that the president had not been hit.

I found out later that for the first few blocks of the ride to the airport, Ford was stretched out on the floor of his car with Rumsfeld and the two agents on top of him, shielding him with their bodies.

"You guys sure are heavy," Ford cracked, keeping his sense of humor even in those circumstances. "Can we turn on the air conditioning? It's getting stuffy in here."

When the danger of possible additional assassins was considered passed, Ford was allowed to sit up in the back seat, but in the middle, flanked by two agents, in case someone tried to fire through the windows.

As the limousine pulled up close to the stairway of *Air Force One* at the airport, Ford ordered agent Pontius to radio the president's appreciation to all the security forces involved in his protection during the San Francisco stop. Although the Secret Service tried to hurry Ford into the safety of *Air Force One*, he insisted on shaking hands with all the motorcycle policemen who had escorted his motorcade to the airport and others guarding the aircraft.

Once on the plane, Ford went directly to his cabin. Rumsfeld, Hartmann, Lukash, Kennerly and I followed him into the small compartment. Almost as soon as the president dropped into his high-backed swivel lounge chair, a steward appeared with an icy martini. Ford gulped a large swallow. The rest of us ordered drinks, too.

At that moment Betty Ford arrived. She had spent the day in Monterey relaxing. She stepped into the president's cabin wearing a white suede outfit, sat down across the table from Ford and struggled out of her coat with Hartmann's assistance. A tall drink appeared in front of her. "How did they treat you in San Francisco, dear?" Mrs. Ford asked her husband in her languorous way, smiling broadly.

"You mean you haven't heard?" Ford replied.

"Heard what?" Mrs. Ford asked, still smiling.

It was obvious that no one had told her about the assassination attempt, even though the president had ordered the news radioed to the plane bringing her from Monterey. There was a strained silence in the cabin. The president was not able to tell his wife that some-one had just shot at him.

Rumsfeld started to tell her, in a convoluted way, beginning with Ford's leaving the TV interview.

"Why are you taking so long?" Hartmann cut in impatiently. "Get to the point."

"Do *you* want to tell her?" Rumsfeld snapped. Hartmann sub-sided and Rumsfeld quickly came to the point. "Don't you know someone took a shot at the president?" Rumsfeld asked the First Lady.

I watched her face intently to see what her reaction would be. She never changed her expression. She just kept smiling and took a sip of her drink.

Pontius, the Secret Service agent, came to the president's cabin to give a report on the incident, radioed from the ground. I noticed there was a closeness between the men, almost affection. They held on to each other's arms. It was a gesture of the very special relation-ship between a president and the men assigned to protect his life.

There was an edginess, almost hysteria, among the staff on the flight home, far more so than after the Sacramento assassination attempt. Many staffers on the flight from San Francisco drank enough to get tipsy. There was plenty of gallows humor during the flight, too, in an attempt to exorcise the fright. Someone wanted to know if the president's life insurance was paid up. Another staffer thought it was only natural in a time of women's liberation that women should have an equal right to take a shot at the president.

Ford phoned his children Susan and Jack from the plane to let them know he was all right, ate a steak dinner and went to sleep, telling the radio operator to wake him twenty minutes before landing in Washington.

The TV networks carried live broadcasts of the president's re-turn to Washington. A number of presidential aides and other government officials had gathered spontaneously in the Diplomatic Reception Room, just inside the ground-floor south entrance of the White House, shortly before midnight to welcome the president and Mrs. Ford home and to express their gratitude for the president's escape from death. Ford made a short speech before the cameras. His remarks were like a replay of his statement just seventeen days earlier in Sacramento: He praised the Secret Service, said San Francisco's hospitality was great and promised to keep traveling.

"I don't think any person as president or any person in any other major political office ought to cower in the face of a limited number of people, out of two hundred and fourteen million Americans, who want to take the law into their own hands," Ford declared.

Whenever I recall the shooting in San Francisco, I can hear that loud pop echoing in my head and the instant of silence that followed, and I can see again that fraction of a second frozen in time when nobody moved, when nobody knew whether the president was hit.

As a result of the two assassination attempts, the White House press corps took particular notice of any changes in security procedures or in the president's travel plans. We had to walk a narrow line so as not to give the impression that Ford either had been frightened away from public appearances or was acting foolhardy, ignoring real danger.

A few trips that presented especially difficult security problems were canceled, notably attendance at the Michigan–Michigan State football game. For a while we stopped announcing presidential trips far in advance so as to reduce the amount of time a would-be assassin had to make plans.

The reporters were especially curious about whether Ford wore a bulletproof vest after the California incidents. On a trip to New Hampshire to campaign for Republican Senate candidate Louis Wyman shortly after the scare in Sacramento, the Secret Service insisted that Ford wear a bulletproof vest under his shirt. It was bulky and showed clearly through his clothes. It also was so heavy and hot that Ford sweated profusely and became dehydrated. The president had to drink extra amounts of water and soft drinks to restore his body fluids.

Later the president was fitted with a bulletproof garment, woven from a lightweight material, that looked and fit like an undershirt. It was strong enough to stop all but the largest-caliber bullets, but it was so thin that it was undetectable under his clothes. He followed the Secret Service recommendation and wore it whenever he appeared before large crowds where it was impossible to check every spectator. Bulletproof linings also were sewn into the regular vests of Ford's three-piece suits.

Another effect of the assassination attempts was to increase the number of journalists signing up for presidential trips, especially foreign journalists. Reporters and TV teams from England, Canada, Italy, Germany, Australia, France and Japan, who rarely or never made a presidential trip, started traveling with Ford. If anything else happened to him, they didn't want to miss it.

On October 14, less than a month after the San Francisco shooting, they got their chance.

As Ford was driving away from the Civic Center in Hartford, Connecticut, after addressing a Republican fund-raising dinner, his limousine was hit full-force in the side by a 1967 Buick driving through an intersection left unguarded by local police.

Secret Service agents, thinking it might be another attempt to kill Ford, jumped out and surrounded the Buick with guns drawn. But the car contained only six teen-agers out for a ride. The driver, a nineteen-year-old sheet-metal worker named James Salamites, was driving through the intersection legally with the green light when the president's limousine crossed in front of him.

There were no injuries, except for a jammed finger suffered by Fred Biebel, Jr., Republican state chairman, who was riding with Ford. The president's $500,000 armor-plated, bulletproof Lincoln limousine was dented behind the right front fender but was able to continue on to the Hartford airport after a brief stop. Salamites's yellow Buick was a total wreck, its front jammed in.

Ford phoned Salamites the next day to express his concern and say he was grateful that neither the driver nor his passengers had been hurt.

Salamites made a little money exhibiting his wrecked car at auto shows and other events for a while before public curiosity waned.

For a time after Sacramento, San Francisco and Hartford, the press became obsessed with presidential security, writing at length about routine incidents that almost always occurred during White House trips, but which previously had been ignored as unimportant. This eventually became frustrating to Ford and his White House staff

because the president's substantive actions and statements sometimes were lost in the mania for reporting the arrest of suspicious
characters or the supposed threat of minor episodes.

A ridiculous instance of this press preoccupation occurred during
a presidential trip to Massachusetts in November 1975. A major
speech on Ford's defense policy was buried in the coverage given
to a little boy who accidentally tapped the president with a minia-
ture flag at Westover Air Force Base:

> *Springfield, Mass.* (UPI)—President Ford was rapped on
> the side of the head today with a 24-inch flag staff by an ex-
> cited youngster. . . . A secret service bodyguard slapped the
> small flag to the ground, yelling, "Get that thing out of here!"
> Three agents stepped in front of the President, pushing away
> the small but sharp flag sticks that greeters waved. . . . There
> was no blood where Ford was struck on the right temple and
> there was no sign that he was injured. . . . The boy was not
> immediately identified and there was no indication or evidence
> that it was anything but an accident.

An even sillier example of stretching the news to connect Ford
with mishaps appeared during a later presidential trip to Connecticut. A UPI story about that trip began:
"While President Ford's motorcade swept North along Inter-
state 91, an accident occurred in the opposite lane which police
said had 'nothing whatsoever to do with the motorcade.' But reporters with the motorcade said the collision happened because one
of the drivers was gawking at the presidential motorcade in the
northbound lane."

Also damaging to Ford's image were the news photos of him at
the instant he saw the gun in Sacramento and at the instant he
heard the shot in San Francisco. In both pictures his eyes were
blank, his face white and slack, his expression dazed and frightened.
It was not a "presidential" look to inspire confidence.

In the autumn and winter of 1975, Ford's public standing
slumped. Some members of the White House staff blamed this on
the assassination attempts and the auto accident, which they felt
had created an impression that Ford was an unpresidential klutz
forever stumbling into some kind of accident.

In December, *Newsweek* ran a cover story on the president entitled, "Ford in Trouble." It listed his difficulties during that period,

including clashes with Congress over the economy, energy and foreign policy; Reagan's good showing in the polls; and what the magazine referred to as Ford's "Bozo the President" image.

"Whether the President has been playing the clown or whether he has become the victim of a cycle of downbeat politics and trendy journalism remains very much an open question," *Newsweek* declared.

What was "trendy journalism" and how did it affect the public perception of the Ford presidency?

What was "a cycle of downbeat politics" and how was Ford a victim of it?

Newsweek didn't say.

Periodically, even now, I see a newspaper photo or a TV news story showing a spectator getting beaned by one of Ford's golf drives.

Why do these things keep happening?

CHAPTER FIFTEEN

President Reagan?

The first big news story of the 1976 presidential election campaign was an article in *Newsweek* in April 1975 quoting Ford as telling friends he would not try for a full term as president.

According to *Newsweek*'s unnamed "source," Ford told two senior White House advisers and four outsiders at a meeting that he had decided unequivocally not to run because of Mrs. Ford's uncertain health and his own lack of money and enthusiasm for a national campaign.

Just hours before the magazine containing the article went to press, Thomas DeFrank, *Newsweek*'s White House correspondent, informed me of the story and asked for White House reaction. The reaction was swift and unanimous. I informed DeFrank that he could use the following quotes:

FORD: Absolutely not true.
HARTMANN: Not true.
NESSEN: Certainly not true.
CHENEY: Absolute bullshit.

The story had an insidious twist which made the denials suspect. According to *Newsweek*'s source, Ford planned to announce his candidacy, set up a campaign organization, select a campaign chairman and actually run in some primaries before dropping out of the race. The way the story was written, it would take a year before its falsity could be demonstrated.

I argued all afternoon and into the evening with DeFrank and by phone with Mel Elfin, the magazine's Washington bureau chief, and Osborn Elliott, then the editor in New York, that Ford was not capable of such a charade. They were adamant about running the story. They said they had checked back with their source four times and he stuck to his story, though they conceded that all efforts to confirm it through others had failed.

Elfin claimed *Newsweek* had the story earlier but decided to run it only after the magazine's editors heard Ford make what they considered an ambiguous statement about his candidacy in a CBS television interview with Walter Cronkite, Eric Sevareid and Bob Schieffer. In an excess of coyness on the TV program, Ford had said, "Walter, I have indicated that I intend to be a candidate. I have not made any categorical legal determination that I will be a candidate. . . . I haven't decided categorically I am going to be a candidate."

Ford was trying to say that he had not decided when to officially announce his candidacy. The president wanted to put off the announcement as long as possible because the new federal election law imposed certain legal and financial restrictions on official candidates. Besides, Ford knew that once he was a declared candidate all presidential actions and statements would be viewed in the context of election-year politics.

Encouraged by the president's fuzzy statement on CBS, *Newsweek* ran its story.

At a damage-assessment meeting the day the magazine hit the newsstands, Ford and his advisers agreed the article could harm his candidacy. It could hamper the effort to raise campaign funds; potential supporters and campaign workers might hesitate to commit themselves; other Republicans would be encouraged to jump into the presidential race. Bob Hartmann described the story as a deliberate effort to "sabotage" Ford's candidacy, and he and others suspected someone connected with Ronald Reagan was the likely source. A minority view was that a friend of the president, perhaps Melvin Laird, leaked the story to *Newsweek* as a way of nudging Ford to devote more attention to organizing his campaign. (Even now, DeFrank and Elfin refuse to reveal the identity of the "source" who stuck them with the bum story.)

The day the article appeared, Lou Cannon of the *Washington Post* told me someone had tried to peddle the same story to his newspaper the week before. The *Post* turned it down. Sarah McClendon and others informed me of a vicious whispering campaign about the state of Mrs. Ford's health and its possible effect on the president's plans. "Somebody is playing politics very rough in this town," I observed to some of my staff colleagues.

While most of the White House suspicions about the source of the Ford-won't-run rumors focused on the Reagan forces, at least some of the lingering doubts about his candidacy could be traced back to a statement Ford himself made in 1973 at his vice-presidential confirmation hearings. He told the hearings that he did not intend to run for president in 1976 regardless of whether Nixon finished out his term or departed prematurely.

But shortly after he moved to the White House, Ford instructed Jerry terHorst to inform the press that he "probably" would run. And late in 1974 he had me announce that he definitely would run.

The president often was asked why he changed his mind. He sometimes replied that he wanted a full four years to carry out a number of policies he'd started, but more often he answered simply, "I like being president." Some thought he meant he liked the limousines, the helicopters and *Air Force One*—the pomp and pageantry. But what Ford really liked was the work.

After a quarter of a century in Congress, Ford considered himself a public servant in the best sense of the term, a man devoted to solving the public's problems. He often spoke enthusiastically of the pleasure he felt when he strode into the Oval Office each morning and found the desk piled high with documents requiring his attention. He loved working his way through the stack of papers, and knowing there would be another stack waiting for him the next morning.

Ford made his presidential candidacy official first by filing documents with the Federal Election Commission on June 20, 1975, establishing his campaign organization, simply named the President Ford Committee (PFC), and then by reading the ritual announcement on July 8, 1975, in the Oval Office for the television cameras.

Today, I am officially announcing that I am a candidate for the Republican nomination for president in nineteen seventy-six. I do this with the strong support of my family and my friends. . . .

I am determined never to neglect my first duty as president. After eleven months in this office, I know full well that the obligations of the presidency require most of the stamina and concentration one human being can muster, but it is also the duty of all Americans to participate fully in our free elective process, and I will do so enthusiastically.

In all the thirteen election campaigns I have undertaken, my basic conviction has been that the best politics is always to do the best job I can for all the people. I see no reason to change that successful philosophy.

The statement, delivered from the president's desk, lasted only three minutes. There were no crowds, no campaign hoopla. We staged the event so as to convey the impression of a busy president stealing a few moments from official business to make a routine announcement of his candidacy, then quickly returning to the burdens of his awesome duties.

That was, after all, Ford's chief selling point: He was the president, with experience in the job. He wasn't doing badly in a difficult situation. He was a likable, down-to-earth man who had restored trust and normalcy after the nightmare of Nixon. He certainly hadn't done anything that justified turning him out of the White House.

And yet, a fellow Republican decided to try. Ronald Reagan—former movie actor, former governor of California, darling of the conservatives—loomed larger and larger through 1975 as a threat to Ford for the nomination of his own party. At first the Ford White House refused to believe that Reagan would challenge an incumbent conservative Republican president. When the reality of the threat sank in, various strategies were tried to discourage Reagan from entering the race and to win his constituency over to Ford.

—An indirect effort was made to talk Reagan out of running.

—Ford selected a conservative southerner as his campaign manager, Army Secretary Howard "Bo" Callaway of Georgia.

—Ford did not interfere when Callaway suggested that Vice President Nelson Rockefeller, detested by conservatives, was a hindrance to Ford's nomination, at least in the South.

—The president issued his own arm's-length statement saying the delegates at the convention would decide whether Rockefeller would be his running mate. And when Rockefeller finally decided he'd had enough humiliation and withdrew from contention for the vice-presidential nomination, Ford did not try to talk him out of it.

—Public statements of support for the president were solicited from leading Republicans across the country. The Ford campaign organization in California conspicuously included several prominent former Reagan backers.

—The president shifted some of his policies further to the right.

None of this worked. (And Ford aides later shook their heads in wonder that they had been so naïve as to think it would work.) Reagan announced he was a candidate for the Republican presidential nomination on November 20, 1975.

As the 1976 election year began, Ford's pollster, Robert Teeter, presented to the president and his aides the results of a comprehensive survey of public attitudes toward Ford. It was depressing.

To the question "What has Ford done that particularly impresses you?" 61 percent replied, "Nothing." The next-largest group was 4 percent, which liked the tax cut; 3 percent praised Ford's honesty and integrity; 2 percent mentioned the rescue of the *Mayaguez*.

To the question "What has Ford done that you don't like?" 41 percent responded, "Nothing"; 16 percent objected to the Nixon pardon; 5 percent complained Ford had not stopped inflation; 4 percent didn't like his handling of New York City's financial crisis.

The Teeter poll asked, "When you think of President Ford, what is your first reaction?" Half the respondents said they had a negative reaction, mentioning lack of leadership, indecisiveness and lack of competence, and 10 percent reported a neutral reaction. Only 33 percent had a positive reaction: They said Ford looked like a president, was honest and open, and had integrity.

"There is no clear perception of his presidency, of his goals, of where he is going," Teeter concluded.

On that discouraging note, the serious campaigning began for the first primary, February 24, 1976, in New Hampshire, a tiny, chilly and unrepresentative state of conservative but maverick voters, where the governor, Meldrim Thomson, and William Loeb, the publisher of the vicious, widely read *Manchester Union-Leader*, were all-out Reagan supporters.

As the campaign began, I unintentionally created another problem for Ford in New Hampshire by deprecating the state's ski industry, a source of pride and tourist dollars. Lowell Thomas, the old-time radio newscaster and a ski enthusiast, asked Ford during an Oval Office conversation whether he planned to ski in New Hampshire that winter. No, the president replied, when he'd skied there while attending Yale Law School he found the slopes icy and the snow uncertain; he'd stick to the powder of Vail. Later that day, when an AP reporter asked me if Ford planned to ski in New Hampshire before the primary, I unthinkingly repeated the president's private remark about icy slopes and uncertain snow.

My slur made big news in New Hampshire. I was denounced in editorials and columns, lampooned in cartoons and criticized by Reagan supporters for slandering an important state industry. Radio reports of good ski conditions were sneeringly dedicated to me. The Mt. Sunapee Area Ski Club gave my name to a slope "on the icy section of the upper bonanza trail." Ford campaign advisers were genuinely concerned that my gaffe could hurt the president in a tight race with Reagan. I lived in fear that if Ford lost the primary by a few votes, I would be blamed for the outcome.

When Ford made his first campaign trip to New Hampshire, the campaign organization forced me to wear on my coat a large badge proclaiming, "Ski New Hampshire." That, and a visit to a New Hampshire ski resort by Susan Ford, ended the embarrassing episode—almost.

Ford wasn't quite ready to let me off the hook. Stepping off *Air Force One* in Manchester for a campaign swing, he told local reporters, "I am surprised that some of you haven't asked about my good press secretary Ron Nessen's comment."

"Is he going to ski?" a newsman asked.

"I have been thinking of taking him up to the headwall and throwing him over," Ford threatened. And I don't think he was entirely kidding.

A far more serious potential problem for Ford in New Hampshire was former president Nixon's acceptance of an invitation to visit mainland China just before the primary voting. Months before, Herb Klein, director of communications in the Nixon White House, and other intermediaries passed the word to Ford aides that Nixon would not go to China or participate in public events until after the 1976 election. But Nixon changed his mind. Some White House aides suspected Nixon undertook the China trip to hurt Ford and boost the prospects of John Connally for the Republican nomination.

Advisers warned Ford that the Nixon trip would dominate news coverage during the final days of the New Hampshire primary and revive memories of the pardon. While Nixon aides were in jail or on their way to jail, the former president would be on the front pages and the TV news shows being wined and dined in Peking because Ford let him off scot-free. That could hurt in the New Hampshire voting, the president was advised.

A number of meetings, among the staff and with the president, were held to discuss the problem. There was talk of forbidding a Chinese airplane to land in the United States to pick up Nixon, or of allowing U.S. marshals to seize the plane as payment for old debts owed by China to American creditors, or of quietly asking China to withdraw its invitation. But nothing came of those schemes.

Publicly, Ford put the best face on the Nixon trip when questioned about the former president's visit to China.

"President Nixon is going there as a private citizen," he told reporters in Manchester. "I certainly am delighted that his health is such that he could go and I asked him to extend my best wishes to Chairman Mao and others."

Privately, Ford's judgment was harsher. When news accounts (inaccurately) interpreted Nixon's toast at a Peking banquet as being critical of U.S. policy toward Russia, Ford steamed to his aides, "If he keeps this up, we are going to crack him."

During one White House discussion of the Nixon problem, John Marsh complained that the former president was like an albatross around Ford's neck. Brent Scowcroft, normally a mild-tempered man, snapped, "Nixon is a shit."

Reagan, meanwhile, had his own problem in New Hampshire. Several months before the primary, he had proposed in a speech that $90 billion in federal programs—food stamps, housing, welfare, education, Medicaid, community and regional development, etc.—be transferred to the states to run, pay for, modify or terminate as they wished. The Ford campaign leaped on the proposal as a major issue in New Hampshire, arguing that the state would have to impose an income tax and sales tax for the first time to pay for the programs transferred from the federal government. Reagan was kept on the defensive, explaining his plan, instead of being able to go on the attack.

Ford's personal campaigning in New Hampshire was severely limited by the new election finance law, enacted in response to the Nixon campaign abuses. The law set state-by-state spending ceilings for each primary. Because it cost the president more to take his

White House entourage on the road than it cost Reagan to travel with a few aides, the challenger was able to campaign twenty-one days in New Hampshire, while Ford could barely afford two trips. Indeed, after an initial trip to New Hampshire, Ford was so close to his spending ceiling that a second trip depended partly on whether the phone company would return the Ford campaign's deposit in time to use the money for another visit. When enough money was scraped together for a second campaign swing, the high cost of renting sound equipment and lights for a presidential appearance limited Ford to only one major speech.

Pennies literally were pinched because of the new spending ceilings. For example, I spent hours haggling with the campaign press staff over whether they had the money to pay eighty cents apiece to print photos of the president for a press kit. They couldn't afford it, and used old pictures from their files.

The importance of winning the New Hampshire primary far exceeded the twenty-one convention delegates at stake. Massive news coverage of New Hampshire would exaggerate the significance of the outcome. Studies showed that the TV networks devoted more than three times as many news stories to the primary in tiny New Hampshire as they did to the primary in New York State, where eleven times more delegates were at stake.

And being perceived as the winner was as important as winning. In the 1968 Democratic primary, Eugene McCarthy was declared the "moral winner" by the press, although he received 7½ percent fewer votes than Lyndon Johnson. In 1972, George McGovern was perceived to have scored an important victory despite finishing almost ten percentage points behind Edmund Muskie.

We did not want a similar effect in 1976. To avoid building up expectations of a strong showing by the president, Ford campaign aides engaged in some last-minute psychological warfare, refusing to predict any victory margin, saying they would be happy with 50 percent plus one. Luckily for us, Reagan's chief New Hampshire supporter, Governor Thomson, made a mistake in the perception game. He publicly predicted that Reagan would win by at least five percentage points. Thus, Thomson made the president the underdog. A narrower Reagan victory, or a loss, would be interpreted as falling below expectations.

Winning in New Hampshire, and being perceived as the winner, was critical for both Ford and Reagan. Ford needed to win to show he could appeal to voters outside his Grand Rapids congressional district. Reagan needed to win to demonstrate he was a credible rival for an incumbent president.

On the night of the New Hampshire primary, the returns came in agonizingly slowly and, at first, disappointingly. Reagan held the lead through the evening and past midnight. Ford did not bother to wait up for the final results. He went to sleep in his bedroom on the second floor of the White House at his regular hour, 11:30 P.M. He was behind Reagan in the returns when he retired for the night.

After the president went to sleep, I and other aides continued a vigil over the wire-service Teletype machines and television sets, following the vote count. We were heartened when the news reports showed Ford pulling ahead early in the morning. But we were dismayed when the president quickly slipped behind again. By 3:30 A.M., with the outcome still in doubt, it was clear that the final results would not be known for several more hours. So I curled up on the couch in my office, pulled a raincoat over me to keep warm and tried to sleep for a while.

I was shaken awake at 6:30 A.M. by an assistant because I had promised the TV networks I would provide them with White House reaction to the New Hampshire voting for their early-morning news shows. I stumbled to the wire-service machines and through bleary eyes tried to find a report on the final outcome of the primary. I located the bulletin and was jolted wide awake. The bulletin reported that Ford had won, by just 1587 votes!

I raced through the empty corridors to Cheney's office, where he also was sacked out on his couch. I woke him up and showed him the good news. Excitedly we asked the White House phone operator to ring the president in his quarters. Ford came on the line immediately. He had been up for more than an hour and had heard the news of his victory on a radio newscast at 5:30 A.M., while Cheney and I were still tossing in a worried sleep on our couches.

The press might understandably have interpreted such a close call for an incumbent president as a "moral victory" for his challenger. Reagan tried to encourage the idea, telling reporters that if the McCarthy and McGovern showings were "victories," so was his. But Thomson's blunder of predicting a five-point Reagan win undercut that argument.

Another reason why Reagan was not proclaimed the "moral victor" in the press, even though he lost by only 0.8 percent, was that the president and his staff acted like the narrow win was a solid victory. Reporters, looking for guidance on the meaning of the close vote, were swayed by our enthusiasm. For example, I made sure the press corps knew that Ford had walked in unannounced at the regular 8 A.M. senior staff meeting the morning after the New Hampshire vote and been greeted by a standing ovation from the staff. The president was exuberant at the meeting, I related to the press; he told his aides that the New Hampshire victory was "a great springboard." "If we win a couple more, and I think we will, we will be ready for the finals," meaning the November election, "and I think we will win there, too," the president enthused to his staff.

Indeed, the New Hampshire victory was crucial. Several times in the days ahead, Ford commented accurately to aides, "We'd be in real bad shape if we hadn't won in New Hampshire."

Despite earlier concern by Ford and his campaign aides, a survey in New Hampshire by the president's pollster, Bob Teeter, after the primary, found that Nixon's visit to China had no effect on the voting. But the aftermath of the Nixon trip almost caused me to resign from the White House.

There was a lot of press interest in Nixon's report to the Ford administration on his observations in China. Originally Vernon Walters, then deputy director of the CIA, was assigned to fly to San Clemente to receive whatever information the former president had. Nixon vetoed that plan and insisted he wanted to send a written report to the State Department. Later Nixon changed his mind and decided to send his information directly to the White House.

An aide was dispatched to San Clemente to pick up the sixty-page report. It was flown to the White House, read by Ford, Kissinger, Scowcroft and CIA Director George Bush, found to contain little of value, and returned to Nixon before I was told about it.

I was furious. I had been asked daily by the press corps whether the Nixon report had arrived. Now, I knew I faced a brutal briefing, trying to explain why I had "inadvertently" not alerted the newsmen when the report reached the White House.

I learned that the president's legal counsel, Philip Buchen, was partly responsible for the decision not to notify me. Since the report was from a private citizen, the White House had no right to withhold it if a reporter requested a copy under the Freedom of Information Act. Buchen and others wanted to get it in and out of the White House before any reporter learned of its presence and demanded a copy.

For a time after terHorst's resignation, I was the beneficiary of a bend-over-backward attitude by senior White House staff members. They were careful to keep me informed of what was going on as a precaution against another devastating protest resignation by a press secretary. However, by the time of Nixon's China report, a lot of that attitude had worn off.

Once I learned that the Nixon report had come and gone, I notified the White House press corps at my next briefing. My anticipation of a grueling briefing was justified, as these excerpts illustrate:

Q.: Ron, when did you first find out about this?

NESSEN: I would just prefer not to go down that track now.

Q.: Well, your credibility is at stake here.

Q.: . . . Ron, would you deny this has the appearance of a conspiracy in the White House to cover up Mr. Nixon's report?

NESSEN: I would, Tom.

Q.: Why would the NSC keep you from having information about the report being here, knowing about our interest?

NESSEN: . . . I will find that out. I intend to find it out. I have told a lot of people of my displeasure and it will not happen again.

Q.: Even the president has chosen not to keep you fully informed.

NESSEN: I disagree with that. . . .

Q.: How can you say he keeps you fully informed when you did not know about this and the president read the report and did not bother to tell you? . . . Now, how are we to believe that you are fully informed?

The grilling increased my anger. I decided to go home for the rest of the day and think about resigning. I could not continue to function as an effective White House spokesman if the reporters did not believe me and the staff thought I would meekly acquiesce to being cut out of important information.

I was home mulling over whether to quit when Cheney phoned late that afternoon and asked me to come back to the White House to discuss the problem with Ford.

We met over drinks in the sun-bright solarium on the third floor of the White House, overlooking the Washington Monument and the Potomac River beyond. I explained my displeasure in strong terms, complaining that the press secretary's difficult job was made more difficult when the staff put him in the position of appearing not to know what was going on. I said I didn't see how I could stay if I continued to be cut off from important information.

The president replied that he didn't want me to leave and would take steps to make sure I was better informed. On the spot, he gave orders that Cheney and Scowcroft should provide more information to me. He also directed that I should be added to the list of those receiving the CIA's highly classified daily intelligence report, sent to only nineteen other persons in the government. (I already was reading the less-secret weekly CIA roundup, but, as I once complained to Scowcroft, it was about as informative as *Newsweek*.)

After ninety minutes, the martinis and conversation had created a mellow mood. My anger abated. I agreed to continue as press secretary on the promise that I would not be kept in the dark about major developments in the future.

But over my years in the White House, I became resigned to the fact that the completeness of my knowledge came in cycles. After an episode like the blowup over the Nixon China report, members of the staff were sensitive to the need to keep me informed. However, as delicate new issues arose and fear of leaks grew, I was again cut out of some information. Eventually I'd explode and then the cycle would start again. It was an unending struggle to make sure I knew what was going on.

With the victory in New Hampshire boosting the president's hopes, the goal of the Ford campaign was to defeat Reagan in Florida on March 9, 1976, and in Illinois on March 16, 1976. By beating his opponent in a northern state, a southern state and a midwestern state, it was believed, Ford could destroy the Reagan challenge.

But the Ford campaign in Florida, headed by Congressman Louis Frey and an inexperienced man named Oscar Juarez, was in bad shape a few weeks before the primary. Frey, who was anxious to run for statewide office—governor or senator—and afraid to offend any segment of the Republican party, served as master of ceremonies at a banquet at which Ronald Reagan was the chief speaker.

He also was quoted as saying that although he was supporting Ford, he didn't think Reagan was really such a bad guy. Some campaign chairman. An adroit political consultant, Bill Roberts, was dispatched to Florida to take the Ford campaign out of the hands of the inept Frey.

Meanwhile, Reagan had his own share of difficulties in Florida. His $90-billion problem followed him from New Hampshire, and he also created a new problem for himself, in a state heavily populated with retired persons, by seeming to suggest that the Social Security system should invest its funds in the stock market. Ford and his supporters criticized this idea on grounds that the return from the stock market was unreliable and that such an investment would amount to "back-door socialism," making the government the owner of many companies.

Reagan's Florida campaign manager, E. L. "Tommy" Thomas, repeated another New Hampshire mistake: He predicted that Reagan would win big in Florida, first claiming a two-to-one margin, later cutting that back to 55 percent. Again, Reagan would appear to fall below expectations if he won narrowly or lost.

On two campaign trips to Florida, Ford trumpeted his success in reducing inflation, reversing the recession, keeping America's military forces strong and attempting to keep the Social Security system solvent—all popular themes in the state.

The highlight of the president's Florida campaign was a six-hour motorcade, in the rain, from Palm Beach to Fort Lauderdale, with fourteen stops along the way for rallies at shopping centers, town halls, condominiums and a fishing pier. Sixty thousand people saw Ford in person and hundreds of thousands watched the TV coverage. It was a great media event, made irresistible to photographers and TV cameramen by Ford's insistence on standing up and waving through the open hatch in the roof of his limousine despite the steady rain.

In a short time the president was drenched. Standing in soggy clothes with his hair plastered down, he told one roadside crowd, "I don't look very good, but I think I'm a darned good president." (Under his clothes, Ford's bulletproof T-shirt kept him warm and partially dry.)

Campaigning always charged up Ford. By the last stop of the last trip to Florida, he was bubbling over with optimism. He told a meeting of campaign workers in Tampa, "When I came down from Washington I thought we were going to win. Today, I am absolutely certain we are going to win. We have got the momentum.

"Florida is really the key," he told them. "If we win, and win very well, in Florida," the Reagan forces would know they couldn't win the nomination. It was high-risk rhetoric, given Ford's narrow victory in New Hampshire and Reagan's early lead in Florida.

But the president did win well in Florida, 53 percent to Reagan's 47 percent.

Next, on to Illinois. Even though the state was Reagan's birthplace, Ford expected his momentum from the New Hampshire and Florida victories to help him win in Illinois, perhaps delivering the knockout blow to Reagan's challenge.

Then trouble struck. During a presidential trip to Illinois on March 12, 1976, press reports appeared alleging that Ford's campaign chairman, Bo Callaway, had used his position as army secretary to pressure the Agriculture Department and the Forest Service to approve an extension of his Crested Butte, Colorado, ski resort on federal land.

That night and the next morning, Callaway, who was along on the president's trip, was questioned about the allegations by Cheney and Peter Kaye, the campaign press spokesman. Callaway explained his actions in a way that made them sound innocuous. But Cheney, who was ice-hard beneath his relaxed manner, decided the Ford campaign could not afford even the suspicion of impropriety, with memories of the Nixon scandals so fresh.

Callaway was told by Cheney that he had to go. Bo agreed reluctantly.

Cheney had kept Ford out of the matter up to then. On a flight from Illinois to North Carolina for more campaigning, the day after the first press reports about Crested Butte, Callaway met with Ford in his cabin aboard *Air Force One*. Callaway went through the formality of notifying the president that he had made the decision to step aside as campaign chairman. Ford did not try to talk him out of it.

After the meeting, Bo sat in the plane's guest lounge wiping away tears that rolled down his cheeks and the sides of his nose. Then he pulled himself together and, dry-eyed, walked to the rear of the plane to read the press pool a statement:

"I am absolutely confident that there's been no impropriety whatsoever, but this president quite properly has the support of the American people for an honest and open administration of the highest honor and integrity and therefore I think it's important to go the extra mile and at the first hint of any impropriety take every action that we possibly can to ensure that there's no appearance of impropriety in the campaign."*

Ford appointed as his new campaign chief Rogers C. B. Morton, a huge, shambling, white-haired bear of a man who had been a colleague of Ford's in the House and Nixon's interior secretary.

Despite the distraction of the Callaway affair, Ford won the Illinois primary by a wide margin. After three big victories in a row, to none for Reagan, the Ford campaign grew overconfident, almost cocky, about the next primary, in North Carolina on March 23. Reflecting this overconfidence, Ford's advertising and polling were cut back in North Carolina and the campaign effort was generally eased up. The president's supporters meanwhile launched a heavy-handed effort to pressure Reagan to drop out of the race. Morton asked several Republican congressional leaders to contact the Reagan camp to persuade the Californian to give up his campaign; Republican mayors and governors were recruited to issue public statements urging Reagan to quit.

But the pressure backfired, only stiffening Reagan's determination to stay in the contest. He had attacked Ford's foreign and military policies in Florida and Illinois without much effect, but he stepped up his criticism in North Carolina. A thirty-minute TV program, taped in Florida, was run on more than a dozen North Carolina stations in prime time in the last days of the campaign. Reagan's message was that Ford and Kissinger were dangerously weakening America's defenses, caving in to Soviet demands and negotiating to give away the Panama Canal to a tin-horn leftist dictator. Reagan turned the Panama Canal into a major issue with his demogogic cry, "We built it, we paid for it, it's ours and we are going to keep it!"

Reagan won the North Carolina primary, catching the White House, the press and even Reagan by surprise. The seeming invulnerability of a popular incumbent president was punctured. The sputtering Reagan candidacy was revived.

The press called it a stunning upset. Richard Reeves, corrosive critic of politicians and journalists, wrote in *New York* magazine that there is no such thing as an upset in politics; that the term was

---

* Nine days before Carter's inauguration, long after it made any difference, the Justice Department announced that the Crested Butte matter "is no longer under active investigation and . . . no further action is contemplated at this time." Callaway was absolved. A little late.

just an excuse used to hide bad reporting by newsmen who failed to spot the factor which produced the outcome. I agreed with that.

Reporters attributed Reagan's "upset" victory in North Carolina to his last-minute television blitz. But the blitz was never reported before the voting. A few days after the primary, I asked Tom Pettit, a solid correspondent who had covered the North Carolina election for NBC, whether he'd been aware of the Reagan TV barrage. He said no. He and the rest of the press pack had covered the candidate in the traditional way, trailing him around in the press bus, covering his rallies and public speeches.

But far more people make up their minds about candidates by watching them on TV than by seeing them in person. Journalists need to develop new coverage methods which will allow them to report and gauge a candidate's impact via TV.

At the White House, we decided to salvage what little public-relations benefit we could by being frank in our reaction to the North Carolina loss.

"The president had expected a close race, but he expected to win. So naturally we are disappointed," I told the reporters. "The point is we lost, and there are no excuses and no alibis."

The next big confrontation between Ford and Reagan was in Texas on May 1, the first primary in the state's history. Reagan found a responsive audience for his conservative issues in Texas.

Unfortunately, Ford allowed himself to be put on the defensive, responding to Reagan's choice of issues. While Reagan appealed to the voters' emotions with charges that the president had let U.S. military power fall behind Russia's and was preparing to give away the Panama Canal, Ford tried to answer with a glut of facts and logic. The president was advised to give shorter, punchier answers, but he overdid it during a news conference in Dallas by declaring, "The United States will never give up its defense right in the Panama Canal and never give up its operational rights as far as Panama is concerned."

That was an incorrect statement of American policy. It was shown to be incorrect within a few days when congressional testimony revealed that the chief American negotiator for a new Panama Canal treaty was under instructions from Ford to work out a deal that would turn over the canal to Panama around the end of the century.

When the president's Dallas news conference remarks were

shown to be overzealous, I proposed to Ford that the White House stop trying to match Reagan's rhetoric on the Panama Canal and start talking sense to the voters, explaining why it was necessary to negotiate a new treaty. Ford agreed I should tell the press that what he meant at the Dallas news conference was that the United States would insist on the right to defend, operate and maintain the canal during the term of any new treaty. I was deliberately to leave vague what would happen when the treaty ran out, but the clear implication was that Panama would take over.

Then, there was the "Kissinger problem." Shortly before the Texas primary, Kissinger made a trip to Africa and delivered a speech in Nairobi calling for black majority rule in white-run countries of southern Africa. This irritated some campaign officials. They were sure Kissinger's African safari would stampede the conservative voters of Texas into Ronald Reagan's arms.

Private campaign polls showed that many voters believed that Kissinger, not Ford, was running American foreign policy. To counter this image, we considered allowing reporters and cameramen to attend the beginning of a National Security meeting—an unprecedented idea—to witness a staged dialogue in which the president would give Kissinger instructions for the secretary's trip to Africa. The plan was finally rejected as too transparent.

The periodic demand by some presidential advisers and political strategists that Ford fire Kissinger was revived. The president concluded, however, that he would suffer worse damage by unloading Kissinger. He would appear to have panicked and made the decision for purely political reasons to appease the right wing. Besides, any short-term political benefits were not worth the loss of Kissinger's diplomatic skills.

The night of the Texas primary, Ford and many White House and campaign officials attended the annual black-tie dinner of the White House Correspondents Association at a Washington hotel. Returning to the White House shortly after 11 P.M., the president invited Cheney, Kennerly and me to watch the vote results with him and Mrs. Ford on TV in his residence. I stopped at my office first to check the latest wire-service stories. They were bad. Ford was losing in every district.

When I arrived at Ford's living room—really one end of the hall which ran the full length of the second floor—the others were sipping drinks and watching television, all in formal clothes. Kennerly wore a denim tuxedo.

"Mr. President, in the old days the kings used to shoot the messenger who brought bad news," I said.

"Do you have bad news?" he asked.

I showed him the wire copy from Texas. He didn't say a word.

"I also have some good news," I advised him, trying to cheer him up with another wire-service story saying he had won more delegates than expected in a caucus in Maine. That didn't lighten the mood much.

It was clear from the 11:30 P.M. TV specials that the Texas primary was a disaster for Ford. Reagan won all ninety-six delegates at stake. With George Wallace no longer a serious contender for the Democratic presidential nomination, thousands of his supporters crossed over—as the rules allowed—and voted in the Republican primary for the conservative Reagan. John Connally's refusal, in his home state, to endorse Ford hurt too.

The president was alternately glum, silent, angry and profane. "God damn it!" he exploded periodically. When the results were conclusive, the only phone call the president accepted was from Senator John Tower, his pint-size Texas campaign chairman, who was deeply distressed. The phone conversation consisted mostly of Ford trying to cheer up Tower, rather than the other way around. Mrs. Ford got on a white Princess extension phone and tried to cheer up Mrs. Tower.

As Cheney, Kennerly and I departed after midnight, Ford tried to put a good face on the setback. "This is just one primary," he consoled. "We are going to be back in there. We are going to win more primaries and we are going to win the nomination."

But the news got much worse, rapidly.

Three days later Ford lost the primaries in Alabama and Georgia, as expected, and unexpectedly in Indiana, where many Democrats, without a viable conservative left in the race for their party's nomination, crossed over and voted for Reagan. A week later the president lost again to Reagan in Nebraska, where crossovers were not allowed.

Reagan surged ahead of Ford in delegates. The president was in trouble, in danger of losing the nomination. *Newsweek* ran a cover story on Ford's skidding quest, entitled, "A President in Jeopardy."

A string of little things went wrong, along with the big things. For example, the night of the Alabama-Georgia-Indiana loss, campaign chairman Rogers Morton was caught by news photographers looking bleary-eyed and dismayed, in front of a batch of empty liquor bottles and beer cans in his office. The photo was misleading; reporters had helped drink the booze. But the picture appeared on front pages of newspapers all over the country and on the TV news, giving the impression the Ford campaign was drowning its sorrows.

At a Ford rally in the War Memorial Coliseum in Fort Wayne before the Indiana primary, the climactic cascade of balloons from the ceiling failed because the mesh net holding them refused to open.

Back in his hotel suite, Ford was uncharacteristically testy. With an edge in his voice, the president threatened to send chief advance man Red Cavaney up to the ceiling of the arena the next time a balloon drop was attempted "and if the balloons don't drop, we are going to drop Red Cavaney."

Before the aborted balloon drop at that Fort Wayne rally, Ford answered questions from the audience, which struck me as a particularly mean-faced and mean-spirited crowd. The first five questions sounded suspiciously like Reagan plants. The first two were duplicates, about the Panama Canal. The third was about Kissinger's trip to Africa. The fourth was, "Do you plan to continue to lead this country to full socialism?" And the fifth was about busing for school integration.

I complained to some White House reporters about Reagan's campaign apparently rigging the questions. The newsmen shrugged it off. "I'd be very surprised if some of the questions weren't planted," one reporter told me. I couldn't understand that attitude, in view of the post-Nixon sensitivity to campaign dirty tricks.

I also grumbled about the reporters' failure to demand from Reagan a detailed financial statement and a response to allegations that he avoided most income taxes during one period by using loopholes and write-offs. I asked Richard Lerner of the UPI why his wire service did not press Reagan on these matters as hard as it pushed Ford on his finances.

"We can't afford to have a reporter travel with Reagan like we do with the president," Lerner replied.

In the midst of these multiplying troubles, *Newsweek* came sniffing around with rumors that someone on Ford's congressional staff had arranged dates for constituents with party girl Elizabeth Ray, or that Ford himself had seen her socially. Nothing was found to substantiate the gossip, but in the course of checking it out, we discovered that Kennerly had taken nude photographs of Ray during sessions at her apartment and his house. He foolishly had sent his film rolls for development to the Navy Film Lab, which is supposed to handle only official government work. When this was discovered, Kennerly sheepishly mailed the government a check for $4.50 for the developing.

The president, in his primary battle with Reagan, continued to be haunted by Nixon. Just before Ford's string of primary losses, sensational excerpts from Woodward and Bernstein's new book, *The Final Days*, were published and the movie of their previous work, *All the President's Men*, had its premiere at the Kennedy Center, reviving memories of Nixon yet again, and of Ford's connection with Nixon.

Cheney and I discussed the possibility of Ford attending the movie premiere as a gesture of his break with Nixon and as a way of avoiding charges that the movie was an embarrassment to the president. But when a friend, a top White House official in a former Democratic administration, advised me privately that the movie would be a very painful experience for Ford, we decided to give the presidential box at the Kennedy Center for the premiere to Katherine Graham, publisher of the *Washington Post*.

Cheney, Kennerly and I joined the president in his residence to follow the returns on TV the night he lost the Alabama, Georgia and Indiana primaries, May 4. We watched in the homey den, cluttered like any suburban family room with odds and ends from the Fords' Virginia home. One by one, the states were declared by the TV anchormen to be in Reagan's column. The president, tieless, in the wrinkled shirt he'd worn in the office all day, was gloomy and quiet. The painful silence was heightened by the absence of Mrs. Ford, who was in California campaigning.

Ford said it was a "damn shame" that he and Reagan were still engaged in a bloody primary battle while Jimmy Carter had seemingly locked up the Democratic nomination. The president said enviously that Carter had a full month before the Democratic Convention to unite his party and plan his fall campaign, while the Republicans were still fighting over their nominee.

After the 11:30 P.M. TV specials confirmed Ford's three primary losses, Cheney, Kennerly and I rose to go. The president said, "I've got to lay out my clothes for the morning. It lets me sleep five minutes extra."

We watched him take shorts, socks and shirt from his dresser drawers and place them where he could slip into them in the morning. It was sad to see him following this lonesome routine, alone with his defeat in that big house.

Some of Ford's White House and campaign aides responded badly as the president's political situation worsened.

Two days after Ford lost the Indiana, Georgia and Alabama primaries, Defense Secretary Rumsfeld phoned me from the Pentagon. He said he'd spotted me at a White House reception looking depressed.

"You looked very glum and down today. You looked whipped," he said. "You shouldn't look that way, because your own appearance and attitude transmits itself to the people on your staff and throughout the White House, and it can start a panic."

There already was a panic in the White House and the campaign organization. And as Ford's losses mounted, the panic grew. We turned on each other and sought scapegoats.

"This White House is not showing grace under fire," I wrote in a note to myself at the time. I described those weeks as a "cannibalistic, self-devouring period."

Indeed, almost daily, columns and articles quoted anonymous inside sources as blaming Kissinger for the string of primary losses, or saying I was inept as press secretary, or claiming that Cheney didn't know anything about national politics, or fingering Hartmann for poor speeches. Within hours after Ford's Campaign Advisory Committee concluded a closed meeting at the Mayflower Hotel to examine why Ford was floundering in the primaries, participants leaked that the committee blamed Kissinger, Cheney and Nessen for the president's declining fortunes.

On the other hand, Hartmann grumped to me during a shared car ride home one night during that period that people running Ford's campaign were a bunch of losers. Morton, he complained, didn't know anything about running a national campaign. The only Republicans who understood how to run a winning campaign were those who had worked for Nixon, "and most of them are in jail," Hartmann said.

Indeed, the president and his closest White House advisers concluded during the string of primary losses that the Ford campaign committee was performing poorly. After that, more and more of the management of the campaign was directed from the White

House. The most dramatic gesture of no-confidence in the campaign committee occurred one night in May when the president returned from a campaign trip shortly before midnight. Waiting for Ford's helicopter on the south lawn were Kennerly and his friend Don Penny, a diminutive, curly-haired former TV actor and comedian, a producer of commercials who had been brought to the White House to coach the president on his speech delivery. Kennerly and Penny were about to stage a coup against the campaign advertising organization, run by Peter Dailey and Bruce Wagner.

Kennerly and Penny ushered Ford, Cheney, me and others from the president's helicopter into the Map Room on the ground floor of the White House. Tape machines and speakers had been set up to play a set of commercials made secretly and hurriedly by Penny. They consisted of actors pretending to be ordinary people—housewives, executives in a car pool, hardhat workers—overheard discussing why they thought Ford was the best choice. Penny called them "slice of life" commercials. They reminded others of phony conversations between "ordinary people" in commercials for toothpaste or underarm deodorant.

Wagner, who had been invited to the midnight meeting, defended his existing commercials, which were montages of still pictures and film of Ford in his most presidential moments. Wagner claimed they set the right tone for the incumbent of the Oval Office. But Penny snapped at Ford, "If you stick to those commercials, you are going to lose. That is all there is to it. Those commercials haven't worked. You are going to lose."

The president went around the room, asking the opinion of each person.

Cheney worried, "We don't have any specific evidence to show that the so-called slice-of-life approach is better than the approach of Bruce Wagner's commercials."

Nevertheless, Ford liked Penny's commercials. He ordered that some of them be put on the air, along with Wagner's, in the remaining primary states.

But officials at the President Ford Committee, irritated by Penny's interference and unconvinced of his commercials' impact and taste, dragged their feet on using them in the next primary states— Michigan and Maryland. Besides, Penny's commercials cost more to broadcast than Wagner's because stations were allowed to charge more when the candidate's voice and picture did not appear, and the Ford Committee was beginning to be very tightfisted. The committee now realized that the president was not likely to nail down the nomination during the primaries; therefore some of the $13.1 million allowed by the federal election law for spending during the period before the fall campaign had to be set aside to woo delegates at the state and national Republican conventions.

Dailey and Wagner were fired as the campaign advertising managers soon after the Kennerly-Penny revolt. They were replaced for a time by James J. Jordan, president of the Batten, Barton, Durstine & Osborn agency, a Penny recommendation. Jordan eventually was replaced by John Deardourff and Doug Bailey, a talented and successful team of campaign advertising and media experts.

In the darkest hours of the president's downward tumble in the primaries, I was visited by David Belin, a friend of Ford's, a counsel for the Warren and Rockefeller commissions and an active Republican of the moderate persuasion in his home state of Iowa.

"I wonder what would happen if the president lost the nomination," I asked, trying to sound casual about a far-out possibility I wanted to broach. "I wonder if there would be any way for him to run for president."

It was an idea I had been thinking about since Ford's fortunes took a disastrous turn. After all, when Theodore Roosevelt was denied the nomination of his Republican party in 1912, he ran on the third-party Bull Moose ticket. I asked Belin to research the legal questions involved in Ford running for president as an independent if Reagan beat him for the Republican nomination.

"I think it's something that has to be kept very, very quiet," I cautioned. Belin said he would treat it as a private client-lawyer conversation.

I'm sure that Ford, with his strong sense of loyalty to the Republican party, would have rejected the idea of running on a third-party ticket if Reagan had won the Republican nomination. But the fact that I asked Belin to look into the possibility shows how low the mood was in the White House after the string of primary losses.

Ford's survival as a contender for the presidential nomination ultimately hinged on the primary in Michigan on May 18, 1976. If he could not win his home state, he would very likely be out of the running; Reagan almost certainly would be the Republican nominee and possibly the next president.

Four years earlier, George Wallace had won an astonishingly high number of votes in the Michigan Democratic primary. Now, with Wallace out of it and Carter all but assured of the Democratic nomination, Michigan's conservatives—Republicans and Democrats—might line up solidly for Reagan, sending Ford into retirement.

Ford's staff and supporters disagreed on the proper strategy to meet this threat in Michigan. State GOP chairman William McLaughlin declared that Democrats ought to stay out of the Republican primary, mind their own business and let Republicans choose their own candidates.

This approach was rejected by Ford and his campaign staff, who realized that McLaughlin's "stay out" warning would alienate Democrats whose votes Ford needed in the November election against Carter. Instead, the president adopted the strategy of making a hard pitch for Democrats and independents to vote for him in the primary.

The Ford campaign's need to conserve money led to another spat among Ford's supporters planning the Michigan strategy. Governor William Milliken, Senator Robert Griffin and other friends from the state, complaining that the White House advance men and staff were incompetent, urged Ford to campaign by whistle-stop train. The Washington campaign chiefs said it would cost too much.

The train won, thank goodness.

Named the *Presidential Express*, the train had the same dramatic effect on Michigan voters and Ford's spirits as the rain-drenched motorcade in Florida. Jammed with newsmen, Republican officials, popular sports figures, bands and cheerleaders, the train crossed Michigan the Saturday before the primary from Flint in the east to Niles in the west, with stops at Durand, Lansing, Battle Creek and Kalamazoo. More than 50,000 people lined the tracks and jammed the stations in an intermittent rain. There were so many colorful scenes that the TV news programs and the Sunday papers gave the whistle-stop journey heavy coverage, carrying the president's campaign pitch to hundreds of thousands of Michigan voters who didn't see the train in person.

Ford's message was an unapologetic appeal for Michigan voters to help the home-state boy. "Let me say at the outset how wonderful it is to be back in Michigan, our home state," the president told the crowd from the rear platform of the train before pulling out of the Amtrak station in Flint. "I ask you to help us on Tuesday. We must win in Michigan."

The upbeat mood of the whistle-stop trip was marred briefly by an incident in Battle Creek as the president spoke to a trackside crowd.

"You blew it!" a heckler shouted as Ford listed his White House accomplishments.

"We blew it in the right direction, young man," Ford shouted back at the heckler, "and those of you who don't agree . . . if you would go out and look for a job, you would get one."

Many reporters thought the president's put-down had a harsh Nixonian tone to it. Ford's retort seemed to assume that the heckler was not employed, although there was no obvious reason to make that assumption.

The episode did not dampen the high spirits generated by an invigorating day of campaigning across the president's home state. Someone brought a bunch of fake black handlebar mustaches aboard *Air Force One* for the flight home. Mrs. Ford and Susan each put on a mustache and paraded around the plane. The president was so charged up by the day that he didn't notice for a few minutes that his wife and daughter had suddenly sprouted thick black cardboard mustaches.

The morning of the crucial Michigan primary, the president unexpectedly walked in on the senior staff meeting in the Roosevelt Room at the White House. Like a general talking to his troops on the eve of a big battle, not knowing whether they would survive, Ford thanked his staff for their hard work and devotion.

"If we can get the nomination, I believe we will have an easier time in the election than we are having in the primaries," Ford said. He cited what he called his good performance in the White House. There was a puzzled note in his voice, as if he were wondering how his primary campaign had gone so wrong.

About 5 P.M. on the afternoon of the Michigan primary, a number of staff members learned simultaneously from friends at NBC and CBS that network surveys of voters leaving the polling places showed Ford winning in a landslide.

The findings put Ford and his aides in an optimistic mood during a fancy-dress banquet given that night by visiting French president Giscard d'Estaing. The dinner was held on the grounds of the

French Embassy in a lavishly furnished tent hung with tapestries and paintings and carpeted with oriental rugs.

There was a lot of happy whispering back and forth among Ford staff members during the dinner. Messages containing fresh returns were passed to the president. By the time we returned to the White House from the banquet, the outcome was clear: Ford had won Michigan by a huge margin, 65 percent to Reagan's 34. The voters of Ford's home state had kept his candidacy alive.

Ford and his aides were bubbling—laughing and joking in the marble corridor on the ground floor of the White House upon their return from the French banquet.

"We have sat upstairs during a couple of weeks when the news was bad," the president said. "Why don't you come up with me tonight, when the news is good?"

So we joined him and Mrs. Ford—Cheney, Appointments Secretary Terry O'Donnell and I in uncomfortable white-tie evening clothes, army aide Robert Barrett in formal military uniform and Kennerly in khakis and sport jacket. In the Fords' living room we watched TV, drank, laughed, talked excitedly and savored victory. When Reagan appeared on the television screen claiming he was pleased with his showing, Ford cracked, "I'm glad he's pleased with thirty-four percent. I hope we can keep him that pleased in the other primaries."

What a contrast with the other nights when Ford had watched dismayed as his chances for the nomination sank.

The president's candidacy had survived, but it was still on the critical list. Coming up were primaries in a number of border and western states, where Reagan had strong appeal.

During that period the White House launched a strange exercise, which the participants insisted was a legitimate effort to find an appropriate case to challenge excessive school-busing for integration, in keeping with the president's long-held views. But the matter was handled so clumsily that many reporters viewed it as a naked political appeal for the votes of parents opposed to busing in primary states.

The tempest began when Republican Senator Edward Brooke of Massachusetts, a black, leaked the news that Attorney General Edward Levi was examining the Boston integration case for possible intervention by the Justice Department on behalf of less or no busing. I confirmed at my briefing that Ford had asked Levi six months previously to look for a case that was suitable for a Ford administration legal challenge asking the Supreme Court to re-examine its busing edicts. Reporters at the briefing were skeptical of my insistence that campaign politics was not involved.

Q.: Does the fact we are getting the president's views or participa-tion in this today . . . have any connection with the fact there is an important primary in Kentucky next week and busing is a very hot issue in Louisville?

NESSEN: . . . The answer to your question is no. . . . What I sense you are suggesting by your questions is that this is some kind of public-relations plot, and I submit that it is not.

My contention was undermined when, at a news conference for Kentucky reporters a few days before that state's primary, Ford suggested that Louisville, rather than Boston, might be a possible case for the government to challenge the court's busing orders. This mention of Louisville for the first time shortly before the Kentucky primary convinced some critics that Ford was playing politics with the busing issue in an effort to appeal to Reagan's conservative supporters.

Levi never did find a suitable case, heightening press suspicion that the issue had been raised only for the purpose of winning anti-busing votes in the primaries.

The president compounded the sticky situation when, during a news conference in Columbus, Ohio, he mistakenly stated that the attorney general was searching for an appropriate case on which to ask the Supreme Court to reconsider its 1954 Brown decision, the original ruling declaring segregated schools to be unconstitutional.

I had to make a rare, flat-out admission of presidential error: "The reference to the Brown case was not correct."

Looking back at our handling of the busing matter, I believe the White House came close to improperly exploiting an emotional issue for political purposes and to encouraging violent protests by busing opponents. It was not the only time the Ford White House took a position on an issue which seemed to offer short-term po-litical benefits, without calculating the possible longer-term lia-bilities or the eventual need to make a responsible policy decision.

Despite his Michigan victory, Ford trailed Reagan in delegates and was expected to fall further behind after the six primaries on May 25, in Kentucky, Tennessee, Arkansas, Idaho, Nevada and Oregon. To avoid the psychological impact of that, the squeeze was put on

Ford supporters in the big New York and Pennsylvania delegations to give up their official uncommitted status and publicly endorse the president. The New York chairman, bald, baby-faced Richard Rosenbaum, delivered 119 delegates, and Pennsylvania produced 88 more, putting Ford comfortably ahead of Reagan in the delegate count once more.

Ford and Reagan split the May 25 primaries, the president winning Oregon and, unexpectedly, Tennessee and Kentucky, while the challenger took Arkansas, Idaho and Nevada.

Finally, the last primary Tuesday arrived, June 8, with voting in the large, delegate-rich states of California, Ohio and New Jersey. Reagan needed to win in his home state of California to stay in contention, just as Ford had needed Michigan.

For a time, the polls indicated Ford had a chance in California, but as the voting approached, it became clear that Reagan would carry the state. Nevertheless, the president made a foray to California. By then, campaign funds were running so low that we had to persuade the local Public Broadcasting TV outlet in Anaheim to provide the lights and sound equipment for a Ford speech in return for giving the station an interview with the president.

With the budget so tight, we decided to take advantage of some free TV time on the eve of the final three primaries by accepting a long-standing invitation for Ford to appear on the CBS Sunday panel show "Face the Nation."

The associate producer, Joan Barone, sounded thrilled when I phoned her to accept. I explained that the program had to be taped ahead of time at the White House because Ford would be campaigning in New Jersey the day it went on the air. But Bill Small, a hard-nosed CBS vice president, who was ever alert for real or fancied efforts by the White House to misuse CBS for political purposes, insisted that Ford must tape the show at the network studio. Small said I was trying to make the president look more presidential by requesting that the program be taped in the White House.

"That's silly," I replied. "How do you make a president look presidential? He *is* the president. Even if the program were taped on a street corner, he'd still be the president."

I tried a bluff: I told Joan Barone the president would accept an invitation from ABC's "Issues and Answers" rather than come to the CBS studio.

She was crestfallen. "I've been trying for two years to get the president on our show," she moaned.

"Don't blame me," I replied. "Blame Bill Small."

"Yes, I know what you mean," she agreed. "I know. But why take it out on me?"

Ultimately, Small called our bluff and the White House gave in to his demand. The president drove to the CBS studio to tape "Face the Nation" because it had a bigger audience than "Issues and Answers."

Reagan gave Ford's hopes in California a last-minute lift when he became embroiled in a controversy over what he would do about the agitation for black rule in Rhodesia. In response to persistent press questions, Reagan seemed to suggest that he might send a token force of American troops there.

At the urging of Stuart Spencer—the president's deputy campaign director and a Californian—the Ford campaign rushed out a new set of commercials advising Californians, "When you vote Tuesday, remember: Governor Reagan couldn't start a war. President Reagan could." The injection of such an emotional appeal at the last minute may have boomeranged and hurt the president.

While Susan Ford and her friends held a roller-skating party around the White House south lawn driveway, the final primary returns came in. Reagan won California handily, capturing all 167 delegates. The president took all 67 delegates in New Jersey. They split Ohio, 88 for Ford, 9 for Reagan.

Four months of hand-to-hand combat in the primaries were over. Ford was ahead in delegates. But neither he nor Reagan had accumulated enough delegates to win the nomination.

The candidates turned their attention to the 400 delegates who remained uncommitted or were still to be chosen at state conventions.

The original Ford campaign strategy had been to knock Reagan out of the race in the early primaries. Therefore the president's campaign organizers had not paid much attention to the state conventions, thinking Ford would have the nomination locked up by the time that phase of the delegate-selection process rolled around. Reagan did not make that mistake. He courted the state convention delegates, and that attention paid dividends. Four days after the last primaries, Reagan won eighteen of the nineteen at-large delegates picked by the Missouri convention, despite a last-minute personal appearance by Ford.

In mid-June the president planned to fly to Des Moines to appeal for delegates at Iowa's convention. But two days before the convention opened, the American ambassador to Lebanon, Francis E. Meloy; his economic counsellor, Robert O. Waring; and their Lebanese chauffeur were kidnapped and murdered in Beirut.

One of the first presidential decisions in the crisis was that all statements on the episode should come out of the White House, so Kissinger would not appear to be managing the American response from the State Department, and so political considerations would be taken into account. Ford convened a meeting in the Oval Office to draft a statement on the killings. The problem was to make the statement responsible but at the same time tough enough to head off a Reagan charge that the president was not showing sufficient backbone. After a good deal of haggling, writing and rewriting, softening and hardening, the president walked to the White House press briefing room to read his statement for the cameras:

"I have . . . ordered that all appropriate resources of the United States undertake immediately to identify the persons or group responsible for this vicious act. Those responsible for these brutal assassinations must be brought to justice. At the same time, we must continue our policy of seeking a peaceful solution in Lebanon. That is the way we can best honor the brave men who gave their lives for this country and for the cause of peace."

Two days later Ford decided the situation in Beirut was so dangerous that private American citizens should be evacuated. He canceled his trip to the Iowa delegate-selection convention to oversee the delicate withdrawal operation, which required the tacit cooperation of the Palestinian guerrillas.

Cancellation of the Iowa trip brought a rash of press speculation about possible political motives and implications of Ford's actions. Tom Brokaw, for example, told his NBC viewers, "One of the president's campaign spokesmen said the decision to stay in Washington probably helped Mr. Ford because it would remind people that he's the president living with hard decisions." And Godfrey Sperling, Jr., wrote in the *Christian Science Monitor* that the evacuation of Americans from Beirut "was precisely what Republican leaders across the U.S. have been saying Ford needed to lift his campaign in coming weeks."

The evacuation of Americans and Europeans from Beirut was carried out without a hitch by unarmed U.S. Navy landing craft. Ford sat up all night in the NSC office, following reports from the scene.

Some of the evacuees told reporters they were going to Europe for vacations or business, and planned to return to Beirut later, which reinforced speculation that Ford had ordered an unnecessary evacuation for political purposes. But the fighting in Beirut grew much worse immediately after the evacuation, making the city extremely dangerous. Water and electricity were cut off. Food was scarce. The hospitals looked like slaughterhouses. Ford had ordered the evacuation of Americans just in time. The talk about political motives stopped.

While the president was occupied with the evacuation, Mrs. Ford flew to Des Moines on June 18 to act as stand-in for her husband at the Iowa convention. Her appeal to delegates to support her husband was marginally successful: Ford won nineteen delegates, Reagan seventeen.

Every weekend through June and into July, state conventions met to select their delegates. The political pros of the Ford and Reagan camps maneuvered publicly and privately, twisting arms, cajoling, threatening, promising, calling debts, incurring debts, pulling deals and tricks.

Ford flew to Connecticut and Mississippi to plead his case in person. He also appealed to individual uncommitted delegates by phone. He invited many delegates to the White House—sometimes entire state delegations—to explain his policies, answer questions and ask for votes. Reagan and his organization made the same appeal. It was called "nickel-and-diming," trying to win the necessary delegates one by one. It's what the battle for the Republican nomination had come to.

A joke went around illustrating how some uncommitted delegates played hard-to-get. It seems one delegate from New Jersey received a phone call from the president inviting him to a reception and state banquet for Queen Elizabeth at the White House. There was a long pause of indecision and then, according to the gag, the delegate asked Ford, "What's for dinner?"

All through the long struggle for the nomination, Ford was accused of using his White House powers to influence voters, by inviting uncommitted delegates to glittery social events, promising to consider a new veterans hospital in Florida, announcing approval of a nuclear power plant in Ohio, designating a national historic landmark in New Jersey, throwing the switch on a new fountain in a redevelopment area in Tennessee, and so on. Perhaps. But then he was the only candidate being judged on presidential performance, not mere promises. Ford bore the liabilities of incumbency as well as the advantages. He was the only candidate who had to accept responsibility for the consequences of his official policies. Reagan didn't have to worry about being blamed for unemployment or for the death of marines rescuing the *Mayaguez*.

When the state conventions ended, Ford had over 1100 delegates, but not quite the 1130 needed to win the nomination. Reagan had more than 1050. Fewer than 100 delegates, who had not publicly revealed their preferences, would determine the winner.

Then Reagan made a mistake. He announced that if he won the nomination, his vice-presidential running mate would be Richard Schweiker, a liberal senator from Pennsylvania.

Reagan's advisers, convinced that they could not acquire enough delegates without some dramatic change of tactics, decided to gamble that the Schweiker selection would shake loose some of Ford's delegates in the liberal Northeast, particularly in Pennsylvania, without losing Reagan's conservative supporters in the South.

The strategy did not work. There were only minor defections from Ford in the Northeast, but there were screams of outrage in the South.

The other effect of the Schweiker blunder was to send John Connally flying to the White House to endorse the president. Connally had been sitting on the fence, perhaps waiting to see who would win the nomination, or whether there was a chance he could win it himself in the case of a deadlock between Ford and Reagan. His decision to support Ford was a strong sign that he thought, after Reagan's Schweiker choice, that the president would win the nomination.

Ford and Connally held a joint news conference on July 27 at which Connally announced his support of the president and made clear that Reagan's choice of the liberal Schweiker as his running mate had propelled him into Ford's corner. "It is quite clear now," Connally told the reporters in his rich Texas voice, "that the president is the better choice, not only for the party but for the country."

Entering a postmortem meeting in Cheney's office, I jumped up and clicked my heels together in the air. Staff members were buzzing with excitement, feeling the Schweiker choice had started an irreversible break toward Ford, with Connally the first big convert. There was talk of changing Ford's campaign strategy now that the nomination seemed finally in sight.

"Look," Cheney interrupted gruffly, "we have to keep the same posture we have had. We are working hard to lock up the delegates. We don't have the nomination. Let's not go overboard. Let's not get euphoric. Let's just stick to the same hard work we have been doing.

"Remember North Carolina."

Near the end of that long, hard winter and spring of politics, I wrote a note to myself: "The White House doesn't seem to be as much fun anymore as it used to be."

There was no time anymore for the little perquisites of the job—like having drinks with Robert Redford when he visited the White House to research his role in *All the President's Men*, or chatting with Elizabeth Taylor in the White House mess. There was no time anymore for an afternoon game of tennis on the White House court, the most exclusive court in town. The White House had become all work, pressure and tension.

For Ford, too. He frowned a lot. At times he was impatient. He seemed unable to relax, and by the end of the final, grueling primary campaign trip to Ohio and New Jersey, he was irritable. "I don't want to see one more person!" he barked to his appointments secretary, Terry O'Donnell.

One day during the struggle with Reagan, I had to visit the White House dentist for some painful scraping and drilling. The dentist could tell I was harried and worried about the president's troubles.

"I'll bet this is the most relaxing part of the day for you," he observed. "It's too bad you have to come to the dentist's chair to get away from your problems."

I laughed at the thought that a painful visit to the dentist was a welcome interlude in those days.

CHAPTER SIXTEEN

Kansas City, Here We Come

Neither Ford nor Reagan had enough delegates to win the presidential nomination when the primaries and state conventions ended. The long struggle was going right down to the wire; the winner would be decided at the Republican National Convention in Kansas City in August.

Early in the primary season some Ford aides had thought a brief, unsuccessful Reagan challenge might be helpful to the president, demonstrating that he could win against a tough opponent and serving as a dress rehearsal for the campaign organization. But as the Republican convention approached, it was clear that the primary battle had hurt Ford, making him appear to be such a weak leader he couldn't even control his own party from the White House, and forcing him to spend large amounts of time on politics, which our polls showed damaged his public standing.

In the days immediately before Kansas City, with the nomination hanging on the decisions of a handful of delegates, a number of news developments that ordinarily would not have been considered in a political context were examined closely in the White House for possible political benefit.

For instance, when twenty-six children were kidnapped on their school bus in Chowchilla, California, it was suggested that if the kidnappers turned out to be terrorists, the president might have to order an Entebbe-like rescue raid—an opportunity for Ford to demonstrate strong leadership.

As a first step, to position Ford for possible involvement in the kidnapping, a statement was prepared saying the president was "quite concerned" and wanted a written report from Attorney

General Levi. The press office issued the statement without checking with Ford, although he said later it reflected his views.

When Cheney learned what we had done, he worried that the press might recognize the intent of the statement and accuse the White House of trying to exploit the kidnapping for political purposes. But the children soon escaped unharmed and there was no further excuse for White House involvement.

There were less momentous problems to consider on the eve of the Republican convention as well. I sent my assistant, Connie Gerrard, a note: "Please inquire discreetly of the Republican National Committee what they plan to do about press credentials requested by Elizabeth Ray and other such nonjournalists."

Ray, Wayne Hays's blonde congressional secretary with round heels and a yen for money and publicity, had signed up to cover the convention for a skin magazine called *Genesis*. Given the press mania for gossip and trivia, any pictures of her near the president in her role as "reporter" would surely be splashed on front pages and TV shows all over the country. I hoped to avoid that distraction.

The Republican National Committee reported to me that it had granted *Genesis* a limited press credential allowing Ray only in the fringe areas of the convention. (One day, however, as Ford was pushing through a jammed hotel lobby in Kansas City, I spotted Ray heading for him. Some quiet blocking by White House staff members and Secret Service agents prevented her from getting near the president.)

Two weeks before the Republican convention opened, a White House committee, including the president's son Jack, sent Ford a long memo outlining its suggestions for the Kansas City meeting. Some excerpts from that fascinating document:

The theme of the Democratic convention was perhaps "The Coronation of Jimmy Carter." What we would like to see in Kansas City is a story entitled "The Triumph of Gerald Ford." It would be the personal triumph not so much of a President but of a field general who has figured out how to turn back a heavy attack and overwhelm the opposition. . . .

Leadership, control, intelligence, competence, vision—these

are the personal qualities we would like to have you project.

As for the GOP, we believe it is essential that the party not only be re-united in Kansas City but that it also project an image of being a party with a future, a party with a broad base, a party which can provide a home for the average American—not the party of the has-beens, the party of WASPs, nor the party of the comfortable. . . .

New faces, representing young people, athletes, celebrities, and various constituent groups, would be suggested for such things as the Pledge of Allegiance, "Star Spangled Banner," invocations, and benedictions in an attempt to appeal both to interest groups and to make the convention as interesting as possible.

The memo also informed the president that he needed to decide when to go to Kansas City—a matter complicated by financial, political and public-relations considerations. The Ford campaign was so close to the spending ceiling set by the Federal Election Commission that it could not afford accommodations for the president and his entourage in Kansas City for a long period. The Crown Center Hotel, the Ford headquarters at the convention, demanded payment in advance for the rooms, including the president's $350-a-day suite.

Aside from the money question, campaign chairman Rogers Morton felt Ford would give the impression of being overly concerned about his prospects of winning the nomination if he flew to Kansas City too far ahead of the convention opening. On the other hand, the chief of Ford's convention team, William Timmons, argued that the president might have to go to Kansas City early to compete with Reagan for media exposure and to appeal in person to the last uncommitted delegates.

Eventually it was decided that Ford would fly to Kansas City on Sunday afternoon, August 15, 1976, the day before the convention opened. We timed his arrival so he was welcomed by thousands of screaming, banner-waving supporters at the Crown Center, to whom he responded with a pep speech, right in the middle of the TV networks' special convention-eve broadcasts. The networks were forced to cut live to the colorful and enthusiastic rally because we had turned down all requests for pretaped presidential interviews. We wanted Ford to appear on the broadcasts in a flattering setting we controlled.

Kansas City steamed in the August heat. Thousands of people jammed the city to take part in the colorful process of selecting a candidate for president and to report that process to the rest of the world.

Kansas City was selected for the Republican convention partly because it symbolized stable, conservative Middle America, distant from bureaucratic and corrupt Washington, distant from alien and frightening New York City. Some parts of Kansas City still had the flavor of a cattle town and a grain hub, although the downtown was being renewed with modern skyscrapers, including attractive and efficient hotels. (There were not enough hotel rooms, however, and many delegates were put up in outlying cities more than an hour's bus ride from the Kemper Arena convention hall.) Kansas City also had some first-rate resturants and enticing bars, but few members of the Ford staff had time for them during convention week. A relaxed meal was a room-service cheeseburger and a bottle of beer gulped down while juggling phone calls and crises.

Ford and his campaign strategists braced for Reagan's final efforts to overcome the Schweiker goof and win the nomination. The Ford camp suspected the Reagan maneuvers would involve forcing the delegates to vote on a procedural or ideological issue which would demonstrate Reagan strength and thereby might stampede the convention for the Californian.

A week before the convention began, Reagan's strategist, John Sears, unveiled his first gambit. He proposed that the convention adopt a new rule, Rule 16-C, requiring Ford to announce the name of his vice-presidential running mate before the balloting for the presidential nomination.

Sears's motive was to force the president to alienate one batch of delegates or another with a vice-presidential choice they didn't like, just as Reagan had alienated some southern and conservative delegates with Schweiker. Some delegates joked that 16-C was the "misery loves company" rule. Obviously, the Ford forces resisted the rule change.

The president's supporters were able to defeat Sears's proposal in the Convention Rules Committee. But 16-C received enough votes to allow Sears to demand consideration by the full convention the night before the balloting for the presidential nomination. That would be an all-important test of strength between Ford and Reagan.

Reagan disclosed his second ploy the day the convention opened. He proposed that a new plank, entitled "Morality in Foreign Policy," be added to the Republican platform. The proposed plank read:

The goal of Republican foreign policy is the achievement of liberty under law and a just and lasting peace in the world. The principles by which we act to achieve peace and to protect the interests of the United States must merit the restored confidence of our people.

We recognize and commend that great beacon of human courage and morality, Alexander Solzhenitsyn, for his compelling message that we must face the world with no illusions about the nature of tyranny. Ours will be a foreign policy that keeps this ever in mind.

Ours will be a foreign policy which recognizes that in international negotiations we must make no undue concessions, that in pursuing detente we must not grant unilateral favors with only the hope of getting future favors in return.

Agreements that are negotiated, such as the one signed in Helsinki, must not take from those who do not have freedom the hope of one day gaining it.

Finally, we are firmly committed to a foreign policy in which secret agreements, hidden from our people, will have no part.

It was, of course, a critcism of Ford's foreign policy, especially of Kissinger, cleverly written in temperate language to appeal to moderate delegates.

Reagan claimed he proposed the plank in order to make the GOP platform "reflect the mainstream of thought in this country today." Actually, Reagan's goal was to provoke Ford into an all-out fight against the plank. If Reagan could win a convention vote on the reasonable-sounding foreign-policy plank, he would demonstrate strength and popularity which might attract enough wavering delegates to give him the nomination.

A copy of the so-called morality plank arrived at Ford headquarters just as the president was leaving the Crown Center to attend a reception for Republican VIPs at the grand old Muelbach Hotel. Cheney and I grabbed Brent Scowcroft of the NSC and dragged him along so the three of us could discuss in the staff van driving to the reception what Ford's response to the plank should be.

Cheney and I argued that Ford should accept the plank without a fight because he could lose only if he opposed it and was beaten in a convention vote; if he welcomed the plank, Reagan's effort to provoke a test of strength would evaporate. Scowcroft replied that Ford should fight the plank on principle because it was a repudiation of his foreign policy and a repudiation of Kissinger.

"Principle is okay up to a certain point," Cheney said as the van bounced along the Kansas City streets, "but principle doesn't do any good if you lose the nomination." Besides, Cheney declared, "platforms don't mean anything; they are forgotten the day after the convention."

We continued the argument on the fringes of the reception while Ford circulated through the mob of Republican governors, senators, members of Congress, and state delegation chairmen. When the reception ended, Cheney, Scowcroft and I still had not been able to resolve our difference of opinion. Therefore we decided the best approach would be to stall for time by telling reporters that Ford was studying Reagan's foreign-policy plank and would express an opinion on it later. I was assigned to return with Ford to his hotel after the reception and get his approval for that response to the press.

Back in his modernistically furnished eighteenth-floor suite at the Crown Center, Ford read the Reagan plank for the first time.

"I don't like it," he snapped. "I'll fight it."

He especially did not like the sentence about the need to restore the confidence of the American people in U.S. foreign policy. "We have already restored confidence," he insisted.

I explained that Cheney, Scowcroft and I recommended he take no public position on the plank that night until he and his advisers had time to sift through the political implications.

Ford agreed, grudgingly.

"But if you have to, you can indicate I am leaning toward opposing the plank," he instructed.

I rushed down to the press center in a ballroom on the hotel's mezzanine and hurriedly summoned a news briefing. Just as the convention's Monday evening session was beginning, I told the assembled reporters, "The platform, as approved by the Platform Committee today, is acceptable to the president. . . . If any amendments are offered on the convention floor, we will study each proposal and determine our position." In other words, we hadn't decided yet what to do about Reagan's foreign-policy plank.

The vote on Rule 16-C, Reagan's other proposal, to force Ford to name his vice-presidential running mate in advance of the nomination, was scheduled for the second night of the convention, Tuesday. It would be the most important vote of the convention. If the proposal was defeated, Ford would demonstrate his control of the convention and would likely sweep on to win the nomination. If 16-C was approved, showing Reagan's strength, it could ignite an emotional switch to the Californian.

Both sides lobbied intensely. Ford and Reagan met in person with delegates to push their opposing views on 16-C. The president's major arguments were reduced to a written script and distributed to members of Ford's convention team to use in buttonholing delegates:

1. Fairness. We should not change rules in the middle of the game.

2. Sears's mistake. Sears is trying to make up for the Schweiker maneuver.

3. Restrictive. It would prevent a Ford/Reagan ticket now and in the future prevent the two strongest candidates from getting together.

4. Hurtful of Party Unity. It eliminates consultation with Governor Reagan for the President's Vice Presidential recommendation. Such consultation is needed to unify the party.

The Mississippi delegation, with thirty votes, was the focus of the heaviest lobbying on 16-C. The colorful and complex chairman of the delegation, Clarke Reed, was badgered by Ford and Reagan agents virtually nonstop. Reed originally had favored Reagan for the nomination but had endorsed Ford, under heavy White House pressure, after the Schweiker choice.

The Mississippi delegation met at its hotel Tuesday afternoon, about four hours before the convention session on 16-C, and voted thirty-one to twenty-eight (one abstention) to oppose Reagan's rule change. Under the delegation's unit rule, that meant all thirty Mississippi votes would be cast against 16-C. By Ford's calculation, that meant 16-C probably would be defeated and he would go on to win the nomination.

But as the delegates gathered in the arena that Tuesday night to vote on 16-C, an old ailment of the Ford campaign—foot-in-the-mouth disease—threatened to wreck the hard-won victory. Copies of Alabama's *Birmingham News* appeared on the convention floor with the headline, "Ford Would Write Off Cotton South?" The article reported that Rogers Morton had told a breakfast meeting with newsmen that Ford's presidential campaign would be aimed at winning the northern industrial states, with some chance of carrying states of the "peripheral" South. According to the article, Morton seemed to be suggesting that the president was writing off any effort to win the Carter deep South.

The Reagan forces seized on the *Birmingham News* headline to launch a renewed effort to win support for Rule 16-C in the Missssippi delegation. It was the final pitch of the final inning for the Reagan team.

The Ford strategists pressed equally hard for Mississippi and other wavering delegates to maintain their opposition to 16-C. The president himself phoned Mississippi chairman Reed to assure him that the Ford campaign was not going to write off Dixie.

Dan Rather of CBS spotted the shirt-sleeved Morton on the sweltering convention floor during the furor and rushed him onto the air for a live interview. Morton insisted to Rather that the Ford campaign would not ignore the deep South. Well, then, Rather suggested, he would escort Morton over to where the Mississippi delegates were seated and let him try to explain that to them while millions of CBS viewers watched live. Rather began leading Morton toward the Mississippi delegation. Cheney saw what was happening on TV and rushed an aide to the convention floor to rescue Morton from Rather's effort to stage a news event.

After the flurry over the *Birmingham News* report on Morton's remarks, the time arrived for the convention to vote on 16-C. Ford followed the proceedings in his office at the Crown Center on a large three-screen television set that allowed him to view the coverage of CBS, NBC and ABC simultaneously. The president was more tense than I'd ever seen him as he settled into a red leather easy chair in front of the TV. Mrs. Ford, their son Mike, Mike's pretty wife, Gayle, and a few aides joined the president in his office for the 16-C showdown.

As the roll of states was called, Ford did not utter a word. He sat tight-faced, peering at the TV screen through his glasses, keeping a running tally of the delegates' votes. Near the end of the roll call, when it was almost certain that 16-C would be defeated, Kennerly began to chatter.

"Shut up!" Ford barked. I'd never heard him use such a harsh tone before.

The delegates defeated 16-C by a vote of 1180 to 1069, fifty votes more than necessary. (In the end, Reed and his Mississippi delegates stuck with Ford, but their thirty votes didn't make any difference.) There was no explosion of jubilation in the president's suite, just a quiet exchange of congratulations, a phone call to the convention hall to thank Ford's team of strategists, and the weary knowledge that after so many months of struggle the president was going to win the nomination.

Ford sent me down to the press room to express his appreciation for the 16-C victory.

"Obviously, the president is delighted by the victory," I told the reporters and TV cameras, "and he believes it is a good indication of how the final vote will turn out when the delegates vote on the nomination tomorrow night."

With the GOP nomination virtually locked up as a result of his 16-C triumph, the president decided it was time to start healing the split between the Ford and Reagan wings of the Republican party. He instructed me to read a unity statement to the newsmen at the late-night briefing.

"Nothing has happened during the primary campaign and nothing has happened here in Kansas City that divides the Republican party," I declared on Ford's behalf. "The party will emerge from this convention, the president believes, united to begin the campaign for the fall election."

I continued: "This has been a healthy competition. It has been a competition between two strong, articulate leaders who hold principles very strongly and there has been nothing divisive about this. It has only been healthy for the party to have this kind of competition."

Somehow, I read it with a straight face.

Immediately after the 16-C vote, the convention took up Reagan's "morality" plank on foreign policy. Ford and his aides still had not decided whether to fight it or accept it. Kissinger, feeling he was the target of the plank, wanted the president to oppose it. So did Vice President Rockefeller, initially.

But the political strategists could see nothing to be gained by fighting the plank at that late hour, after already defeating Reagan on 16-C, the key test of strength. To fight the foreign-policy plank was to risk losing, thereby reviving Reagan's chances. There was nothing in the wording of the plank that Ford could not swallow (perhaps holding his nose). Even Rockefeller came around.

Instructions were flashed to Ford's team at the convention hall: Try for a compromise by eliminating the specific reference to the Helsinki agreement. If not, accept it as is.

As Cheney put it delicately, "We are going to take a dive."

The convention adopted Reagan's foreign-policy "morality" plank without opposition from the Ford forces.

With Reagan's final maneuvers thus disposed of, the convention turned to the business of nominating the Republican presidential candidate the next night, Wednesday.

Ford had agreed that a few reporters could watch the roll call on TV with him at his Crown Center office. The president approved Strobe Talbot of *Time* and Tom DeFrank of *Newsweek*, friends who needed a lot of color detail for their magazine articles; and John Mashek of *U.S. News & World Report*, who would be the pool reporter for all the other journalists. Ford did not want network TV cameras, partly because he did not want his moment of victory endlessly compared to Jimmy Carter's reaction, televised from his hotel room during the Democratic convention.

This arrangement for limited press coverage set off a revolt among the excluded reporters. The wire services screamed that it would be the first time they had been barred from witnessing such a historic moment on behalf of their hundreds of client publications. When I agreed to allow the AP and UPI each to send a reporter to the president's office, they refused to go unless I also accepted pool reporters representing the daily newspapers. I agreed. But then the newspaper reporters wouldn't go unless I also agreed to let in television correspondents. Then the radio reporters demanded representation, then local newspapers, then photographers.

Ford ended up watching the roll call with a herd of twenty-five reporters, four photographers and network minicameras jammed into the entrance hall of his office. It was an outrageous case of press arrogance, but I gave in because I was anxious to avoid a distracting fight with the press at the sweet moment of the president's victory.

The actual roll call on the nomination for president was almost an anticlimax, the result a foregone conclusion by then. Nevertheless, the Ford and Reagan organizations went through the ritual of staging noisy demonstrations at the arena for their candidates. A few Reaganites still hoped the demonstrations might ignite an emotional spark that would start a clamor for their man. But it was a vain hope.

Relaxed now, coatless, tieless, in his Crown Center office, Ford watched on TV as the state delegations were called one by one by the convention chairman to cast their votes. Ford clutched in his hand a slip of paper on which he had scrawled the number of delegate votes he expected to receive: 1179. Actually, when the roll call was completed and the outcome was announced, the president had 1187 delegate votes, 57 more than he needed to win the nomination. Reagan received 1070. The long battle for the nomination was over at last. Around the TV set in the Crown Center office, Ford's staff applauded happily.

As usual, Ford was restrained in his reaction. "I hope nobody demands a recount," he joked. Grinning, he turned to Don Penny, his speech coach, and cracked, "I guess we don't have to change the [acceptance] speech."

The other staff members crowded around, congratulating Ford and shaking his hand.

"It's been long and tough," the president told his aides, "but it was great."

The TV screens continued to show the scene at the arena, where a radiant Mrs. Ford was being mobbed by well-wishers and peppered with congratulatory kisses. Entertainer Sonny Bono appeared in the television pictures standing beside Mrs. Ford in the VIP box amidst the pandemonium of triumph.

"Look at the wonderful first family," I joked. "Mrs. Ford, Sonny Bono . . ." The president broke up laughing at the crack.

By prearrangement Ford left his office shortly after the roll call to drive the twenty-two blocks to Reagan's headquarters at the Alameda Plaza Hotel for a unity meeting with the loser. Reagan did not come to the Alameda lobby to greet Ford, but sent an assistant to escort the president to the Californian's ninth-floor suite. Reagan met Ford at the door of the suite and led him to a sofa in the living room, where they talked alone. Their conversation was beyond the hearing of their aides, who clustered, whispering awkwardly, in a dining-room/bar alcove and in the corridor.

Up and down the hallway, the doors stood open to the rooms of Reagan's staff members. In some of the rooms aides were weeping. I wondered how I would have acted if Ford had lost.

Lyn Nofziger of Reagan's staff, who had the reputation of being one of the hardest of political hardball players, offered me a drink.

"Gee, Lyn, thanks. That's probably the nicest thing you ever did," I replied stupidly.

The chief subject of discussion between the president and Reagan was the GOP vice-presidential choice. Reagan was not asked to run. John Sears had advised Cheney that Reagan would go through with the meeting only if he had an ironclad promise in advance that Ford would not offer him the number two spot on the ticket. Reagan had proclaimed again and again during the campaign and the convention that he was not interested in the second spot. But even if that could be dismissed as necessary public rhetoric to avoid undercutting the credibility of Reagan's presidential campaign, his aides told Ford campaign officials the same thing privately.

There was another reason why Ford did not ask Reagan to be his running mate. During the long campaign, the president began to resent Reagan's attacks on his abilities and accomplishments. By the time the nomination fight was over, Ford didn't like Reagan very much.

During their meeting at the Alameda Plaza, Ford reviewed with Reagan some names he was considering for his running mate. Reagan didn't like Elliot Richardson or former deputy attorney general William Ruckelshaus. He did like Senator Robert Dole of Kansas. After discussing the vice-presidential nomination and other matters for about fifteen minutes, Ford and Reagan adjourned to a hot and crowded meeting room of the hotel at 2:05 A.M. for a news conference to publicly kiss and make up.

"Governor Reagan, I came over to the hotel for the purpose of congratulating you on a very fine campaign and expressing to you our compliments for the outstanding organization that you had," Ford informed Reagan for the benefit of the reporters and cameras. "I think the campaign you waged and the organization you put together was beneficial to the campaign that we have, beginning right away, to defeat the Democratic nominee."

"Mr. President, my congratulations to you," Reagan replied. "It was a good fight, mom, and he won. My congratulations and, of course . . . as we both agreed all the way from the very beginning, once the fight was over, we are on the same side and we go forward together."

For Reagan, with his dream of the presidency thwarted, and for Ford, with his dream of election clouded, the honey-dipped words must have stuck in their throats.

By the time the president returned from the news conference to the Crown Center, family, staff and friends were celebrating his nomination victory.

"Where's my daddy?" Mrs. Ford shouted. Locating the president, she threw her arms around him and gave him a hug of congratulations.

Fifteen Republican officials trooped into Ford's office to perform the official notification that Ford was the convention nominee.

"Mr. President, we are here to tell you you were nominated, in case you didn't know it," announced Senator Robert Griffin of Michigan. Some of the delegation wore yellow or red baseball caps, the color-coded identification emblems of Ford's team of troubleshooters who roamed the floor of the convention. The president complied with requests that he autograph the caps.

The celebrations in the hotel rooms and offices of the president's headquarters picked up steam as the night wore on. But at about 3:15 A.M., Ford broke away from the partying and sat down at the conference table in his office to select a vice-presidential running mate. Around the table were his closest political advisers: Rockefeller; Cheney; deputy campaign director Stuart Spencer; pollster Bob Teeter; Senator Griffin; Senator John Tower of Texas; White House Counsellor John Marsh; former defense secretary Melvin Laird; and Bryce Harlow, Washington lobbyist for Proctor and Gamble, aide to Eisenhower and Nixon, one of the wisest political heads in Washington.

The process of picking a vice-presidential nominee had begun several weeks before when Ford invited Republican governors, senators, House members, convention delegates and other party luminaries to send him their suggestions. Ford said he was looking for a running mate who had the ability to take over as president, if necessary; shared his general political ideology; and was a good campaigner—in that order.

More than a thousand replies had come in. When the list was pruned to about two dozen—most of the nationally known Republicans—those still in the running were asked whether they would be willing to submit certain financial and other personal information. At least one well-known figure had informed the White House that he preferred to drop out of contention rather than expose his financial dealings.

Naturally, the names of those asked to supply information had leaked to the press. And for once, the White House was delighted with the leaks; Republicans who thought they had a chance to be Ford's running mate were likely to stick with the president in the battle against Reagan.

The list of semifinalists in the vice-presidential sweepstakes included senators Robert Dole, Edward Brooke of Massachusetts, Lowell C. Weiker of Connecticut, John Tower of Texas, Charles Percy of Illinois, Howard Baker and William Brock of Tennessee, Mark Hatfield of Oregon and Pete Domenici of New Mexico; governors Christopher Bond of Missouri and Robert Ray of Iowa; mayor Pete Wilson of San Diego; John Connally; Melvin Laird; William Ruckelshaus; Anne Armstrong of Texas, the U.S. ambassador to London and former White House counselor to Nixon and Ford; Don Rumsfeld; Elliot Richardson; and Nelson Rockefeller. Most of the people on the list were serious contenders for the vice-presidential nomination, but some were there primarily because Ford's strategists believed it would flatter them into supporting the president against Reagan.

By the time Ford sat down in the middle of the night in Kansas City to make his choice, the contenders for vice president were down to four: Dole, Ruckelshaus, Baker and Armstrong.

Ford listened as the participants discussed the pros and cons of the four.

Ruckelshaus, supported strongly by Teeter, was a Catholic, thought to be helpful in the quest for blue-collar and ethnic votes.* Ruckelshaus also would help erase some of the Nixon taint clinging to Ford, because he had resigned from the Justice Department rather than carry out Nixon's order to fire Special Prosecutor Archibald Cox. On the downside, Ruckelshaus would draw opposition from Reagan and other conservatives.

Armstrong, backed by Spencer, was an effective campaigner, a proven administrator, and popular in her home state of Texas, which Ford needed to carry. By nominating the first woman vice-presidential candidate of a major party, Ford might shed his public image as an unimaginative and cautious man. On the other hand, Teeter's polls showed Armstrong had no special appeal to women voters and hurt Ford among men voters.

Baker was from a border state, which might help undercut Carter's southern appeal, although there was considerable doubt about that. Baker had served visibly on Senator Sam Ervin's committee

---

* Treasury Secretary William Simon had been considered earlier because of his Catholic faith as well as his conservative philosophy. A friend told Ford that Simon had a double appeal: "He's a Catholic with a Jewish name."

investigating Watergate, but his role was ambiguous and possibly open to Democratic criticism. (Shortly after the convention had opened, a news story had appeared revealing that Baker's wife previously had a drinking problem. No one participating in the vice-presidential selection meeting with Ford acknowledged that this matter was considered.)

Dole was found by Teeter's polls to hurt Ford the least among voters. He was a true conservative, acceptable to the Reaganites, a hard-hitting campaigner, a friend and supporter of Ford, and a midwesterner who could appeal to farmers who were angry at the president for imposing a two-month embargo on grain sales to the Soviet Union.

After listening to his advisers discuss these merits and drawbacks of the candidates for nearly two hours, Ford suggested at 5 A.M. that everybody get some sleep and reassemble in about four hours to make a decision on the vice-presidential candidate. The president indicated no preference as the session broke up. Different participants left with different ideas of whom he favored.

The flood of news stories from Kansas City throughout convention week, purporting to reveal who was ahead and who was behind in the competition for the number two place on the ticket, were pure guesswork. No journalist and no "source" could authoritatively report which contender would be selected for the vice-presidential nomination because Ford himself didn't know until the last minute. As the *Washington Post*'s media critic Charles Seib complained, the press played an endless game of "let's pretend," pretending that a meaningful answer could somehow be discovered by asking every leading Republican in Kansas City whom Ford was going to select.

Carter phoned the Crown Center from Georgia at 8 A.M. the morning after Ford's nomination to congratulate him, but the president was still asleep. He returned the call when he got up.

"Good morning, Jimmy," Ford boomed in his loud telephone voice.

Carter congratulated him on winning the nomination.

"Aren't you kind," Ford replied. "We had a good convention. It was a rough, tough go."

Ford informed Carter that he was going to announce his vice-presidential choice at noon, but he didn't reveal whom it would be.

"Thanks for your thoughtfulness," Ford concluded. "My best to your family."

The president reconvened the vice-presidential selection meeting about 9:30 A.M. It was clear to the participants almost immediately that Ford was leaning strongly toward Dole. Within a half-hour the president made his selection.

Ford phoned Dole in his suite at the Muelbach about 10:30 A.M.

"Bob, I would like you to be on the ticket with me," the president announced.

"Certainly," Dole accepted immediately. He had been hoping for the call.

"I think we will make a great team," Ford said.

Explaining the choice later, some Ford aides claimed the president had been virtually forced to pick the conservative Kansas senator in order to prevent the convention from revolting and drafting Reagan for the vice-presidential nomination.

Having won the nomination and picked a suitable vice-presidential running mate, Ford turned to the third and final goal of his strategy for Kansas City: to deliver an acceptance speech that would launch his underdog campaign against Carter with a bang.

Bob Hartmann had begun writing the speech weeks before. It went through innumerable drafts. Once it was close to the final form, the president started rehearsing under the coaching of Don Penny. Ford read the speech several times in front of a TV camera which recorded it on videotape, then the tape was played back while Penny pointed out in his blunt manner where the president needed to improve his delivery. Ford had never before prepared so carefully for a speech. The stakes had never before been so high.

The acceptance speech was scheduled to be delivered to the convention and broadcast on TV on Thursday, the night after Ford won the nomination. But one paragraph of the speech was deliberately omitted from the advance text distributed to reporters late Thursday afternoon. Ford wanted to spring it as a dramatic surprise.

"I am ready, I am eager to go before the American people and debate the real issues face-to-face with Jimmy Carter," the missing paragraph declared.

The president had for some time been considering challenging Carter to televised debates. He had even hinted at his inclination in several press interviews. Traditionally, an incumbent does not debate his opponent, on the theory that debates give free publicity to the lesser-known challenger. But Ford's circumstances were different from those of any previous president: He was far behind

Carter in the polls, down more than thirty points before the Democratic convention; he'd never been elected to the White House; and the voters had doubts about his intelligence and competence.

Needing to convert 125,000 Carter supporters a day, by one aide's estimate, yet limited by the new campaign-spending law on how much television time he could buy, Ford saw the debates as a way to get a lot of free TV time with a guaranteed large audience. The format would allow him to demonstrate his knowledge of complex issues and, perhaps, expose Carter's lack of knowledge. The clincher was a tip reaching the Ford camp that Carter was preparing to challenge the president to debate. Rather than appearing to respond to Carter's idea, the president decided to seize the initiative.

Ford's strategy of using the acceptance speech as an attention-grabbing kickoff for his campaign depended on its being delivered in prime television time, when the largest number of voters would be watching. He did not want a repetition of George McGovern's disastrous experience four years earlier, when skirmishing at the Democratic convention delayed the acceptance speech until 3:30 A.M., when even most West Coast viewers had gone to bed.

All week in Kansas City, Ford's tall, cool, efficient TV adviser, William Carruthers, ran a masterful operation to make sure the president's campaign got the most and the best television coverage. Using direct phone lines to the NBC and ABC anchormen's booths, Carruthers made sure the president's activities were timed for maximum TV exposure. Carruthers also quarterbacked a team of Ford spokesmen who rushed in front of the cameras for interviews whenever the convention hit a slow period or when the president's strategists wanted to divert attention from harmful developments.

But as the time came for the acceptance speech, the most crucial moment of Ford's TV master plan, Carruthers lost his tight control. This occurred when Reagan's last-ditch supporters at the convention clapped, cheered and demonstrated, demanding that he leave his box and come to the podium to speak before Ford did. Chairman John Rhodes invited him to the microphone. Reagan declined. The Reaganites demonstrated some more. Rhodes invited him again. Reagan declined again.

The drama was using up the president's prime TV time!

Ford sat on a sofa in his hotel suite watching the time-wasting demonstration for Reagan on TV, growing grim and tight-jawed as the clock ticked away. As the deadline approached for morning newspapers, the president summoned me to his suite and directed me to leak the news of his debate challenge to as many reporters as I could reach. At least that story would be circulated, no matter how long the acceptance speech was delayed.

I ran to another room and began phoning reporters with the tip about the debates.

At last, the Reagan demonstration subsided. As the next event on the convention schedule, a twenty-minute film was shown in the arena, depicting the president's life, with endorsements from friends and formal and informal shots of Ford and his family in the White House and at Camp David. Carruthers insisted that every light in the arena be switched off during the film so the networks could not pick up interviews or analysis from their correspondents and would be forced to broadcast the film, which was really a long commercial for Ford.

By the time the film ended and the president stepped out on the podium to deliver his acceptance speech, it was twenty minutes before midnight in the East, past prime TV time. Thanks, Ronald Reagan.

The ovation for Ford died out and, spotlighted at the enormous rostrum, the president began reading his acceptance speech.

It was obvious as soon as he started speaking that this was a different Jerry Ford—forceful, polished, articulate, in command, *presidential.*

"We will wage a winning campaign in every region of this country from the snowy banks of Minnesota to the sandy plains of Georgia," he thundered. "We concede not a single state. We concede not a single vote.

"I seek not a Republican victory, but a victory for the American people. You at home listening tonight, you are the people who pay the taxes and obey the laws. You are the people who make our system work. You are the people who make America what it is," Ford intoned in a mesmerizing cadence.

"It is from your ranks that I come and on your side I stand. . . .

"It is not the power and the glamour of the presidency that leads me to ask for another four years. It is something every hardworking American will understand—the challenge of a job well begun but far from finished. . . .

"I faced many tough problems. I probably made some mistakes, but on balance, America and Americans have made an incredible comeback since August 1974," Ford recalled.

"My record is one of progress, not platitudes. My record is one of specifics, not smiles. My record is one of performance, not promises," Ford proclaimed in an indirect crack at Carter. "It is a record I am proud to run on. It is a record the American people—Democrat, Independent and Republican alike—will support on November second. . . .

"Right now I predict that the American people are going to say that night: 'Jerry, you have done a good job. Keep right on doing it.' "

It was the best speech of his life, well written, delivered brilliantly, exceeding even the hopes of his campaign strategists. All through his public career, at moments that demanded an extraordinary effort, Ford rose to the occasion. He did it again in Kansas City.

Then came the emotional climax of that bitter Republican convention: On cue, Republican leaders of every ideological persuasion poured onto the podium and crowded around Ford and Dole in a live, onstage, on-camera love fest.

The president waved Reagan up to the stage, and this time the loser came. He spoke, a little too long, a little too self-servingly, using excerpts from what must have been his acceptance speech. But he was spellbinding, as usual, and he used his influence to encourage harmony by telling the delegates, "Go forth in unity."

Following the closing session of the convention, ABC gave a party in a park across the street from the Crown Center, starting at midnight. The party was held in the park because, under the peculiar drinking laws of Kansas City, booze cannot be consumed indoors after 2 A.M., but it can be consumed outdoors until 5 A.M.

By dawn, just about everybody who was anybody in the press or on the campaign staffs, plus a large number of hangers-on, had made it to the party. After months of hard work and pressure, it was time to unwind.

I got back to my room in time for about one hour's sleep before I had to board Ford's motorcade for the departure from Kansas City. Naturally, I overslept. I was awakened by the phone ringing. Staggering around trying to answer it, I jammed my foot under a door, slicing my toes open. I had only a few minutes to pack, shave and shower, dress and make it to the motorcade. I was in pain.

I couldn't find anything to bandage my toes. Everywhere I stepped I left a bloody footprint.

I made it to the motorcade, somehow.

Ford originally was supposed to fly directly from Kansas City to Vail for a vacation and a series of meetings with aides to plan his campaign. But after talking to Dole on Thursday, the president decided to stop on his way to Colorado at his running mate's tiny hometown, Russell, Kansas. Cheney told him there wasn't enough time for the exhausted advance men to make the necessary arrangements, but the president, in his new forceful, take-charge mood, said he damn well *was* going to Russell, so the advance men better get busy.

The advance men did get busy, and one of the first things they discovered was that Russell, population 5631, did not have an airport large enough for Ford's plane. So, the day after the Republican convention ended, *Air Force One* landed at Salinas, Kansas, forcing Ford and Dole to drive the eighty miles to Russell. Arriving at the dusty Main Street of the wheat-country town, the president and his new running mate found people had come from miles around to honor the hometown boy at an old-fashioned political rally and picnic. Ford and Dole got right into the spirit of the occasion, munching hot dogs and barbecue on the courthouse lawn.

Standing on the bunting-draped platform, looking out at his friends and neighbors, Dole wept as he recalled the help he'd received from his hometown when he returned, horribly wounded, from World War II.

On his way out of town after the rally, the president stopped his limousine on a quiet side street to drop off Dole's seventy-three-year-old mother at her home. She let Ford into the house with a key hidden in the drainpipe over the front door. It was a nostalgic, mellow, happy day in the heart of Middle America, which added to the upbeat feeling of the convention's conclusion.

But beating Carter would require more than an upbeat mood. So, from Kansas, Ford flew to Vail to plan his campaign to keep the White House.

The date for the Republican convention had been chosen at a time when it was assumed that Ford would be the uncontested nominee. By scheduling the convention so late, it was reasoned, Ford would have more time to build his presidential record and less time to be portrayed as a politician campaigning for election. As it turned out, the late convention was harmful to Ford's election prospects. By the time he beat Reagan and flew to Vail, the president had only seventy-three days to unite a divided party, plan his campaign strategy and overcome a large Carter lead. It was a perilously short length of time.

True, the polls had changed dramatically; immediately after the Republican convention, Ford was found to have pulled within eight to fourteen points of Carter, cutting the Democrat's lead by more than half. But the Ford forces had far more sophisticated polling results which showed the president suffering serious and perhaps fatal weaknesses in the race with Carter. A blunt appraisal of Ford's chances was assembled by Cheney's staff and pollster Bob Teeter, and was given to the president in a loose-leaf notebook:

> You are not perceived as being a strong, decisive leader by anywhere near a majority of the American people. These perceptions do not necessarily reflect your true character or style as President. They are a reflection of how the TV viewer and newspaper reader "sees" you. We have presented this with the "bark" off because we must solve this perception problem in order to successfully communicate your leadership qualities. This obstacle must be overcome or there is no chance for victory. . . .
>
> There is one disturbing factor beginning to show up in Bob Teeter's latest data. Some of those polled are beginning to raise the question of whether the President is considered smart enough for the job. Also, he apparently has lost a great deal of his perception of being open. This has contributed to the President's decline. This is linked to the President being perceived as becoming more political (especially when he goes on the attack in a partisan, strident manner). This is why the primary campaigns have really hurt the President's national standings.
>
> Also, there is a clear public perception that no one is in control of this administration—no one in the White House, in the campaign, or anywhere. This is a major negative.
>
> To some he doesn't seem good enough to be President, indecisive, reactive, not smart.

Nevertheless, the campaign planners concluded, "We firmly believe that you can win."

CHAPTER SEVENTEEN

What a Way to Start
a Campaign

In the cool, clear summer air of the Rockies, between golf games, tennis matches and dinner parties, Ford met daily in Vail with his political strategists to review their recommendations and make decisions on his campaign plan.

The president agreed that his campaign should not waste time or money in those states where he was a sure winner (Nebraska, Kansas, Vermont, Idaho, North Dakota, Utah, Wyoming, Arizona, South Dakota, Oklahoma, Indiana, Colorado, New Hampshire, Maine and Iowa—total eighty-three electoral votes) or in those states that Carter had locked up (Georgia, Minnesota, District of Columbia, Alabama, Arkansas, Louisiana, Mississippi, South Carolina, Massachusetts, Rhode Island and Hawaii—total eighty-seven electoral votes).

The presidency would be won or lost in the remaining states, especially in California, Illinois, Michigan, New York, New Jersey, Ohio, Pennsylvania and Texas, the big "swing states" with the largest number of electoral votes. The Ford campaign would concentrate there.

Nearly half the $21.8 million the Federal Election Commission allowed each presidential ticket to spend would be allocated by the Ford campaign to TV commercials and other advertising, with much of the media budget hoarded for the last weeks of the campaign. Senator Dole and a team of presidential advocates would do most of the campaigning while Ford stayed in the White House demonstrating his competence and achievements as president.

Ford was reminded again at Vail that, despite his zest for the stump, the polls showed him losing popularity every time he campaigned heavily. The president's personal campaigning would be limited mostly to the last ten days before the election, and then only in those states where the latest polls showed that a presidential visit could swing the outcome. He was warned in Vail that he would be besieged by old friends from Congress telling him they guaranteed he would win the election if he only campaigned in their districts. But the president must resist and say no, painful as that might be for him. He promised to stick to the plan. The plan relied heavily on Ford making a good showing in the debates with Carter.

The second half of the campaign strategy was to deflate Carter's support by attacking him for being "devious and arrogant, driven by personal ambition in ruthless pursuit of power," and for being a far-out liberal, as demonstrated by his selection of Senator Walter Mondale as his running mate.

"We should try to characterize Carter's campaign as a mirror image of Nixon's '68 and '72 campaigns," Ford was advised in a campaign-strategy memo. "The following similarities should be pointed out: a candidate who tries to be all things to all people; avoids specifics on issues . . . ; driven by personal ambition—harsh and manipulative; secretive and surrounded by a protective and fiercely loyal staff."

As Ford put together his campaign team and plan at Vail, he had the unpleasant task of removing his old friend Rogers Morton as campaign chairman. Morton, slow-moving, ailing, lacking administrative talents, with a penchant for saying the wrong things to reporters, just didn't fit the fast-paced, tightly organized, error-free campaign Ford needed. To replace him, the president wisely selected James Baker, an impressive Houston lawyer and former undersecretary of commerce, who had established a record of accomplishment and of credibility with the press as the Ford campaign's chief delegate-hunter during the primaries and convention. Morton was kicked upstairs to a face-saving job as chairman of the Ford Steering Committee, a large advisory group set up to give prominent Republicans an outlet for their campaign suggestions.

The change in campaign leadership was announced at a unity news conference in Vail on the street in front of Ford's rented chalet with the mountains as a backdrop for the cameras. Arrayed around the president were Rockefeller, Dole, Connally, Morton and Baker. Reagan was not there; in fact, he had not been invited. Although Lyn Nofziger and a few other Reagan aides crossed over to work for Ford or Dole, the president's strategists bobbled the ball by not recruiting Reagan and his top advisers, John Sears and Senator Paul Laxalt, to campaign hard for Ford.

The *Dallas-Times Herald* was given a leaked story right after the convention saying Connally had turned down an invitation from Ford to become chairman of the Republican National Committee because he expected the president to lose the election. The White House suspected the leak came from Connally himself because he was angry that he had not been selected as Ford's vice-presidential running mate. But by the time he arrived in Vail for the unity session, Connally was on board. Following the newly adopted anti-Carter strategy to the letter, he told reporters at the street-corner news conference, "Everywhere I have gone throughout the country, in every stratum of society, I have detected a note of fear about Governor Carter and an uncertainty about Governor Carter."

A major recommendation of the campaign planners was that Ford get tough about the sniping and feuds among his staff members. Nevertheless, the jockeying continued at Vail. Sensitivity over news leaks rose almost to the paranoid level, particularly among Cheney's assistants, nicknamed the "junior varsity." They were especially upset by leaks of parts of the campaign strategy. They blamed the Press Office, although with newsmen and staff members spending so much time mingling at Vail's restaurants, bars and tennis courts, it was impossible to trace the leaks.

One CBS story that angered the campaign planners showed film of Don Penny walking through Vail in a tennis outfit while the correspondent reported that the actor/comedian/producer/speech coach planned to master Carter's mannerisms and voice patterns so he could play the part of the Democratic candidate in dress rehearsals to help Ford prepare for the debates. Penny was suspected by other White House aides of unthinkingly leaking the story himself to publicize his role in the campaign. The story was potentially damaging to Ford, since a good showing in the debates might be written off by the press as the result of careful rehearsing. Carter alertly jumped on the Penny story, saying he didn't plan to stage any rehearsals with an actor playing the role of Ford.

I became conscious at Vail that my authority in the area of press relations had been diluted by the addition to the staff of others assigned to media matters: a TV adviser, a press spokesman for the campaign committee, and a new White House director of communications who ostensibly worked for me but in reality was virtually independent. In addition, Cheney and his assistants dabbled incessantly in my business. However, with only two months remaining before the election and plenty of press and TV problems to go around, I decided to let it pass for the time being and straighten out the rivalries after November 2.

By the time of Ford's Vail interlude, there was no question that Dick Cheney was firmly atop the White House chain of command. Cheney had taken on more and more power until he was running the White House staff and overseeing the campaign in an authoritative manner—his easygoing style had disappeared. Although he kept a low public profile, Cheney had accumulated as much control as some of the better-known chiefs of staff. Some reporters privately started calling him the Grand Teuton, a complex pun referring to his mountainous home state of Wyoming and the Germanic style of his predecessor, H. R. Haldeman.

On the way back to Washington from Vail, *Air Force One* landed at Ellsworth Air Force Base near Rapid City, South Dakota, to refuel. Ford wanted to use the rows of B-52 bombers lined up at the SAC base as the setting for a speech on the need for a strong defense. On the flight to Ellsworth, Communications Director David Gergen, Don Penny and I discussed what the president should say. We agreed that he should mention the SAC motto, Peace Is Our Profession, and declare, "Peace is my profession, too."

Standing on a platform at the edge of the windswept runway, the president told the crowd of airmen and their families and townspeople, "Peace is your motto and I want you to know peace is my motto, too."

"He blew it," Gergen blurted. He did indeed.

Gergen, Cheney's assistant James Cavanaugh and I stood silently under the low, dark, late-afternoon prairie sky, worrying how many other slips of the tongue Ford would make during the hard days of campaigning ahead.

Ford was inundated with a flood of bad news in early September:

—The Labor Department announced on September 13 that unemployment in August went up for the third month in a row, to 7.9 percent, the highest rate of the year. It was the last unemployment report before the Ford-Carter debate on the economy and domestic matters, and the next to-the-last shot at a better unemployment rate before the election.

—After narrowing the gap in the polls at a phenomenal rate after the Democratic and Republican conventions, Ford seemed to slip again. A Gallup poll published on September 2 showed Carter increasing his lead from ten points to fifteen points, 52–37.

—The Securities and Exchange Commission on September 1 accused the accounting firm formerly headed by Ford's friend and White House adviser William Seidman of negligence for failing to detect "fraudulent conduct" by four corporate clients. There was no suggestion that Seidman or the company was involved in fraud, but in the post-Watergate atmosphere the faintest hint of wrongdoing attracted heavy press attention.

—FBI Director Clarence Kelley conceded at the end of August that the bureau's carpentry shop had constructed some drapery valances for his apartment at government expense.

—The president's program to inoculate every man, woman and child in America against swine flu hit still another snag in early September. Ford had been talked into the unprecedented mass inoculation project by HEW and a panel of independent scientists because they feared an outbreak of flu similar to the 1918 influenza epidemic. The swine-flu inoculations finally were abandoned when some people died and others became temporarily paralyzed after receiving their shots. There never was a swine-flu epidemic. The whole thing became the butt of jokes and, to critics, a confirmation of the Ford administration's incompetence.

The worst problem in early September was arranging the official kickoff speech for the Ford campaign. The campaign kickoff was of more symbolic importance to reporters than it was of strategic importance to the Ford campaign, since the president's plan was to stay off the hustings. But when Labor Day, the traditional day for launching presidential campaigns, passed without Ford stirring from the White House, stories began to appear saying the president's campaign was so disorganized he couldn't even figure out how and where to stage his kickoff speech. The stories died out after we announced that the president would officially launch his campaign with a speech at his alma mater, the University of Michigan, on September 15.*

The University of Michigan speech was almost a disaster. The Ford campaign had virtually invited itself to the campus, which angered a group of student political activists who promised protest demonstrations. The school newspaper, the *Michigan Daily*, ran an editorial saying that Ford launching his campaign on a college campus was like Adolf Hitler making the first contribution to the United Jewish Appeal.

Concerned about an embarrassing student demonstration during the president's speech, the campaign committee canceled plans to buy TV time to broadcast the address. The speech had been scheduled for 7:30 P.M. because that is a good television period in the East and Midwest, even though it is too late for coverage on the regular evening TV news shows. But after the live broadcast was scrubbed, the school refused to let Ford change the time for fear of further irritating the protestors. So the president was stuck giving a campaign kickoff speech that would be seen by only a small audience on the morning TV news shows and would be dead news by the next evening's newscasts.

In an effort to salvage some coverage on the news programs on the evening of the speech, the president agreed to meet informally with about two dozen students in midafternoon to answer their questions while the TV cameras rolled. However, the advance team picked up indications that the most radical students on campus had been selected as the questioners. Worried that the students would walk out on the president or stage some other dramatic gesture of protest, we canceled TV coverage of that event, too.

The speech came off as well as could be expected under the circumstances. Buoyed by dinner with the Michigan football team, the president strode into the crowded Crisler Arena with Mrs. Ford at his side to the blaring sound of the university's victory march. Some students booed and heckled during Ford's speech, but far more cheered and applauded, trying to drown out the demonstrators.

---

* Carter made his campaign kickoff speech on Labor Day at Warm Springs, Georgia, Franklin D. Roosevelt's summer home. He did everything to invoke the memory of the founder of the Democratic coalition except roll out in a wheelchair puffing on a cigarette through a long holder.

Near the end of the speech, a firecracker exploded under a seat high up in the arena. For an instant, that frightened look which photographs had captured in Sacramento and San Francisco appeared again on the president's face. But he kept reading his speech, barely missing a beat.

Afterward, reporters didn't know what to make of the audience's response to Ford's speech. Most of the newsmen allowed themselves to be persuaded by members of the Ford staff that the booing had been confined to a few dozen students and did not justify stories saying Ford's campaign kickoff had been rudely disrupted by hecklers at his own university. Flying back to Washington that night, I told the press pool on *Air Force One* that the president was "very pleased" by his reception and felt he was "well received." The booing, I told the reporters, had been "fully expected" and was really mild compared to the almost continuous heckling Ford received when he made the commencement speech at Michigan as vice president in 1974.

"It would have been so easy to find a hundred-percent supportive audience," I argued. "He could have gone to a Republican fundraiser. But he wanted to go to his own university to start the campaign. We all expected much worse [from the demonstrators]."

For once, the reporters gave our line the benefit of the doubt.

However, back in the White House, where a number of staff members listened to the speech over a loudspeaker hookup, the booing sounded worse than it was. Doug Smith, Hartmann's deputy in the speechwriting office, flew into a rage, charging that the campaign kickoff was badly planned and should never have been given at Michigan. The next morning, at the senior staff meeting, he launched into a tirade about the speechwriters being kept out of scheduling discussions. (Cheney had done that to stop leaks.)

Later that morning, Ford intervened to head off anticipated news leaks from the speechwriting office about alleged poor planning of the campaign kickoff.

"I don't want any leaks saying anybody is unhappy with the way the speech went over," Ford declared during an Oval Office meeting, looking directly at Smith. "I want positive stories. I am very happy with the reception. I think it was a good reception. It was a good event. I am very pleased and I don't want anybody telling reporters otherwise. If they do, I'm going to be damned mad. Do you understand?"

"Yes, sir," Smith answered.

Besides the kickoff-speech difficulties, the Ford campaign had other shakedown problems during September.

An almost continual round of planning meetings was held in the White House from early morning to early evening. It was just about possible to spend the entire day going from one meeting to another without doing any work. In fact, at one point consideration was given to setting up a campaign "war room" manned ten or twelve hours a day. This control center would follow and react to campaign developments minute by minute. But nothing came of the idea.

The Ford "Advocates Program," which was supposed to schedule leading Republicans for speeches and news conferences around the country in the president's behalf—in the manner of the efficient Nixon "Surrogates Program" in 1972—limped along. For one thing, the White House and the campaign committee dueled over who was in charge. Secondly, the White House Counsel's Office ruled that the original plan—to send cabinet members around the country several days a week at government expense to speak about the president and his record—was illegal and had to be revised "if you don't want to go to jail."

I conducted a meeting in my office every morning, usually lasting well over an hour, with a half-dozen White House and campaign aides to decide what lines Ford and his advocates should emphasize, how to attack Carter and respond to his charges, and how to get maximum favorable media attention for the president. A similar group in the Nixon White House was called the Attack Group. We carefully called our meeting the Communications Strategy Group. However, we had trouble getting our strategy decisions carried out.

For instance, one of our earlier decisions was that Rockefeller should deliver the major response to Carter's Warm Springs kickoff speech. We suggested a line of attack, but Rockefeller declined to do it. Another time, I gave Connally the outline of a speech we wanted him to make. Connally said he was certainly glad to get the assignment and stuffed the outline in his pocket. But as far as I know, he never used it.

Often decisions reached at the Communications Strategy meeting were mysteriously canceled. Attacks that were supposed to be made, statements that were supposed to be written, events that were supposed to be staged, never were.

The Campaign Committee's press spokesman, William Greener,

was proud of a fat loose-leaf notebook he prepared for the Advocates Program listing where every Republican luminary was every day of the campaign, what media events they had scheduled and how to reach them with instructions. The book was supposed to make it possible for my daily Communications Strategy meeting to program the advocates to say what we wanted them to say, when and where we wanted them to say it.

The concept sounded great, but it rarely worked. Greener seemed reluctant to get his hands dirty. He almost never put out a statement in his own name criticizing Carter, and he appeared to drag his feet in asking Ford's advocates to challenge Carter on such potential problems as his large income-tax deductions, his secret 1970 gubernatorial campaign contributions or the thousands of dollars his campaign paid to black ministers in California who supported him.

I once griped to Cheney that the president was the only advocate we could count on.

"Yes," Cheney agreed, "he has to do it all himself."

Ford did get campaign help from Dole, an effective and hard-hitting spokesman who usually followed our suggestions for attacking Carter. However, Dole was forced onto the defensive early in the campaign by a *New York Times* story alleging that he had accepted illegal campaign contributions from Gulf Oil as a senator.

After Dole denied the charge, we sent instructions to Larry Speakes, Dole's press secretary, to make sure the vice-presidential candidate said nothing more about the allegation so as not to feed press stories that would distract from his role as an attacker. However, Dole declared he had nothing to hide and insisted on answering every question about Gulf. Every time he talked about it, he provided fresh quotes for another cycle of newspaper and TV stories. This kept Dole on the defensive and neutralized him as the hitman for the anti-Carter campaign.

"The only way I can shut him up is to tape his mouth shut," Speakes' moaned to me in one frustrated phone call.

Dole's effectiveness was further undermined by the hostility of his personal aides toward the Ford and Reagan people assigned to him for the duration of the campaign. White House advance people who questioned arrangements for Dole's campaign appearances were told by the senator's longtime aides, "If you don't like the way we do things here, go back to the White House."

According to Cheney, Lyn Nofziger, a diehard Reagan aide

working in the Dole campaign, once handed the vice-presidential candidate a speech he'd written and said, "You put something in there good about Ford. I can't think of anything."

My Communications Strategy Group finally scored its first big success one Saturday in mid-September when we spotted and exploited a Carter answer in an AP interview which seemed to say he would raise income taxes for everybody earning over about $14,000 a year. In the interview, promoted by the AP for a big spread in Sunday newspapers, Carter said that as president he would reform the income-tax system "to shift a substantial increase toward those who have higher incomes" and reduce taxes for low- and middle-income families.

Q.: What do you mean when you say "shift the burden"?
CARTER: I don't know. I would take the mean or median level of income and anything above that would be higher and anything below that would be lower.
Q.: The median family income today is somewhere around twelve thousand dollars. Somebody earning fifteen thousand dollars a year is not what people commonly think of as rich.
CARTER: I understand. I can't answer that question because I haven't gone into it. I don't know how to write the tax code in specific terms. It is just not possible to do that on a campaign trail. But I am committed to do it.

Carter's commitment to raise the income taxes of all those above the median—half the American families—did not impress AP correspondent Walter Mears enough for him to give much attention to those answers in his news story about the interview. But James Reichley, a former *Fortune* editor on Cheney's staff who was assigned by the Communications Strategy Group to read the transcript of the Carter interview, spotted the blunder right away. He underlined it, put brackets around it in the margins and excitedly brought his find to the Communications Strategy Group meeting in my office.

We mobilized all the forces we could find quickly on that Saturday morning. Dole, our heaviest hitter, happened to be in the White House for a meeting with Ford. We drafted a suggested attack and sent him out to tell the reporters and cameras what he thought of Carter's tax plan.

"I'm astounded to read here that he's going to raise taxes for half the American families, anyone above the median income," Dole declared, waving the AP wire copy at the TV cameras.

We recruited Treasury Secretary Simon and Budget Director James Lynn to express similar disbelief at Carter's answer on taxes. Having long since abandoned my apolitical stance, I joined in, telling reporters that Carter's proposal was a major blunder similar to McGovern's 1972 plan to give $1000 to every American.

The attack was blunted slightly by the disclosure that the AP had inadvertently dropped the words "middle income" in printing Carter's promise to reduce taxes for low- and middle-income families. But we insisted, correctly, that the error did not invalidate our criticism of Carter's promise to raise taxes for everyone above the median income.

By coincidence, an interview Ford had given months before to *Reader's Digest* was published that weekend. In it the president said, "I favor giving greater tax relief to the so-called middle-income taxpayers—those in the earning brackets of $8,000 to $30,000." Nice timing.

In his first public appearance the following week, Ford joined the attack on Carter's tax plan.

"Our middle-income taxpayers have been shortchanged in the last ten years," Ford told a Rose Garden audience. "I believe that this group ought to get additional tax relief. Those who advocate additional expenditures have now suggested there should be an additional levy on middle-income people, representing about fifty percent of the families in the United States."

The issue kept Carter on the defensive for days. He was forced at every campaign stop to try to explain away his gaffe.

All through September, up to the first debate, Ford followed the "Rose Garden strategy," avoiding campaign trips, staying in the White House and taking part frequently in official presidential functions, at which press coverage was welcomed. The strategy brought cries of complaint from Carter and the press.

September 7 was probably as good an illustration as any, although we may have laid it on a little thick that day.

At 11:03 that morning, in the Rose Garden, surrounded by members of Congress, administration officials and representatives of private charitable organizations, Ford signed a bill to pay tens of millions of dollars in compensation to victims of the Teton Dam disaster in Wyoming. Press and cameras were invited, of course.

An hour later the president was back in the Rose Garden, surrounded by a different group of officials and guests, signing a bill to help working parents pay child-care expenses.

Later that afternoon, popping into the press briefing room, Ford read a statement complimenting North Vietnam for providing information on twelve American men missing in action, but demanding a full accounting of the rest of the missing.

In between, Ford issued a proclamation designating October 11 as Columbus Day and another proclamation designating October 24 as United Nations Day.

The president also sent Jeno Palucci, national chairman of the Italian-American Foundation, on a mission to Italy to determine what U.S. help was needed following a bad earthquake.

The next day at a news conference Ford was asked whether he was "abusing" his powers "by controlling the media" through the Rose Garden strategy.

"I apologize if I am using the American press," Ford replied. "I am trying to do the job as president of the United States. And I hope that between the American press and the president we can convey important information to the American people."

The press charges of White House manipulation, and complaints by Carter that Ford was getting a free ride on the evening TV shows by making statements in the Rose Garden, exaggerated the success of the president's strategy. In fact, the Rose Garden strategy backfired to a great extent. The reporters and TV correspondents were so anxious to point out that Ford was using the White House as a campaign platform that the substance of his presidential actions and statements was often obscured by a blizzard of cynical cracks.

Thus, when Ford held a long cabinet meeting to catch up with developments after the convention and his Vail vacation, Bob Schieffer told his CBS viewers what it was really all about: "When you are the incumbent, you campaign from the Cabinet Room." And when the president sent Congress a proposal to double the size of the national-parks program, Schieffer made sure his audience understood "the president has decided that improving the quality of life will be one of his major campaign themes. Hence, the bill's Rose Garden send-off."

If the Rose Garden setting was an advantage of incumbency, it was more than offset by the disadvantages, namely that Ford was required to make policy decisions every day and accept the blame for whatever decisions went wrong. Carter was not saddled with that responsibility. Besides, the press undercut any benefit to the White House by suggesting political motives for even Ford's purely presidential activities.

If reporters and TV correspondents truly believed they were being manipulated to cover phony White House events for political purposes, their response should have been to ignore the events, rather than using them as a vehicle to raise doubts about the president's sincerity.

All the maneuvering during those weeks in September was just marking time until the first Ford-Carter debate. As I noted to myself at the time, "All the eggs are being placed in one basket with the debates." The hope was to close the gap in the polls by conclusively demonstrating Ford's competence and intelligence to the huge TV audience, and raising doubts about Carter's.

Ford's original proposal, announced at Vail, was for four debates, at least ninety minutes each, with the first one on the subject of national defense immediately after Labor Day. That would give Ford the advantage of talking about a subject he knew thoroughly while leaving little preparation time for the less knowledgeable Carter. (But that was an opening negotiating position more than anything else.)

With remarkably few snags, negotiators representing Ford, Carter and the League of Women Voters, sponsor of the debates, agreed on three presidential debates—in Philadelphia on September 23 on the economy and domestic matters; in San Francisco on October 6 on foreign and defense policies; and on October 22 in Williamsburg, Virginia, on any subject. A vice-presidential debate between Dole and Walter Mondale was scheduled in Houston for October 19. Each debate would be ninety minutes long with questions from a panel of newsmen and no direct cross-examination between the candidates.

Ford strategists, who had originally pressed for early debates to catch Carter unprepared, now said they were happy with the September 23 starting date because that would keep public opinion fluid and prevent Carter from hardening his lead while the president's late-starting campaign got organized. In light of the nagging unemployment problem, Carter seemed to have an advantage by focusing the first debate on the economy.

The TV networks and secondary candidates Eugene McCarthy and Lester Maddox griped justifiably that the debates were organized as a charade to get around the Federal Communications Commission's equal-time requirements. The pretense was that the League of Women Voters was staging the debates as a news event which the networks had decided to cover. In fact, of course, the debates were staged primarily for television coverage, although the charade allowed the League to exclude McCarthy and Maddox and dictate coverage restrictions to the networks.

The negotiators were exasperated at times by the conduct of Carter's TV adviser, Barry Jagoda, a short, stocky former network producer with salt-and-pepper beard and hair. Jagoda demanded that the panel of journalist-questioners address the president as "Mister Ford" instead of "Mister President" to assure Carter of complete equality. The negotiators decided to let the questioners address Ford and Carter as they pleased.

Jagoda's silliest demand was that Ford be required to stand in a depression in the stage or that Carter be allowed to stand on a riser so the 6'2" President and the 5'10½" Carter would appear to be the same height.

Jagoda was laughed out of the meeting.

The method of selecting the journalists for the coveted roles of questioners was kept a mystery from the public. The League of Women Voters chose the panels from suggestions submitted by its officers and by the Ford and Carter camps. Ford and Carter were allowed to veto any panelists they strongly opposed.

Carter's staff vetoed from the economic debate Eileen Shanahan of the *New York Times* even though she was recognized as one of the most knowledgeable reporters on the subject. (Ironically, the Carter administration later appointed Shanahan to be assistant secretary of HEW for public affairs. Two other newsmen on the Ford list of suggested debate panelists also went to work later in the Carter administration: Jerrold Schecter of *Time* and Leslie Gelb of the *New York Times*.)

The Ford managers vetoed no one, although they considered objecting to Jack Nelson, Washington bureau chief of the *Los Angeles Times*, on grounds that he was pro-Carter. The decision was made not to strike him from the panel at the Williamsburg debate on the theory that if he displayed pro-Carter sentiments too blatantly, it would build sympathy for the president.

During September, while arrangements for the debates were being completed, Milton Pitts, the White House barber, visited

Richard Nixon at San Clemente. Knowing that Pitts cut Ford's hair regularly, Nixon asked him to relay to the president his recommendations on the debates.

Back in Washington, the next time Pitts had Ford in his barber chair in the White House basement, he passed on Nixon's words of advice.

"Prepare, prepare, prepare" was the message Nixon sent Ford through the barber. "Take the amount of time you plan for preparation and double it."

Nixon ought to know. He blamed his loss to John Kennedy in the 1960 election on his poor appearance and lack of preparation for their first debate.

That precedent was very much on the minds of Ford's handlers as the president began serious preparations for the first round in Philadelphia.

CHAPTER EIGHTEEN

"Are There Any Soviet Troops in Poland?"

Nixon's big mistake was thinking his debates with Kennedy were debates, to be judged and scored like some college forensic competition.

Ford and his strategists knew better. The judges were 100 million TV viewers—the voters—and they would decide the winner, not on debater's points, but on appearance, personality, demeanor, image, good vibes, bad vibes, gut instinct.

To make sure the lessons of the past were well understood, Ford watched a grainy, black-and-white kinescope of the first Nixon-Kennedy debate, and staff members looked at kinescopes of all four 1960 debates.

Doug Bailey, the president's brilliant advertising and media consultant, wrote the following memo a week before the first Ford-Carter debate:

Winning the debate will result from the President seeing it not as a contest with Carter but as an opportunity to communicate with the people, regardless of what Carter does. The goal, therefore, is for the President to know exactly what he wants to communicate and to do so—without trying to influence what Carter does.

The dominant fact of the debate will be that it is not between two candidates but between one candidate and the president. Everything said, done and projected by the President should emphasize that fact. If the President is consistently, persistently Presidential, Carter (no matter what he does) will not measure up.

No one at the White House worried about Ford's ability to answer factual questions. He knew the material, dealt with it every day in the Oval Office. He had handled tough questions dozens of times at news conferences, campaign rallies and meetings with citizens' groups. In fact he often answered in too much detail, with a glut of statistics. The president knew *what* to answer; in preparing for the debates, he needed to master *how* to answer, in order to emphasize his strong points and emphasize Carter's weak points, in memorable language.

Bailey produced a chart listing seven points—the "basic message" —Ford should communicate. No matter what specific question was asked, the president was to answer it briefly, then slip into one of the seven points:

—America's recovery during the Ford presidency, from Vietnam, Watergate and deep economic recession, had been extraordinary.

—Ford wanted to lead the nation into a new age of freedom: freedom from too much government and freedom from crime.

—A president, unlike a candidate, must make tough decisions. He cannot evade issues or try to make everybody happy.

—A president has no choice but to veto legislation when it adds to the burden of inflation.

—Ford would not be satisfied as long as one willing worker couldn't find a job. But he was proud that more Americans had jobs than ever before.

—Economic problems came from Vietnam, congressional spending and zigzag policies of previous presidents. Recovery came from Ford's steady policy.

—The president should concede that his decision to embargo grain sales to the Soviet Union for a period in 1975 was wrong. (But Ford rejected that suggestion and refused to go that far.)

Bailey suggested several quotable expressions the president should use in making these points: "A president cannot be all things to all people"; "There is no button in the Oval Office marked 'maybe' "; "Surely Mr. Carter understands why vetoes are necessary. As governor of Georgia he vetoed his own legislature 138 times in four years."

As for the mechanics, Ford was advised to stand at all times during the debates, assume that a camera was always focused on him, make notes while Carter spoke, avoid telling anecdotes about his years in Congress and stay away from direct attacks on Carter unless Carter attacked him first.

Rehearsals were held in the Family Theater on the ground floor of the White House, where a replica of the stage layout for the debates was constructed. This permitted Ford to familiarize himself with the setting, get the feel of his podium and of the location of Carter's podium, and try out the signal-light system which indicated how much time was left to complete the three-minute answers and two-minute rebuttals. During the rehearsals, aides took turns firing questions at the president for hours while he developed and sharpened his answers. The sessions were videotaped and played back for criticism.

While reporters accepted the claims by Carter's aides that he was not rehearsing, details of Ford's preparations were leaked and reported extensively, raising again the danger that a good performance by the president might be discounted. I could never figure out why reporters made such a fuss about the president rehearsing. TV correspondents and anchormen rehearsed to polish their performance for a big program. Why shouldn't the president rehearse before the debates? The stakes on a good showing were enormous.

Ford flew to Philadelphia at midafternoon on September 23, 1976, the day of the first debate. He drove to the Walnut Street Theater, near Independence Hall, shortly before 4 P.M. to check the microphones and lighting and let his TV adviser, William Carruthers, see how he looked on the cameras. (The Walnut Street Theater, opened in 1809 as a circus and now completely modernized, was said to be the oldest theater in continuous use in the English-speaking world.) During the microphone and light check the president seemed to be concentrating hard, but he was not tense. He bantered with me and other staff members who acted as stand-ins for the panel during the brief dry run and he was calm when he returned to his rented residence to wait out the five hours before the debate.

In contrast, there was a carnival mood at the aging Benjamin Franklin Hotel, headquarters for the hundreds of reporters covering the debates. Three separate press rooms were in operation: one for the White House press corps, one for the Carter press corps and one for everybody else accredited by the League of Women Voters. The place was jammed with reporters, both famous and anonymous, political celebrities, groupies and curiosity seekers. It throbbed with expectation, like the atmosphere before a Super Bowl.

Ford's campaign spokesman, William Greener, invited me, Carter's press secretary Jody Powell and Jim King, Carter's chief advance man, to join him for drinks at the bar in the middle of the hotel lobby. King, a big, merry, Boston Irish imp, made funny announcements over his ever-present portable bullhorn. Powell seemed uptight. It was difficult to carry on a coherent conversation with reporters surrounding us, taking notes.

The fun and sideshows evaporated as 9:30 P.M approached, starting time for the debate. The moderator for the first debate was Edwin Newman, the respected NBC correspondent. The panel was composed of Frank Reynolds of ABC News, James Gannon of the *Wall Street Journal* and Elizabeth Drew of *The New Yorker*. In the audience were several hundred guests, invited by the candidates and the League of Women Voters and given strict instructions before air time not to react in any audible way to what they were about to see.

Carter walked on stage first, grinning but looking uncomfortable. Then the president entered, exuding authority and presidential presence, tall, athletic, dressed in an impeccable blue suit, quiet tie and —the impact was immediate—a *vest*, which created the overpowering image of a self-assured executive. TV adviser William Carruthers had also persuaded the president to abandon his resistance to television makeup.

Ford reached to shake hands with Carter. Carter shook briefly and stiffly. Carter said later he was awed and nervous to be on the same stage with the president and had treated Ford too deferentially —which was the exact reaction we intended.

Most members of Ford's staff who had come to Philadelphia watched the debate on TV sets in a room backstage, rather than in the audience, so we could see it exactly as the viewers at home were seeing it. Four television receivers—one for each network plus the public broadcasting channel—were set up in front of rows of folding chairs in the staff room. Along the back wall a buffet and a bar were laid out. Sipping beer and drinks, munching potato chips, the staff cheered, moaned and kept up a running commentary as the program unfolded.

Carter got the first question as the result of a coin toss before the broadcast. Reynolds of ABC asked for his specific plans to reduce unemployment.

"First of all is to recognize the tremendous economic strength of this country and to set putting back to work our people as a top priority," Carter responded. "This is an effort that ought to be done primarily by strong leadership in the White House, the inspiration of our people and the tapping of business, agriculture, industry, labor and government at all levels to work on this project."

Carter seemed to swallow his words, stammer, hesitate in his answer. His voice was difficult to understand as he talked in general terms about stimulating the housing industry and focusing job-creation programs in ghettos where unemployment was extremely high.

Ford got two minutes to comment.

"I don't believe that Mr. Carter has been any more specific in this case than he has been in many other instances," Ford said, his voice forceful and confident.

It was a strong start for Ford, following his game plan. The president would have given a variation of that remark no matter what Carter's first reply had been.

A little later in the debate, Ford got an opportunity to use another preplanned answer after Carter promised to cut government spending, reorganize the bureaucracy, reduce the size of the White House staff and eliminate useless agencies.

"In the four years that Governor Carter was governor of the state of Georgia," Ford retorted, "expenditures by the [state] government went up over fifty percent. Employees of the government of Georgia during his term of office went up over twenty-five percent and the figures also show that the bonded indebtedness of the state of Georgia, during his government, went up over twenty percent."

"*Zap!*" I cried. Ford's backstage cheering section gave its loudest cheer.

Carter seemed to lose his jitters and gain confidence as the program progressed. He hit Ford hard on the high unemployment rate and large budget deficits, dragged the Nixon pardon into an answer about Vietnam draft evaders, and even managed to bring up the names of Herbert Hoover and Alf Landon as regressive leaders of Ford's Republican party.

In his hardest shot, Carter claimed, "Mr. Ford, so far as I know, except for avoiding another Watergate, has not accomplished one single major program for this country."

As the debate neared the end, by prearrangement, Ford aides at the theater and others at the White House were hooked up on a telephone conference call to review the program and agree on a line everyone would follow in comments to reporters.

We decided to declare flatly that the president was the clear winner—decisive, specific, in control of the situation and in command of the facts. Our theory was that our own enthusiasm would sway the judgments of voters and press commentators trying to decide who won, just as our jubilant attitude after the New Hampshire primary persuaded doubters that Ford's tiny margin over Reagan represented a victory.

We were just hanging up on the conference call, about eight minutes before the debate was scheduled to conclude, when the sound on the TV suddenly went dead, due to an electronic breakdown. Ford and Carter remained stiffly at their rostrums, not speaking because they didn't know when their microphones would come on again, barely moving because they didn't know what the cameras were picking up.

The Ford staff realized almost immediately that the networks would have to fill the air time. So Michael Duval—a Cheney aide who was in charge of White House debate preparations—Campaign Chairman James Baker and I rushed to the lobby, where, as we had expected, the network TV correspondents were fairly panting for someone to interview. The three of us rotated among ABC, CBS and NBC, explaining why we thought Ford was the big winner, for nearly ten minutes before Jody Powell and other Carterites caught on to what was happening and showed up at the cameras.

The TV sound from the stage came on after twenty-seven minutes. Ford and Carter delivered their prepared closing remarks, but their concentration had been broken and they were both flat.

After the program went off the air, the panelists and officials of the League of Women Voters came up on the stage to have their photos taken with the candidates. When the picture taking was over, Ford stood alone at his podium for a moment, waiting for his aides to arrive from offstage.

"Look at him," Carter's TV adviser, Barry Jagoda, sneered at the president under his breath. "He doesn't know what to do with himself."

As Ford was leaving the theater, a reporter called out, "Who won?"

"The American people," the president replied.

That was a more sensible appraisal of the real value of the extended discussion of issues in the debate than the media's all-out scramble to declare a "winner" and a "loser," as if it were a political heavyweight championship bout. (At a postdebate news briefing, reporters asked Ford strategists to "score" the debate by "rounds," estimating how many questions each candidate "won" and "lost.")

The press gave wide circulation to an instant poll of 600 viewers by the Roper organization within minutes after the debate went off the air. It showed Ford was perceived to be the winner, 39 to 30, with 30 percent calling it a draw. Later, polls by the AP, CBS and NBC's "Today Show" reached similar conclusions.

These poll results suggested that Ford benefited from the public expectation that he would not do well in the first debate because the economy and domestic problems were supposed to be Carter's strongest issues. The president also had the image of being a plodding speaker, slow-witted and clumsy. Thus, when he did not trip or bump his head, when he spoke with style and clarity, he appeared to be doing even better than he really was. In short, the *incumbent* proved his competence to be considered a serious candidate. The first Gallup poll after the debate showed the president had cut Carter's lead in half again and now trailed by only eight points.

As Ford was helped by exceeding expectations in Philadelphia, he was hurt by not living up to expectations at the second debate, in San Francisco. The subject was foreign and defense policy, on which the president was considered to be knowledgeable since he regularly read intelligence reports and made decisions on these matters. Indeed, the White House staff contributed to the inflation of expectations by reiterating to the press that Ford dealt with national defense and foreign-policy affairs every day and even in Congress was an expert in these fields.

"The president expects to do well in the debate," I told the reporters on *Air Force One* on the flight to San Francisco.

We should have seen the warning signs. The president devoted much less time to preparing for the second debate than he did for the first. He also was distracted by a series of nagging campaign problems, including the resignation of Earl Butz as agriculture secretary; charges that Ford accepted free golfing holidays from corporate friends when he was in Congress; and a special prosecutor's investigation of allegations that Ford misused congressional campaign contributions.

The second debate was staged at the ornate Palace of Fine Arts overlooking San Francisco Bay. Pauline Frederick of National

Public Radio was the moderator, and the panelists were Max Frankel of the *New York Times*, Henry L. Trewhitt of the *Baltimore Sun* and Richard Valeriani of NBC. The austere stage set had been hauled by truck from Philadelphia to San Francisco; the only change was that the backdrop was repainted a slightly darker shade of blue, which the handlers agreed would improve the appearance of the two debaters.

Carter walked out from the wings and took his place behind his rostrum at stage right, acting more confident than he had in Philadelphia. Ford, again dressed in a dark three-piece suit to emphasize his aura of leadership, stepped behind his podium ten feet away from Carter. At 6:30 P.M. Pacific time the red lights on the cameras blinked on and the second debate was under way.

As a result of a coin toss, Carter again got the first question. Frankel asked why Carter quarreled with the recent Republican record in foreign policy, which included withdrawing from Vietnam, ending the draft, opening negotiations with Russia on arms control, reopening relations with China, arranging peace moves in the Middle East and encouraging the change to black rule in southern Africa.

Carter demonstrated immediately that his strategy for the second debate was to go on the attack, to shed the deferential manner he had displayed in Philadelphia.

"Our country is not strong anymore," Carter responded to Frankel's opening question. "We are not respected anymore. . . . Mr. Ford, Mr. Kissinger have continued on with the policies and failures of Richard Nixon. . . . As far as foreign policy goes, Mr. Kissinger has been the president of this country. Mr. Ford has shown an absence of leadership and absence of a grasp of what this country is and what it ought to be."

About twenty minutes into the debate, Frankel got his next chance to ask a question, this time of Ford. The exchange was to be one of the most controversial moments of the campaign, and for the president, one of the most damaging.

Frankel asked Ford whether the Helsinki agreement and other dealings between the United States and Russia were more advantageous to Moscow than to Washington.

In defending the Helsinki agreement against charges that it recognized permanent Soviet domination of Eastern Europe, Ford declared, "There is no Soviet domination of Eastern Europe, and there never will be under the Ford administration."

Everyone knew that since the end of World War II the Communist governments of Eastern Europe had been satellites of the Soviet Union because of outright occupation by Russian troops or the threat of occupation. Therefore Frankel, thinking the president must have misspoken, asked a second question which offered Ford a chance to correct his mistake.

"Did I understand you to say, sir, that the Russians are not using Eastern Europe as their own sphere of influence and occupying most of the countries there and making sure with their troops that it is a Communist zone . . . ?"

Given this second chance, the president did not retrieve his gaffe.

"I don't believe, Mr. Frankel, that the Yugoslavians consider themselves dominated by the Soviet Union. I don't believe the Rumanians consider themselves dominated by the Soviet Union. I don't believe that the Poles consider themselves dominated by the Soviet Union.

"Each of these countries is independent, autonomous. It has its own territorial integrity and the United States does not concede that those countries are under the domination of the Soviet Union."

The moderator called on Carter for his rebuttal. He recognized and seized the opportunity. "I would like to see Mr. Ford convince the Polish-Americans and the Czech-Americans and Hungarian-Americans in this country that those countries don't live under the domination and supervision of the Soviet Union behind the Iron Curtain."

Why had the president said Eastern Europe was not dominated by the Soviet Union when he knew it was? Ford had been primed for a question on the so-called Sonnenfeldt doctrine, named for Kissinger aide Helmut Sonnenfeldt, who once was quoted in a news story as advocating that the United States accommodate to the fact that Eastern Europe is a Russian sphere of influence. The president was so intent on rejecting the Sonnenfeldt doctrine that he insisted there was no Soviet domination of Eastern Europe. What he meant to say was that the United States did not *accept* Russian domination of Eastern Europe.

The Ford staff, watching the debate on TV in a small auditorium down the hall from the theater, did not immediately sense the significance of the president's mistake, although Scowcroft grimaced when he heard Ford's answer. A group of reporters watched with the Ford people and did not display any unusual interest in the answer either. During a telephone conference call among Ford staff members near the end of the debate, nobody suggested that the Eastern Europe answer was a major problem. We decided we again would declare the president the uncontested winner, using the rhetorical flourish that "Ford won by a TKO in the first round because Carter never came out of his corner."

But some reporters were already focusing on the president's Eastern Europe answer as a blunder. As Ford left the theater a reporter asked him, "Do you think that you did a good enough job of discussing Eastern Europe, or do you think you left some confusion?"

"I answered all of the question," the president responded, unaware of the gathering storm. In the president's limousine, Ford and Cheney discussed the debate, but Eastern Europe was not mentioned. Kissinger phoned his congratulations later and did not sound a warning.

Our recognition of the error, and its seriousness, was further hampered by the fact that the president's entourage was scattered all over San Francisco following the debate. Ford first dropped in at a "victory" rally at the St. Francis Hotel, then drove to his rented house in Pacific Heights to unwind with friends. Cheney, Baker, Scowcroft, Spencer, Duval and I climbed into press buses and rode to the Holiday Inn, the White House press headquarters, for a postdebate press briefing promised long before.

When we got there my deputy, John Carlson, intercepted us in the lobby and gave us the first inkling that the president's Eastern Europe answer was a major problem. Carlson, who had watched the debate on TV with the press corps, advised us that the reporters had concluded overwhelmingly that Ford made a blunder with that answer.

By then, Scowcroft had come to the same conclusion.

"Let's just face it right now," Scowcroft told the huddle of presidential aides outside the press briefing room at the Holiday Inn, "the president made a bad mistake. So before we go in there and try to explain it away, we ought to understand clearly in our minds that he was wrong. He made a mistake."

That was a sound analysis. Unfortunately, we didn't act accordingly. No one went to the phone, called the president and suggested that we acknowledge publicly that he made a mistake. If we had, I feel sure the story of the president's Eastern Europe gaffe would have faded quickly, probably in one day. Instead we trooped into the briefing and tried to pretend there was no mistake.

The briefing was held in a large room with a high ceiling and mirrored walls, usually rented out by the hotel as a ballroom for conventions. Now it was lined with long tables laden with typewriters, telephones, tape recorders and all the other paraphernalia of the press corps. Across the back of the room, raised platforms held the TV cameras. When the Ford staff members entered the room for the briefing, we found it jammed with reporters who were drawn by the scent of a hot story that might be embarrassing, perhaps fatal, to the president. The very first question from the press let us know the Eastern Europe remark was going to be a big problem.

Q.: Are there any Soviet troops in Poland?
SCOWCROFT: Yes.
Q.: How many would you say?
SCOWCROFT: Offhand I don't recall. There are four divisions. I am not sure, but a substantial number.
Q.: Do you think that would imply some Soviet dominance of Poland?
SCOWCROFT: I think what the president was trying to say is that we do not recognize Soviet dominance of Europe. . . .
Q.: Don't you think you should issue a clarification on that?
CHENEY: No. I thought he was clear in terms of what he meant. . . .

That question to Cheney had been our chance to recoup by acknowledging Ford's mistake and asserting that of course he understood Russia dominated Eastern Europe. But we blew it.

Meanwhile, the pollsters were busy. Most of the first quick polls indicated that Carter was considered the winner by a small margin. However, a survey by Ford's pollster, Bob Teeter, immediately after the debate, showed the president to be the winner by eleven points. (Teeter took subsequent polls and found that as press coverage concentrated heavily on Ford's Eastern Europe mistake, public opinion swung around until Ford was perceived to be the loser by an enormous margin.)

By the morning after the debate, the Ford staff fully understood that it had a major political problem. Teeter phoned Cheney to alert him. So did staff members at the White House and in the campaign organization, especially those assigned to work with ethnic groups. They were getting complaints from spokesmen for those important blocs of voters.

Ford left San Francisco early on the morning after the debate to fly to Los Angeles for a series of campaign appearances. On the plane, Cheney went to the president's cabin and urged him to issue a clarification, to acknowledge that he had misspoken concerning the situation in Eastern Europe. Ford refused. He didn't think his answers needed clarification.

"He is stubborn," Cheney reported to the rest of us after his visit to Ford's cabin. "He doesn't want to clear it up."

Nevertheless, Scowcroft drafted a statement in case the president changed his mind. Just as the plane was landing, Cheney and Spencer tried again to talk the president into acknowledging his mistake. Ford's answer was still no.

After inspecting a plywood mock-up of the B-1 bomber at the North American Rockwell plant near the Los Angeles airport, Ford drove to the University of Southern California campus to deliver a speech from the steps of the library. He had nearly two hours to kill in an office set aside for him at the university, and during that time he was urged again by his staff to correct his Eastern Europe remarks. He agreed, grudgingly, to state clearly his attitude toward Eastern Europe in the USC speech. But he refused to admit he had made a mistake in the debate.

After much haggling, drafting, rewriting and negotiating, the president accepted this four-paragraph insert in his speech:

> Last night in the debate I spoke of America's firm support for the aspirations for independence of the nations of Eastern Europe. The United States has never conceded and never will concede their domination by the Soviet Union.
>
> I admire the courage of the Polish people and have always supported the hopes of Polish-Americans for freedom for their ancestral homeland.
>
> It is our policy to use every peaceful means to assist countries in Eastern Europe in their efforts to become less dependent on the Soviet Union and to establish closer ties with the West.
>
> I am very much aware of the present plight of the Eastern European nations. . . .

But it wasn't good enough for the press. There is an unwritten rule among reporters that when a public figure makes a mistake, or does something the press corps overwhelmingly considers a mistake, he must perform the ritual of a public confession of error before the story will be allowed to fade away.

Typical of the press reaction to the president's failure to make the ritual admission of error in his USC speech was Phil Jones's report on CBS: "Ford did not say flat out that he had goofed in last night's debate." Consequently, the Eastern Europe story was kept alive.

Even if the press had not locked onto the story with full intensity, Carter would have made sure it did not disappear from the headlines. In his first campaign appearances after the debate, Carter leaped on Ford's Eastern Europe misstatement with a new hard edge of criticism and sarcasm, calling it "ridiculous" and a "disgrace" to America. Carter joked that Mondale was going to a Polish bar because he was sure the drinks would be on the house for Democrats.

Indeed, in press interviews and private complaints to Ford aides, spokesmen for Polish-American and other ethnic organizations expressed shock at the president's Eastern Europe remark and said it would hurt him among voters of East European ancestry. Feeling the heat from these ethnic groups, White House and campaign aides burned up the phone lines to Los Angeles, almost in a panic, sometimes on a speaker phone so several could speak at once, pleading with Cheney and other staff members to persuade the president to admit his mistake. They warned that the Eastern Europe gaffe could cost Ford Illinois and other northern industrial states with large blocs of ethnic voters.

The president got his next chance to clear up the growing controversy on his second day of campaigning in Los Angeles, at a breakfast with 150 members of the San Fernando Valley Business and Professional Association. Before the breakfast, Ford met with aides to discuss what questions he was likely to be asked by the group and how he should respond. He went over some issues of local interest concerning migrant farm workers, illegal Mexican immigrants and the Burbank airport.

Then I spoke up. "The senior staff recommends that you say your remarks about Eastern Europe in the debate were a misstatement, or that you were not very precise, or something like that," I advised.

"You know I'm not inclined to do that," Ford responded firmly.

It was clear that the president still was not ready to admit publicly that he had made a mistake on Eastern Europe. I could see no point in pressing the matter while Ford was in that mood, so I dropped it.

The setting for the breakfast was the roof-garden restaurant of the Sheraton Universal Hotel, overlooking smoggy Burbank. After picking at his scrambled eggs, Ford stepped up to the rostrum at the head table, ran through a short version of his standard campaign speech and then invited questions. He had reached the next-to-the-last question before someone asked for his views on "the Communist rule" of East European countries.

"This administration does not concede that there should be Soviet domination of the Eastern European countries," the president responded. "It has been alleged by some that I was not [as] precise as I should have been the other day. But let me explain what I really meant."

That grabbed my attention. Perhaps he was going to acknowledge his error after all and thereby end the controversy. But instead, Ford continued his answer in a way that made his problem even worse.

"I was in Poland a year ago and I had the opportunity to talk with a number of citizens of Poland, and believe me, they are courageous; they are strong people. They don't believe that they are going to be forever dominated—if they are—by the Soviet Union. They believe in the independence of that great country, and so do I, and we are going to make certain to the best of our ability that any allegation of domination is not a fact."

I couldn't believe my ears. Ford had referred to the "allegation" of Soviet domination of Poland and seemingly raised doubts that the Poles were really dominated by Russia with the expression "if they are." He had compounded his gaffe.

Within moments after Ford's new mistake, I was called out of the breakfast to take a phone call from my deputy, John Carlson, who was at the White House press center in another hotel, listening with the reporters to the president's remarks over a loudspeaker. When I picked up the phone, Carlson tried to convey the scene at the press center, and his helpless anguish, as a result of the president's new Eastern Europe bobble.

"Ron, this is just unbelievable!" Carlson shouted. "The place is going wild! The reporters are racing around the press room, laughing and playing their tapes over and over and filing bulletins saying the president put his foot even deeper into his mouth! Ron, he's got to do something to straighten it out!"

But there was no time to straighten it out immediately. As soon as the breakfast appearance was over, the president left by limousine for a campaign rally in front of the Glendale, California, City Hall. As soon as the motorcade arrived in Glendale, Cheney and I went to the temporary press center on the patio of the County Building to determine whether Carlson was exaggerating or whether Ford had indeed seriously worsened his problem with his breakfast answer on Eastern Europe.

Amid the noise and confusion of the rally, with a band blaring right next to the press facilities, Cheney and I were surrounded by hordes of reporters demanding to know why Ford had used the terms "if they are" and "allegation" in referring to Soviet domination of the Poles. After a few minutes in that maelstrom, Cheney and I concluded that Carlson was right. The president needed to straighten out the controversy before it caused further damage to his campaign.

After the rally, Cheney and Spencer led Ford into the City Hall, to the mayor's office, closed the door and lectured him on what he must do. They showed him a stenographic transcript of his remarks at the breakfast that morning and explained that he had worsened his problem. The two aides told the president he must now admit publicly that he had made a mistake in the debate and at the breakfast. He must state clearly that Russia dominated Eastern Europe. Otherwise, Ford was warned, the issue would contine to haunt him, possibly costing him his chance to win the election.

Ford finally gave in and agreed to make the necessary statement to the press before leaving Glendale.

The press corps was already on buses several blocks away, waiting to depart for the next stop. I had to scramble to round up reporters and cameras to cover Ford's *mea culpa* while Cheney and Spencer painstakingly drilled the president on exactly what he should say.

"Have you got straight in your mind now what you are going to say?" Cheney asked.

"Yeah. I'm going to say Poland is not dominated by the Soviet Union," Ford teased, breaking into what Cheney described as a "shitty grin." Ford still had his sense of humor, even at a time like that.

A makeshift news conference was hurriedly assembled in the parking lot behind City Hall. With his words relayed by walkie-talkie to loudspeakers on the press buses, Ford delivered his statement slowly and carefully.

"Perhaps I could have been more precise in what I said concerning Soviet domination of Poland. . . . I recognize that . . . in Poland there are Soviet divisions. . . . It is tragic that the Soviet Union does have some divisions in Poland. . . . President Ford does not believe that the Polish people over the long run—whether they are in Poland or whether they are Polish-Americans here—will ever condone domination by any foreign force. . . . There are several other countries in Eastern Europe that tragically have Soviet military forces in their country. That is not what President Ford wants and that is not what the American people want."

A reporter asked, "Did you come out to put an end to this misunderstanding?"

"I hope and trust that my observations this morning will put an end to a misunderstanding," Ford replied dryly. "It was a misunderstanding."

The president took the last step and closed the controversy four days later when he invited seventeen leaders of East European ethnic organizations to the White House and confessed, "The original mistake was mine. I did not express myself clearly—I admit it."

After Ford had met the press demand for this ritual admission of error, Cheney commented, in a bitter private moment, that the reporters had exacted their "pound of flesh."

Ford was so angered by what he considered unfair and exaggerated press treatment of his Eastern Europe remarks that he broke one of his basic rules of political life and openly criticized reporters. "I am frankly disappointed that there was not a better, more thoughtful analysis [of the second debate] in the news media," he told a meeting of New York newspaper and broadcast executives. "Ninety percent of what has been written . . . involved . . . one sentence. . . . There was such a concentration on that one point, ignoring virtually everything else, that I think the news media didn't give a full and accurate picture of the substance in many of the questions and many of the answers."

For Ford, who normally concealed his critical feelings about the press, that was a strong complaint. (Even after leaving the White House, Ford continued to nurse a grudge over press treatment of that episode.)

The controversy over the Eastern Europe gaffe was not about the president's policy. The real damage of the Eastern Europe error was that it revived doubts about Ford's intelligence and competence. And the controversy was kept alive by the president's refusal to admit he'd made a mistake.

The last presidential debate was held in Phi Beta Kappa Hall on the campus of the College of William and Mary in Williamsburg, a reconstructed colonial town in Virginia. The set had been trucked back from San Francisco. (It ended up as a gift to the Smithsonian Institution.) Barbara Walters, then with NBC, was the moderator. The panelists were columnist Joseph Kraft, Robert Maynard of the *Washington Post* and Jack Nelson, Washington bureau chief of the *Los Angeles Times*.

When Ford went to the hall in the afternoon for the lighting and microphone check, Mrs. Ford went with him. Standing at Carter's podium while Ford tested the mike at his podium, the First Lady mischievously scrawled a message on Carter's light-blue note pad: "Dear Mr. Carter—May I wish you the best tonight. I'm sure the best man will win. I happen to have a favorite candidate—my husband President Ford. Best of luck, Betty Ford." Worried that someone might steal the note from the podium as a souvenir before Carter arrived, I took it with me and delivered it to Jody Powell, who passed it on to Carter. It was another delightful example of Betty Ford's unpredictable free spirit.

The Williamsburg debate was judged by the press to be the least newsworthy, even dull. But it probably was the most informative. With the subject matter unlimited, both candidates spent the ninety minutes giving careful explanations of their positions on the issues, and being extremely careful not to make a mistake. The Roper instant poll found Carter to be the winner, although many reporters felt it was a draw.

In mid-October, between the San Francisco and Williamsburg presidential debates, the vice-presidential candidates, Dole and Mondale, held their own televised debate in Houston, Texas. White House and Ford-campaign officials were apprehensive about going through with the vice-presidential debate, on the theory that a good performance by Dole wouldn't help the president much and a bad performance could hurt. We tried to talk Dole out of the debate, but he insisted on doing it because he considered himself a skilled debater, based on his experience as a Senate candidate in

Kansas. Dole, an engaging man in private conversation, did not realize that he came across on television as abrasive and sarcastic.

The White House prepared briefing books for Dole to help him bone up for the debate, but when the first batch of books was delivered to him, he complained that they contained too much material for him to read on the campaign trail. White House aides then sharply reduced the amount of material in the briefing papers and sent them back to Dole. This time he complained that he wasn't given enough information to prepare adequately.

During the vice-presidential debate, Dole tried some humor, referring to the vice presidency as a job that's "mostly indoors and there's no heavy lifting." But near the end of the program he took a harsh crack at the Democrats. Himself a badly wounded World War II veteran, Dole described World Wars I and II and Korea as "all Democrat wars."

"I figured it up the other day, we added up the killed and wounded," he said. "In Democrat wars in this century it would be 1.6 million Americans, enough to fill the city of Detroit."

That unfair reference to "Democrat" wars may have turned off a number of voters otherwise attracted to the Ford-Dole ticket. Our apprehensions before the vice-presidential debate, that the possible benefits did not justify the possible risks of a mistake, appeared to be well founded.

However, the three presidential debates achieved for Ford just about what he'd hoped when he challenged Carter: They gave him extensive free television time to demonstrate his knowledge of complex issues. Even with the negative effect of the Eastern Europe bobble, overall Ford displayed to the large audience his intelligence and competence, and his presidential bearing. And by the time the last debate ended, the confrontations had helped Ford pull almost even with Carter in the polls.

CHAPTER NINETEEN

Troubles

In September and October, the Ford campaign was plagued by a series of highly publicized developments that raised questions about the president's commitment to morality, propriety and even legality, while Carter stumped the country as the apostle of a new, higher standard of ethical conduct for government officials.

—Agriculture Secretary Earl Butz was forced to resign after he was quoted using obscene language to describe blacks.

—Ford acknowledged accepting, while he was in Congress, free golf holidays and plane flights from friends who were corporate executives.

—The Watergate special prosecutor did clear the president of charges that he misused campaign contributions in his congressional races, but only after an agonizingly slow investigation.

—John Dean, drumming up sales for his book, revived an old allegation that the Nixon White House recruited Ford to squelch an early congressional investigation of Watergate.

Ford was not found to have done anything wrong. But these episodes kept the president on the defensive during much of the campaign, revived memories of Nixon and distracted voters' attention from his record of accomplishments in the White House.

The Butz episode grew out of an article on the Republican convention in *Rolling Stone*, by its special correspondent John Dean. Near the end of the article Dean reported a postconvention conversation he'd had aboard a California-bound airliner with entertainers Pat Boone and Sonny Bono and a "distinguished member of Ford's cabinet (who shall remain nameless, unless he chooses to be otherwise)." According to Dean, Boone asked the "shirt-sleeved cabinet member" why Republicans, party of Abraham Lincoln, couldn't attract more support from blacks.

" 'I'll tell you why you can't attract coloreds,' the secretary proclaimed as his mischievous smile returned, 'because coloreds only want three things . . . first, a tight pussy; second, loose shoes; and third, a warm place to shit. That's all.' "

The article was read by journalists and others in Washington, who guessed the unnamed cabinet member was Agriculture Secretary Earl Butz, because he was the only one known to talk that way. Several news stories were written about Dean's article. None mentioned the offensive reference to blacks. I read the article and didn't bother to mention it to anyone else at the White House. In a day or so, Dean's journalistic debut was forgotten.

A couple of weeks later, Butz came to the White House to inform Cheney that he was the cabinet member in the Dean article and that he believed *New Times* was going to identify him. Cheney notified the president, who was outraged by the quoted remarks. Ford summoned Butz to the Oval Office and told him that such language was offensive to him and intolerable from a member of the cabinet. Butz apologized and offered to issue a public apology.

However, the language in the Butz quote was so vile that we doubted that newspapers and networks could use it; hence the story might not surface. So although Butz drafted his apology and Cheney ordered me to write a statement of condemnation from the president, we decided not to say anything publicly for the time being.

A day or so after his dressing down by Ford, Butz received a tip that in its issue of Friday, October 1, the *New York Post* was going to name him as the cabinet member in the Dean article. To find out how the newspaper handled the story, press office staff members phoned friends in New York and asked them to buy each edition of the *Post* that Friday and report to me any article on Butz. But none appeared.

That Friday afternoon, however, I received a phone call from Judy Woodruff, an NBC correspondent based in Atlanta, who was covering the Carter campaign.

"Do you have anything on the Butz thing?" she asked.

"What Butz thing?" I answered innocently.

"You know, the joke," Woodruff said.

"Are you going to use the story?" I asked, wondering how a network could broadcast Butz's language.

"I don't know yet," Woodruff replied.

"Well, if you decide to use it, call me back and I might have something to say," I stalled. "By the way," I added, "I thought you were covering Carter. Why are you working on a Butz story?"

There was a pause at the other end of the line. Then, "I have some friends at *New Times*," Woodruff answered lamely.

"Yes, and you also have some friends in the Carter camp," I shot back. (NBC promoted Woodruff after the election, moving her to Washington to cover the Carter White House.)

I quickly phoned Butz and urged him not to say anything to Woodruff that she could quote on the air in a way that would allow her to back into the story without actually quoting his obscene joke. He promised he wouldn't.

But about 6 P.M., Butz called back and said he had just hung up from talking to Woodruff. He'd told her he was sorry for his crude remark and revealed to her that he had apologized to William Coleman, the black secretary of transportation, and was trying to reach black Republican Senator Edward Brooke to apologize.

That was it. Now NBC could break the story without having to use the language. I phoned the producer of the NBC "Nightly News," which was going on the air momentarily, and dictated Ford's statement condemning Butz.

"The president informed the secretary that such language and attitudes were not acceptable from a member of his administration," the statement said. "The president told the secretary the remarks were highly offensive to him and to the American people. The president's statement to Secretary Butz amounted to a severe reprimand."

As soon as the NBC story appeared, other reporters rushed to my office for confirmation. Within a few hours, everyone had the Butz story.

Later that night, when the excitement died down a little, I went to Cheney's office and reported that many newsmen and some staff members felt Butz couldn't stay in the cabinet under the circumstances. But if Butz was going to be fired, it should be done quickly, I urged. That way, Ford would be seen as acting decisively to deal with an embarrassment in his administration. If Ford waited a few days before firing Butz, he would appear merely to be responding to the public outrage that was sure to build up.

"Don't worry," Cheney replied when I offered this advice. "It's being taken care of."

The newspapers and networks had to resort to euphemisms to explain what the Butz story was all about. The Associated Press said Butz's remark about blacks "described in derogatory and vulgar terms what he said were their sexual, dress and bathroom preferences." However, the AP sent Butz's actual words over its wire in a private advisory to editors.

Some of the coverage had a leering quality. On NBC's "Meet the Press" that Sunday, former U.N. ambassador William Scranton, a Ford campaign adviser, was asked what he thought of the Butz joke. He replied he hadn't read it. Bill Monroe, the moderator, shoved a copy in front of Scranton to scan while the live cameras focused on his reaction.

On the "Today Show" an NBC correspondent asked a farmer if he knew what Butz had said in his joke. The farmer didn't.

"Here, I'll whisper it to you," the reporter said. He did, while the camera rolled.

Ford decided not to fire Butz right away. It was his style not to react quickly in a crisis until he'd pondered all the alternatives, not to "shoot from the hip," as he phrased it. The president felt a strong sense of loyalty to his team and resisted throwing a valued aide overboard. Despite his penchant for vulgar and tasteless jokes, Butz was a likable man and a good agriculture secretary. He had presided over a historic reduction of government control over farming. Costly subsidy and storage programs had been phased down and a healthy free-market, full-production system had been expanded under his management. Butz also was politically astute and could help Ford win back the farmers who were angry about the president's 1975 embargo on grain sales to Russia.

Butz phoned me several times daily over the weekend after NBC broke the story, asking me what the news stories were saying and what the reaction was. Normally ebullient, he sounded subdued, almost crushed, by the jam he had gotten himself into. He insisted plaintively that what he'd really said in response to Pat Boone's question about attracting more blacks to the Republican party was that Negroes have come a long way in American political life since a Chicago alderman had told him thirty years ago that "coloreds only want three things. . . ." I agreed that was significantly different from Dean's version, but I advised him it would be useless to try to defend his remark at that late date on the basis of such a distinction.

In his phone calls, Butz asked me several times, "What do you think I ought to do? Do you think I ought to resign?" I declined to offer any advice at first, but I reported his query to Cheney. Saturday evening Cheney advised me that if Butz asked again, I should suggest it might be best if he quit so his remark would not become an issue in the campaign. But Cheney cautioned me to do it in a way that did not sound like the White House was ordering him to resign. I phoned Butz and passed the word.

But the next morning, Sunday, Butz seemed to get a reprieve. While Bob Teeter took a quick poll of opinion in two farm states, Cheney and campaign managers James Baker and Stuart Spencer gathered in Cheney's office to check the views of Republicans and farm leaders around the country by telephone.

They found surprising support for the secretary, which they suspected had been partly inspired by Butz's aides. Connally phoned and said Butz should stay. Baker and Spencer said they were leaning toward that position, too.

Cheney suggested that one scenario the president could follow would be for Butz to submit his resignation and for Ford to reject it on grounds that, while he condemned Butz's joke, the one indiscretion should not deprive the country of his skills as agriculture secretary. Cheney said Butz's remark wasn't much worse than Carter's language in a PLAYBOY magazine interview or Joan Mondale's crack on a TV talk show that the Democrats were doing to their secretaries what the Republicans were doing to the country.

Cheney also contended that firing Butz would appease the *New York Times* and the *Washington Post*, and the liberals and blacks who weren't going to vote for Ford anyhow, but would offend many farmers who probably used the same kind of language themselves. Cheney was afraid that a Butz resignation or the suggestion of White House pressure on Butz to resign might turn rural voters against the president.

Ford weighed his decision all weekend. It was, as Cheney said, a "close call," certain to make some people mad no matter which way Ford decided. But by Monday morning Ford had decided he wanted Butz's resignation. One factor in the president's decision was Mrs. Ford's strong aversion to the sexist connotations of the Butz joke.

With Ford's decision made and communicated to Butz, all that remained was for the secretary to quit officially. Monday afternoon Butz came to the White House press briefing room and, with tears in his eyes, announced his resignation to the reporters.

"This is the price I pay for a gross indiscretion in a private conversation," he said in a low, choked voice. "The use of a bad racial commentary in no way reflects my real attitude. By taking this action, I hope to remove even the appearance of racism as an issue in the Ford campaign."

As Butz walked back to my office, stricken, I put my arm around his shoulders and said, "You are a hell of a man, Earl." Cheney came up and tried to comfort him, too. Even though Butz had caused embarrassment to the president, there was a sense of protectiveness and sympathy for a man whose distinguished career of more than twenty years in public service and in the academic world had been ended by a stupid joke. Contemporary history would certainly remember him as that man who made the awful crack about blacks, and not as the agriculture secretary who restored the free-market system to American farmers.

Maybe Butz's biggest mistake was saying anything at all in front of John Dean.

There were two things I didn't understand about the Butz affair. First, why did an NBC reporter covering Carter break the story? And second, why wasn't the obscene remark news when *Rolling Stone* first published it?

I asked some reporters why several weeks had passed between the time Dean's account of Butz's joke appeared in *Rolling Stone* and the time it became big news.

"A mass failure of our professional judgment," one of the reporters replied.

The next episode raising questions about the president's integrity occurred just before the first presidential debate when the UPI, Jack Anderson and other journalists came out with a series of stories alleging that Ford, while a member of Congress, accepted free golfing holidays from a friend, William Whyte, vice president and chief Washington lobbyist of U.S. Steel.

"I get so tired of this horseshit!" the president snapped when I informed him of the charges.

Ford and Whyte and their families had been extremely close friends for more than twenty-five years, since shortly after Ford came to Washington for his first term in Congress. The families often spent holidays and vacations together. The two men loved golf and played whenever they got the chance, sometimes Ford paying, sometimes Whyte paying.

Ford authorized me to tell my press briefing that he had played golf twice as Whyte's guest at the Pine Valley Golf Club near Clementon, New Jersey, once in 1964 and again in 1971. The 1971 outing was somewhat troublesome because it occurred three years after the House passed a code of ethics stating, "A member . . . shall accept no gift of substantial value, directly or indirectly, from any person, organization or corporation having a direct interest in legislation before the Congress."

Ford's attitude on the matter was old-fashioned, midwestern, middle-class: Old friends played golf together because they liked the game and each other's company, and it never entered their minds to expect anything or grant anything in return. Furthermore, was a golf game a gift of "substantial value"?

When the stories about the golf trips with Whyte first broke, the president told me to inform the reporters that he never considered the expenses of the game to be gifts of substantial value, in the terms of the House code of ethics. But that did not satisfy the press search for wrongdoing in the golf games. At my press briefings I tried to defuse the controversy by taking a low-key approach—without much success, as this excerpt demonstrates:

Q.: In view of the president's statement on June 15 to the Baptists, "We cannot stand very long on the shifting sands of situation ethics," . . . how can you justify the violation of the House ethics code by virtue of the fact that this man just happens to be a longtime friend of the president?

Q.: . . . Ron, all I was asking you to say was that . . . there was nothing wrong in what he did. . . .

NESSEN: But who said there was?

Q.: Can you not say that he finds nothing wrong with what occurred?

NESSEN: . . . It has always been my policy not to deny things that are never charged.

Q.: Obviously, there is some question about a member of Congress accepting—

NESSEN: Questions are not charges. You will agree to that.

Q.: . . . I am just asking you, in general, can the president not say that he feels there was nothing wrong in what he did?

NESSEN: . . . It is obvious that if the president thought there was anything wrong, he would not have done it.

Q.: That was then. We are talking about now.

Precisely. Innocent golf outings with an old friend years before were being judged retroactively in the post-Watergate atmosphere of suspicion and less-tolerant ethical standards.

Somehow, Ford kept his sense of humor through the tempest. When Cheney asked him whom he wanted to sit in the seats reserved for presidential guests at the first debate, Ford suggested slyly, "Let's invite Bill Whyte."

A week after the first stories about Ford's golf outings with Whyte, we learned that Jack Anderson and others were collecting information about other golf holidays Ford had taken as the guest of other friends who were corporate executives.

We decided a preemptive disclosure by the White House would put a better face on the news than a revelation in Anderson's column. So, after a search of memories and records, I announced to my press briefing that Ford had accepted the hospitality of friends to play golf at courses owned by the Firestone Tire and Rubber Company, Alcoa, and Bethlehem Steel, and had stayed in U.S. Steel's guest quarters at Disney World in Florida while playing golf nearby.

Naturally, Carter attacked Ford for the golf outings. "You can't expect any better from political leadership that has been bogged down in Washington for twenty-five or thirty years, drawing their advice, their counsel, their financial support from lobbyists for special interests," the Democratic candidate proclaimed, playing on his anti-Washington theme. "They go to the same restaurants, belong to the same clubs, play golf at the same golf clubs."

Carter muted his criticism, however, after it was disclosed that he had accepted free transportation on corporate airplanes owned by Lockheed and Coca-Cola, had some expenses paid by the governments of England and Israel during an overseas trip, and was a guest at vacation lodges owned by the Union Camp Corporation and the Brunswick Paper and Pulp Company while governor of Georgia.

Carter defended himself on grounds that he had accepted this hospitality strictly in the pursuit of official business—which seemed to me to make it worse than Ford's purely social outings with friends. (More than six months after the election, it was revealed that on at least five trips during the campaign Carter had flown free aboard an airplane owned by Bert Lance's National Bank of Georgia. The new president denied any illegality, but agreed to reimburse the bank almost $1800 from personal and campaign funds.)

A far more serious challenge to the president's reputation for honesty was raised when Watergate Special Prosecutor Charles Ruff launched a secret investigation in July 1976 into charges that Ford misused contributions to his congressional campaigns in Michigan. An FBI informant alleged that Ford had diverted to his personal use money from his campaign funds, including contributions from the Marine Engineers Beneficial Association, a maritime union. Attorney General Edward Levi, a man of total integrity and little concern about politics, referred the charge to the special prosecutor for investigation.

The first hint the White House had of the investigation came when some of the president's friends and election workers in Grand Rapids phoned White House Counsel Philip Buchen to tell him the FBI was questioning them about Ford's campaign contributions and seizing campaign records going back to 1964.

Then an article in the *Wall Street Journal* publicly revealed the investigation on September 21, 1976, two days before the first presidential debate and exactly six weeks before Election Day.

"That is just plain not true!" Ford exploded in outrage when he heard about the allegation.

The investigation couldn't have come at a worse time or raised a more damaging issue. The very name "Watergate special prosecutor" rekindled all the bad memories of Nixon. We knew that whatever public statement we made on the investigation would be compared to Nixon's early reaction to the Watergate scandal. For instance, we were reluctant to issue a strong public declaration of Ford's innocence because it would recall Nixon's "Your president is no crook." And a statement demanding that Ruff clear the president quickly might appear similar to Nixon's pressure on the special prosecutor.

The only course open to us was to stay calm and hope that Ruff would hurry his investigation and clear Ford before the doubts began to hurt his election chances. But Ruff, who taught law at Georgetown University while running the Special Prosecutor's Office part-time, kept the president on the hook for weeks.

The wait was particularly frustrating because the charges had already been thoroughly checked, and ruled unfounded, three years earlier at the time of Ford's nomination for vice president. During Ford's vice-presidential confirmation hearings, the House Judiciary Committee and the Senate Rules Committee had examined voluminous FBI reports and campaign records of the House clerk and the state of Michigan going back to 1952. The committees concluded that Ford had handled his campaign contributions properly.

When Ruff's new investigation was revealed, Leon Jaworski, the highly respected former Watergate special prosecutor, came to Ford's aid. Jaworski told reporters he had looked into the maritime union's contributions to Ford's congressional campaigns and found nothing that called for further action.

Carter, of course, needled Ford about the unresolved allegations during Ruff's lingering investigation, at one point calling on the president to "tell the truth, the whole truth and nothing but the truth."

Ford had hoped to delay his next news conference until Ruff cleared him, and then go before the reporters vindicated. But Carter's cracks goaded him into inviting newsmen to a question-and-answer session to give his views of the investigation. Seated behind his desk in the Oval Office, the president told the reporters gathered around him, "There is a saying that is prevalent in the law that 'justice delayed is justice denied.'" Ford spoke in a tone of bitter frustration.

The president seethed in private because the newspapers and TV news programs rehashed the allegations against him daily while Ruff's investigation dragged on. Ford was particularly angered by Fred Graham's frequent reports on Walter Cronkite's "CBS Evening News," which Ford felt contained no new facts but merely repeated night after night the original charges. (Even a year after leaving the White House, Ford still nursed a sense of outrage over Graham's reports.)

Bob Woodward of the *Washington Post* phoned me when the investigation was first revealed, seeking information. He sounded very sympathetic toward the president, and in fact said he hoped to write a story that would clear Ford. I wondered whether that was a tactic Woodward used when he and Carl Bernstein investigated Watergate, persuading people to open up by pretending to be friendly and understanding.

Woodward had only one minor scoop on the Ford investigation, an interview with Deputy Attorney General Harold Tyler, Jr., in which Tyler revealed that Attorney General Levi had initiated the special prosecutor's inquiry. The *New York Post* ran the interview under a banner headline that implied Ford faced serious charges. That touched off a rumor which swept through Wall Street that Woodward and Bernstein were coming out with a story so damaging to Ford that he might resign. The stock market dropped ten points in a half-hour. When I learned of the panic on Wall Street, I phoned Woodward. He said he'd heard the rumor, too, but was not working on any such story.

The Tyler interview brought a fresh flood of press questions and I went to Philip Buchen's paneled, book-lined office on the second floor of the White House office wing to get some answers. I was astounded when he informed me that two weeks before, during a conversation on another matter, and apparently without the president's knowledge, he had asked Tyler by what authority the special prosecutor was conducting the investigation of Ford.

I had been telling my briefing daily that the White House had scrupulously avoided talking to the Justice Department or the special prosecutor about the inquiry so as not to give the impression of applying pressure. Now I learned that Buchen had talked to the Justice Department about the investigation two weeks before, making me an inadvertent liar again.

"This White House lost one press secretary this way and you're going to lose another one," I told Buchen in a low, emotional tone. "This is the last time I'm going to let this happen to me. I won't go out there and ruin my reputation to cover up other people."

Cheney, who had listened to my outburst to Buchen in silence, informed me that what I'd said in the past about the White House not being in touch with the special prosecutor was outdated anyhow because Ruff had met the night before with Buchen for the first time to explain the investigation and to request additional information on the president's tax returns and other financial records.

"Since you have to go out there and take the heat, I thought you ought to know what's going on," Cheney told me.

After I had been informed of Buchen's meeting with the special prosecutor, I could not longer tell the press truthfully that Ruff had not contacted the White House. But I also did not want to publicly confirm the meeting, because that might imply that Ruff had found evidence substantiating the charges against Ford. So I started answering all questions about the investigation by saying I had nothing to add to my previous statements.

However, a more elaborate answer obviously was needed when Dean Fischer, White House correspondent for *Time*, informed me during a presidential trip to Texas on October 9, 1976, that his magazine planned to run a story alleging that Ford had received an illegal $2000 monthly "retainer" from a maritime union for years when he was in Congress.

It took several hours for the White House to check out the charge and determine it had been disproved two years earlier by a U.S. attorney in New Jersey. By the time we'd prepared a denial, Ford was in the grandstand at the Cotton Bowl watching the traditional Texas-Oklahoma football game. Cheney, angry, almost trembling with indignation, called Fischer to a concrete tunnel under the stands and gave him our response to *Time*'s charge: "It's so ridiculous and so vile it doesn't even warrant an answer."

That night, in the penthouse bar of the hotel where the president was staying, Fischer informed Cheney that *Time* had reduced its story to two sentences discrediting the charge that Ford had taken union payoffs.

"One of these days the special prosecutor is going to clear the president," Cheney snarled at the reporter loudly enough to be heard over the band, "and we expect you to devote as much ink in your magazines to that as to all these charges you've been printing."

While Ford and his aides waited for Ruff's clearance with growing impatience and concern about possible political damage, still another series of stories raising suspicions about the president's probity appeared. Citing as their source "a supporter of the Jimmy Carter presidential campaign," Woodward and Bernstein reported details of an Internal Revenue Service audit of Ford's tax returns from 1965 to 1972, which had been submitted to the congressional committees considering his nomination as vice president three years before. The House Judiciary Committee concluded at the time that Ford's tax returns were in order.

Nevertheless, authors of the new round of stories were intrigued by the IRS finding that Ford seemed to get by on $5 a week pocket money when he was House Republican leader. This suggested to some reporters that someone was paying his bills or else he had a secret source of income.

In fact, many top government officials carry little or no cash because they have almost no opportunity to spend it. Meals at the congressional dining rooms and the White House mess are billed monthly. Transportation is by government car or plane. Even newspapers are delivered to the office. Secretaries normally keep a pretty-cash box to pay minor incidentals.

The silly and unjustified revival of the three-year-old "walking-around money" story soon collapsed from lack of evidence.

On the night of October 13, 1976, just nineteen days before the election, the Watergate special prosecutor finally notified the White House that he was on his way over with a letter exonerating the president of any wrongdoing in connection with his congressional campaign contributions.

For more than three weeks Ruff had let the president dangle in public, his honesty in question, while suspicion built and Carter exploited Ford's dilemma. Bitterness toward Ruff had grown daily in the White House. When Ruff phoned to say he was driving over with the letter of exoneration, Edward Schmults, Ford's deputy legal counsel, walked down the darkened West Executive Avenue to the Southwest Gate of the White House to meet the special prosecutor. Schmults wanted to get into Ruff's car, read the letter and ask any questions he had, but Ruff refused to remove his brief-case from the passenger seat. So Schmults had to read the letter by the illumination of the streetlight, then lean through the car window to ask his questions.

Schmults trudged back to Cheney's office and passed the letter around to a half-dozen staff members waiting there to read it, including Buchen, who had returned to the White House from a dinner party dressed in a velvet tuxedo.

The letter was terse:

Dear Mr. Buchen:
    As you requested, this is to advise you concerning the status of the investigation by this office into an allegation that certain contributions made to political committees in Michigan were improperly diverted to the personal use of President Ford.
    The investigation of that allegation is now complete, and the evidence developed has disclosed no violation of law on the part of President Ford. The matter has therefore been closed.

The next morning Ruff issued a longer statement declaring, "The evidence developed during this investigation was not corroborative of the allegation on which it was predicated. Nor did evidence disclosed during the inquiry into that allegation give reason to believe that any other violations of law had occurred. Accordingly, the matter has now been closed."

And what about the anonymous informant whose false tip had started the investigation, wronging and damaging the president?

"Investigation has revealed no apparent motive on the part of this individual to fabricate," Ruff explained blandly.

Ford held a news conference that evening to attract maximum public attention to the exoneration and to attempt to use it to wipe away all the "suspicions" plaguing him: the golf holidays, Butz's delayed resignation, the "pocket money" matter, and the charge by John Dean that the Nixon White House had recruited Congressman Ford to kill an early Watergate investigation.

"Today's announcement by the special prosecutor reaffirms the original findings of my vice-presidential confirmation hearings," Ford declared to his news conference in a prepared opening statement. "I hope that today's announcement will accomplish one other major task—that it will elevate the presidential campaign to a level befitting the American people and the American political tradition.

"For too many days this campaign has been mired in questions that have little bearing upon the future of the nation. The people of this country deserve better than that. They deserve a campaign that focuses on the most serious issues of our time."

Cheney had an idea to dramatize the president's desire to shift the focus of the campaign to serious issues. He considered recommending that Ford cancel all further campaign travel, return $10 million in unspent campaign funds to the Federal Election Commission and ask the voters to judge him solely on his record as president.

Cheney dropped the idea as too risky on the morning of Ford's news conference.

A maddening element of the special prosecutor's inquiry was that, while almost daily stories were written about charges that Ford had pocketed contributions from the Marine Engineers Beneficial Association, almost nothing was written about the fact that the union raised $150,000 for the Carter campaign.

As far as I could tell, only two news stories discussed in detail the maritime union's contribution to Carter, and Carter's statement to the union that he supported its demand for a law guaranteeing that a certain amount of cargo would be shipped on American vessels. One unsigned story was in the small-circulation *National Journal* and the other was by Robert Schanke on CBS.

Ford had vetoed this so-called cargo-preference bill, favored by the maritime union, which should have ended speculation that his views on the legislation were influenced by union contributions to his congressional campaign.

But Carter kept his promise to his maritime union contributors once he became president. He supported the legislation, even though it would have cost consumers an estimated $240 million a year in higher cargo charges on imported oil alone. (Congress eventually killed the bill despite Carter's support.)

The day before Ruff issued his public statement clearing Ford, still another damaging charge of a past impropriety was leveled at the president, further hobbling his campaign effort. The charge was made by John Dean on the "Today Show" in a heavily promoted interview designed to whip up sales for his just-published book, *Blind Ambition*, and to help NBC in its ratings battle with ABC's increasingly popular "Good Morning America."

On the program and in the book, Dean embroidered his earlier Senate testimony that the Nixon White House had put pressure on Republican congressional leaders to quash a House Banking Committee investigation of the Watergate break-in. Dean testified that he had looked into alleged campaign-contribution violations by Committee Chairman Wright Patman as a possible lever to persuade him to drop the investigation.

"I discussed this matter with Bill Timmons [then head of the White House Congressional Liaison Office] and we concluded that several Republicans would probably have a similar problem, so that matter was dropped," Dean testified.

In that appearance before the Senate Watergate hearings, Dean gave no indication that Ford was involved; in fact, he did not mention Ford's name. But in writing his book, Dean seemed to recall much more explicitly what he claimed were Timmons's arguments against using Patman's campaign contributions as a threat.

"Jerry [Ford] doesn't think it would be such a good idea. And, frankly, I'll tell you the problem is that, uh, Jerry himself might have some problems in this area and so might some of our guys on the committee. I don't think we ought to open this up."

There were other discrepancies in Dean's various versions of the episode. In his book Dean claimed that Timmons was the White House contact with Ford in attempting to scuttle the House Banking Committee investigation. On the "Today Show," Dean changed his story and said Timmons's assistant, Richard Cook, was the contact.

Timmons and Cook both denied Dean's account.

Carl Stern, NBC's legal correspondent, reminded Dean during the "Today" interview that Ford had told his vice-presidential confirmation hearings that he did not recall discussing the Patman Committee investigation with anyone at the White House.* Stern pressed Dean to say Ford's denial was a lie.

STERN: Do you believe that Mr. Ford did not tell the truth when he said to this [confirmation] committee under oath that he did not recall any such contact [with the White House]?

DEAN: I believe not recollecting is a very safe answer for him.

STERN: My question is do you believe he lied?

DEAN: I don't want to say that. I'll stand on the facts, as I know them.

STERN: . . . I don't want to harp on that, but it's an awfully important point. . . . If he didn't tell the whole truth on that occasion, that's a pretty big matter.

DEAN: Yes, indeed, it is.

Yes, indeed, it is.

But NBC never pursued the story beyond the "Today" interview, demonstrating that it did not really consider Dean's charge against Ford to be a "pretty big matter."

The president was campaigning in New York City the morning of Dean's "Today" interview. The first item on Ford's schedule that day was a videotaped interview at his hotel with Barbara Walters for use on the "ABC Evening News," of which she had recently become the million-dollar coanchorperson. Shaving and dressing in my hotel room, I switched on "Today" to catch up on the latest news, and saw the Dean segment. I warned the president that Walters probably would ask him about Dean's charges.

---

* Ford insisted then and afterward that he called two meetings of Republican members of the Patman Committee, at their request, to discuss what position they should take on the inquiry, which they considered an anti-GOP "fishing expedition."

Incredibly, she either had not watched "Today" or she did not want to mention Dean because he had been on a rival network from which she had just departed. The first reporter with a chance to confront the president with Dean's charges, Walters never asked the question!

But later that morning, as Ford's motorcade pulled away from the hotel for a day of campaign appearances in New York City and the suburbs, Walter Cronkite alertly hopped aboard the press bus. He immediately began trying to wangle a chance to talk to the president privately. Cronkite got his chance during a lunch break at the Rockland County Court House. Ford sent me to escort the newscaster to a tiny office in the courthouse where the president was taking a breather before his next speech.

"Why are you pushing so hard for a talk with the president?" I asked Cronkite in the parking lot outside the courthouse.

"Well, you know the name of this game, don't you?" he replied.

"What is it?" I asked. "Beat Barbara Walters?"

"That's it," Cronkite explained.

However, Ford thought Cronkite was dropping in for a friendly, off-the-record chat, so the cameraman and sound technician Cronkite brought with him were shooed out after only a short time, just long enough for Cronkite to ask the president about the swine-flu program. But Ford and the anchorman talked privately about Dean's charges after the camera had withdrawn.

Later that day, while Ford was resting at a restored Revolutionary period house near Union, New Jersey, I learned that Cronkite had given some information to the president as well as obtaining information. Ford called me into the bedroom and advised me that Cronkite had told him NBC paid Dean $7000 or $8000 for the interview.

"If that's true, we ought to get that information out," the president instructed.

I phoned "Today" host Tom Brokaw, who had conducted the interview with Carl Stern, and asked him whether NBC had paid Dean. He denied it.

I asked to be switched to Richard Wald, president of NBC News. He readily admitted that NBC had paid Dean $7500 the year before for an option on the TV rights to his book. I suggested that NBC's news judgment had been affected by this secret financial interest in publicizing Dean's book. The phone conversation with Wald grew progressively nastier. I argued that since Ford, Timmons and Cook had all denied Dean's charges, and with the election only three weeks away, NBC had a special obligation to be extremely careful with such unsupported allegations.

Wald replied, "Well, Dean made some charges against Nixon, too, and Nixon denied them and they turned out to be true."

After we'd argued for a while I told Wald, "We are not getting anywhere this way. I am just going to tell you we are going to win this election and you are going to be left with shit on your face." I slammed down the phone.

On the flight back to Washington after his day of campaigning in New York and New Jersey, Ford delivered a diatribe against Dean and NBC. Still later that night, back in the White House, the president kept up a shower of denunciatory phone calls to Cheney and me—one placed from the swimming pool. Ford was particularly upset by a long-distance phone call from his son Steve, who had seen the "Today" interview and wanted his father to level with him.

At one point that night, White House Counsellor John Marsh went to Ford's residence to discuss another matter. The president snarled to him that Dean was "a low-down, no-good, son of a bitch, a sniveling bastard."

Ford had worked himself into a rage over the "Today" interview. He was composing in his head an angry statement attacking Dean, which he wanted to deliver at a news conference the following day. But by the time he walked into the auditorium of the Executive Office Building for the news conference the next morning, Ford had been talked out of a harsh public attack on Dean. The staff convinced the president that such an attack would be reminiscent of the reaction by the Nixon White House to Dean's Watergate testimony.

Unfortunately, this staff warning made the president too cautious. When a reporter asked him at the news conference whether he would like to "set the record straight" on Dean's charges, Ford made the mistake of being overly timid in his denial.

"I have reviewed the testimony that I gave both the House and the Senate [confirmation] committees and those questions were asked. I responded fully," the president told the reporters. "A majority of the members of the House committee and the Senate committee, after full investigation, came to the conclusion that there was no substance to those allegations. I do not believe they are any more pertinent today than they were then, and my record was fully cleared at that time."

The answer, simply referring back to the previous congressional clearance, was too weak. Ford should have forcefully denied Dean's allegations.

Despite the weak answer, however, the Dean charges faded from the headlines and news shows within a few days, further evidence that NBC and the other news organizations didn't seriously believe Dean's accusations. Certainly, charges that the president of the United States had skirted close to perjury during his confirmation hearings should have propelled NBC into an unrelenting effort to expose the truth. Instead, after a few days of milking the Dean interview (and two others on subsequent "Today" shows) for their publicity and audience-building value, NBC dropped the sensational allegations and never pursued them. Neither did any other news organization. It was hit-and-run journalism at its worst.

Indeed, there wasn't much for NBC to pursue. Ford, Timmons and Cook all denied Dean's allegations. Watergate special prosecutor Ruff ruled there was no cause to investigate the Dean charges. And former special prosecutor Leon Jaworski, ever a man of fairness and integrity, pointed out the suspicious timing of Dean's accusations.

"What bothers me is why hold a matter of this kind for several years," Jaworski complained in an interview, "especially when the man is nominated for vice president, succeeds to the presidency and it's still withheld. And then, here shortly before the election, it comes out in connection with the sale of a book."

Dean's motives for the "Today Show" episode were obvious. Forever the hustler, driven by self-confessed "blind ambition," unemployed after his jail term, Dean needed all the publicity he could get to promote his book for royalties and future writing and lecture fees.

What were NBC's motives for going along? By owning the option on the TV rights to Dean's book, NBC stood to profit by stimulating interest in the book, boosting it onto the best-seller list and thereby building a larger audience for the TV show it was considering making.

Until the end of the campaign we tried without much success to interest reporters and TV columnists in reporting the $7500 NBC payment to Dean, which would have raised questions about Dean's and NBC's motives.

Many other questions about the episode also remained unanswered. For example: What role had the Carter campaign played in promoting the Dean allegations? Why did Associated Press stories on September 23 and 24, 1976, reporting Dean's charges against Ford, leaked from the book manuscript, appear under a Plains, Georgia, dateline? Why was the book's publication date, originally scheduled for January 1977, after the election, moved back to November and then October 1976, before the election?

The episode did not catch the White House entirely by surprise. Weeks before, White House staff members had been tipped by friends in the publishing industry that the Dean book was going to be used for political purposes to harm the president.

In the midst of the Dean controversy, I mentioned to Cheney that the Carter campaign was benefiting from the various allegations of wrongdoing against Ford, if the Democrats were not actually responsible for the charges.

"They have a lot of shit flying at us," Cheney advised, "and what we have to do is to get a lot of shit flying back at them."

However, we were never very successful in the shit-flinging competition.

Some of my White House colleagues—and on occasion Ford himself—complained in private that the press followed a double standard, by pursuing allegations of Ford's wrongdoing far more vigorously than they did with Carter. A bitter, resentful attitude toward the press spread through many White House offices.

I wrote in my private notes during those troubled October days: "For a long time I resisted and fought against the antipress, kind of paranoid bunker mentality. But I find now I have caught that mentality along with the rest."

Certainly the White House press corps' deep mistrust of Nixon spilled over into lingering suspicion about Ford, who had been picked by Nixon and had pardoned Nixon. Meanwhile, Carter successfully created an image for himself of the untainted outsider who would bring morality and honesty to Washington. I blame my Communications Strategy Group, in part, for failing to prod or entice reporters into investigating Carter's blemishes.

One of the few efforts by the campaign organization to demonstrate that the pious Carter might not be so pure involved gossip that he once had a mistress. But attempts to persuade reporters to look into this rumor were done so heavy-handedly that they backfired: The news stories which resulted were about how the Ford campaign tried to pull a dirty trick by spreading suggestions that Carter had a mistress.

The alleged mistress's name was Irene. The height of our ingenuity was an idea of campaign spokesman William Greener that a group of Ford campaign workers should go to a Carter rally and serenade him with "Goodnight, Irene."

While that effort was sophomoric, there were legitimate grounds for the Ford campaign to raise questions about Carter's integrity. An unsigned document circulated in the White House a few days after Dean's "Today" interview, saying Carter was vulnerable on the issue of character and honesty.

"Jimmy Carter has a long history of personal improprieties which illustrate the fact that he is not worthy of the trust he has asked the American voters to place in him," the document declared. "These improprieties should be stressed in order to raise doubts about Carter's own character and integrity, which he has made the leading issue in this campaign."

Because of lack of press interest, and our own inability to stimulate interest, none of the alleged improprieties was much of a problem for Carter. Nor was the well-hidden fact that he was a millionaire, personally worth $5 million as an agri-business corporate executive, in contrast to the poor-peanut-farmer image he liked to project.

The best the Ford campaign could manage in their endeavor to puncture Carter's facade of rectitude was a suggested list of pejorative adjectives distributed to Ford spokesman for use in attacking the Democratic candidate: "weird . . . erratic . . . strange . . . compulsive . . . odd . . . bizarre . . . unbalanced . . . twisted . . . manic . . . dangerous . . . irrational . . . peculiar."

The only sustained public scrutiny of Carter's character during the campaign came about not because of anything the Republicans did, but because Carter granted an interview to PLAYBOY.

At the very end of the last in a series of question-and-answer sessions, Carter told interviewers Barry Golson and Robert Scheer:

> I try not to commit a deliberate sin. I recognize that I'm going to do it anyhow, because I'm human and I'm tempted. And Christ set some almost impossible standards for us. Christ said, "I tell you that anyone who looks on a woman with lust has in his heart already committed adultery." I've looked on a lot of women with lust. I've committed adultery in my heart

many times. This is something that God recognizes I will do—
and I have done it—and God forgives me for it. But that
doesn't mean that I condemn someone who not only looks on
a woman with lust but leaves his wife and shacks up with
somebody out of wedlock.

Christ says don't consider yourself better than someone else
because one guy screws a whole bunch of women while the
other guy is loyal to his wife. The guy who's loyal to his wife
ought not to be condescending or proud because of the relative degree of sinfulness.

Read in its entirety, the interview was an excellent and far-rang-
ing insight into Carter's personality. But press reports on the interview dealt almost entirely with his remarks about lust, shacking up
and screwing.

PLAYBOY, in a later issue, ran an article by Golson criticizing the
press for going "berserk" in its coverage of those parts of the interview dealing with Carter's views on sex while virtually ignoring
the rest of the interview. But PLAYBOY itself contributed to the press
hysteria by giving a preview of the sexual remarks on the "Today
Show" shortly before the first presidential debate.

Carter's views on sex were a sensation. Never before had a presidential candidate used such blunt language publicly. Never before
had a presidential candidate revealed such an intimate view of his
deepest religious convictions in the area of sexual attraction.

The uproar was enormous. For weeks, everywhere Carter went
he was questioned about the interview. Mrs. Carter, the Carter sons,
practically everyone and anyone in political life was sought out for
reaction. Religious leaders, including some from Carter's own
Southern Baptist denomination, expressed shock. Some thought
Carter's worst mistake was talking to PLAYBOY at all. Jokes and
cartoons proliferated, including a devastating drawing by cartoonist Paul Conrad of the *Los Angeles Times* showing Carter visualiz-
ing a naked Statue of Liberty. The interview provided Johnny
Carson with monologue material night after night. Bumper stickers
sprouted: "In his heart he knows your wife."

In addition, another portion of the interview, ignored initially in
the furor over Carter's remarks about sex, soon began to hurt the
candidate in Texas. He had told his interviewers, "I don't think I
would ever take on the same frame of mind that Nixon and Johnson
did, lying, cheating and distorting the truth." Texans didn't take

kindly to that kind of criticism of their LBJ, and Carter was forced to apologize to Lady Bird Johnson.

The press, of course, would not let the PLAYBOY story go until Carter made the ritual public confession of error, which he finally did in the last debate.

"In retrospect, from hindsight, I would not have given that interview had I to do it over again," Carter admitted. "If I should ever decide in the future to discuss my deep Christian beliefs and condemnation and sinfulness, I'll use another forum besides PLAYBOY."

Ford's reaction to the PLAYBOY interview caused him (and me) trouble. When asked during interviews and public question sessions for his opinion of the interview, the president usually responded by stating that he also had been asked to do a PLAYBOY interview, but had turned it down and never would do an interview with that magazine.

PLAYBOY decided to contest that assertion. Golson phoned me at the White House one night to inform me that he intended to issue a statement to reporters denying that Ford had ever been asked to do the main PLAYBOY interview. I grew angry and profane because Golson said he was going to issue his statement immediately, before I had a chance to search the files for a copy of an interview request from PLAYBOY and my rejection. I told Golson if he issued his statement I would issue my letters and then he would look like a "fucking idiot."

A search of the White House files showed PLAYBOY originally contacted me in July 1975 in a letter from articles editor Geoffrey Norman, requesting White House cooperation with an author named Richard Rhodes, who was preparing an article on Ford. Rhodes wanted interviews with White House staff members and twenty to thirty minutes with the president.

"We would like PLAYBOY to have a small slice of the president's time, which we know is very dear," Norman wrote.

I had responded that Ford would be on a trip to Europe and in Vail during the period when Rhodes wanted his interview. "I am sorry we are not able to arrange the interview for Mr. Rhodes," I wrote to PLAYBOY.

As usual, I had tried to find a polite excuse for rejecting an interview the president didn't want to do. Polite, but still a firm turndown.

As promised, Golson issued his statement denying that Ford had ever been invited to take part in *the* PLAYBOY interview, and I issued copies of the correspondence showing I had rejected an invitation for Ford to take part in a PLAYBOY interview. The minicontroversy ended in a standoff.

The Ford campaign had decided initially to keep out of the public furor over Carter's PLAYBOY interview. The reasoning was that whatever damage it was going to cause Carter could only be lessened if the Ford campaign turned it into a partisan matter.

But toward the end of the campaign the Ford organization ran an advertisement showing the cover of PLAYBOY—picturing a seductive girl unbuttoning her top and a plug for the interview with "The *Real* Jimmy Carter"—and the cover of *Newsweek*, which had a close-up photo of Ford and the headline "How Good a President?" The only text in the ad said, "*One* good way to decide this election. Read last week's *Newsweek*. Read this month's PLAYBOY."

Carter's supporters screamed, "Dirty trick!" But it was a damned effective ad.

Back in July 1976, when Carter won the Democratic nomination, Ford had phoned to congratulate him. "I'm looking forward to a good, high-level campaign," the president told his opponent.

I recalled that phone conversation in a note to myself in the midst of the controversies over PLAYBOY, Earl Butz, golf holidays, John Dean and old campaign contributions.

"It just seems there is not a single serious issue being discussed in this campaign," I noted ruefully. "I don't know whose fault that is: the press for only covering the sensational things or the candidates for not really dealing with serious issues."

CHAPTER TWENTY

The Ten-Day Orgasm

Immediately after the last presidential debate, in Williamsburg, Ford set out on a final, ten-day campaign swing that would end on election eve in his hometown of Grand Rapids, Michigan. In a last quiet moment before beginning the trip, Cheney and I chatted about the experience we were about to undergo.

"It's too bad it's not possible to sit back and savor what we are living through as an historic experience," Cheney mused. "But if you like politics, there is not anything comparable to the experience you are about to have. It's going to be a ten-day orgasm."

My own image of the campaign trip on which we were embarking was that it was like a roller-coaster ride. Once aboard, there would be no stopping and no getting off until the end of the line, ten days away.

My only concern was that Ford seemed to be hyperactive, his motor racing, anxious to hit the road. I worried that he was not preparing adequately for the final debate and that his excitement would sweep him into making a damaging statement.

I expressed my concerns to Cheney, who assured me that the president would have time to rest and calm down before the trip. Cheney said one reason Ford seemed charged with excess energy was that he had taken a dislike to Carter as a result of his opponent's campaign tactics and statements. It was one of the few times in his life that easygoing Jerry Ford felt genuine animosity toward another person. He was champing to get out on the last campaign trip to start swinging at Carter.

After Carter's harsh attacks on Ford's Eastern Europe comments following the second debate, the president's public denunciations of his opponent had grown increasingly sharp, especially in questioning the Georgian's truthfulness. Ford's aides held their breath as he edged closer and closer to the unpresidential posture of calling Carter, outright, a liar. He stopped just short.

As the last campaign swing began, the president had pulled close to Carter in the polls and was still gaining. The rash of stories casting suspicion on Ford's integrity had finally faded. The president's campaign, having hoarded its advertising money, had plenty of cash to spend on a last-minute media blitz, while Carter had used up a lot of his funds on advertising early in the campaign. Polls suggested Carter's support in his native South might be slipping, forcing him to divert some of his energies from essential campaigning in the large industrial states.

Thus, Ford and his staff began the trip in high spirits.

From Williamsburg, Ford motored to Richmond, stayed overnight at the Governor's Mansion, then addressed a rally on the State Capitol grounds. From there he flew to another rally at the North Carolina State Fair in Raleigh, and on to the South Carolina–Notre Dame football game in Columbia, South Carolina, hoping to cut into Carter's southern strength. Still the same day, Ford flew across the country to Burbank, California, before he slept.

The next day, Sunday, the president attended church at the San Gabriel mission, motored to a rally with John Wayne at a recreation center in Fountain Valley, then flew to another rally at a shopping center in San Diego.

Monday, Ford toured the shipyards and spoke in Seattle, Washington; answered questions from the National Association of Broadcasters in Portland, Oregon; and flew back across the country to spend the night in Pittsburgh.

The pace grew faster: from a steel mill in Pittsburgh—to Chicago—to the boardwalk in Atlantic City, New Jersey (with Miss America on the platform). Then, in one day, Philadelphia, Indianapolis, Cincinnati and Cleveland.

The next day, an even longer itinerary: Milwaukee, St. Louis, Houston and a high-school football game in Baytown, Texas. Back in Philadelphia, Syracuse, Buffalo (Saturday night in Buffalo!). Then, after attending mass the Sunday before election day at the Polish Saint Stanislaus Church in Buffalo (remember the ethnic voters), Ford plowed on to Rochester, Long Island, New York City and Akron.

Finally, the last day of the campaign, Monday, November 1, the president hit Columbus, Ohio, and Detroit, before arriving the night before the election in Grand Rapids.

My memories of that incredible 15,705-mile odyssey are a kaleidoscope of fragments, surreal impressions, meaningless and memorable moments:

—Ford's limousine was rigged with loudspeakers hidden inside the fenders and a microphone in the back seat so he could speak to the startled crowds along his motorcade route. We called it "The Amazing Talking Car."

—A radio reporter was shoved into the back seat of the limousine to tape an interview while Ford was driving from one event to another in Detroit. It was a frantic scene—the nervous reporter stammering his questions, the president trying to answer, talk to the crowds along the street through his loudspeakers, wave, and prepare for the next appearance, all at the same time. The reporter got a scoop, but didn't know it, when Ford offered his one and only prediction of how many electoral votes he would win—278.

—One hotel assigned Ford to its Emperor Suite. He told his appointments secretary, Terry O'Donnell, to do something about that name emblazoned on the door. The Emperor Suite nameplate was covered with a piece of cardboard taped up and marked with a felt-tip pen, "Jerry Ford's Room."

—Doug Blaser, the tireless and superbly efficient press office advance man, slipped in his shower during the president's stop in Houston, slitting his eyebrow open. But the campaign came first. He taped up the gash with a Band-Aid, worked all day herding reporters around and, when he finally got a breather, had four stitches taken over his eye, then immediately returned to work.

—The White House schedule for the Milwaukee stop, abbreviating the name of the Milwaukee Exposition, Convention Center and Arena, read, "8:30 A.M. Motorcade arrives Mecca."

—I spent half of one night trying to appease Tom Vail, publisher of the *Cleveland Plain Dealer*, who refused to accept an invitation to breakfast with the president or let his editors attend if representatives of Cleveland's other paper, *The Press*, were invited. We eventually caved in to Vail's demand. Discussing U.S. dependence on Middle East oil at the breakfast, the president told news executives, "The Saudis have us by the balls."

—In San Diego, Jim Naughton of the *New York Times*, the

champion practical joker of the White House press corps, paid $100 for the gigantic head of a chicken costume used to promote a local radio station. The president never faltered when Naughton wore the head to a Ford news conference the next day at the Portland airport. "Are you going to put this on your expense account?" Ford laughed. Naughton did.

—When Ford developed laryngitis from too many campaign speeches, Saul Kohler of the Newhouse Newspapers sent the White House doctor a joking memo reading, "The Jewish voters of America recommend the ultimate and heroic remedy—chicken soup." Dr. Lukash passed on the memo to Naughton with his own spoofing note typed at the bottom: "Mr. Naughton—We have decided to accept the above suggestion. May we borrow your chicken for a short time?"

—The Ford entourage, grown flaky from lack of sleep and constant travel, amused itself during the long hours on *Air Force One* by making up fantastic news stories. One of the best was, "In his sharpest attack yet on his Democratic opponent, President Ford today ordered Air Force F-4 Phantom jets to shoot down Jimmy Carter's plane. The Democrats immediately charged this was a Republican dirty trick."

The president had polished his basic stump speech so that he made pretty much the same pitch at every stop. One of the most memorable recitations of The Speech was delivered at the Valley Forge Music Fair near Philadelphia. Standing alone, spotlighted on the small stage of the theater-in-the-round, the president spoke softly into a hand-held microphone for twenty-seven minutes without notes.

"I would like to hear a pin drop," Ford breathed into his mike. The 2700 people surrounding the stage in the dark honored his request.

"I would like to talk very seriously and very straight from the shoulder and let you refresh your memory, if you would, for just a moment," Ford said, looking like a star entertainer, totally commanding the stage. "Go back to August of nineteen seventy-four. . . . America was in very deep trouble. Faith and confidence in the White House had been lost. . . . We certainly were suffering the worst inflation since the turn of the century—over twelve percent. We were on the brink of the worst economic recession in forty years and we were still involved very substantially in Vietnam. . . .

"Slowly but surely, because the American people felt they had a new trust in the White House itself . . . there was this restoration of confidence in America, its government, its people, its principles, its aims, its objectives."

Holding the audience spellbound with his slow, quiet delivery, Ford ticked off his accomplishments: inflation coming down; unemployment stubbornly and erratically coming down; the Vietnam War ended; America's allies and adversaries convinced that the United States intended to play a strong role in the world.

"What you do between now and November second, when the polls close, will make a significant difference in the third century of America's future. I know you won't let America down, and, as the next president, I won't let you down."

It was probably the best distillation of his basic speech of the entire campaign. Unfortunately, the extraordinarily effective performance did not begin until nearly 10 P.M., so there was almost no TV news coverage.

Ford's strategists recognized that the president would reach only a tiny fraction of the voters in person during his final campaign swing. He needed to get through to millions on TV, and he could not rely on the fifteen- or twenty-second clips from his campaign speeches which were used on the network news shows, often on some trivial matter.

Thus was born the only media innovation of the 1976 campaign, "The Jerry and Joe Show."

Joe Garagiola, a balding, genial former baseball player making good as a sportscaster and TV star, and Edith Green, a grandmotherly former congresswoman from Oregon who was the most visible Democrat for Ford, appeared with the president in a series of half-hour television shows broadcast by the campaign in six key states. The programs, which were watched by roughly a million people in each state, were produced by Ford's TV adviser, William Carruthers, and his hardworking team, which had T-shirts made advertising themselves as President Ford's "Traveling TV Circus."

Each program began with a well-edited videotape of Ford's campaign appearances in the state earlier that day, narrated by Garagiola or one of Ford's sons. Then Garagiola, Green and sometimes a popular local Republican asked the president questions.

Garagiola—who is really bright, even shrewd—has cultivated the image of being an ungrammatical, unsophisticated "Joe Six-Pack" just like any guy watching the game on TV down at the corner bar. Playing that role, Garagiola asked Ford questions that the voter in front of the TV set would have liked to ask, the way the voter would have asked them.

The program came across as relaxed and light, like a good talk show, as if the participants were making it up as they went along. Actually, of course, the broadcasts were carefully orchestrated and ran with deceptive smoothness because of Garagiola's masterful professionalism.

Some reporters grumbled that the programs were thirty-minute commercials disguised as legitimate question-and-answer sessions with a well-known TV personality. There were jokes about the former baseball player tossing softballs to the president. But most newsmen admired the inventiveness of the format and Garagiola's engaging personality. And they'd have to agree—having devoted so much of their campaign coverage to trivia and hoopla—that the programs gave Ford a chance to outline his policies at length. Two political science professors at Syracuse—Thomas E. Patterson and Robert D. McClure—concluded in their book *The Unseeing Eye* that voters learn more about candidates' positions on the issues from paid political commercials than they do from the evening TV news coverage.

The "Jerry and Joe" shows were paid commercials that gave Ford the opportunity to inform voters of his stand on the issues without having his remarks chopped down to meaninglessness or by-passed in favor of trivia by the TV news programs.

Six days before the election, the Ford campaign got an unexpected late break when Herb Hafif, former California finance chairman of the Carter campaign, forked out $8000 of his own money to buy a full-page ad in the *Los Angeles Times* to deliver "a personal warning about Jimmy Carter." The ad appeared under the headline "Can a man no longer trusted by the Co-Chairman of his National Steering Committee be trusted by you?" It featured two pictures of Hafif with Carter and one photo of Hafif with Rosalynn Carter.

In the ad Hafif wrote: "I am a Democrat and I would like to see a Democratic President. But I am now convinced that it would be a disaster if that Democratic President was Jimmy Carter. . . . Independent of character flaws, the man is simply not capable by experience or ability to be President of this country.

"This country is not being asked to elect a Democratic President but to elect another imperial president who will promise anything to get elected but whose words stand in stark contrast to his record and actions."

The Ford campaign expected the ad to be a bombshell, comparable to, say, former Ford campaign chairman Rogers Morton publicly turning against the president. But Hafif's public defection was largely ignored by the national press. In fact, to give the disillusioned Carter official's views some circulation, the Ford campaign again had to buy advertising, full-page reproductions of the Hafif ad in forty newspapers the day before the election.

Another ticklish last-minute problem, for both Ford and Carter, suddenly popped up the Sunday before the voting when a black minister, the Reverend Clennon King, and three other blacks tried to attend services at Carter's Plains Baptist Church. Church deacons canceled services rather than admit the blacks.

Concerned that the episode could damage his strong support among blacks, Carter issued a statement disagreeing with the deacon's decision and pointing out that he had voted ten years earlier against the white-only policy of his church. However, he said, he would not resign from the church but would work from within to alter its segregation rules. Carter also said that he thought King's attempt to integrate the church the Sunday before the election was "partially at least politically motivated."

Some of Carter's supporters were more blunt. "This is obviously a continuation of Watergate," Coleman Young, the black mayor of Detroit, charged, "a last-minute dirty trick."

"It's just kind of fishy," Rosalynn Carter commented.

The Ford campaign denied any role in King's attempt to attend church services. The president's strategists realized that any appearance of involvement in the episode would surely backfire and hurt the Ford campaign. Consequently, orders were sent to everyone in the upper levels of the White House and campaign staff not to say or do anything that could be construed as exploiting the King incident.

But in the confusion of the campaign's last hours somebody in the campaign office didn't get the word. Telegrams were sent to several hundred black ministers and other black leaders, over the signature of campaign chairman James Baker, questioning Carter's commitment to racial equality.

A copy of the telegram quickly reached the Carter campaign,

which rushed it to reporters. The focus of press accounts shifted from Carter's views on integration of the church to an alleged unethical maneuver by the Ford campaign. The president's entourage felt that the press, particularly NBC, went overboard in discrediting King and suggesting that the Ford campaign was behind the episode, without any evidence.

The net effect of the episode probably was harmful to Ford by raising at the very end of the campaign the suggestion of a Nixonian dirty trick.

The president arrived in his hometown the night before the election in a dead heat with Carter, according to the polls—the most amazing comeback in American political history.

The final Gallup poll had Ford ahead by one point; the final Harris poll had Carter ahead by one point. Allowing for statistical error, the pollsters agreed it was too close to call a winner.

After a motorcade through friendly crowds from the airport, Ford strode out onto a platform in front of the old Pantlind Hotel in Grand Rapids, where he had awaited the results of so many congressional elections. Pinpointed in the TV lights, his voice nearly gone, achingly tired, drained, washed by the cheers of his friends and neighbors, he tried to tell what he felt.

"I don't think I can adequately express in words tonight Betty's appreciation and mine for this tremendous welcome to the home that we love so much, Grand Rapids," the president rasped, tears glistening in his eyes.

"I have made a lot of speeches and this is the hardest one to make—" His voice faltered. This stolid man, who kept his emotions under such tight control, was overcome by the occasion and by the affection expressed by his hometown. He wept openly.

While the flashbulbs blazed in the chill night air, Betty moved to his side and gave him a kiss to steady him.

"You know, I had a speech I was going to make," Ford declared when he could continue. "But I threw it away." The crowd loved him all the more.

The president struggled through a speech, trying to hold back his tears, speaking from the heart.

The next morning, after voting, Ford drove to a rustic restaurant called Granny's Kitchen and ordered blueberry pancakes, not on his usual weight-conscious menu but a superstitious tradition he had followed over the years on the day of his congressional elections.

With the nostalgic stay in Grand Rapids over, the president drove to the airport for the flight back to Washington to await the election returns. Just before boarding *Air Force One*, the president dedicated a mural in the airport terminal, depicting highlights of his life. Again, he was overcome by emotion. With Betty gripping his hand, with tears streaming down his cheeks, Ford said the mural "brought back so many, many memories, and I could tell a little story about each and every one of them. . . .

"It will mean much to me because of the name Gerald R. Ford and Dorothy Ford, my mother and father," the president said in a hoarse voice. "I owe everything to them and to the training, the love, the leadership. And whatever has been done by me in any way whatsoever, it is because of Jerry Ford Senior and Dorothy Ford. And that is what that mural will always mean to me in the years ahead."

The president was crying. In the audience and behind the curtains surrounding the ceremony, many of Ford's friends and staff members, and even some reporters, were also weeping. When the moving dedication was over and we were flying back to Washington, I told Ford, "You did the impossible. You made Helen Thomas cry."

Before leaving Grand Rapids, the reporters covering Ford's last campaign swing organized a betting pool on the outcome of the election. It cost $5 to enter. The pot would go to the person who correctly predicted the outcome of the election and came closest to guessing the number of states and the number of electoral votes the winner captured. Staff members were invited to enter. So, as a gag, Cheney placed a bet in pollster Bob Teeter's name predicting that Ford would carry 36 states and win 371 electoral votes.

Word quickly spread through the press corps of this confident bet by Ford's reliable pollster. As a result, reporters started writing stories saying the president's strategists were optimistic about winning the election by a wide margin. When Cheney and I learned of the erroneous stories, we got cold feet and told the reporters it was a joke.

As we'd raced through that final ten-day campaign swing, there had seemed to be less and less for the president's staff to do; it was as if the campaign were on automatic pilot. During that final countdown there were no new strategies to devise and implement, no more campaign speeches to write or rallies to plan, no new issues to raise.

In the last days, the staff traveling with Ford withdrew increasingly into its own little group. We stuck together, sometimes literally huddled together, on *Air Force One*, in motorcades, in strange hotels. The mood was subdued and quiet. We didn't talk much to each other and we pulled away from contact with reporters and other outsiders.

By the time we returned to Washington on Election Day, it seemed to me we had cut ourselves off from all those who did not share our deep, personal hopes and fears for the counting of the ballots that night.

CHAPTER TWENTY-ONE

Defeat

The president followed the returns in his White House residence with Mrs. Ford, their four children and relatives and friends, including Senator and Mrs. Dole, entertainer Pearl Bailey and Joe Garagiola. The guests nibbled from a buffet and watched the results on TV sets placed in the living room, hallway and family room. For a long time Mrs. Ford and Pearl Bailey sat on the floor of the family room, their arms around each other, staring at the television.

I shuttled between my office, with its three TV sets and two wire-service Teletype machines, and Cheney's office, where the campaign strategists were gathered. Periodically I walked to the president's residence to give him printed results or interesting stories from the wire machines.

In the first hours Carter swept most of the South and border states, as expected. Ford won Indiana, Kansas, Colorado, Nebraska and Connecticut.

The big states were still up for grabs.

I told reporters at midevening that the election was "unfolding just about according to plan. We haven't lost any states we expected to win."

But we hadn't made a breakthrough either, by winning states we had expected to lose. The polls had been right—it was tight; the race was going right down to the wire. The night of waiting would be long.

After midnight, Carter captured New York and Pennsylvania, big prizes. Fred Perrotta, a New York lawyer and Republican activist, phoned the White House and asked the president's permission to have all the voting machines in New York impounded because of suspected irregularities. Ford approved.

Another phone call put through to the president in his residence was from John Connally. He assured Ford that Texas looked good for the GOP. He was wrong. Texas went for Carter, another damaging loss for the president.

Then, in the first hours of the morning, Ford began to gain on Carter. The president and his guests watched the TV anchormen report that Ford had won his home state of Michigan, New Jersey and most of the states west of the Mississippi. One of the networks, which had awarded Oregon to Carter, conceded that was a mistake and declared Ford the winner there. Hopes at the White House rose, cautiously.

However, the president still trailed, and by 2 A.M. the computer at CBS projected that if Carter won all the states he was expected to win, he'd be within three electoral votes of capturing the presidency. The atmosphere in the White House offices was subdued and concerned after that news broadcast. At the party in Ford's residence the mood of gaiety seemed forced. Dole phoned from the party to the campaign chiefs in Cheney's office to ask, "Does it look any better down there than it does upstairs?" He was told it didn't.

The problem was that the vote count was coming to an end. There weren't many states left undecided where Ford could win enough electoral votes to overtake Carter. The outcome could be determined by one of the small states where the results were still in doubt—Mississippi with seven votes or Alaska with just three.

Shortly before 3 A.M. the bells on my UPI machine clanged. A secretary ripped off the bulletin and threw it down on my desk. It read:

FLASH

WASHINGTON—CARTER WINS PRESIDENCY.

UPI   11-03   02:57   AES

"Based on what?" I shouted.

An assistant rushed off to contact UPI. He returned soon and reported that Carter had been declared the winner of the election on the basis of Mississippi going for the Democrat.

I scrawled across the bottom of the UPI flash, "On the basis of Miss.," and hurried to Cheney's office to show him the dispatch. When I got there, his secretary informed me that Cheney and pollster Bob Teeter had gone to the residence to give Ford a progress report on the returns.

I learned later that Ford had led them away from the party and into the family dining room so he could receive their report in private. The president invited only Senator Jacob Javits of New York to join him in the dining room to hear the prognosis from Cheney and Teeter.

"It doesn't look good," Teeter began. To win, he explained, Ford would have to carry all the states still undecided, including three big ones—Illinois, California and Ohio—and at least one small state in which Carter was leading would have to turn around and go for the president.

Cheney recalled later that Ford took the news in a businesslike way, showing no emotion. Then he asked Teeter to step into the hallway and give the pessimistic report to the other guests.

Learning that Cheney and Teeter were with Ford and that the president was unaware of the UPI flash declaring Carter the winner, I hurried to the residence with the wire-service bulletin. Cheney and Teeter must have left the president's quarters by the stairway as I rode up on the elevator, because I never saw them. Instead, when I stepped off the elevator into the foyer of the residence at 3:15 A.M., I found the president bidding his guests goodnight.

He grasped my arm and squeezed. "I'm going to bed," he whispered, his voice virtually gone from so much campaign speaking. "If I'm going to be worth a damn tomorrow, I better go to bed."

I had the UPI flash in my hand, officially declaring him the loser. I didn't have the heart to show it to him.

I returned to Cheney's office. The campaign strategists decided I should call a press briefing to announce that the president had turned in and was not going to a "victory celebration" at the Sheraton-Park Hotel. Hundreds of disappointed supporters and campaign workers were still milling around the hotel ballroom, trying to keep their hopes up.

At my press briefing a reporter asked me whether Ford had felt he still had a chance to win when he went to bed.

"Yes," I replied. Victory was still possible, but, we all knew, not probable.

Cheney and the other campaign managers slipped away quickly. Nobody said much. But Communications Director David Gergen and I lingered in Cheney's office until 5 A.M. discussing all the things that would have to be done when Washington awoke in just a few hours. Gergen told me he had already drafted a telegram of concession for Ford to send to Carter. I felt like Gergen and I were making funeral arrangements for a relative who had died.

At 8:30 A.M., about the time Ford was awakening, Cheney convened a meeting in his office of nearly a dozen White House and campaign officials. The purpose was to review the vote in each state to determine whether uncounted or absentee ballots, or challenges, might change the result.

Of the major states in doubt when Ford went to bed, he won Illinois and California, but lost Ohio by 11,000 votes, a margin of only two-tenths of one percent. Ohio and one small state would have meant victory for Ford.

Carter won the electoral vote 297 to 241, the popular vote 40.8 million to Ford's 39.1 million. Ford carried four of the eight biggest states. But he needed five or six. We found that Carter won New York by 289,000 votes, so the White House dropped its complaint of fraud. We figured *that* many votes couldn't have been stolen.

A Republican leader in Mississippi phoned Cheney to complain of vote fraud there, which he said could switch the state to Ford. We checked the charge and found it was unjustified. Calls were made to Republican leaders in several states where Carter won narrowly to find out if a recount would change the result. The answer was negative every time.

We went through the list of states over and over again, looking for a chance to reverse the outcome. It wasn't there.

Finally, shortly before ten o'clock, Cheney said with a sigh, "Gentlemen, we have to hoist our flag"—the white flag of surrender.

Cheney and several others from the group went to the Oval Office to inform the president. It was time to publicly acknowledge defeat and congratulate the winner. Cheney phoned me from Ford's office and directed me to write a presidential statement to go with Gergen's concession telegram.

There was a lengthy discussion among presidential aides about who would read the statement for the TV cameras. The president had almost no voice left. Some staff members were concerned that Mrs. Ford might go to pieces if she read it. There was a discussion of using Jack Ford, who had campaigned hard for his father; or Mike Ford, the president's eldest son, a seminary student, the least political member of the family.

There was no immediate decision from the Oval Office, so when the statement was ready, Cheney's secretary typed three different versions on 5-by-7 cards, suitable for the president, Mrs. Ford or one of their sons.

While the problems of the statement were being hashed out,

there was a funereal mood in the White House, with plenty of tears from secretaries and staff members. But we also made a few attempts at humor to relieve the crushing disappointment. When it appeared that Carter might win by only one or two electoral votes, we kidded about using invitations to White House social events to woo electors away from Carter, as we had wooed convention delegates.

"Bring back the queen!" somebody cracked.

For others, Ford's defeat was not a sorrow but an opportunity. For instance, that morning a Virginia real-estate agent phoned the press office and requested the names of all White House staff members who would be selling their houses as a result of the election outcome. One of my assistants told him where he could stuff his multiple listings.

A little after 11 A.M. a deeply disappointed Ford phoned Carter and congratulated him. The president's voice was so bad and his hurt was so painful that he put Cheney on an extension phone to read the telegram of concession to Carter:

Dear Jimmy:

It is apparent now that you have won our long and intense struggle for the presidency. I congratulate you on your victory.

As one who has been honored to serve the people of this great land——both in Congress and as president—I believe that we must now put the divisions of the campaign behind us and unite the country once again in the common pursuit of peace and prosperity.

Although there will continue to be disagreements over the best means to use in pursuing our goals, I want to assure you that you will have my complete and wholehearted support as you take the oath of office this January.

I also pledge to you that I and all members of my administration will do all that we can to insure that you begin your term as smoothly and effectively as possible.

May God bless you and your family as you undertake your new responsibilities.

The antagonists were beginning to put their campaign rancor behind them in the interest of continuity.

At noon, Cheney, Appointments Secretary Terry O'Donnell and I went to the Oval Office to make final arrangements for the president's public statement. We found David Kennerly posing the president, Mrs. Ford, their four children and Mike's wife, Gayle, behind the desk, trying to duplicate a photo he had taken on Ford's first day as president. He was having trouble catching a shot in which someone wasn't crying or near tears. The family hugged and kissed each other, giving each other support and strength at that terribly sad moment, as I had seen them do before at difficult times.

When the photo session was over, the president made the decision that Mrs. Ford would read his statement for the cameras. I gave her the appropriate set of cards to rehearse and she read them aloud, stumbling badly through the words. Cheney and I exchanged a worried look. But Ford was firm—his wife was going to read his statement—so I riffled through the cards one more time to make sure they were in the proper order, inked in a minor change and handed them back to the First Lady.

"Ready to go?" Ford croaked.

He and the family trooped into the briefing room. The passage was lined with aides and secretaries from all over the White House, many of them weeping. The briefing room was packed solid with reporters, cameras and TV technicians.

"It is perfectly obvious that my voice isn't up to par and I shouldn't be making very many comments, and I won't," Ford whispered into the microphones on the raised stage. "But I do want to express on a personal basis my appreciation and that of my family for the friendship that all of us have had. . . . Let me call on the real spokesman for the family, Betty."

Mrs. Ford took a step forward and spread her typed cards on the wooden rostrum. Without a tear, with a little smile on her face, she read the statement flawlessly in her soft, lilting voice.

"The president . . . wants to thank all those thousands of people who worked so hard on his behalf and the millions who supported him with their votes. It has been the greatest honor of my husband's life to have served his fellow Americans during two of the most difficult years in our history.

"The president urges all Americans to join him in giving your united support to President-elect Carter as he prepares to assume his new responsibilities."

Then she read the president's telegram to Carter.

Ford and the family stood behind her, Susan sobbing softly, the boys fighting to control their emotions, the president biting his lip with a terrible look of hurt and bewilderment in his eyes. He didn't understand why he'd been turned out of office. Those who saw the look on his face that day will never forget it.

"Let's have a little applause," I hissed to the staff jammed in the doorway as soon as Mrs. Ford finished reading the telegram. I wanted the applause to drown out any reporters trying to fire questions at the president at that painful moment.

While the staff clapped, Ford and his family stepped off the platform and circulated through the crowd of reporters, photographers and technicians. With each person, the Fords shook hands, exchanged a few words, chatted about the future. Despite the pain of defeat he was suffering, despite private complaints he nursed about unfair press coverage, Ford insisted on spending that time with the men and women who had reported on his presidency. Many of the reporters were moved to tears. Ford's graceful gesture explains as well as anything why relations between the White House and the press improved so much while he was president.

Until then, I had been too busy to absorb fully the fact that Ford had been defeated. But after the president and his family left the briefing room and went off to be alone for a while, I walked to my office, locked the door and cried.

About two hours after Ford's concession statement, Cheney summoned the senior staff to a meeting in the Roosevelt Room.

He said the President, not able to attend because his voice was gone, wanted the staff to know it had been a great try, there was nothing to be ashamed of. Cheney relayed Ford's instructions that the transition was to be smooth. But he also wanted everyone to understand that he had full responsibility as president until January 20.

Just then, the door from the Oval Office opened and Ford walked in.

"I had not intended to come, but I just felt I had to," he rasped. "I want to thank everybody for their service, both in the campaign and to the nation. We took the ball right down to the goal line, but we couldn't get it over. We gave it a hell of a shot. We have nothing to be ashamed of. We should all be very proud."

The president walked around the room shaking hands with each staff member, sharing a few words in his hoarse whisper. Everyone got very teary.

Ford still had the hurt look in his eyes. It didn't fade for days. He was puzzled about why he had been rejected. He felt he had done a good job as president during a difficult two and a half years. He believed he deserved to be rewarded with a full four-year term. He sincerely believed he was a better man and a better leader than Jimmy Carter.

Ford's assessment of himself was echoed in an outpouring of praise for him in columns, editorials and news articles printed right after the election, some of it from news organizations that had been critical before the election.

A *New York Times* editorial declared, "Mr. Ford today enjoys the respect and affection of his fellow citizens. Moreover, he leaves the country in better shape than he found it."

Joseph Kraft wrote: "He personally exemplified truth, openness and affection for other Americans. He democratized the White House and appointed independent persons of rare qualities to the highest offices. . . . If . . . the state of the union is more perfect, it is due in large measure to the innate goodness of Jerry Ford."

The most heartbreaking post-election reevaluation of the Ford presidency was by David Broder in the *Washington Post.*

"In an odd, inexplicable way," said Broder, "the truth has begun to dawn on people in the final days of Gerald R. Ford's tenure that he was the kind of President Americans wanted—and didn't know they had."

Naturally, Ford wondered bitterly where all this praise had been when he needed it.

As always in times of trouble, Ford staff members used gallows humor to brighten the dark hours.

"The hell with this 'orderly transition' shit," one wit declared. "Let's get the Eighty-second Airborne, barricade ourselves in here and make the Carter people come and get us out."

Another time, noting that NBC's election-night TV coverage featured a map with Ford's states in blue and Carter's states in red, someone suggested that Ford proclaim himself president of the United Blue States of America.

The black humor could not soften the knowledge that losing was like death, or like a sentence of death. Despite brief, irrational flickers of hope that vote canvasses might reverse the outcome, we all knew that on January 20 at noon it was going to end, beyond stay or appeal.

The reality was underscored by the memos that began to circulate: "Employment Opportunities," "Payment for Unused Annual

Leave," "Civil Service Retirement Fund," "Severance Pay," "Unemployment Compensation," "Diagram Indicating the Location of the Live Cameras to Be Used the Morning of January 20."

Those things had a wonderful way of focusing the mind.

One of the aspects of defeat most difficult to get used to was not having much to do after the jam-packed days and nights of the past two and a half years. I held press briefings only sporadically. The White House continued to work on routine matters, but there was no future to plan for. The machinery was slowing down. The phones in the office and the White House phone on my bedside table at home didn't ring much anymore. The little paging "beeper" device I carried on my belt rarely went off.

I felt a great emptiness in my life. My days had been filled with excitement and decisions and clashes and important work on historic matters. Now there was a void. I realized I had to fill it by reviving a private life, which had been abandoned during my White House service. A few days after the election I went to lunch with the secretaries from my office. We discussed what we were going to do with our free time when Carter took over. An outsider would have found the plans laughably mundane: start going to movies again, read long-postponed books, resume piano lessons, get bicycles out of storage—simple things that most people took for granted. But to people who had devoted all their time to the White House, they seemed rare pleasures. We were like inmates being set free from prison.

I used my newfound spare time to rekindle my neglected relationship with my wife, Cindy, and to get to know my son, Edward. He had been a baby a year and a half old when I went to work in the White House. Now he was a bright boy of nearly four. He knew who I was, of course, but he didn't really know me as a daily presence in his life. He was shy around me at first, not knowing how to respond, when I started spending more time at home. Getting reacquainted with Edward and Cindy was my first step back into a normal life.

I indulged myself in one last perquisite before leaving the White House. I accepted a long-standing invitation to tour the secret, bombproof emergency headquarters carved inside Mount Weather in Virginia, from which the remnants of the American government would operate in case of nuclear attack.

Riding past the enormous steel blast-resistant doors and through long, dim tunnels stacked with emergency rations, I felt like I was in a science-fiction movie. Sitting all alone in a huge, two-story briefing room, from which a future president could command what was left of the nation, I was taken through a simulated alert, evacuation and attack.

I was shown the more than twenty barracks built inside the mountain, including a fully equipped hospital, cafeteria, offices, a TV studio for postattack broadcasts, and luxury quarters for the president and the highest officials. I was taken to the bedroom cubicle assigned to me in case of war. What an eerie feeling it was to stroll around the wartime press office, set up and ready.

When I first went to work at the White House, I received memos notifying me that I had been designated a member of the "Presidential Emergency Staff" and instructing me how to reach the evacuation headquarters.

The last line of the instructions was chilling: "There are no provisions for families at the relocation or assembly sites."

Carter and his wife accepted an invitation from the president to visit the White House on November 22. The president-elect would discuss Oval Office problems and the transition with Ford while Mrs. Carter would take a tour of the White House to familiarize herself with the rooms and furnishings.

That morning the White House and the Carter staff jockeyed over plans for the meeting. The White House wanted President-elect and Mrs. Carter to arrive by car at the south driveway. Barry Jagoda, Carter's TV adviser, informed me by phone that the president-elect intended to walk across Pennsylvania Avenue and up the north driveway from his temporary residence at Blair House.

I argued that the walk would dominate press coverage and detract from the primary purpose of the visit, which was to project the Ford-Carter meeting as a symbol of national unity and the orderly transfer of power. After a lot of phoning back and forth, the Carter camp agreed to abandon the walk.

"Some of the people down the line here don't always get the word of the decisions made by the people at the top," Jagoda grumbled.

I smiled to myself. The new guys had started elbowing each other already.

Early that morning, Dr. Lukash had phoned me to report that Mrs. Ford was ill. She had been up most of the night suffering nausea, possibly a reaction to an antibiotic she was taking for a bladder infection. Lukash said it was doubtful that Mrs. Ford would be well enough to receive Mrs. Carter, but he planned to examine her again in the late morning before making a final decision.

Around noon, Cheney, Lukash and I met with the president to determine whether Mrs. Ford was well enough to see Mrs. Carter. If not, we would have to announce it in a way that would head off speculation that she was snubbing the new First Lady.

Actually, the president acknowledged that Mrs. Ford's indisposition *was* caused, at least partly, by displeasure at the idea of having Mrs. Carter in the White House. But, refreshed by a nap, Mrs. Ford decided at nearly the last minute that she felt well enough to receive Mrs. Carter after all.

"Just let her do it the way she wants to do it," the president instructed. "Let them have tea, and then someone else can show Mrs. Carter the state rooms, but not the living quarters.

"We are just not going to have her in the residence, and that's all there is to it," he declared firmly.

The president and Mrs. Ford awaited the Carters' arrival just inside the Diplomatic Reception Hall. Sheila Weidenfeld, Mrs. Ford's press secretary, and I lurked nearby. On dozens of previous occasions the four of us had swapped wisecracks while waiting for official functions to begin. Now the atmosphere was so strained no one said a word.

The Fords stepped out under the canopy of the diplomatic entrance to greet the Carters just as the Secret Service sedan delivering the visitors rolled to a stop. Jimmy Carter popped out of the back seat, shook hands with the president and kissed Mrs. Ford on the cheek. That struck me as a presumptuous gesture. Meanwhile, Mrs. Carter trailed along behind her husband, looking as though she didn't quite know what to do. Ford, more restrained than Carter, shook her hand. Then the incoming and outgoing First Ladies went off together while Ford and Carter strode through the Rose Garden to the Oval Office.

The president and the president-elect spent an hour together, exactly the time allotted, chatting in wing chairs in front of a crackling fire in the Oval Office. They were alone except for the last few minutes, when they called in a few aides to make sure there were no hitches in the transition.

Afterward, Ford said Carter had steered the meeting by asking questions, mostly about foreign policy. "He will do all right," the president said reflectively. "He knows all the right questions to ask."

Carter's first appointment to his White House staff was Jody Powell as press secretary. I had struck up an acquaintance with Powell by chatting with him before each of the presidential debates. Two weeks after the election I invited him to visit the White House to look over the sprawling press office operation and discuss the transfer of duties.

He arrived in time for my late-morning briefing, but declined to attend for fear of distracting the reporters' attention. Instead, he listened on an intercom hookup in my office.

At my briefing, some reporters who had learned that Powell was visiting demanded that he appear for questioning:

Q.: Ron, is Jody Powell in the White House right now?
NESSEN: Yes.
Q.: Is he listening to this briefing?
NESSEN: Maybe.
Q.: . . . If you are listening, Jody, thump twice.
Q.: . . . Could we make a request that Mr. Powell come out?
NESSEN: I will relay your message to him.

After the briefing, I asked Powell if he wanted to meet the White House press corps.

"No, one feeding a day for them is enough," he replied.

I announced over the loudspeaker in the press room, "Mr. Powell has declined to come down to talk to you, on grounds that you've been fed once today and that's enough."

After dealing with that, I planned to take Powell to the White House mess for lunch. However, just before leaving I had to step out of my office briefly. When I returned I found about a dozen reporters had invaded my outer office, surrounded Powell and were interviewing him.

"Come on, this is not fair!" I exclaimed. "This is my office and he's my guest. We are trying to conduct business. He already said he didn't want to be interviewed."

"This is not your office," replied Phil Jones of CBS, "so just go away and leave us alone."

"What do you mean this is not my office?"

"It's the taxpayers' office," the CBS correspondent replied.

I was enraged. A dozen reporters would not have been allowed to invade Cronkite's office at CBS. They would have been stopped by the building guards. But here was a squad of reporters refusing to let me conduct business with a guest in my own office at the White House. I threatened to summon the White House police if the reporters didn't leave, but Jones instructed me not to interrupt while Powell was answering questions.

The clash had one beneficial effect. This run-in with the White House press corps convinced me I'd had enough. When January 20 came, I would be happy to give up the job as press secretary.

"I have made a kind of peace with myself," I wrote in my private notes. "I have concluded that I am ready to give up this burden."

CHAPTER TWENTY-TWO

Why; and What If ...?

Ford lost the election, in my view, for these reasons:

—Millions of voters in the South chose Jimmy Carter because of strong regional pride for their native son. Carter's campaign advertisements in the South played upon this regional pride.

—The economy, which had been recovering steadily from the recession, hit a plateau and even dipped a bit just before the election.

—Ford was hurt by lingering hostility toward anyone connected with Nixon and by the unpopular pardon. The special prosecutor's investigation and the other questions raised about Ford's honesty further tarnished his clean reputation. It just wasn't a good year to be the candidate of Nixon's Republican party, or to have spent a generation as an insider in supposedly wicked Washington.

—The image of Ford as a bumbler, reinforced by the Eastern Europe flub, was damaging.

—Maneuvering in the courts by Democrats, which kept Eugene McCarthy's name off the ballot in New York State, may have been decisive. McCarthy probably would have attracted enough votes from Carter in New York's liberal precincts to give Ford the state. Its forty-one electoral votes would have reversed the outcome of the election.

—Ronald Reagan's challenge in the primaries gave Ford an image of weakness. The Reagan threat forced the president to spend months in the role of hard-running politician when he should have been in the White House demonstrating his abilities as president. It also forced him to make a special appeal in the primaries to the most conservative Republicans, at the cost of losing more moderate voters in the race with Carter.

—Reagan did almost nothing to help Ford against Carter, possibly because of mishandling by the president's campaign strategists. Reagan would have been particularly helpful in Texas, Louisiana, Mississippi, South Carolina and other states where he is idolized by conservatives.

—Inept staff members at the White House and in the campaign organization, feuding among the president's associates and harmful and self-serving leaks to the press undermined Ford's credibility as a strong leader.

—The president failed almost totally to attract blacks. Carter was the choice of more than 90 percent of black voters. This overwhelming black vote provided Carter with his margin of victory in more than a dozen states.

A popular pastime among journalists and other political observers after the election was to play "What if?" with Ford's choice of Senator Dole as his running mate.

Would the election outcome have been different, the players speculated,

—if Nelson Rockefeller had not taken himself out of contention for the vice-presidential nomination?

—if George Bush had not eliminated himself from consideration for the number two spot on the ticket by becoming CIA director?

—if Ford had picked Anne Armstrong, William Ruckelshaus or some other Republican with a more middle-of-the-road appeal and a more easygoing manner than Dole?

—if Ford had selected Ronald Reagan as his running mate?

We'll never know the answers to those questions. However, in my opinion, Dole probably helped the president, despite his abrasive style and his harsh attack on "Democrat wars" in the debate with Mondale. Ford's success in the farm states and the West had to be attributed, in part, to Dole's popularity there.

Dole kept his sardonic wit in defeat. After the election he joked that he was going to write a book about his campaign and call it *The Hatchet Man.*

Doug Bailey, the Ford media consultant, had a fascinating theory that the late polls showing Ford even or ahead reversed the tide running for the president.

"The wide coverage of the last-minute dead-heat national polls and forecasts was a principal reason for President Carter's victory," Bailey said in a paper for a post-election NBC forum.

"When Carter was leading in the polls, the natural question in the minds of the undecided voters was, 'Am I sure enough about Carter to want him for the president?'

"The media attention given to last-minute polls and forecasts suggesting a dramatic Ford win changed the question to, 'Do I really want Gerald Ford for four more years?'

"A different question, a different answer and a different outcome."

Bailey and some others in the Ford campaign believed the president was ahead and would have won if the voting had been held three days earlier.

CHAPTER TWENTY-THREE

Press Secretary to Superman

The night before Carter's inauguration, members of Ford's press staff gathered in my private office for a farewell party. First, we drank several bottles of champagne purchased for the party. When that was gone, we drank whatever liquor could be found in the cabinets and desks. And when that was gone, in desperation, we even drank an old bottle of fizzy white wine brought home from a presidential trip to Rumania and forgotten in my refrigerator.

Someone turned down the dimmer switch on the chandelier in my office. The darkness matched our mood. Signs of our imminent departure were everywhere. The viewing stands along Pennsylvania Avenue for Carter's inaugural parade shone in the TV lights outside the window. Installers from the telephone company were putting the names of Carter's press staff members on the telephone pushbuttons. And Carter aides had already moved into a cubbyhole office next to mine to supervise the typing and duplication of the new president's inaugural speech.

Connie Gerrard, my thoughtful assistant, had tried to spare my feelings by closing the door of the tiny office while she typed the mimeograph stencil of Carter's speech. When I peeked in and saw what she was doing, I had to fight down an irrational flash of anger at Connie for seeming to switch her loyalties so easily while the rest of us were in such pain.

I returned to the farewell party. The participants felt sad and alone, like the remnants of a vanquished army, holed up, drinking the night away, before surrender and retreat tomorrow.

On the day of Carter's inauguration, Ford began his last morning as president by following virtually the same routine he'd followed every morning in the White House. He awoke at 6 A.M., about forty-five minutes later than usual, and performed his exercises. Since his stationary exercise bicycle had already been packed and shipped with the rest of the Fords' personal belongings, the president worked out by doing calisthenics.

After shaving, showering and dressing, Ford sat down to his usual breakfast of grapefruit, English muffin and tea. As he ate, he flipped through the *Washington Post*, the *New York Times*, his news summary and the CIA's daily intelligence report.

Shortly after 8 A.M., Ford rode the elevator down from his residence to the main floor of the White House, strode along the marble hallway and entered the State Dining Room. About seventy-five cabinet members and senior White House aides were gathered there for a farewell meeting with the president. When Ford entered, the aides were milling around a long table in the center of the room set with coffee urns, glasses of fruit juice and silver trays of sweet rolls.

Without stopping at the buffet table, Ford moved around the room shaking hands and saying goodbye to each person. Some aides became emotional; their eyes brimmed with tears. When Ford got to me, I couldn't say goodbye. In fact, I couldn't think of anything appropriate to say. Instead I babbled about the Bing Crosby Pro-Amateur Golf Championship in Monterey, California, where Ford was going to play immediately after the inaugural ceremonies. I felt like an idiot running off at the mouth about a golf tournament at what was supposed to be a solemn moment of farewell. But Ford seemed to enjoy it.

Then he moved on to the next staff member. I couldn't hear his conversations with the others. But I wondered how many were making small talk because they also couldn't say goodbye.

After Ford had made his circuit of the room, he ended up near the head of the breakfast buffet table, where Vice President Rockefeller was waiting to serve as master of ceremonies. Rockefeller tapped on something for quiet.

"Mr. President, this is the proudest moment of our lives," Rockefeller rasped. "Your presidency has brought a restoration of faith. Pride has been brought back to our country. It is typical of your thoughtfulness to have us to breakfast."

At that point the doors opened and the high-backed leather chair which had been assigned to Ford in the Cabinet Room when he was vice president was rolled in and presented to him as a gift from the staff. (We had chipped in $10 apiece to buy the chair for $730.50 from the General Services Administration.)*

It was Ford's turn to respond. He gazed around the large, formal room, at the men and women who were his closest aides and closest friends, there to hear his last speech as president.

"I'm not very good at putting words together on an occasion like this," he began.

People swallowed hard, cleared their throats, wiped their eyes. Some just let go and let their tears flow. The president seemed in control of himself. Only a little of the hurt look remained in his eyes.

"I've tried to thank you all in person or by letter or both," he continued firmly.

"I've enjoyed the White House, mainly because of the fine people. The days were long, but they were lightened by the people.

"You all contributed to an administration which I think was good and which history will treat kindly. I hope to see you all again. I believe the friendships we made here will go well beyond January twentieth."

He moved toward the door, shaking a few last hands. At the door he stopped, waved, and shouted in a very loud voice, really his campaign voice, "Goodbye, everybody! Thank you all very, very much!"

He was gone quickly, down the elevator, around the Rose Garden, to the Oval Office.

I think he had to boom out that last goodbye, as if he were addressing a rally, to keep from crying. Many of the staffers were weeping.

After Ford left the State Dining Room, I drifted toward my office to give my last press briefing in the White House, to report on the president's activities that morning. As I walked through the historic corridors, I thought about my time as press secretary during the past twenty-eight months. I had taken over the job at a time when the relationship between the White House and the press corps was at an all-time low as a result of Vietnam, Watergate and

---

* The Cabinet Room chair Ford used as president had been purchased by the University of Michigan for the Ford Presidential Library.

the Nixon pardon. Many journalists no longer trusted the president or the press secretary to tell the truth.

On that last morning, thinking back, I realized that my short temper, thin skin, sarcastic sense of humor and impatience with reporters I considered stupid or niggling were not the ideal qualities for a press secretary trying to soothe the hostility of the White House press corps. Still, because of Ford's candor, accessibility and friendship toward reporters, the battered relationship between the White House and the press had improved greatly during his presidency.

Shortly before the end of the administration, Larry O'Rourke of the *Philadelphia Bulletin,* in his capacity as president of the White House Correspondents Association, wrote Ford: "I want to express to you as you leave office the gratitude of working reporters at the White House. You have provided opportunities for reporters to meet with you and members of your staff in an open and honest manner. In turn, there has been a rebuilding of the healthy tension that must exist between the government and the press in a free society, to the benefit of the country."

Returning from Ford's farewell meeting with his staff, I confronted the "healthy tension" one last time. I stepped up to the podium in the press room for my five hundred and eighty-third, and final, news briefing.

The place was packed with at least a hundred reporters, TV correspondents, radio newsmen, photographers and cameramen, far too many for the room. Press coverage of Gerald Ford's last hours in the White House was typical of the press coverage of his presidency: some rancor, some humor, some sympathetic understanding, some trivia, and some of the best stories missed entirely.

I began my briefing by running through a description of the president's morning activities—getting up, exercising, eating breakfast, etc.

"Did he do push-ups?" a reporter asked.

No, I answered. He never did push-ups.

"Did he fix his own English muffin?" another newsman joked, referring to the PR campaign during Ford's first days in the White House to depict him as an ordinary, nonimperial guy who fixed his own breakfast.

Next, I gave my briefing a bland report on Ford's farewell meeting with the cabinet and senior staff members, not mentioning the tears shed by some persons there or the mood of sadness and finality.

I promised the reporters at my briefing that I would keep them informed for the rest of the morning as Ford concluded his final White House duties.

Questions?

"When did the president take his last swim in the White House pool?" asked a reporter who obviously had been assigned to write a minute-by-minute account of Ford's last day in the White House.

"Last night at five forty-five P.M.," I replied, "and returned to the office at six P.M."

"Ron," a reporter called out, "would you tell us why Sheila Weidenfeld was put on the International Investment Commission?"

Christ! At my final briefing it looked like I was going to have to present a full-scale defense of Ford's last-minute appointments of many friends and staff members to long terms on various commissions and boards.

Sheila Weidenfeld, Mrs. Ford's press secretary, happened to be in the briefing room. She popped up and explained that the announcement of her appointment to the International Investment Commission had been a mistake. Actually, Ford had appointed her to the Historic Preservation Commission, she said, a more suitable plum. Her explanation seemed to take the heat out of the press queries and the matter was dropped.

Finally, Frances Lewine of the Associated Press asked me, "Do you have anything else, Ron?"

"Not right now, Fran."

"Thank you."

It was over. My last briefing. I hesitated a moment at the podium, thinking one of the reporters might say "Good luck" or "See you around." I even thought there might be applause. But there was nothing. Just "Thank you," and the reporters drifted away.

About an hour later, I was at my desk when I heard a high-pitched electronic tone go off. It was a Secret Service device signaling that the president had left his office. I knew he had left for the last time.

I walked the forty or fifty feet from my office to the Oval Office and peered in through the open door. A half-dozen workers were wrapping in protective, padded plastic the few remaining family photos and some pipes the president had kept on his desk until the end. The packers put the items in cardboard boxes for shipment to Ford's retirement home in Palm Springs. The final packing took only a few moments. When it was finished, there was no physical sign left that Gerald R. Ford had served in that office as president of the United States. In a few hours the workers would unwrap Jimmy Carter's things in the Oval Office. It was the physical manifestation of the orderly transfer of power.

I returned to my office, picked up the microphone hooked to the public-address system in the press room and announced that President Ford had left the Oval Office for the last time.

I prepared to leave my own office for the last time. It was a wonderful pale-blue and white office with a high ceiling, floor-to-ceiling windows and a fireplace. It was equipped with a huge horseshoe desk, three TV sets with remote control for watching the three network evening news simultaneously, a refrigerator and a wet bar. I had one of the best views in the White House, overlooking the front lawn and Lafayette Park.

I'd spent twelve to twenty hours a day in that office, six and seven days a week, for more than two years. I'd even slept there some nights, on the red and gray sofa, during international and political crises.

In my last moments there I called in my secretary and dictated a final letter—a congratulatory message to Tom Ross, former Washington bureau chief of the *Chicago Sun-Times*, who had just been appointed chief press spokesman for the Pentagon by the Carter administration.

"I know you will find the experience as stimulating and instructive as I did," I wrote ambiguously. I wondered if he also would find it as maddening on occasion as I did.

My office looked bare and impersonal. I'd taken home my books, pictures, framed cartoons and mementos the previous weekend. Still, I checked the desk drawers and bookshelves for the tenth time to make sure I hadn't forgotten anything. In the closet, I left for Carter's press secretary, Jody Powell, a blue brocade bulletproof vest which had been given to me by some friends from the Justice Department after I'd had a particularly nasty news briefing. I pinned on a note:

> Jody—
> I hope you won't need this.
> Good luck.
>
> Ron

"I guess I'll go," I said to my secretary. I looked around one last time and walked out.

From my office, I walked out past the Rose Garden and up the stairs to the great marble entrance hall of the White House.

President and Mrs. Ford were supposed to be in the hall, at the North Portico entrance, the one facing Pennsylvania Avenue, at precisely 10:30 A.M. to greet Jimmy and Rosalynn Carter for the traditional pre-Inaugural coffee. But Mrs. Ford was late, as she often was for official functions. She had lingered in the State Dining Room, saying goodbye to the maids, butlers and other members of the household staff. She hugged and kissed each servant while the White House photographer and the Instamatics clicked away. There were plenty of tears. The household staff, which had seen many presidential families come and go, had grown particularly fond of the unpretentious Fords.

"Let's go, Betty!" the president snapped in undisguised irritation. "You can't be late this time."

The Carters were on their way, walking from Blair House, across Pennsylvania Avenue, up the curving driveway. We followed their progress on a television set in the chief usher's office next to the entrance hall. You could barely see the Carters in the roiling mass of cameras, reporters, microphone booms and Secret Service agents.

Mrs. Ford was in a playful mood, perhaps to relieve the tension. Just seconds before the Carters arrived, she grabbed her press secretary around the waist and spanked her fanny as mock punishment for some minor misdeed.

The Carters arrived at the portico, their party colliding with the Fords' party packed in the doorway, while dozens of reporters and cameramen, behind rope barriers on either side of the entranceway, surged forward. In the confusion I couldn't hear anything anybody said. I don't think any memorable words were exchanged.

The Fords and the Carters moved to the Blue Room to sip coffee and make small talk, along with the Rockefellers, the Mondales and assorted other dignitaries, until it was time to drive to the Capitol for the inauguration. Various staff members of the incoming and outgoing administrations drifted around uncomfortably in the entrance hall.

I didn't feel like talking to anyone. I just slumped in a chair waiting for it to be over. I had worn a black suit for the final day, as if it were a funeral.

Suddenly, up the marble stairway from the lower lobby came two workmen lugging a double-size mattress. They carried it right across the entrance hall and up another set of red-carpeted marble stairs leading to the family living quarters on the second floor. It was the Carters' bed arriving. What a great human-interest picture! But all the reporters, TV cameramen and photographers jammed on the portico only a few feet away outside the huge front window missed it.

As I went out the front door of the White House to find my place in the motorcade for the ride to the Capitol, the last person I said goodbye to was Freddie Mayfield, one of the doormen. His eyes overflowed with tears and his usually beaming black face looked stricken. Ford had urged Freddie for months to try out the White House swimming pool. One day, near the end, Freddie brought his bathing suit from home and went swimming with the president of the United States. We never told anyone. It was not a media event. It was not a symbol. It was just two men who liked and respected each other having some fun together splashing in the pool.

Ford and Carter rode together in the lead limousine along Pennsylvania Avenue to the Capitol for the inauguration. Rockefeller, Mondale, congressional leaders and all the wives followed in other cars. The handful of Ford staff members who were accompanying the outgoing president to the end were segregated in separate cars from the Carter staff people. As we rode to the Capitol, I peered out at the crowds already taking their places along Pennsylvania Avenue for Carter's Inaugural Parade.

Once the motorcade reached the Capitol and everyone trooped inside, efficient escorts took over and lined up the dignitaries in the proper order for the march out onto the inaugural platform, which had been erected over the long staircase on the east front of the building.

For Carter and his people, the dream was about to be fulfilled. For Ford and his aides, the dream was about to end. But neither side showed what it was feeling. Behind the scenes, as the inauguration ceremony was about to begin, everyone seemed silent and stiff, being moved along according to the inevitable program. But the importance of the moment should not be underestimated. One leader was turning over the power to another peacefully, according to the will of the people. One political party was giving up the executive authority to another. The orderly transfer of power is one of the great accomplishments of the American system. There are so few countries in the world where such a ceremony could take place.

When it came time for the Ford aides to march out onto the inaugural platform, we found that no seats had been provided for us. So we wandered around the rear of the platform looking for a good spot from which to view the ceremony. Most of us ended up crouching under a wooden press stand. Several stories down, tens of thousands of spectators jammed the Capitol plaza and the parks for blocks around to see Carter sworn in.

I noticed Ford and Carter were seated side-by-side in easy chairs at the front of the platform, talking intently during the preliminaries. A microphone was pointed directly at them. If I had spotted that situation during the previous twenty-eight months, I would have slipped a note to Ford or crept up and whispered to him to be careful what he said, TV might be picking it up. But I decided, the hell with it, I'm off duty in a couple of minutes. He's on his own now.

At precisely the instant Carter concluded his oath with "So help me God," Ford's marine aide, Captain Lee Domina, handed to Carter's naval aide, Lieutenant Commander J. Paul Reason, a leather briefcase, code-named the "Football," containing the secret instructions needed to launch a nuclear attack. The briefcase would be within a few feet of Carter, wherever he went, day and night, as long as he was president. The power had passed.

When the inaugural ceremony ended and the dignitaries began filing off the platform, I took a position along the walkway leading into the Capitol so I could fall in behind Ford. But the new president and Mrs. Carter came along first and stopped directly in front of me. Carter stuck out his hand. I shook it.

"Congratulations and good luck, Mr. President," I said.

The "Mr. President" came naturally, a sign of respect. But I could feel Ford's appointments secretary, Terry O'Donnell, on one side of me, and Ford's chief advance man, Red Cavaney, on the other side, stiffen at the courtesy. They were not yet reconciled.

While Carter went off to a lunch in the Capitol to celebrate his inauguration, Ford, Mrs. Ford, Mr. and Mrs. Rockefeller and a small group of outgoing White House aides marched through the building and down a long hill on the Pennsylvania Avenue side to a military helicopter waiting on the lawn to fly them to Andrews Air Force Base outside Washington.

Ford boarded the chopper dry-eyed but shivering. "Whew, it's cold," he exclaimed.

As the helicopter lifted off, Ford put on his glasses. He can't see anything at a distance without them. The flight plan called for the chopper to make a low, slow pass over the Capitol, Pennsylvania Avenue, the White House and the other government buildings on the way to Andrews. It gave Ford a farewell look at the power centers where he had served for nearly three decades, and it gave the people on the ground a chance to wave goodbye to their retiring president.

Ford stared down at the heart of the capital city.

"I've seen more of Washington in the last ten minutes than I saw in thirty years," he commented during the fly-over. He reminisced about coming to Washington in December 1948, a month after his first election to Congress, to look for a house for himself and his new bride. Suddenly it must have hit him that twenty-eight years of his life—Washington, elective politics, public service, climbing the ladder, power—were over. He turned to Rockefeller, who was seated to his right, grasped his hand and squeezed hard. Ford didn't say a word. He pressed his lips into a thin, tight line. Tears welled in his eyes.

Then the moment passed and he turned back to the window.

From where I was sitting, halfway back in the chopper, I noticed David Kennerly snapping dozens of photos of those historic moments and stuffing his exposed film into an envelope for *Time* magazine. Kennerly shouted to the pilot in the cockpit to make another pass over the White House. He had missed the shot he wanted of Ford looking down the first time.

"No, let's not waste any time," Ford fumed impatiently.

But the pilot followed Kennerly's orders and ignored, or didn't hear, Ford's. We made a second pass over the White House.

When the helicopter landed at Andrews, it rolled to a stop just off the nose of the presidential jetliner on the tarmac near the military-VIP passenger terminal. As I popped out of the chopper, I saw that hundreds of White House staff members, administration officials, secretaries, wives and children had turned out even though no well-wishers were supposed to come to the air base for the departure. The crowd was penned inside metal barricades so they couldn't mob Ford.

Ford had decided he wanted a brief, tasteful ceremony at Andrews with no speeches and no handshakes. He had turned down invitations from friends who wanted to give lunches or receptions in his honor, because he wanted to get to California as fast as possible to start playing golf. And he had turned down proposals for elaborate and maudlin farewell ceremonies because he wanted to give the impression of a still youthful, active political figure leaving town for a while, rather than an old man going into permanent retirement.

A red carpet was laid out on the tarmac. Ford and Rockefeller stood at attention as the honor guard marched past with their flags and guns. Then the former president and the former vice president walked along the red carpet reviewing the contingent of troops standing at attention. At the end of the red carpet, Ford and Rockefeller did an about-face and headed back toward the plane.

At the foot of the ramp, Betty Ford took her place at her husband's side. They stood at attention while a battery of howitzers across the airfield pounded out a twenty-one-gun salute. Smoke from the guns enveloped the couple in a white cloud, giving the scene a dreamlike fantasy quality.

The staff members who had flown to Andrews with Ford on the helicopter—Cheney, O'Donnell, Cavaney and me—huddled on the tarmac watching the ceremony. And, typically, we went out with a wisecrack. Cavaney suggested that Rockefeller—who had never liked Cheney—had whispered to Ford as they trooped along the red carpet, "I'm glad you finally had the good sense to get rid of Cheney." We cracked up, laughing with tears in our eyes.

At the bottom of the ramp the Fords said goodbye to the Rockefellers. Happy gave Betty a bouquet of red roses. Ford and Betty climbed the steps, turned, waved, and stepped inside the plane. Carter's people had declined to let Ford use *Air Force One*. They provided, instead, the primary backup jet.

I watched the beautiful silver, blue and white plane taxi out, take off and head for California. Many people in the crowd were weeping. I was trying not to cry as I pushed through the mob, looking for my wife. When I found her, I buried my face in her rough wool hat and bawled.

The Fords, a good man and a good woman, were gone from public life, at least for a while. And my great adventure as an outsider on the inside of the White House was over.

I got a job offer right away.

The president of Rogers & Cowan, Inc., a Hollywood public-relations firm, wrote offering me $25,000 to become international press officer for the big movie *Superman*.

"You would act as the official 'Superman' spokesman. Press releases . . . would be sent out under your name. . . . We would also like you to talk about the film in major broadcast and print interviews."

After being press secretary to the president of the United States, what's left?

Press secretary to Superman!

CHAPTER TWENTY-FOUR

Gossip and Trivia

During the Ford years a great deal of press coverage at the White House concentrated on gossipy and trivial items about the president, his family and the staff. Therefore, it seems only right for me to offer some gossip and trivia that didn't get reported at the time:

Ford's suit was stained by cow manure during a visit to a dairy farm in Wisconsin.

"A cow just shit on the president," one member of the president's entourage whispered.

"Why not?" a Secret Service agent quipped. "Everybody else does."

After Ford returned to Washington from a ski vacation in Vail, a conservative columnist phoned the White House and threatened to charge David Kennerly with violating the Mann Act for taking a girl friend on the presidential trip "for immoral purposes." Kennerly paid the air force for the girl's fare on the presidential jet and the columnist was talked out of pressing the case.

Ford was scheduled to get his swine flu inoculation with full press and TV coverage just a few hours before an important news conference. I suggested to Dr. Lukash that he inject the president with plain water to avoid even the 2-percent chance that Ford would have a bad reaction to the flu shot and be below par for the news conference.

Lukash refused and gave Ford a real inoculation. There was no reaction.

The White House phone operators usually switched crank calls to the press office, where my staff devised ingenious strategies to get rid of them. Larry Speakes and Janice Barbieri of the press office once informed a persistent crank caller that he had inadvertently reached Buckingham Palace and was talking to Queen Elizabeth and Prince Philip. The caller hung up and sent a telegram to the queen and prince, care of the White House press office, reading, "Let Them Eat Cake."

There was a serious security breach during a Ford visit to France in November 1975. When Ford disembarked from *Air Force One* at Orly Field in Paris and boarded his motorcade, the "Football"— the leather briefcase containing the codes necessary to order a nuclear strike—was accidentally left behind on the plane.

When the president's military aide, who was supposed to keep the briefcase close to Ford at all times, discovered it was missing, he radioed the plane and had the "Football" rushed to him in another car. But for about an hour Ford would have been unable to send the coded signal for atomic retaliation if the Russians had chosen that time for an attack.

Ford's army aide, Major Robert Barrett, normally carried the large "Football" briefcase containing the nuclear codes in one hand and a small leather case containing Ford's pipes and tobacco in the other hand.

Tired of explaining to questioners what was in the cases, Barrett developed a gag reply: The large case was for starting large nuclear wars and the small case was for starting small conventional wars.

Ford's code name was PASSKEY. Mrs. Ford's was PINAFORE, Susan's PANDA.

Some White House code names seemed to have been selected as descriptions of the person's characteristics. Ford's son Michael, then a seminary student, was PROFESSOR. Jack Ford, who liked the outdoor life, was PACKMAN.

Kissinger was WOODCUTTER, perhaps in recognition of his ability to cut through the thicket of foreign-policy problems. Irrepressible Kennerly was HOT SHOT. Eric Rosenberger, a press office aide whose job was to herd reporters and cameramen from event to event, was COWPUNCHER. My deputy, John Carlson, a physical-fitness nut, was WEIGHT LIFTER.

Some code names had no special meaning. Rockefeller was SAND STORM, Earl Butz was FAN JET and I was SUNBURN. Since a sunburn is a red, angry-looking condition that causes pain and irritation, my code name obviously was not descriptive.

Israel's Ambassador Simchat Dinitz was once flown on an unmarked U.S. Air Force plane to Caneel Bay in the Virgin Islands for a secret meeting with Kissinger.

When it was time to return Dinitz to Washington, the only jet fuel the pilot could find was 250 gallons stored by Pan Am at an Esso depot for emergencies. The pilot had to charge it to his personal gas-station credit card to avoid revealing his mission.

One night after an NBC-TV interview, Ford invited John Chancellor to stay for a drink. John stayed and stayed and stayed and stayed.

The president somehow managed to smile politely as Chancellor rambled through one story after another, including one about how he learned to speak Serbo-Croatian from listening to cassette tapes while doing his morning exercises.

Long past midnight, Chancellor decided it was time to go.

Members of the White House inner circle sometimes, literally, saw the emperor had no clothes. Cheney and I once briefed Ford for a news conference while he showered and dressed.

A Secret Service agent who, shortly before the resignation, accompanied Nixon on his trip to Egypt, during which the president deliberately appeared before large crowds which had not been checked for assassins, was quoted in Woodward and Bernstein's *The Final Days* as saying, "I can't protect a man who wants to kill himself."

That agent confided to friends in the Ford White House that

Nixon told him the Egyptian trip would have been even more successful "if somebody had taken a shot at me."

The agent quoted Nixon as saying the visit had polished his image as a foreign-policy expert, world leader and peacemaker.

"The trip would have had the same effect if I'd come home in a pine box," Nixon mused to the Secret Service man.

Ben Bradlee, editor of the *Washington Post*, had his graphics department produce a poster showing a picture of Ford and the caption, "I got my job through the *Post*," an obvious reference to the Woodward and Bernstein role in forcing Nixon's resignation.

Bradlee asked me to have Ford autograph the poster, but I kept it in my office for nearly a year, uncertain what the president's reaction would be. Just before Ford left office, I finally showed him the poster and suggested he sign it with a sarcastic inscription. He signed it with a gracious inscription.

The American defense attaché's office in Israel (presumably a CIA cover) alertly noticed some unexplained troop and plane movements in July 1976 and tipped off Washington more than twenty-four hours in advance that the Israelis probably would try to rescue the airliner hostages at Entebbe.

A meeting between the president and the Japanese ambassador was inadvertently scheduled for December 7, 1976, at noon, thirty-five years to the minute after the Japanese attacked Pearl Harbor. Brent Scowcroft of the NSC noticed the unfortunate timing and rescheduled the meeting for another day.

Some Well-Deserved Awards

—Most outrageous suggestion made to the president in an interview: "I am wondering if you don't owe it to yourself . . . to take in an X-rated movie to find out what the country is talking about." Bill Walker, WSOC-TV, Charlotte, North Carolina.

—Most outrageous question asked the president in an interview: "Do you ever say to yourself after a real hectic day and you are tired, 'I really need a drink . . . a couple of good belts,' say, before going to bed?" Jerry Dunphy, KABC-TV, Los Angeles.

—Most tasteless question at a White House briefing (when Interior Secretary Stanley Hathaway was in Bethesda Naval Hospital being treated for exhaustion and mild depression caused by grueling confirmation hearings): "Would you say you are behind him one thousand percent?" Tom Brokaw, NBC.

—Most inaccurate press story printed despite strong White House denials (tie): to the *Boston Globe* for its report that Leonid Brezhnev was on his way to Boston for treatment for cancer, and to John Scali of ABC for his report that Spain's Francisco Franco was dead, weeks before he actually expired.

—Worst misuse of a question at a presidential news conference to advocate a personal point of view: "Can I ask you, Mr. President, why . . . you lend the prestige of your high office to discrimination by golfing at Burning Tree Country Club, which excludes women?" Frances Lewine, Associated Press.

—Best preemptive leak: To Jack Ford, for deliberately revealing in an interview with the *Portland Oregonian* that he had smoked marijuana, thus blunting an impending Jack Anderson exposé of his pot use.

—Best put-down of a press secretary by a hot-tempered Italian woman journalist: To Oriana Fallaci, who, after being notified that her request for an interview with Ford had been rejected, wrote, "You seem to forget that I am Oriana Fallaci and that you are only a Mr. Nessen."

Some Other, Nonjournalism Awards

—Grand Prize for calling a spade a spade: To Gerald R. Ford for referring to Alexander Solzhenitsyn in a private meeting as "a goddamn horse's ass." Ford complained that the dissident Russian writer wanted to visit the White House primarily to publicize his books and drum up lecture dates.

—Grand Prize for best assessment of Soviet economic officials: To George Meany for saying during a Cabinet Room discussion with Ford, "They may be Commie sons of bitches but they are goddamn good capitalists."

—My favorite political maxim: "Every day is filled with numerous opportunities for serious, if not fatal, error. Enjoy it." Don Rumsfeld.

—Government staff title of which I was most envious: Naraichi Fuyiyama, spokesman for Emperor Hirohito, the "Imperial Press Secretary."

Some of the expressions most commonly used by Ford and his aides were metaphors of violence, particularly the violence of the football field. Here is a short glossary of phrases often heard in the Ford White House:

—"Welcome to the NFL." This was said to a fellow staff member, in an ironic tone, whenever he complained about a critical press story, a difficult assignment, etc. It was to remind him that at the White House he was playing in the big leagues and should expect rough treatment.

—"Blindsided." Used to describe a situation in which the president or an aide was caught by surprise by an unexpected development, the sudden need for an immediate decision, an unanticipated press question, etc.

—"Broke your pick." This meant a staff member had tried, unsuccessfully, to talk the president into or out of a course of action.

—"To throw yourself under the wheels." For an aide to use every bit of influence and persuasion he had to try to stop the president from doing something he intended to do.

—"He doesn't know his ass from page eight." This odd phrase was used only by Gerald Ford. Its exact meaning was unknown, but it was thought to signify the president's attitude toward those who broke their picks or threw themselves under the wheels.

Fame is fleeting.

Any White House aide who doesn't believe that ought to count the social invitations he received in a week *after* leaving the White House and compare them to the number in a week *before* leaving the White House.

But some aspects of fame also persist.

Nearly a year after Ford left the White House, I still received letters addressed to me as "White House Press Secretary," asking for information about President Carter.

And I received a letter from a doctoral candidate at Columbia University asking my help in obtaining information about the 1973

Middle East War, since I had served "in the key position of President Nixon's press secretary."

Once a press secretary always a press secretary, I guess.

CHAPTER TWENTY-FIVE

Q and A

Q.: If you're finished with your announcements, we'd like to ask a few questions.

NESSEN: Fire away.

Q.: In this book you seem to display the same pomposity, pettiness, vindictiveness and ill temper that you had in the White House.

NESSEN: Is that a question?

Q.: Don't you?

NESSEN: I thought when I left the White House I didn't have to answer any more questions.

Q.: Come on, Ron!

Q.: Seriously, do you think the criticism of your performance as press secretary was inaccurate?

NESSEN: Of course not. Look, there is nothing like the constant pressure and scrutiny of the White House to expose the limitations of the people who serve there. And that includes presidents. A person just can't hide his true character, from the world or from himself, in that fishbowl.

Q.: So what did you discover was your true character?

NESSEN: Okay. I found that I had a short temper, which grew even shorter when I was tired or had a few drinks. I learned that I wasn't very tolerant of criticism—of myself or the president. I was often vindictive toward the critics. I suppose on occasion I gave the impression of being pompous.

Q.: That's the most accurate thing I've ever heard you say.

Q.: Be quiet and let him finish. Anything else?

NESSEN: I wasn't a very good administrator. I let myself get bogged down in minutiae and paper work instead of spending my time dealing with the broader issues of the president's communications with the press and public. And I sometimes gave the president bad advice, not adequately thought out.

Q.: What about your feuds with other members of the staff?

NESSEN: Well, I know I had the reputation of being a constant intriguer against my colleagues on the staff. But actually I wasn't very good at that game. I was inexperienced at it and I usually acted out of emotion instead of calculation.

Q.: I want to ask you a personal question.

NESSEN: Go ahead.

Q.: You wrote in your book about, well, about the difficulties you and your wife had when you were press secretary. Did the White House job ruin your marriage?

NESSEN: No, I wouldn't say that. My wife and I had problems before I went to the White House. But the lack of time together during the White House years aggravated the problems. I was working sixteen, eighteen, twenty hours a day, seven days a week. The White House is heaven for a workaholic, but hell on a marriage. We simply did not see each other enough to keep up any sustained effort to resolve our difficulties. When we did see each other, she was overburdened with the tensions of carrying my share of the household responsibilities and I was preoccupied with the pressures of the White House.

Q.: Didn't Ford say one time he wanted his staff to work shorter hours so they could lead more normal lives and keep their family relationships healthy?

NESSEN: Every president says that. But it never happens. There's too much work.

Q.: I want to get back to that negative report card you gave yourself at—

NESSEN: Yes, I almost forgot. I want to add something to that. Sure, I have regrets about my flawed performance as press secretary. But I'm also proud of the role I played in helping Ford improve the relationship between the White House and the press after Nixon. I think that was one of Ford's outstanding accomplishments.

Q.: How did he improve the relationship?

NESSEN: A lot of ways. By being very accessible, for one thing. He held thirty-nine news conferences, granted two hundred interviews and had one hundred and thirty-three other contacts with the press in twenty-nine months, about one meeting with newsmen every two and a half days—not a bad record. He let John Hersey sit in the Oval Office all day every day for a week to gather material for a *New York Times* magazine article and a book, and he gave photographers backstairs access for weeks and months at a time.

Ford also introduced a number of improvements in White House press coverage, including follow-up questions at news conferences, which reporters had been demanding for years, and interviews and news conferences with local reporters and anchormen, who usually didn't get a chance to question a president. I don't think I ever suggested an innovation in press relations when Ford didn't say, "Let's try it." And he restored the custom of inviting journalists to White House social events as guests, which symbolized his attitude that reporters were friends, not enemies.

Q.: If Ford had such a great relationship with reporters, how come you had such a lousy relationship?

NESSEN: That just showed I was successfully fulfilling one of my functions as press secretary.

Q.: Don't be funny.

NESSEN: I'm not. That's true. In fact, it's an unspoken duty of all senior White House aides to act as lightning rods, to soak up criticism that might otherwise be directed at the president. White House staff members are supposed to take the blame for what goes wrong and make sure the president gets credit for what goes right.

Q.: In the Ford White House it was sometimes just the opposite.

NESSEN: You can say that again.

Q.: Do you remember an article Bill Moyers wrote in *Newsweek* shortly after you became press secretary, entitled "Poor Ron Nessen," in which he predicted the time would come when you would have to choose between your duty to the press and your duty to the president?

NESSEN: Yes, I remember it.

Q.: Did that time ever come, when you had to choose?

NESSEN: Well, most of the time there was no conflict. But once in a while I did have to choose.

Q.: What was your choice?

NESSEN: I never had an instant's doubt that my loyalty belonged to the man I worked for, the president of the United States.

Q.: Well, at least you're being honest.

Q.: Let's talk about honesty. Did you ever lie for Ford?

NESSEN: Not, not really.

Q.: What does that mean, "not really"?

NESSEN: Occasionally I told a little white fib, mostly out of misguided oversensitivity.

Q.: Like what?

NESSEN: I told you in the book I sometimes stalled or played down information about the phone calls between Nixon and Ford.

Q.: Any other "white fibs"?

NESSEN: Mostly minor matters. Like one time when Ford went to Florida to play golf in the Jackie Gleason Inverrary Tournament I tried to make it sound like he took the opportunity to play while he was in Florida to attend a community leaders conference. Actually, the conference was arranged as an excuse for him to play in the tournament.

Q.: So you violated your promise never to lie and never to mislead us.

NESSEN: Without ever losing sight of my responsibilities to the press and the public, I was guilty of some relatively minor deviations from that promise.

Q.: Confession is good for the soul.

NESSEN: Thanks.

Q.: What about your relationship with Kissinger? Didn't he keep you in the dark about a lot of foreign-policy developments?

NESSEN: Oh, I talked enough about Henry in the book. Besides, my problem was more with the system for handling foreign-policy and national-security information than it was with Kissinger personally. The system was based on a myth, that foreign policy must be handled differently than domestic policy, with more secrecy, less explanation to the American people and less consultation within the White House.

Q.: Why do you call that a myth?

NESSEN: There are some matters that must legitimately be kept secret in order not to destroy a worthwhile foreign-policy goal. But far fewer matters fall into that category than officials like to pretend. Even the White House staff organizations for handling domestic and foreign-policy information were different. I had people on my staff whose responsibility it was to track down information on domestic issues and the economy in order to brief me, prepare presidential announcements and answer reporters' questions. Those staff members had the needs of the press as their primary concern. But the person assigned to do the same job in the area of foreign policy worked for the National Security Council, not the press office, and had as a primary concern the wishes of Kissinger.

Q.: So, Kissinger didn't let you know much about what was going on in foreign policy, right?

NESSEN: I wasn't totally dependent on Kissinger for my information. I talked to the president every day, of course, and I developed my own private sources of information in the pentagon, the CIA and even inside Kissinger's State Department.

Q.: It sounds like you really had to dig hard to get information on foreign policy.

NESSEN: I did. The difficulty I had in obtaining information about foreign relations was one of my greatest frustrations in the White House. I believe it reflected the wishes of Kissinger, who wanted to control the information himself in a way he felt best served his foreign-policy objectives. But sometimes that tight hold on foreign-policy information backfired and resulted in a lack of public understanding and public support. That was the case with the Helsinki agreement on East-West relations in Europe and the Panama Canal treaty.

Q.: In other words—

NESSEN: Wait a minute. Let me make one other point. The fact that information about foreign policy and domestic issues was handled differently grew out of the fact that decisions in the two areas were handled differently. At least until the big cabinet shake-up, Ford consulted far fewer advisers on foreign-policy and national-security decisions, mostly Kissinger and the NSC, even though advice from staff members who specialized in dealing with Congress, special-interest groups, politics, the domestic economy and the press would have been beneficial.

Q.: How could you function as press secretary if Kissinger and the NSC didn't trust you?

NESSEN: Look, the press secretary is always the man caught in the middle. I was not fully trusted by either the press or the White House staff. The press considered me to be the flack for the president, selling the good news and covering up the bad news. At the same time, some members of the staff suspected me of telling too much to my former colleagues in the press. And, of course, the staff blamed me for not being able to stop bad stories about the president. Do you realize that the White House press secretary is the only government official who stands up in public every day, defending the administration on any and every issue and answering its critics? No wonder the press secretary steadily burns up his goodwill. Most press secretaries, sooner or later, get crushed under those pressures.

Q.: What was the hardest part of the job, the daily briefings?

NESSEN: They were certainly the most painful part. It wasn't only the rancor and the pettiness that bothered me. I really don't think the White House briefing is the best way to provide accurate information to the public. I spent about five hours a day gathering information in anticipation of questions, but even the most conscientious press secretary can't know everything about everything. Besides, most White House correspondents are generalists. They do not have enough expertise to go into complex issues in depth.

As a result, we ended up discussing subjects at my briefings about which neither I nor the reporters knew very much. The press coverage had to suffer. The news stories that came out of such uninformed exchanges usually just skimmed the surface or concentrated on some trivial or sensational aspect. In my own defense, I will say that I was usually better prepared at my briefings than the reporters. I almost always had more information than I was asked about. Ford found the same thing with his news conferences.

Q.: So what's the solution?

NESSEN: The ritual aspects of the daily White House briefings need to be deflated. Reporters should stop thinking of the briefings as the one place to get information about everything going on in the government. White House reporters ought to get out of the White House more. They should talk to the people in the agencies and departments who are real experts on the issues in the news. They would get a lot more information with a lot less hassle.

Q.: Didn't you recommend to Jody Powell that he cancel the daily briefings?

NESSEN: I did, but I've changed my mind. Despite the shortcomings and the acrimonious atmosphere, I now believe it's important to continue the briefings on a daily basis. The daily briefing is a commitment by the White House to face questions from the press, representing the public, even on those days when officials would rather duck and hide.

Q.: You've been very critical of the press, in your book and elsewhere.

NESSEN: I try not to be. Richard Nixon and Spiro Agnew gave press criticism a bad name.

Q.: Is that one of your famous one-liners?

NESSEN: Let's go on.

Q.: Seriously—

NESSEN: Seriously, my biggest criticism of the press—that television presents complex issues in an oversimplified and trivial way, or doesn't present them at all—predates my time in the White House. That complaint grew out of my experience as an NBC correspondent. After all, there is no greater critic of TV's simplistic approach than the television correspondent whose news editor has just told him he has seventeen seconds to sum up the president's energy program. Watching television coverage from a different perspective, inside the White House, merely reinforced that complaint.

Q.: Come on, Ron, you know you've been a lot harsher than that in your criticism of the press coverage of Ford.

NESSEN: I have. I honestly believe the Ford administration was constantly scrutinized by the press through a lens of suspicion, which was a poisonous legacy of Nixon. One reporter wrote that Ford had the misfortune to be president during an era when the press was pervaded by "cynical chic." Since Jimmy Carter was campaigning against corruption and politics-as-usual, the post-Watergate suspicion and cynicism in the press coverage of the Ford White House contributed to Carter's appealing image as a spotless outsider who would bring to Washington a higher standard of honest conduct.

Q.: So you think the press helped Carter?

NESSEN: Not deliberately, no. In fact, Carter was very critical of the press reporting of *his* campaign. But when the coverage concentrated on Ford's stumbles, I wondered what would have been the reaction if a network news story showing Ford making a slip of the tongue or banging his head on the helicopter door had been run as a paid commercial by the Carter campaign. The press would have denounced it as a dirty trick!

Q.: What else could the networks show? The candidates weren't talking about any issues.

NESSEN: Baloney! Both Ford and Carter spent enormous amounts of time, effort, manpower and money developing and explaining their policies, their positions on the issues. No, the problem was that the networks thought things like Earl Butz jokes, juicy quotes from PLAYBOY, mistakes, slips of the tongue, falls, Amy Carter's lemonade stand, Billy Carter's beer drinking, Susan Ford's "affairs," et cetera, et cetera, made more interesting TV stories than where Ford and Carter stood on the issues.

Q.: You really sound bitter. How can you go back to journalism with that attitude?

NESSEN: Oh, I could go back to journalism and be a better reporter for my experience in the White House.

Q.: In what way?

NESSEN: I would try to reflect the complexities of what I now know are enormously complex issues. I would avoid depicting situations in simplistic, black and white terms. And I would resist a current trend among journalists, especially among young journalists, to skip over the basic function of telling readers and viewers what happened in order to get into more exciting speculation about backstage maneuvering, who did what to whom and what may happen in the future. That is an especially strong trend among TV correspondents, who are under pressure to draw wide, general conclusions from the smallest development, to tell what it all means in twelve or fifteen seconds on camera.

Q.: Do you really think you can go back to journalism?

NESSEN: I don't know. Some of my friends think I could never be a hard-hitting reporter again because the White House experience blunted my journalistic "killer instinct." Those friends say that having been subjected to press criticism myself, I would be sympathetic toward government officials in the future and would pull my punches.

Q.: You're out of the White House now. You don't have to be loyal anymore. How about an honest appraisal of Jerry Ford as president?

NESSEN: I think he was the right man at the right place at the right time.

Q.: What does that mean?

NESSEN: I mean he had the qualities America needed in its president after Vietnam, the upheavals of the Sixties and the Nixon scandals. The American people yearned for a period of quiet after the trauma, and Ford brought it. You might say he was soothing. His own relaxed personality transmitted a sense of tranquillity. The world seemed normal again. He displayed common sense and a common touch. And he restored to the White House an atmosphere of trust, a high standard of moral conduct.

Q.: What about the pardon of Nixon? That set no moral standard.

NESSEN: Whether you agree with it or not, the pardon accomplished what Ford set out to do: It removed a source of continuing divisiveness and preoccupation from American life. Incidentally, during my twenty-eight months in the White House I never heard anything that led me to doubt Ford's public explanation of the pardon. By my definition, the pardon was an example of courageous political leadership because Ford damaged his personal and political reputation in order to carry out an act he considered in the nation's best interest.

Q.: Bullshit.

Q.: Hey, cool it.

Q.: I'll grant you that Ford restored tranquillity and integrity to the White House. But those qualities relate to mood. What about specific policy accomplishments?

NESSEN: Okay. He presided over the end of the Vietnam war in a way that began to heal the divisions the war had caused in American society. And he insisted, against initial congressional and public opposition, on fulfilling a humanitarian obligation to the refugees. With the *Mayaguez* rescue he demonstrated to potential adversaries that the United States would stand up for its rights in Asia despite the ill-fated Indochina adventure.

Q.: Well, that really—

NESSEN: Wait a minute. Let me finish. Ford cut the inflation rate by more than half. He guided the nation out of the deepest recession since the Thirties with policies that stimulated the economy to recover in a sound, steady way.

Q.: If he was so—

NESSEN: There's more. Ford supervised the public disclosure of excesses by the CIA, FBI and other intelligence and investigative agencies. Then, he proposed reforms to prevent future abuses without wrecking essential government functions. Ford also recruited people of extraordinarily high caliber for top posts in government.

Q.: Like who?

NESSEN: John Paul Stevens for the Supreme Court; Nelson Rockefeller for vice president; Edward Levi, Carla Hills and William Coleman for the cabinet; and so forth. Finally, Ford alerted the nation to two problems on which it is going to have to make hard choices in the near future, namely the energy crisis and the funding of the social security system.

Q.: That's your side of it. But Ford was no innovator.

NESSEN: I'll grant that.

Q.: He didn't stir the nation with visions of a driving dream.

NESSEN: No, he didn't. That wasn't his style.

Q.: He didn't have a questing or creative intellect.

NESSEN: He had a practical intellect and a large fund of knowledge.

Q.: If he was as great as you say, why wasn't he elected in nineteen seventy-six?

NESSEN: I suppose I'm a fatalist. Maybe, having fullfilled the role history assigned him by bringing to the White House the exact characteristics America needed between August 9, 1974, and January 20, 1977, it was his historic role to then move off the stage.

Q.: So how do you think history will remember Ford?

NESSEN: I'd settle for Jimmy Carter's description.

Q.: What?

Q.: What are you talking about?

NESSEN: Jimmy Carter began his inaugural speech by saying, "For myself and for our nation, I want to thank my predecessor for all he has done to heal our land."

Q.: And you think that should be the benediction for the Ford administration?

NESSEN: Amen.

Q.: Thank you.

Index

Abzug, Bella, 33
Agnew, Spiro T., *xi, xii–xiv*, 99, 354,
  resignation, *xiii*, 3
Agronsky, Martin, 171
Akasaka Palace, 43
Alabama, 209
Allende, Salvador, 70
All the President's Men, 211, 224
American Broadcasting Company
  (ABC), 167
Anderson, Gwen, 149
Anderson, Jack, 62, 63, 284, 286, 345
Anderson, Patrick, 5–6
Angelo, Bonnie, 11
Arkansas, 219
Armstrong, Anne, 238, 327
Ash, Roy, 77
Associated Press (AP), 255, 256, 282,
  298

Bailey, Doug, 214, 261–63, 327–28
Bailey, Pearl, 313
Baker, James, 247, 248, 266, 270, 283,
  309
Baker, Howard, 238–39
Barbieri, Janice, 342
Barone, Joan, 219–20
Baroody, William, Jr., 149
Barrett, Robert, 27, 48, 217, 342
Barrett, Rona, 176
Barlett, Charles, 153
Bass, Richard, 79
Beale, Betty, 168
Beame, Abraham, 121, 123
Belin, David, 214
Berger, Marilyn, 172
Bernstein, Carl, 32, 211, 288, 289, 290,
  343, 344
Biden, Joseph, 106
Biebel, Fred, Jr., 189
Birmingham News, 232

Blake, Robert, 166
Blaser, Doug, 305
Blind Ambition, 293
Blumenthal, Michael, 128*n*
Boehm, Edward Marshall, 12
Bond, Christopher, 238
Bono, Sonny, 235, 280
Boone, Pat, 280, 282
Boston Globe, 51, 345
Bowen, David, 25
Braden, Tom, 169
Bradlee, Ben, 344
Breach of Faith, 32
Brezhnev, Leonid, 45–50, 51, 345
Brock, William, 238
Broder, David, 11, 161, 169, 320
Brokaw, Tom, 164–65, 221, 295, 345
Brooke, Edward, 217, 238, 281
Brown, George, 41–43
Brown, Jerry, 179–80
Buchen, Philip, 10, 149, 201, 202, 287,
  289
Buchwald, Art, 168
Buendorf, Larry, 180
Burch, Dean, 37
Burger, Warren, 7
Burns, Arthur, 79, 87, 90
Bush, George, 69, 120, 155, 160, 201,
  327
Business Week, 143, 144
Butz, Earl, 267, 279–84, 302, 343, 355
Byrd, Robert, 124

Carr, Vicki, 24
California, 219, 220
Callaway, Howard "Bo," 159, 195,
  205–6
Cambodia, 92–93
  Phnom Penh evacuation, U.S. aid to
    question, 103–4
  see also Mayaguez incident

Cannon, James, 123
Cannon, Lou, 169, 193
Carey, Hugh, 121
Carlson, John, 270, 274, 275, 343
Carruthers, William, 241, 242, 263, 264, 307
Carson, Johnny, 163, 169, 300
Carter, Amy, 355
Carter, Billy, 355
Carter, Jimmy, *xii*, 6, 14, 178, 211, 215, 232, 234, 239, 243, 244, 245, 246, 247, 248, 250, 253, 254, 256, 257, 258, 273, 279, 281, 286–87, 288, 291, 297–98, 306, 320, 326, 327, 328, 329, 334, 339, 346, 354–55, 357
    character and integrity of, Ford campaign and, 297–98
    Clennon King affair and, 309–10
    debates with Ford, 240–41, 258–60, 261–78
    election returns, his victory, 313–18 *passim*
    Ford's dislike of, 303–4
    Hafif ad attacking, 308–9
    inauguration day, 335, 336–37
    kickoff campaign speech, 251*n*
    Marine Engineers contribution to campaign of, 292–93
    Playboy interview, 299–302
    post-election visit with Ford, 322–24
    tax plan, 255–56
Carter, Rosalynn, 308, 309, 335, 337
    post-election visit to White House, 322, 323
Case, Clifford, 105
Casselman, William, 18
Castro, Fidel, 58, 59–60, 70
Cavanaugh, James, 249
Cavaney, Red, 210, 337, 339
Central Intelligence Agency (CIA), 156
    Bush becomes chief of, 69
    illegal activities question, 54–66
        assassination plots, 57–60, 63, 69–71
        Church Committee report on, 69–71
        classified documents, handling procedures question, 61–62
        congressional investigations of, 61
        domestic spying issue, 54–57, 63, 64–66
        Ford's views on, 60–61
        Glomar Explorer incident, 62–63
        Pike Committee report on, 71–72
        Rockefeller Commission report on, 63–65
    Soviet defense spending gaffe, 72–73
Chancellor, John, 145–46, 147, 343

Chase, Chevy, 163, 172, 173, 174–75, 176–77
Cheney, Richard B., *xii*, 58, 78, 82, 84, 110, 128, 140, 141, 149, 150*n*, 153, 154, 167–69, 192, 200, 202, 203, 205, 208, 209, 211, 212, 224, 226, 229–30, 232, 234, 236, 237, 244, 248, 249, 252, 254, 270, 286, 292, 298, 311, 314, 315, 316, 317, 319, 339, 343
    Butz incident and, 280, 281–82, 283
    cabinet shakeup and, 155, 156, 157, 158, 161
    final campaign swing and, 303
    Ford's Eastern Europe gaffe and, 271, 272, 275, 276
    special prosecutor Ford inquiry and, 289, 290
Cheshire, Maxine, 18
Chicago Sun-Times, 176
Chile, 70–71
China, 137–40
Chowchilla, Calif., 225–26
Church, Frank, 61, 62, 63, 69–71, 105
Churchill, Winston, *xv*
Clawson, Kenneth, 31
Cleveland Plain Dealer, 305
Colby, William, 54, 55, 56, 58, 62–63, 69, 155, 156, 158, 159
Coleman, William, 281, 357
Columbia Broadcasting System (CBS), 72, 80, 193
Compton, Ann, 171
Connally, John, 197, 209, 223–24, 238, 248, 253, 283, 314
Conrad, Paul, 300
Cook, Richard, 294, 295, 297
Cox, Archibald, 238
Cronkite, Walter, 28, 57, 76, 193, 288

Dailey, Peter, 213, 214
Dallas-Times Herald, 248
Daniel, Clifton, 58
Davis, Sid, 45
Deakin, James, 104
Dean, John, 279–80ff., 292, 293–98, 302
Dean, John Gunther, 103
Deardourff, John, 214
DeFrank, Thomas, 97–98, 156, 162, 192, 193, 234
De Gaulle, Charles, 59
Den Uyl, Prime Minister, 127
Denver Post, 167
Dewey, Thomas E., 23
Diem, Ngo Dinh, 60, 70
Dinitz, Simchat, 343
Dobrynin, Anatoly, 40, 48
Dole, Robert, 236, 238, 239, 240, 243, 244, 246, 248, 258, 313, 314, 327

Dole, Robert (*con't.*)
  attacks Carter tax plan, 255–56
  debate with Mondale, 277–78
  effectiveness of in campaign, 254–55
Domenici, Pete, 238
Domina, Lee, 337
Dore, Bob, 146
Drew, Elizabeth, 264
Dunphy, Jerry, 344–45
Dunsmore, Barry, 171
Duval, Michael, 62, 66, 67, 68, 72, 143,
  266, 270
Duvalier, François "Papa Doc," 59, 71

Eastern Europe, 268–77
Ehrlichman, John, 57
Eisenhower, Dwight D., 71
Elfin, Mel, 193
Elliott, Osborn, 193
Ellsworth Air Force Base, 249
Entebbe raid, 344
Enterprise (carrier), 171*n*
Equal Rights Amendment (ERA), 28
Ervin, Sam, 238
Evans, Rowland, Jr., 150, 151, 154
Exner, Judith Campbell, 59

"Face the Nation," 219–20
Fall, Bernard, 95
Fallaci, Oriana, 345
"Family Jewels, The," 56, 58
Federal Bureau of Investigation (FBI),
  287
Federal Election Commission, 246
Final Days, The, 211, 343
Fischer, Dean, 292, 293–98
Florida, 203–5
Ford, Betty, *xi, xii,* 7, 37, 79, 175, 182,
  192, 194, 209, 211, 216, 222, 232,
  235, 237, 251, 277, 283, 310, 311,
  313, 316, 342
  Carters' post-election visit to White
    House and, 323
  family life, relationship with Ford,
    22–26, 28
  health problems, 19–23
  informed of assassination attempt on
    Ford, 186–87
  last day in Washington, 335, 337, 339
  makes Ford's concession statement,
    318–19
  personality traits, 26–28
  political life, her attitude toward,
    3–4
Ford, Dorothy, 311
Ford, Gayle, 232, 318
Ford, Gerald R., *xi,* 11
  assassination attempts on, 179–90
    effect of on the press, 189–90

security procedures prompted by,
    188–89
  author's assessment of as president,
    355–57
  bumbler, his image as, 163, 164–78,
    190–91
  cabinet and staff changeover, 155–61
  car accident in Hartford, 189
  Carter's post-election visit to White
    House and, 322–24
  China trip, 137–40
  dog "accident" anecdote, *xiv*
  economic programs, 74–78, 79, 86–90
  energy program, 79, 86, 89
  as family man, 23–24
  Far East trip, 40–41
    in Japan, 43–45
    in Korea, 45
    SALT II agreement and, 46–52
    in Vladivostok, 45–50
  fireside chat (Jan. 1975), 80–84
  hospital meeting with Nixon, 34–36
  intelligence system operations, his
    views on and plan for, 60–61,
    68–69
  Kennedy assassination, his views on,
    59–60
  last day in office, 329–30
    Carter's inauguration and, 335–37
    departure from Washinton, 337–39
    farewell meeting with staff, 330–31
    leaves Oval Office, 333, 334
    press briefing concerning, 332–33
  Mayaguez incident and, 117–31
  Middle East invasion threat issue,
    144–47
  National Convention and, 225–45
    acceptance speech, 240–43
    foreign policy plank issue, 229–31,
      233–34
    meeting with Reagan, 235–36
    roll call, his nomination, 234–35
    Rule 16-C issue, 228, 231–34
    vice presidential nominee,
      selection of, 237–40
  as negotiator, Kissinger on, 48
  Nessen appointment and, 12–14
  Nixon's effect on his presidency,
    29–36 *passim*
  Nixon pardon, 9–10, 30, 33–34, 158,
    198, 356
  presidency, his accession to, 7–8
  Press Office/Kissinger conflicts and,
    132–33, 134, 135
  press relations, improvement of
    under, 349–50
  SALT II agreement and, 46–52
    passim
  staff infighting and, 148–49, 150, 151,

Ford, Gerald R. (*con't.*)
　152–53, 161–62
　state of the union speech (Jan. 1975),
　　77–78, 84–85
　vice presidency and, 3–5
　see also Ford, Betty; Presidential
　　campaign/elections (1976);
　　Vietnam War; *all related entries*
Ford, Gerald R., Sr., 311
Ford, Jack, 23, 155, 175, 187, 226, 316,
　342, 345
Ford, Michael, 20–21, 23, 232, 316, 342
Ford, Steve, 15–16, 23, 296
Ford, Susan, 23, 28, 187, 197, 216, 220,
　342, 355
Ford, Not a Lincoln, A, 164n
Ford Steering Committee, 247
Franco, Francisco, 345
Frankel, Max, 58, 268, 269
Franken, Al, 173
Frederick, Pauline, 267–68
Freidheim, Jerry, 11
Frey, Louis, 203–4
Friedersdorf, Max, 88–89, 149
Friedman, Milton, 108
Fromme, Lynette Alice, 180, 182
Future Farmers of America, Ford
　speech to, 75–76
Fuyiyama, Naraichi, 346

Gannon, James, 264
Garagiola, Joe, 307–8, 313
Gelb, Leslie, 259
Genesis (magazine), 226
George, Phyllis, 25
Georgia, 209
Gergen, David, 249, 315, 316
Gerrard, Connie, 226, 329
Giancana, Sam, 59
Giscard d'Estaing, Valery, 24, 216
Glomar Explorer (ship), 62–63
Goldwater, Barry, 37
Goldwin, Robert, 81, 82
Golson, Barry, 299, 300, 301–2
"Good Morning America," 293
Graham, Fred, 288
Graham, Katherine, 211
Graham, Martha, 22
Grand Rapids, Mich., 310–11
Grand Rapids Press, 8
Green, Edith, 307
Greene, Jerry, 29
Greener, William, 161, 253–54, 264,
　299
Greenspan, Alan, 76, 77, 78, 81, 82, 84,
　86, 96
Greider, William, 4–5
Griffin, Robert, 215, 237
Griswold, Erwin N., 56–57n

Gromyko, Andrei, 14
Growald, Richard, 43–44, 172

Habib, Philip, 43
Hafif, Herb, 308
Haig, Alexander, 7, 16–17, 29, 31, 33,
　74, 150
Haldeman, H. R., 16, 87, 150, 249
Hansen, Leroy, 49, 50
Harlow, Bryce, 237
Hartmann, Robert T., xi, 11, 12, 16, 20,
　31, 51–52, 86, 87, 107, 134, 135,
　148, 153, 179, 181, 182, 183, 186,
　187, 192, 193, 212, 240
　cabinet shakeup and, 161
　Sinatra affair and, 99, 100
　staff infighting and, 80–82, 84–85,
　　149–51
Hatfield, Mark, 238
Hathaway, Stanley, 345
Helsinki agreement, 268
Henry, Buck, 172
Hersey, John, 350
Hersh, Seymour, 54, 55, 58
Hills, Carla, 357
Hirohito, Emperor, 43, 44, 346
Hoffman, Nicholas von, 163
Holtzman, Elizabeth, 33
Hoover, Herbert, 265
Horrock, Nicholas, 66–67
Howe, James, 27
Howe, Nancy, 27–28
Huang Chen, 120
Hughes, Howard, 62
Hui, Park Bo, 45
Humphrey, Hubert, 22
Hunter, Marjorie, 11
Hushen, John, 13, 55

Idaho, 219
Illinois, 205–6
Indiana, 209
Internal Revenue Service (IRS), 26
"Issues and Answers," 219, 220

Jackson, Henry, 52, 106
Jagoda, Barry, 259, 266, 322
Janka, Les, 41, 91–92
Japan, 39, 40, 43–45, 139
Javits, Jacob, 105, 315
Jaworski, Leon, 288, 297
"Jerry and Joe Show, The," 307–8
Johnson, Lady Byrd, 19, 301
Johnson, Lyndon B., 19, 66, 93, 116,
　164, 199, 300–1
Jones, Jerry, 149
Jones, Phil, 172, 273, 324–25
Jordan, James J., 214
Juarez, Oscar, 203

Kansas City, Kans., *see* Republican National Convention
Kaye, Peter, 205
Keiser, Richard, 180, 182
Kelley, Clarence, 250
Kennedy, John F., 13, 59–60, 70, 116, 260, 261
Kennerly, David Hume, *xii*, 37, 47, 98–99, 108, 110, 113, 115, 116, 127, 181, 182, 183, 186, 208, 209, 210–11, 213, 214, 217, 233, 317, 338, 341, 343
Kentucky, 219
Kerr, Howard, 15
Kim, Hancho, 45
King, Clennon, 309–10
King, Jim, 264
Kissinger, Henry A., *xi*, 7, 24, 39, 40, 44, 45, 47, 61, 68, 92, 108, 127, 149, 165, 201, 206, 212, 221, 268, 269, 270, 342, 343, 351–52
  author's conflicts with, 132–47 *passim*
  cabinet shakeup and, 156, 157, 159, 160
  CIA illegal activities question and, 56, 65, 66
  Ford's China trip and, 137–40, 142–43
  limelight, his need to be in, 136–37
  Mayaguez incident and, 118, 122, 125–26, 129
  Middle East invasion threat issue, 143–45, 146, 147
  on Nixon as negotiator, 48
  presidential campaign of 1976 and, 208, 229, 230, 233
  Press Office leaks concerning, 132–36, 162
  Sinatra affair, and, 99–100
  truthfulness, his view on foreign policy and, 140–43
  Vietnam War and, 98, 101, 103, 105, 106, 109, 110, 111, 112–13
  Vladivostok agreement and, 49–50, 51
Klein, Herb, 197
Kohler, Saul, 306
Korea, 39, 40, 45
Kraft, Joseph, 277, 320
Kreisky, Chancellor, 166

Labor, U.S. Department of, 250
Laird, Melvin, 3, 11, 193, 237, 238
Laitin, Joseph, 121–22, 128
Lance, Bert, 287
Landon, Alf, 265
Laxalt, Paul, 248
League of Women Voters, 258, 259, 264
Lebanon, 221–22

Lerner, Richard, 210
Levi, Edward, 66, 67, 217–18, 226, 287, 289, 357
Lewine, Frances, 333, 345
Liberty (dog), 37
Lincoln, Abraham, 33
Lisagor, Peter, 171
Loeb, William, 196
Lukash, William M., *xii*, 19, 21, 22, 34–35, 182, 184, 185, 186, 306, 322, 341
Lumumba, Patrice, 59, 70
Lynn, James, 86, 256

McCarry, Charles, 60
McCarthy, Eugene, 199, 200, 259, 326
McClellan, John, 124
McClendon, Sarah, 176, 193
McCloskey, Robert, 11
McClure, Robert D., 308
McFarland, Robert C. "Bud," 121
McGovern, George, 199, 200, 241, 256
McLaughlin, John, 31
McLaughlin, William, 215
Maddox, Lester, 259
Manchester Union-Leader, 196
Mansfield, Mike, 123–24
Manson, Charles, 180
Marine Engineers Beneficial Association, 287, 292
Marsh, John O., Jr., *xi*, 15–16, 20, 21, 60, 62, 78, 110, 134, 149, 157, 158, 198, 237, 296
Martin, Graham, 109, 110, 111, 112–13
Mashek, John, 234
Mayaguez incident, 117–31, 196, 356
Mayfield, Freddie, 336
Maynard, Robert, 277
Ma Yu-Chen, 139
Mead, Robert, 186
Meany, George, 345
Mears, Walter, 255
"Meet the Press," 282
Meloy, Francis E., 221
Merchant, Jack, 184
Michaels, Lorne, 173
Michigan, 214–17
Michigan, University of, 251–52
Michigan Daily, 251
Michiko, Princess, 44–45
Milliken, William, 215
Mondale, Joan, 283
Mondale, Walter, 247, 258, 273, 327, 335, 336
  debate with Dole, 277–78
Monroe, Bill, 282
Moore, Sara Jane, 184–85
Morton, Rogers C. B., 156, 206, 209–10, 212, 227, 232, 247, 248, 309

Mt. Sunapee Area Ski Club, 197
Mount Weather, Va., 321–22
Moyers, Bill, 350
Muskie, Edmund, 199

National Broadcasting Company
    (NBC), *xiii, xiv*, 8, 11–12, 281,
    282, 295–96, 297
National Journal, 293
National Security Agency, 66, 67–68
National Security Council, 109, 352
Naughton, James, 142, 305–6
Nebraska, 209
Nelson, Jack, 259
Nessen, Cindy, 94–95, 97, 321
Nessen, Edward, 321
Nessen, Ron
    administrative duties, 15
    appointment of announced, 13–14
    events leading to his appointment,
        xiii–xv, 10–13
    last press briefing, 331–33
    self-interview, 348–57
    Vietnam War and, biographical,
        93–95, 97–98
Nevada, 219
New Hampshire, 196–201
New Jersey, 219, 220
Newman, Edwin, 264
New Republic, 145
Newsweek (magazine), 156, 157,
    190–91, 192–93, 209, 302
New York (magazine), 147
New York Daily News, 51
New York Post, 280, 289
New York Times, 24, 54–55ff., 66–67,
    79, 254, 283, 320
Nixon, Julie, 35
Nixon, Pat, 34, 35
Nixon, Richard M., *xi, xiii, xiv*, 12,
    16, 18, 26, 66, 75, 87, 116, 149,
    162, 194, 195, 196, 211, 247, 279,
    287, 296, 300, 326, 347, 351, 354
    advice to Ford on Carter debates,
        260
    China trip (1975), 197–98, 201
        his report on, author and, 201–3
    debates with Kennedy, 260, 261
    Egyptian trip, 343–44
    Ford pardon, 9–10, 30, 33–34, 198,
        356
    Ford vice presidency and, 3, 4–5
    hospital meeting with Ford, 34–36
    as negotiator, Kissinger on, 48
    private correspondence with Thieu,
        106–7
    relationship with Ford, the press and,
        29–30, 33, 36
    resignation, 7

Vladivostok agreement and, 50, 51,
    52
    see also Watergate
Nixon, Tricia, 35
Nofziger, Lyn, 154, 235–36, 248, 254–55
Norman, Geoffrey, 301
North Carolina, 206–7
Novak, Robert D., 150, 151, 154

Oakes, John B., 58
O'Connor, John J., 176
O'Donnell, Terry, 114, 217, 224, 305,
    317, 337, 339
O'Donoghue, Michael, 176
O'Rourke, Larry, 332
Ohio, 219, 220
Oliphant, Pat, 115
"Operation CHAOS," 64–65
"Operation Frequent Wind," 109–10
"Operation Shamrock," 67–68
Orben, Robert, 81
Oregon, 219
Osborne, John, 142–43
Oswald, Lee Harvey, 59

Palucci, Jeno, 257
Panama Canal, 206, 207–8
Park, Tongsun, 27, 45
Patman, Wright, 293, 294
Patterson, Thomas E., 308
Penny, Don, 213, 235, 240, 248, 249
Pentagon Papers, 66
Percy, Charles, 103, 238
Perle, Richard, 52
Perrotta, Fred, 313
Pettit, Tom, 207
Phnom Penh, *see* Cambodia
Pierpoint, Bob, 170
Pike, Otis, 61, 62, 71
Pitts, Milton, 259–60
Playboy (magazine), 177, 283, 299–302
Poland, 274, 275, 276
Pontius, Ron, 184, 186, 187
Portland Oregonian, 345
Powell, Jody, 264, 266, 277, 324–25, 334,
    353
Press, The, 305
President Ford Committee (PFC), 194,
    212–14
Presidential campaign/elections
    (1976), Ford and, 78, 354–55
    "Advocates Program," 253–54
    announces candidacy, 194–95
    Beirut evacuation and, 221–22
    busing issue and, 217–18
    Butz incident and, 279–84
    California primary, 219, 220
    campaign planning, 246–60 *passim*
    candidacy in question, 192–94

(Presidential campaign/elections
  (*con't.*))
  Carter's *Playboy* interview and,
    299–302
  Carter's tax plan attacked, 255–56
  Clennon King affair and, 309–10
  Dean's Watergate coverup allegation
    and, 293–98
  debates with Carter, 258–60, 261–78,
    303
    Eastern Europe gaffe, 268–77
  decision to run, 38–39, 194
  delegates, battle for, 219, 220–24
  election returns, his defeat, 313–21
    concession telegram to Carter, 317
    concession statement, 318–19
    reasons for defeat evaluated,
      326–28
  final campaign swing, 303–12
    Grand Rapids stop, 310–11
    Valley Forge Music Fair speech,
      306–7
  Florida primary, 203–5
  golfing holidays issue, 279, 284–87
  Hafif anti-Carter ad and, 308–9
  Illinois primary, 205–6
  "The Jerry and Joe Show," 307–8
  kickoff speech, 250–53
  Michigan primary, 214–17
  National Convention, *see* Ford,
    Gerald R.
  New Hampshire primary, 196–201
  New Jersey primary, 219, 220
  Nixon's China trip and, 197–98, 201
  North Carolina primary, 206–7
  Ohio primary, 219, 220
  primary losses/campaign manage-
    ment problems, 209–14
  Reagan challenge, 195–96
  "Rose Garden strategy," 256–58
  special prosecutor's inquiry and,
    287–93
  Texas primary, 207–9
Pueblo incident, 121

Radcliffe, Donnie, 60
Rather, Dan, 232
Ray, Elizabeth, 210–11, 226
Ray, Robert, 238
Reader's Digest, 256
Reagan, Ronald, *xii*, 154, 158, 159, 191,
  193, 214, 248
  campaign of 1976 and, 195–96, 197,
    198–201, 201–12 *passim*, 215, 217,
    218, 219, 220, 221, 222, 223, 225,
    228–34, 235–36, 241–42, 243, 326,
    327
Reason, J. Paul, 337
Reasoner, Harry, 164

Redford, Robert, 224
Reed, Clarke, 231, 232, 233
Reeves, Richard, 161, 164*n*, 177, 206–7
Reichley, James, 255
Reporters Committee for Freedom of
  the Press, 71–72
Republican National Committee, 248
Republican National Convention,
  225–45
  see also Ford, Gerald R.
Reston, "Scotty," 58
Reynolds, Frank, 264, 265
Rhodes, John, 154, 241
Rhodes, Richard, 301
Rhodesia, 220
Richardson, Elliot, 136–37, 156, 236,
  238
Roberts, Bill, 11, 14, 41, 149, 204
Rockefeller, Happy, 22, 337, 339
Rockefeller, Nelson A., *xi*, 26, 56, 62,
  63–64, 77, 122, 154, 156, 158–59,
  195, 233, 234, 237, 238, 248, 253,
  327, 335, 336, 337, 338, 339, 343,
  357
Rockefeller Commission, 62, 63–65
Roderick, John, 142
Rogers & Cowan, Inc., 339
Rogovin, Mitchell, 67
Rolling Stone, 279–80, 284
Roosevelt, Franklin D., 77, 251*n*
Roosevelt, Theodore, 214
Roper organization, 267
Roselli, John, 59
Rosenbaum, Richard, 219
Rosenberger, Eric, 343
Rosenthal, Abe, 58
Ross, Tom, 334
Ruby, Jack, 59
Ruckelshaus, William, 236, 238, 327
Ruff, Charles, 287–92, 297
Rumsfeld, Donald H., *xi*, 29, 30, 31, 47,
  50, 56, 60, 65, 66, 74, 78, 81–82,
  83, 84, 87, 91, 96, 106, 110, 113,
  127, 128, 144, 145, 180, 181, 184,
  186, 187, 212, 238, 345
  cabinet shakeup and, 155, 156, 160,
    161
  Kissinger and, 132, 134–35
  staff infighting and, 149–55
  Vietnam War and, 100, 102
Russell, Kans., 244

Sadat, Anwar, 157, 165
Safer, Morley, 28
Safire, William, 48
Saigon, *see* Vietnam War
Salamites, James, 189
SALT agreements, 46–52 *passim*
Salzburg, Austria, 165–67

"Saturday Night" (Live), 172–77
Scali, John, 345
Schanke, Robert, 293
Schecter, Jerrold, 259
Scheer, Robert, 299
Schieffer, Bob, 133, 167, 170, 172, 193, 257
Schlesinger, James, 56, 66, 122, 127, 128, 147
    dismissed from post, 155, 156, 157, 158, 159
Schmultz, Edward, 291
Schneider, René, 71
Schorr, Daniel, 57–58, 71–72
Schweiker, Richard, 223, 228, 231
Scott, Hugh, 154
Scowcroft, Brent, *xii*, 45, 58, 66, 68, 91, 103, 106, 109, 112, 117, 120–21, 125, 127, 128, 156, 158, 160, 198, 201, 203, 229–30, 344
    Ford's Eastern Europe gaffe and, 270, 271
Scranton, William, 282
Sears, John, 228, 231, 236, 248
Secret Service, 65–66
Securities and Exchange Commission, 250
Seib, Charles, 239
Seidman, William, 82, 84, 136, 149, 151, 250
Sevareid, Eric, 84, 193
Shabecoff, Phil, 76, 143
Shanahan, Eileen, 154, 259
Sharrock, Tom, 167
Sheehan, Neil, 67
Shuman, James, 179
Signals Intelligence Act, 66–67
Sihanouk, Norodom, 59, 120
Silberman, Larry, 141
Simon, William, 87, 149, 151–54, 238*n*, 256
Sinatra, Frank, 99–100
"60 Minutes," 28
Small, Bill, 219–20
Smith, David, 10–11
Smith, Doug, 252
Solomon, Richard, 137
Solzhenitsyn, Alexander, 133, 229, 345
Sommer, Elke, 25
Song of the Yimeng Mountains, 137
Sonnenfeldt, Helmut, 269
Soviet Union, 39, 40, 65, 71, 72–73, 262, 268–69, 274, 275, 276
    see also Vladivostok
Speakes, Larry, 254, 342
Spencer, Stuart, 220, 237, 270, 272, 275, 283
Sperling, Godfrey, Jr., 221
Stern, Carl, 294, 295

Stevens, John Paul, 357
Steward, Douglas J., 32
Squires, Jim, 140
Sukarno, President, 71
Sulzberger, "Punch," 58
Superman (film), 339–40
Swine-flu inoculation program, 250
Szulc, Tad, 66

Talbot, Strobe, 234
Taylor, Arthur, 76
Taylor, Elizabeth, 224
Tears of Autumn, The, 60
Teeter, Robert, 170, 196, 201, 237, 238, 239, 245, 271, 283, 311, 314, 315
Tennessee, 219
terHorst, Jerry, 8, 10, 12–13, 38, 176, 194, 202
Texas, 207–9
Thieu, Nguyen Van, 94, 106–7
Tho, Le Duc, 92
Thomas, E. L. "Tommy," 204
Thomas, Helen, 11, 53, 142, 145, 151–52, 171, 185, 311
Thomson, Meldrim, 196, 199, 200
Time (magazine), 30, 52
Timmons, William, 227, 293, 294, 295, 297
Tito, Josip Broz, 140–41
"Today Show," 282, 293ff.
Tower, John, 209, 237, 238
Trewhitt, Henry L., 268
Trudeau, Garry, 139*n*
Trujillo, Rafael, 59, 70
Truman, Harry S., 67
Tyler, Harold, Jr., 288–89

Udall, Morris, 176
United Press International (UPI), 314, 315
U.S. News & World Report, 38
Unseeing Eye, The, 308
Ursomarso, Frank, 182

Vail, Colorado house, 79–80
Vail, Tom, 305
Valeriani, Richard, 268
Valley Forge Music Fair, 306–7
Vietnam War, Ford and, 91–116, 356
    Bakersfield airport incident, 97
    correspondence with Thieu issue, 107
    fall of Danang, 95–96
    foreign-aid question, 93, 100–3
    Palm Springs vacation, the press and, 95–96
    Tulane University speech, 107–9
    welcome of Vietnamese children, 99
    Weyand's recommendation, 98

Vietnam War, Ford and (*con't*.)
  press briefings on, 91–92, 96–97
  refugees, aid to question, 114–16
  Saigon evacuation, 104–6, 109–14
Village Voice, 71
Vladivostok/Vladivostok agreement,
    40, 45–52, 66–67

Wagner, Bruce, 213, 214
Wald, Richard, 295–96
Waldheim, Kurt, 120
Walker, Bill, 344
Wallace, George, 154, 209, 215
Wall Street Journal, 4, 51, 287
Walnut Street Theater, 263
Walters, Barbara, 277, 294–95
Walters, Vernon, 201
Waring, Robert O., 221
Warren, Jerry, 31
Warren Commission, 59
Washington Post, 27, 31, 41–42, 60,
    163, 167, 176, 283
Washington Star, 134, 176
Watergate, 4, 6–7, 16, 55, 56, 57, 279,
    287, 292
  coverup, Dean's allegation of Ford's
    role in, 293–98
  elections of 1974 and, 36–37
  Ford Administration, effect of on,
    29–36 *passim*
  Ford's position on while vice
    president, 6–7
Wayne, John, 304
Weidenfeld, Sheila, 323, 333
Weiker, Lowell C., 238
Welch, Raquel, 24
Weyand, Frederick C., 93, 98–99, 102,
    116

White, Theodore H., 32
White House
  Oval Office, 12
  press corps, *xiv*, 14
    Ford's China trip and, 137–40,
      142–43
    Ford's Far East trip and, 40–41,
      43–44, 52–53
    interviews Jody Powell in author's
      office, 324–25
  Press Office, 15; *see also* White
    House, staff
  staff, 16–17
    Ford's image as bumbler and, 165
    infighting among, 80–85, 148–62,
      248–49
    Nixon members of, problems
      posed by, 30–32
    speechwriting operation, 80–85,
      151
White House Economic Conference,
    74
Whyte, William, 284–86
Wicker, Tom, 58
Wilson, Pete, 238
WIN program, 74–75
Wood, Rose Mary, 150
Woodruff, Judy, 280–81
Woodward, Bob, 32, 66, 211, 288–89,
    290, 343, 344
Wyman, Louis, 188

Young, Coleman, 309
Yugoslavia, 140–41

Zarb, Frank, 82, 84, 143
Ziegler, Ron, *xiv*, 10, 14, 17, 30, 31,
    32, 35, 36, 58, 92